GY

INTERNATIONAL BUSINESS STRATEGY

John Ellis and David Williams

PITMAN
PUBLISHING

PITMAN PUBLISHING
128 Long Acre, London WC2E 9AN

A Division of Pearson Professional Limited

First published in Great Britain in 1995

ISBN 0 273 60712 X

British Library Cataloguing in Publication Data
A CIP catalogue record for this book can be obtained from the British Library

10 9 8 7 6 5 4 3

Typeset by PanTek Arts, Maidstone, Kent
Printed and bound in Great Britain by Clays Ltd, St Ives plc

The Publishers' policy is to use paper manufactured from sustainable forests.

CONTENTS

PREFACE

Rationale

International Business Strategy provides both lecturers and participants with a core text addressing the strategic challenges surrounding the internationalisation process. The text is explicitly international in the way it considers strategic development across borders. By treating international competition as the norm, the text seeks to meet the increasing need for greater international course content on strategic management programmes. This currently unmet demand reflects the realities of the business environment for many companies and the needs of managers and aspiring managers.

In trying to capture the fluid nature of the strategy process, the text adopts an avowedly cross-disciplinary approach to develop a 'phase model' of international business development. This holistic perspective on cross-border development has been crafted to reflect the needs and realities of international strategic imperatives. Consequently, the cross-disciplinary mindset recognises that managers at all levels need to have a broad perspective of the internationalisation process and understand the contribution to, and demands on, different functional areas of the business in achieving, and sustaining, international business development.

Central to the phase model of international business development is a balanced view of the action, reaction and interaction of internal and external drivers to the internationalisation process. Assessing individual organisational responses focuses on the what, why and how of international strategic management. In offering insights in respect of these key areas, the text seeks to offer a blend of theory and practice, thereby ensuring both the development of an appropriate 'tool kit' and an understanding of when particular approaches are likely to be appropriate.

To assist readers in this process the text is illustrated by numerous examples of current business practice and the strategic dilemmas facing companies operating in an international context. These illustrations, together with the case studies, provide an important bridge between the informing frameworks around which the book is designed and practical business applications.

In writing this text the authors have set out to achieve the following aims:

- to enable managers and aspiring managers to understand those factors which drive the internationalisation process and the reasons why organisations respond in different ways;
- to offer a series of intellectually powerful frameworks which provide important practical insights into the challenges facing international businesses and how these might be managed;
- to provide a variety of truly international case examples to illustrate a range of strategic dilemmas, and to examine how different cross-border opportunities and threats may be managed.

Audience

The book is designed as a main international strategic management text for:

- final year undergraduate business/management programmes;
- postgraduate/experience business/management programmes; and
- specialist courses in international management and/or marketing, including a wide range of in-company and executive programmes.

Content and organisation

The book is organised in three parts. Part I: Strategy, Process and Performance has two chapters. Chapter 1 discusses the nature of international business strategy and distinguishes between corporate, business and functional strategies, and how these are linked to business performance. Chapter 2 introduces some of the key informing frameworks used throughout the text and reviews the factors which cause organisations to seek cross-border markets. The chapter also introduces the phase model of international business development, enabling organisations to be distinguished according to the phase of international business development they have reached.

Part II: International Strategic Analysis examines in greater detail the external and internal triggers to the internationalisation process. Chapter 3 considers the external drivers to meta-level, industry and firm-specific changes. Developments in the world economy are considered in detail together with the balance of forces at the industry level between globalisation and localisation. Chapter 4 reviews the importance of the organisation's internal context, and how this can both drive and prevent change. Particular attention is given to the issues of managing organisational change and the corporate mindset.

Part III: International Business Development is devoted to examining in detail the four stages of the international phase model. Chapter 5 examines the conditions where operating with a restricted national market scope offers a basis for sustainable competitive advantage. Chapter 6 considers the reasons for, and the methods of, international market entry and development. The emergence of international economic regions prompts Chapter 7 to examine the basis for developing international regional strategies. Finally, Chapter 8 considers the strategic options and organisational needs of worldwide competitors.

Style

The structure of each chapter contains the following features:

- a statement of key learning objectives;
- summary of contents;
- clearly written text using key concept diagrams to illustrate major principles and/or frameworks;
- international industry and company vignettes offering practical examples of the concepts introduced;
- chapter summary;
- checklist of key concepts;
- specially written major international case study;
- case questions.

Instructor's manual

An instructor's manual is available from the publishers for qualified adopters of this text. The manual offers suggestions in respect of:

- overall course design based upon the authors' extensive experience in developing international management programmes for undergraduate and postgraduate participants; and in running company-specific management development programmes for international clients;
- alternative approaches to the use of the text and cases in the development of individual teaching programmes, showing how utilising both together can advance participants' understanding of international strategic management issues;
- how the cases may be used in the development of active learning, together with teaching notes to case studies;
- selecting additional teaching and learning resources.

ACKNOWLEDGEMENTS

The breadth of the current text inevitably means that the authors have needed to draw on many sources. In particular, each of the case studies has been researched and written specifically for the present text. Many individuals in different organisations have helped in this task and we owe a particular debt to each. From our own organisation both Jill Beard and James Tudor, tutor librarians, have responded to often unreasonably short deadlines with great professionalism and energy. We would wish to record our special thanks to both of them.

In respect of all the companies used throughout the text we would wish to make clear that the views expressed are the authors' own, and do not necessary reflect the company's position. Indeed, this general disclaimer applies to all examples used, with the responsibility of the views expressed remaining the authors' and the authors' alone. We would wish to emphasise that the choice of individual corporate illustrations and cases throughout the text does not infer either good or indifferent management practice.

Over many years colleagues and participants on the various Dorset Business School postgraduate and undergraduate European Management and Business Studies programmes have provided invaluable help and insights on many aspects of the book. Once again, participants have proved tolerant in allowing us to use earlier drafts of the current text and associated cases with them and to explore areas of shortcomings. To all these individuals we owe a debt of gratitude.

Finally, to our parents, families and friends who have suffered from the unsociable hours and general lack of quality time they have had to endure during the writing of this, our second book, we owe a special thanks. Particular thanks go to our wives Susan and Anne who have been left on their own for so much time.

John Ellis and David Williams
Bournemouth, March 1995

Part I

STRATEGY, PROCESS AND PERFORMANCE

Chapter 1

CORPORATE, BUSINESS AND FUNCTIONAL STRATEGIES

Key learning objectives

To understand:

- different perspectives on the what, why and how of international business strategy
- the characteristics of international business strategy
- the nature of strategy
- corporate, business and functional strategies
- 'same' and 'new' game strategies
- the role of business performance in triggering adjustments to corporate, business and functional strategies

Context

Trapped by self-contained, narrow disciplinary boundaries, central issues relating to international business strategy have been developed by various researchers in almost virtual isolation from one another. Those unconnected islands of insight cannot necessarily be drawn together by merely island hopping. Adopting various contrasting perspectives and frameworks of reference is not sufficient, it is also imperative to draw out their key informing principles and weave them into a broad-based 'holistic' framework; in short, to develop an integrated approach which regards international aspects of industries and competition as the norm.

The development of a holistic approach to international business strategy is long overdue. For far too long a narrow and blinkered approach has been adopted to strategy in general and international business in particular. This chapter seeks to tease out the generic issues central to the development of an integrated viewpoint. The structure of the chapter is as follows:

- *an integrated approach to international business strategy*
- *international business strategy*
- *the nature of strategy*
- *corporate strategy*
- *business strategy*
- *functional strategy*
- *business performance and corrective adjustments*

The chapter begins by reviewing various strategic frameworks and draws out their informing principles with a view to shaping them into a balanced perspective of the role of strategy. This leads naturally to discussion of why international business strategy differs from purely domestic strategy. The distinction between corporate, business and functional strategy is then examined, and key requirements at different levels reviewed. Recognising that even successful management teams need to modify their chosen strategies, reflecting organisational learning and an ever changing external environment, the idea of corrective adjustments is introduced. The chapter concludes with a summary and checklist. Danone SA, an international food and drink manufacturer based in France, is the case featured at the end of the chapter.

An integrated approach to international business strategy

International business strategy is about how firms compete in increasingly internationally competitive markets. It is an emerging subject to the extent that its roots lie in the development of individual disciplines and the extension of analysis and understanding in specific areas. To date, there has been little or no attempt to provide a horizontal linkage of the deepening knowledge base within various narrow discipline boundaries. It is a challenge that this book seeks to address by developing an integrated approach which regards international aspects of firms and their competitive strategies as the norm. Figure 1.1 illustrates the nature of this approach.

A central principle informing this text is the need to adopt a holistic approach. This is grounded in the belief that international business strategy by its very nature is both eclectic and cross-disciplinary. As a first step to identifying the basic building blocks for such a framework, three contrasting paradigms are critiqued:

- external context
- resource based
- process view.

External context Strategic change is regarded mainly as a prescriptive adjustment to external change factors in which competitors play a prominent role (Porter, 1980; Yip 1993). The achievement of competitive advantage focuses on developing a strategy which enables the organisation to position itself advantageously in relation to the competitive forces operating at the level of the industry of which it is part. Superior competitive strategies embrace the notion of a fit between the

Figure 1.1 An integrated approach to international business strategy

company and its external environment, with any strategic change regarded as a reaction to environmental change. It is avowedly an external stimulus response view of the world, and as such tends to neglect internal factors.

Resource-based approach

This is an internal firm-based perspective which views competitive advantage as dependent upon the possession of firm-specific resources and capabilities (e.g. Collis, 1991; Hamel and Prahalad, 1994). These factors modify, and sometimes prevent, the organisation's response to external changes. Moreover, any strategic positioning is merely the expression of the presence or absence of distinctive capabilities over competitors. The resource-based view is not only firm specific, but forward looking. It does not, however, consider in any detail how change can be understood from an analysis of process.

Process view

This viewpoint looks to the management of the process of change and the organisational context in which it occurs (Pettigrew, 1985; Mintzberg and Waters, 1985). The prime focus is on the process of change as it affects the actions, reactions and interactions of people within the organisation. It is appreciated that there is a continuous interaction between external and internal change factors, with the organisation's internal context playing a key role in generating, enabling or preventing strategic responses. While the approach captures the complexity and ambiguity of how strategy is developed, the remit tends to offer less insights into the what and why of strategic imperatives.

Recognising that there is merit to each of the approaches – external context, resource-based approach and process view – suggests that it might be unduly restrictive to choose one at the expense of another. It is far less easy to merge these different strands of thinking, given that the assumptions of one approach are the focus of attention in other. In order to meet this challenge, a number of informing principles have been drawn from the three approaches discussed, namely the view that in the context of international business strategy:

- internal and external contexts cannot be viewed as mutually exclusive. Few organisations are pushed and pulled entirely by internal factors, while few firms have total control over their external environment;
- there is no single exit solution, or one way to manage strategy. Firm-specific factors need to be taken into consideration in the development of organisational strategies, and attention focused on the management of the process of change;
- time and space must be factored into the equation. Throughout the change process the temporal and spatial dimensions of business strategy require attention, both in respect of a particular point in time and the dynamics over time.

Internal resource-based, external and process perspectives are portrayed in Figure 1.2 as three inter-related strands of a rope. The informing principles have been reconfigured in such a way as to be complementary rather than competitive. Throughout the text this holistic approach will be adopted, thereby giving fresh insights into the strategy process.

The metaphor of a rope is adopted to underscore several points. First, while the three strands are separate they are clearly inter-related. In a strategic setting there is a need to examine the complex interplay between the three factors. Secondly, from a distance the individual strands are not distinguishable. In such circumstances it is not possible to become prescriptive about strategic outcomes, since complexity and ambiguity produce a non-prescribed or descriptive outcome. This may result in firms within the same industry adopting different strategic options. Ropes can also become unravelled, particularly when there is a lack of fit between the organisation and the assumptions it makes concerning its external environment. Furthermore, the length of the rope can be linked to

Figure 1.2 The holistic approach to international business strategy

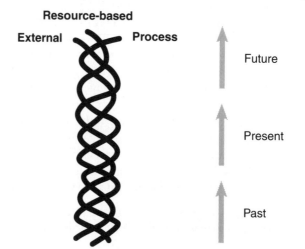

real time. From this perspective the present can only be understood from an appreciation of an earlier period of development, while the value of looking at the present is to provide a window to the future.

The need for managers to take a 'strategic' approach to how they manage their business is emphasised by the need to consider the why, what and how of strategy:

- *why* is the organisation seeking to develop as an international business; what are the external and/or internal change factors to the internationalisation process? Can organisations simply remain focused on their domestic market?
- *what* is the content of the organisation's strategy; will this deliver a satisfactory level of anticipated business performance, and, if so, over what time scale?
- *how* is the organisation's international business development to be achieved; does the organisation recognise a likely discontinuity to the current way it does business in developing cross-border markets? How is the organisation going to configure its resources to meet these new needs; can managers instil the necessary drive and leadership into the organisation to meet these new challenges? How is the international business strategy to be monitored and evaluated and under what circumstances might corrective adjustments be made?

Above all, adopting a 'strategic' approach provides the basis for the organisation to be proactive rather than reactive to events, by which time it may be too late to take effective strategic action. The nature of strategy, its differing levels – corporate, business and functional – and key features are the topics of the remainder of this chapter, which is designed to prepare the reader for considering in subsequent chapters how and why organisations develop an international business strategy.

International business strategy

Definition

> **International business strategy is concerned with the strategic management processes by which firms of all sizes evaluate their changing international business environment and shape an appropriate organisational response that involves the crossing of international borders.**

Integrating international business dynamics and strategic analysis focuses on three key aspects of international business strategy, namely:

- the spatial perception (or mental maps) of managers in assessing competitive opportunities and threats;
- the scope of the organisation's customer base; and
- the increased scale and complexity involved in serving international markets.

Spatial perception of competitive opportunities and threats

Understanding the reasons why, and the process by which, the strategic orientation of a company becomes international requires in the first instance an appreciation of the spatial perception of managers, as a prelude to reviewing the increased complexity associated with the internationalisation process. A broadening of a firm's spatial awareness may be hindered to the extent that senior management and the Board are drawn predominantly from the organisation's country of origin. Thus in German companies German nationals tend to hold the majority of senior positions, and similarly for US companies, US nationals tend to predominate. Other companies, realising the potential danger of only using a single country's nationals to help shape the organisation's strategic direction, have sought to internationalise the composition of their Board of Directors.

In taking an international as a opposed to a local perspective, managers no longer use mental maps of local or national competitors. Both internal and external stimuli result in the acknowledgement of opportunities and threats afforded by a wider market. For example, a European firm may no longer simply look to its national competitors and market place, but focus instead on the opportunities and threats contained within the European Union and the emerging single market in Europe. To assist this process a company may consider moving the locus of its management. Pilkington plc, one of the world's largest glass makers, announced in 1992 that it was moving the headquarters of its European operations away from its founding base in St Helens in the UK to Brussels, at the centre of Europe. The company's move recognised that trying to run the firm's European operations from a geographical location on the edge of the Single European Market was unlikely to create a truly international focus.

Customer base

Similarly, international business strategy looks to a wider customer base than the one which is offered by taking a solely restricted national focus. It is not sufficient to take a market-oriented approach to strategic analysis. Ohmae (1990), for example, has emphasised the need to be equidistant from all customers. He argues that for an organisation to be successful, all customers must be given equal importance, rather than seeing one group of customers, say those in the local market, as more important. The international company recognises these facts and makes sure that no group of customers is disadvantaged when compared to others. For this to happen the organisation's management and employees must disavow any distinction between 'domestic' and 'foreign' customers.

Scope and complexity

It is important to recognise that, as firms seek to move from a restricted focus based on national markets or their sub-markets and enter one or more international markets, they face considerable discontinuity in terms of the *resource needs* and *demands on managers* to develop and maintain a successful international business strategy.

Operating in an international context requires a firm to have a broader scope and to manage a much greater degree of complexity than is the case for a firm with a solely local focus. The increasing complexity of international business strategy as it relates to the functional areas of the business requires management to recognise and manage successfully differences in respect of the regulatory/institutional framework, customer requirements, cultural norms and levels of economic activity as they relate to national markets.

Further, set against the broad business context, each of the key activities of a business needs to be made compatible with the requirements of the international markets into which the company is seeking to make sales and/or locate. As a result, there is an increase in both the scope and complexity in developing and managing each of the functional business areas which enable the business strategy to be operationalised. Examples of the manner in which this happens are shown in Table 1.1.

A company-specific example of international business strategy and its relation to functional areas of business is discussed in Illustration 1.1, which considers the example of Ford of Europe. The illustration also serves to emphasise the importance of communication networks in managing geographically dispersed activities. As firms increase their product range and/or geographical complexity, co-ordinating such activities becomes a key management task.

Table 1.1 *Examples of the increasing complexity of international business strategy as it relates to the functional areas of a business*

- *Marketing:* need to change/adapt price, product and promotion strategies, recognising, for example, the differing competitive pressures, customer bases and media characteristics. For example, the company which fails to take into account attitudes to religion, sexual values or the manner in which business transactions are concluded in a market, risks causing serious offence and undermining any opportunity to gain business.

- *Logistics:* increasing complexity of supply chain management and the likely need to customise in relation to specific characteristics of the distribution channels of a particular country. For example, the presence or absence of different types of intermediaries within a distribution channel will result in different configurations to the supply chain as it relates to a particular market and/or group of customers. Movement of goods across national frontiers is likely to require additional documentation, notwithstanding greater harmonisation between nation-states within trading blocs over the last decade or so.

- *Finance:* the desire and/or ability to tap different capital markets may well place different requirements on the company in the reporting of its business performance. Alternatively, the risk of currency fluctuations brings a further layer of uncertainty influencing sourcing of supply and/or profitability of overseas sales. As a result, companies may well seek to protect themselves from excessive variations in their trading currencies through a variety of financial instruments.

- *Human resource management:* recruitment, training and skills of personnel to manage international operations and strategy; integration of different nationalities and cultures within the business. For example, the company will need to consider the extent to which it intends to develop the so-called footloose 'international manager', or rely on recruiting local managers and subsequently training them in the specific ways of the company.

- *Operations:* the need to serve different market requirements often results in more complicated organisational structures, recognising the necessity of managing both the product and geographical scope of the business. The diffusion of sales and/or production facilities across national boundaries increases the information and co-ordination requirements for successfully managing the business and ensuring operations are both effective and efficient.

Source: The authors

Illustration 1.1

Ford of Europe

Established in 1967, Ford of Europe co-ordinates European product developments, manufacturing and sales and planning. Prior to this date key markets were served by autonomous national subsidiaries that managed a broad range of functional activities. This limited the potential for exploiting economies of scale, pan-European sourcing and sales networks.

Twenty-five years later the same competitive issues continue to challenge Ford: how profitably to provide consumers with more product value for money than competitors; and utilise fully the company's resources to reduce the cost of design and manufacturing. The installation of a fast and flexible centralised communications network has been a central factor in achieving benefits in computer aided design (CAD)/computer aided manufacturing (CAM) across multiple locations – principally between the USA, the UK and Germany.

Information technology also plays a pivotal role in customer-oriented outreach. By the company installing common information technology platforms in its 7000 European dealerships, a car ordered from anywhere in Europe will be delivered to local customer specifications. This not only permits high service levels, but reduces the time lags from vehicle order to delivery. It also reduces the need for the costly stockpiling of finished products, since dealers directly order new cars through the company's computer network, enabling production schedules to reflect actual rather than anticipate demand.

Source: The authors

It is interesting to reflect on whether changes to international business strategy prompt functional changes or vice versa. From Illustration 1.1, the evidence of Ford of Europe suggests that increasing spatial complexity prompted the initial functional reorganisation. Equally, subsequent changes to functional strategies, reflecting rapid advances in information technology and flexible manufacturing systems, have informed and modified the overall strategic thrust. Consequently, readers should be aware that the relationship between the overall business direction and the functional strategies is bi-directional.

The nature of strategy

The term *strategy* is difficult to define and many management texts using the term fail to provide a clear definition. Where texts do define the term, they often do so with reference to a particular view of how strategy should be formed and implemented in an organisation. As a result the term is defined in different ways according to the views and values of the writer concerned. A common denominator is that the art of strategy is about winning. The term strategy comes from the Greek *strategos*, meaning general. Dictionary definitions of strategy also tend to relate the concept to its military origins, for example:

> **Generalship, the art of war, management of an army or armies in a campaign, art of moving or disposing troops or ships or aircraft as to impose upon the enemy the place and time and conditions for fighting preferred by oneself; instance of or plan formed according to this.** (*Concise Oxford Dictionary* (1976), p 1138)

While tactics constitute an operational manoeuvre intended to win a given battle, strategy is concerned with winning the war. The distinction between tactics and strategy should be interpreted with care given, as Rumelt (1979) suggests, 'one person's strategy is another's tactics'. Military strategy yields two important insights concerning organisational strategy. It provides first, a significant directional thrust which cannot be reversed easily; and secondly, an important and sizeable commitment of resources to a 'grand design' where the outcome is necessarily uncertain.

Mintzberg (1994) considers that strategy can be defined using one or more of the following terms:

- plan
- pattern
- position
- perspective

Each of these terms describes a different way of considering what is meant by the term strategy, illustrated in Figure 1.3.

Plan

Considering strategy as a plan emphasises an approach whereby an organisation seeks to take the future into account by explicitly or implicitly having a plan which it is attempting to follow. Recognition of the difficulties of predicting future events, together with the past experiences of overly prescriptive planning processes, has tended to reduce and/or modify the way in which organisations plan.

Figure 1.3 What is meant by the term strategy?

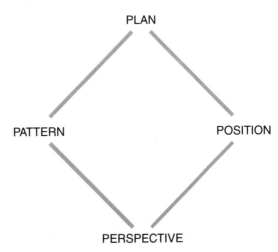

PLAN

PATTERN   POSITION

PERSPECTIVE

Position   Seeing strategy as a position tends to focus on how specific products/services are positioned in particular markets. This view of strategy emerges out of taking an external contextual view of strategy, and emphasises the importance of product-market positioning for the purposes of competitive advantage.

Perspective   Taking strategy as perspective tends to take an internal view, emphasising the organisation's way of doing things, particularly with regard to people and processes. Strategic actions need to be inter-related in the light of organisational culture.

Pattern   Considering strategy as a consistent pattern of behaviour over time permits assessment and evaluation of how a firm operates, and the processes by which different strategies take shape.

Mintzberg and Waters (1985) suggest that the pattern in a stream of strategic decisions tends to be as 'emergent' as they are 'deliberate'. Figure 1.4 shows that emergent strategies are constantly being adjusted and reviewed in the light of experience, while deliberate strategies are those which are both intended (planned) and realised (implemented). Hence the strategies that companies follow may be planned and deliberate, but equally may reflect the organisation's learning in the face of environmental change. More usually, effective strategies are likely to be a mixture of deliberate and emergent, reflecting not least the need to react to unexpected events and organisational learning.

Figure 1.4 Strategy development

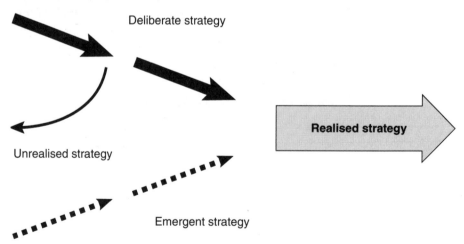

Perhaps one of the best known examples of an emergent strategy is Honda's entry to the American motorcycle market. Details of how the realised strategy was almost wholly emergent are given in Illustration 1.2. Honda's success can of course be rationalised in terms of formal analysis, but that was not how the strategy emerged in practice.

Illustration 1.2

Honda's successful entry to the US motorcycle market

During the 1960s, Honda, a Japanese motorcycle manufacturer, decided to enter the American motorcycle market. Contrary to what many people might imagine, the decision was based on virtually no formal analysis. Indeed, Honda had little idea of how it might build a market position.

On entering the market the company believed that its main chance of success lay in sales of its larger bikes, competing directly with companies which included Harley-Davidson and BSA/Triumph. Rather surprisingly, the company's actual success resulted from sales of its small motorcycles with a 50cc capacity, and then only by accident. Indeed, Honda's executives had considered the company's 50cc 'Supercubs' unsuitable for the US market where everything was bigger and more luxurious.

Interest arose from the fact that the company had imported a number of its 50cc machines for its employees to use for their personal transport in the vicinity of the company's location in California. Soon the company was receiving requests from potential retailers as to how they might buy similar motorcycles. These retailers were not the traditional motorcycle dealers through whom Honda had being trying to sell its larger bikes, but sporting goods stores.

Relatively quickly sales increased and the company realised that the market opportunity in the USA was not in selling large motorcycles, but exploiting an unmet need for small motorcycles, sold through different retail outlets to those traditionally associated with the industry. In other words, there was a gap in the market for which the company had a ready-made product.

As a result the company was able to change its strategy and achieve a successful market entry to the US market. This outcome was virtually wholly emergent, and the company's initial intended strategy was not only unrealised, but was based on a number of falsehoods.

Source: based on Pascale (1984)

The distinctions between deliberate and emergent strategies reflect both the nature of a company's organisational dynamics and the constant change and uncertainty of the business environment. As a consequence, the development of an organisational strategy is a much more uncertain and evolutionary process than the highly rational models of strategic analysis have suggested in the past. The widespread infusion of corporate culture throughout an organisation means that significant shifts in business strategy tend only to occur infrequently, with long periods of incremental and evolutionary adaptation of strategy in the periods in between.

> Organisations go through long periods when strategies develop incrementally, that is decisions build one upon another, so that past decisions mould future strategy. (Johnson (1992), p 28)

As a result, overall strategy tends to evolve slowly over time, reflecting organisational learning and the inability of companies to implement strategies which are inappropriate in the context of the corporate culture. Only infrequently do most organisations experience a fundamental discontinuity in their strategic development, although when such events do occur they can lead to dramatic shifts in strategy.

In summary, being strategic is a unifying theme which gives a clear coherence and sense of direction to where a firm is heading. This may be distanced from the need to plan, which is concerned with the detail of how to achieve the strategy. The term strategy can be redefined further in relation to three interconnected levels of decision making – *corporate, business* and *functional* strategy.

Corporate strategy

As Figure 1.5 shows, *corporate strategy* is concerned with adding value in respect of two equally important key areas of decision making, namely:

- the overall scope of the organisation's activities; and
- corporate parenting.

Overall scope The overall scope of the organisation's activities can be defined in terms of the business the organisation wants to be in. In making additions to, and deletions from, the range of industries and markets in which the firm competes, sources of additional corporate value added will accrue to the extent that corporate managers judge whether individual business are able to achieve acceptable rates of returns. If they cannot, the business should be divested from the company's portfolio. This may result in the business being spun off as a separate entity, sold to another organisation, or in extreme cases closed down. Similarly, acquisitions should be capable of producing acceptable rates of returns in order to justify their purchase.

Corporate strategy becomes international to the extent that an organisation's activities are influenced by three elements, namely:

- competition;
- currency; and
- country.

Competition

The corporate strategy of an organisation will inevitably have an international dimension to the extent that changes to the overall scope of an organisation's activities are influenced by the pressures arising out of international competition. In such circumstances, defence of the domestic market is necessary but not sufficient. Competitive realities will prompt some firms to build their own international capabilities. The overall vision of corporate management will reflect spatial manifestations in accord with their international perception. Today, competitive drivers prompt more and more managers to make explicit

Figure 1.5 Distinguishing between corporate and business strategy

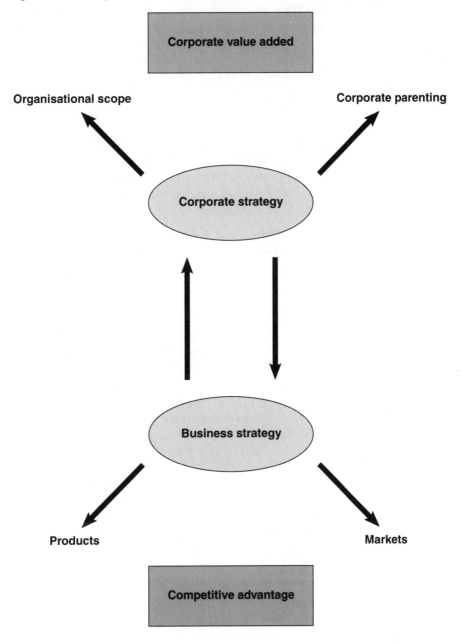

plans concerning their geographical location of activities in the interlinked economy of the Triad (East Asia/South Pacific, European Union and North American Free Trade Area).

Currency

The second element which is likely to exert a considerable influence on international corporate strategy is currency. Foreign exchange markets are increasingly volatile and currency movements can have a profound effect on the profitability of international sales, and/or the costs of producing in different locations. In recent years, the effective devaluation of the major European currencies and the American dollar against the German deutschmark has meant that a German exporter to those markets would have to increase prices by the exchange rate variation simply to maintain revenue.

The cumulative effect of the continuous appreciation of a currency (e.g. Japanese yen, German deutschmark) over time makes it very difficult for an indigenous exporter to neutralise the impact of currency changes. This is not necessarily the case for the international firm with cross-border production and sales. Such international companies are becoming adept at neutralising foreign exchange risk by establishing a presence in all three regions of the Triad and matching production costs to sales revenue. In applying this strategy Hitachi, the Japanese conglomerate, recently stated:

> The company's global thinking is to balance its worldwide distribution between the United States, Europe and Asia. (Kabushiki Kaisha Hitachi Seisakusho, Annual Report 1993, p 20)

Country

Additional to the need to neutralise currency movements is the requirement to recognise broader factors relating to individual countries which have a strong influence in shaping the scope of the organisation's activities. In the past the fear of trade protectionism has persuaded firms to locate production facilities overseas to offset any risk of key markets becoming inaccessible. While this threat has receded for the present following the latest round of the General Agreement on Tariffs and Trade (GATT) talks, the requirement to move close to customer bases continues to exert a strong and powerful pull.

The country variable may also be critical in terms of assessing a country's political risk alongside the attractiveness of any market potential and the intensity of local competition. This is likely to be particularly true where companies are seeking to achieve sales and locate facilities in lesser developed countries.

For larger companies with production and marketing in all areas of the Triad, the crucial issue is the co-ordination and management of separate activities and businesses in a way which achieves corporate added value. These are key issues which will be examined later, following a review of how the corporate centre manages the individual international businesses within its group.

In summary, international corporate strategy determines the composition and balance of the organisation's international business portfolio. It may result in either the disposal of businesses, to reduce the spread of the organisation's activities, or purchases to consolidate or broaden the scope of the organisation's activities. Illustration 1.3 shows how the French company Thomson's scope of activities has changed radically since the early 1980s.

Corporate parenting

The second task of corporate strategy is concerned with how corporate management at head office should manage the various businesses within the

Illustration 1.3

Thomson SA

Since his appointment in 1982, Alain Gomez, chairman and chief executive of the French electronics company Thomson SA, has dramatically reduced the number of major businesses within the group from 20 to 3. As a result the organisation's scope of activities has been reduced allowing it to concentrate on its remaining business activities. Over the same period, the company's consumer electronics business has been developed so that the company now has a worldwide presence. The strategy of building a worldwide consumer electronics business was initially facilitated by acquisitions. For example, in 1987 the company purchased the world's largest television plant from the American company General Electric (GE). GE was willing to sell the plant in Bloomington, Indiana to Thomson following its decision to dispose of its consumer electronics business on the basis of expected future performance. Thomson's purchase of the plant enhanced the company's presence in North America, a major step to developing its business worldwide. All that remains is to secure production and market facilities in SE Asia. In making this and other acquisitions Thomson takes a long-term view of the return it is likely to achieve from its investments.

Source: The authors

organisation. This is a particularly important challenge. If each individual business trades as an independent entity, there would be no co-ordination costs associated with portfolio management. In order to recover such costs and generate further positive financial performance, the potential for corporate intervention with individual businesses needs to be explored. How the centre manages individual business units and/or business divisions is termed *corporate parenting*.

Goold and Campbell (1989) have discerned that a number of principles exist with regard to corporate parenting:

- Parent companies add value ('parenting value') to businesses in their portfolio either because the headquarters team has some special skill which can be used to help the businesses, or because they can create synergy between businesses in the portfolio.
- A company should add a business to its portfolio if it believes it can create more parenting value in relation to the new business than other potential bidders.
- A company should divest a business in its portfolio when it believes the business will perform better as an independent company or as part of the portfolio of some other company.

The appropriate corporate parenting role depends closely upon the way in which corporate management *adds value* to the respective individual businesses. Goold and Campbell (1987) found that large and diversified companies use different 'strategic management styles'. Alternative styles are appropriate to different types of business and corporate management. Strategic management styles can be differentiated according to two dimensions: *planning,* the influence and co-ordination of head office in business strategy formulation; and the type of performance *control* imposed by head office.

On the basis of these two dimensions – planning and control – three broad categories of corporate management styles can be identified, namely:

- strategic planning;
- strategic control; and
- financial control.

Goold and Campbell (1987, chapter 12) further argue that it is important to match the style to the business, recognising both the nature of the business and its resource base. No one style was found suitable for all situations, and each had strengths and weaknesses, as discussed in Illustration 1.4.

Illustration 1.4

Strategic management styles

Strategic planning (also known as Orchestrator)

Characteristics
Corporate headquarters is deeply involved with management at the business level in formally planning strategies. Emphasis is strongly on the planning lever to influence the direction of the business. Centre may provide clear direction to the business unit. Control of the business unit involves using both strategic (e.g. investment, market share) and financial goals.

Performance
Short-term financial performance may suffer to the extent that the organisation takes a longer-term view. Lack of emphasis on financial performance may result in poor cost control. Planning process can be highly time consuming, with the centre losing objectivity. Business unit management may become frustrated by interventions by corporate management in their business.

Corporate example: Hewlett-Packard Inc
Hewlett-Packard Inc is an American company well known for its hardware products in the field of information technology. The company's superior performance in the office electronics industry during the late 1980s is widely attributed to a corporate management who can nurture innovation, and speedily respond to market conditions in order to gain an advantage over competitors. The company is organised into product divisions, with formal management links between divisions to ensure co-ordination of manufacturing policies and diffusion of technological development. Task forces regarding total quality control (TQC) represent a more flexible and less formal mechanism for achieving organisation linkages. This highly centralised management style employs 3000 people at its Palo Alto head office.

Strategic control (also known as Coach)

Characteristics

The strategic development of the business is left to divisional or business unit management. Centre does not set direction for businesses, or seek to co-ordinate synergies between businesses. This is left to the divisional level. Capital projects are generally initiated by the business. Businesses expected to make detailed reports to the centre in relation to performance.

Performance

Style attempts to provide a balance between longer-term (strategic) and shorter-term (financial) goals. Maintaining the balance between the two is, however, difficult. Co-operation between business units may be ineffective in exploiting potential synergies.

Corporate example: Schlumberger SA

Schlumberger SA is world's largest oil field service company, operating in more than a hundred countries. The French company comprises two groups: Schlumberger Industries and Schlumberger Technologies. Despite the technological basis of the company's businesses, corporate staff number less than 200. The company, initially by necessity but later by design, is very decentralised. The heart of its business lies in more than a thousand autonomous profit centres. Roughly ten days into every month, each manager receives a financial statement indicating how well they performed in the previous month. Although the real issue for everyone at Schlumberger is performance and achieving targets, the company's culture encourages managers to support each other. Interaction among various business units has led to co-operation in respect of research and development. Projects are often shared by different separate businesses and between research centres to optimise resources and yield synergies from sharing ideas.

Financial control (also known as Controller)

Characteristics

Strong delegation of responsibility by the corporate centre to management at the business unit. Budget process and agreeing budget with the corporate headquarters are critical. Budget becomes 'contract' between corporate and business levels of management. Strong emphasis on short-term payback for projects requiring investment. Thrust is primarily on the financial controls. Financial performance monitored in detail by the centre.

Performance

Style tends to maximise short-term financial performance, but at the expense of organic growth. Long-term investment opportunities may be lost, and linkages between business units not developed. Business-level management have a strong incentive to 'achieve' agreed budget.

Corporate example: Hanson plc

Hanson plc is a major international business conglomerate operating primarily in the UK and USA, which has grown mainly through acquisition over the last 25

▶

19

> years. The success of Hanson lies in its sophisticated post-acquisition management skills and highly effective systems of short-term financial control. Throughout the year each division's financial performance is monitored closely from the centre against agreed profits, cash flow and capital expenditure targets. There are no links between Hanson's brick businesses in the UK and USA. Hanson has no interest in building synergies between different businesses in the way other conglomerates attempt. For example, Hanson prevents companies within the group from sharing distribution facilities because it believes in intra-organisational competition as opposed to co-operation. By engineering head-to-head competition with other businesses within the group, Hanson believes costs will be driven down and performance enhanced. Hanson, with comparable sales to Hewlett-Packard but a more 'hands off' management style in low technology businesses, has fewer than 200 employees at head office.
>
> *Source:* The authors

To summarise, corporate strategy is concerned with how the corporate centre of the organisation *adds value* through its actions in respect of:

- achieving an appropriate portfolio of business activities, by shaping the organisation's overall scope and locational balance; and
- using a strategic management style compatible with the organisation's resources and culture in order to enhance corporate performance.

Business strategy

In comparison to corporate strategy, *business strategy* relates to how a business seeks to compete in its chosen product-markets. This may, for example, be on the basis of price, quality or service. Used interchangeably with the term business strategy is the term *competitive strategy*. Where a small business only operates in a narrow product-market, and does not have separate business divisions or units, corporate and business strategy are effectively the same. In practice, most larger organisations contain a range of businesses and the distinction between corporate and business strategy is meaningful.

International business strategy is concerned with how the organisation competes in international product-markets. In other words, the scope of *international*, as opposed to *domestic*, business strategy is much broader. The focus of international business or competitive strategy is on how the firm competes and whether it has, or can develop, a sustainable *international competitive advantage* when compared to rivals in its respective markets. Competitive advantage is the ability to outperform rivals consistently over a specified time frame on commonly accepted performance criteria.

In attempting to craft a sustainable competitive advantage, organisations have the choice of either seeking to emulate existing rivals by implementing similar strategic recipes more successfully, or inventing a new way of competing in the market. These two choices may be labelled *same game* or *new game strategies*. Both choices provide the basis for delivering superior business performance. The chief characteristics of each way of achieving competitive advantage are summarised in Table 1.2.

Same game strategies emphasise the need to segment the organisation's customer base and seek to serve the chosen segment more effectively and efficiently through superior market positioning when compared to competitive rivals. Competitive advantage is assumed to derive from a blind pursuit of beating competitors. As a strategic approach it is about improving on the known strategic recipes employed by rivals in order to serve the same group of customers more effectively. At best, this approach of doing the same better leads to incremental advantages, which are often all too quickly replicated by competitors.

By contrast, the emphasis of the *new game* strategy is on strategic innovation. It is about discovering new ways of serving an existing or unexplored customer need. The process by which this occurs may be based upon one or a combination of product, process or marketing innovation. By being the innovator the strategy offers first mover advantage. Successful implementation

Table 1.2 Same and new game strategies leading to competitive advantage

Same game	New game
Characteristics ● Identify market segments ● Decide positioning within segments ● Serve market more effectively and efficiently than competitors	*Characteristics* ● Strategic innovation: product, process or market discovery ● First mover advantage within a market ● Avoidance of head-to-head competition
Strategic intent Strategy of outcompeting rivals using similar strategic approaches (recipes) to those employed by rivals. Approach emphasises assessing what competitors have done and taking appropriate action to doing the same better.	*Strategic intent* Strategy of outcompeting rivals by investing in new strategic recipes. Approach emphasises innovation and vision, as the organisation crafts a new strategic approach to meet consumer needs.
Potential outcomes Business achieves parity or at best an incremental competitive advantage when compared to rivals. Takes an 'incremental' approach to developing a new business strategy.	*Potential outcomes* Business crafts a competitive superiority which places the organisation at a distinct advantage when compared to rivals. Takes a 'fundamental' approach to developing a business strategy.

will yield a competitive advantage which is highly distinctive and often difficult to replicate. The informing principle of new game strategy is to outflank the competition by delivering better value to customers, rather than to engage in a confrontational competitive struggle.

The extent to which a firm is using a same game or new game strategy helps to inform the nature of any existing or developing competitive advantage. Linked to this question is the way an organisation may seek to develop its business strategy in order to achieve competitive advantage. Illustration 1.5 provides an example of same versus new game strategies with reference to the world's piano market.

Illustration 1.5

Yamaha KK: Same and new game strategies in the world's piano market

By the late 1980s Yamaha had captured almost 40 per cent of the world piano market. Having finally achieved market leadership, overall demand started to decline by an estimated 10 per cent every year. What strategic response should Yamaha make?

● *Same game* strategies suggested trying to serve the declining world market even more effectively or efficiently. Unfortunately, the up-market segment of the industry had only limited ability to absorb additional volume, while low-cost South Korean producers were entering the more price-sensitive segments of the market. The prospect of having to fight even harder against an aggressive set of new competitors for their share of the shrinking market was not an encouraging prospect for Yamaha.

● *New game* strategy thinking suggested looking with fresh eyes for opportunities to create value for customers. With 40 million pianos already in existence, Yamaha used a combination of digital and optical technology to produce a piano player with superb acoustics. Using the same kind of 3.5 inch disks that work on personal computers, owners can play music of their choice on their 'techno' acoustic piano.

In terms of the piano market, the new technology created the prospect of Yamaha refitting up to 40 million pianos. Sales in Japan have been dramatic. Moreover, many customers now want their piano tuned to professional standards. As the piano regains popularity, Yamaha is discovering a wide range of additional value-creating opportunities in the digital segment of the piano market. Yamaha's new game strategy helped reshape its source of competitive advantage and increase further its financial performance.

Source: adapted from Ohmae (1990)

In respect of 'same' and 'new' game strategies, it is possible for businesses to find themselves in either a vicious or a virtuous circle. Figure 1.6 shows that operating with a same game strategy may result in a downward spiral. If, for example, rivals in a particular product-market, faced with recessionary trading

Figure 1.6 The 'same' versus 'new' game strategies

The downward spiral   1. Same game

2. Delayering

3. Divestment

4. Deteriorating performance

4. Improving performance

3. New vision and capabilities

2. New strategic recipe

1. New game   **The upward spiral**

conditions, all adopt similar cost-reduction strategies, then individual organisations can find they are running even faster and further just to stand still. More fundamentally, while a downturn in the business cycle is likely to be temporary, if the existing way of competing in the industry/market is becoming less and less appropriate companies wedded to an unchanging same game strategy are likely to find their business performance spiralling downwards.

By contrast, even in otherwise difficult trading conditions, a new game strategy may allow the organisation to advance and strengthen its competitive position. As Figure 1.6 shows, new game strategies may, if successful, result in an upward spiral. This emphasises that new game strategies are about building rather than cutting; and about developing new markets and/or competitive approaches which avoid confrontational 'head-to-head' competition.

Some of the issues raised in comparing and contrasting same and new game strategies have been taken up by Hamel & Prahalad (1994) to suggest how organisations should shape future strategies. They argue that the main competitive threat comes from organisations who develop new business solutions. They further suggest that too much management time, particularly in the USA and the UK, is spent on restructuring and re-engineering the existing business rather creating the new markets of the future. The belief is that too many Anglo-Saxon managers focus on delayering and divestment, key components of the downward spiral depicted in Figure 1.6.

Organisations need to do three things, each to some degree overlapping, if they are going to lock into an upward spiral and shape a strategy which allows them to compete for the future. This is depicted in diagrammatic format in Figure 1.7. First, they must compete for industry foresight and intellectual leadership. This is essential in order to gain a better appreciation and understanding of key external trends, reflecting the likelihood of a major discontinuity; and in order to assess the extent that industry/market boundaries may change and new industries/markets emerge. Key areas of attention might well include technology, demographic and lifestyle changes, which will be examined in greater detail in Chapter 4.

Secondly, to exploit newly emerging industries/markets organisations need to develop the necessary core competences. A core competence is a bundle of constituent skills and technologies which integrate a variety of individual skills, but is not a physical asset. These allow the company to provide particular benefits to its customers through its product/service offer. Core competences can relate to both the corporate and business levels. At corporate level, core competences can provide an entry to new markets. Organisations need to consider which core competences they have and do not have, and the extent to which these are essential/non-essential. Table 1.3 considers these parameters and a range of possible corporate responses.

Figure 1.7 Competing for the future

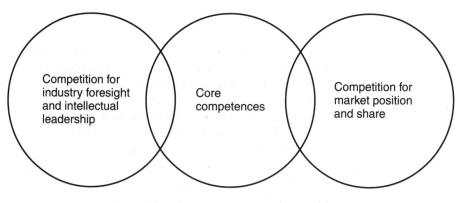

Competition for industry foresight and intellectual leadership

Core competences

Competition for market position and share

STRETCH

Table 1.3 Core competences

	Have	**Have not**
Essential	Develop	Organic growth; acquire; and/or joint venture
Non-essential	Harvest/divest	Buy in

The third stage to developing a competitive strategy for the future is concerned with market positioning and share. This, however, emerges out of the first two factors, rather than being seen as the point of origin in determining a competitive strategy. Hamel and Prahalad (1994) also emphasise that market position is not necessarily assisted by market research, which by its very nature tends to have limitations in respect of new products.

Contrasting their view with the traditional idea of resource 'fit', they further emphasise that strategy is about 'stretch' as well as fit. Arguing that strategic intent is necessary if organisations are to grow and develop, they point to a number of companies who have successfully achieved corporate aims which seemed unrealistic given their resource position. It is unquestionably important to emphasise the need to stretch an organisation's resource base; but it is important to appreciate that there may be limits to this process, and 'fit' and

Figure 1.8 Strategic options

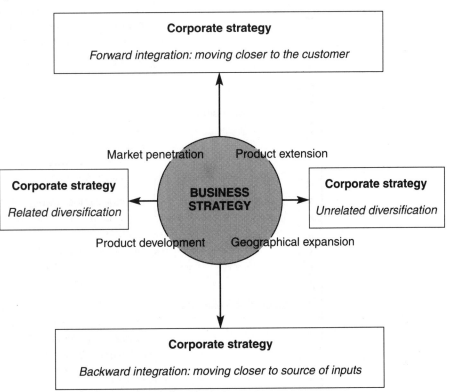

'stretch' need to be balanced if organisations are to grow and function concurrently. Consequently, the degree of stretch and fit in developing a particular strategic option will need to be examined and the tension recognised.

The alternative business strategy options – *market penetration, product expansion, product development* and *geographical expansion* – which each describe the overall strategic thrust at the business level, form the central element of Figure 1.8. Organisations may wish to pursue these options through one or more methods of development, namely organic and external growth and/or the use of international strategic alliances, including joint ventures. Each of these methods of development has strengths and weakness, and these will be examined later in the text.

The range of business strategy options which may be available to an organisation is detailed and illustrated with the help of examples in Table 1.4.

Table 1.4 Strategic options – business strategy

	Strategic options	Product-market implications
	Existing products and/or markets	
B U S I N E S S S T R A T E G Y	Market penetration	The strategy is to increase the company's market share. This may be difficult in a mature market, where any growth is likely to be at the expense of competitors. Such a strategy may bring retaliation from competitors who find their sales falling. Alternatively, companies may 'buy' market share by acquiring existing competitors. *Example: Unilever's acquisition of Ortiz-Miko to enhance its presence in the French ice-cream market*
	Product extension	Derivatives of existing products are developed and sold into the same market. *Example: The American company Coca-Cola developing a related product (Diet Coke) to its main soft drink*
	Product development	Management's strategy is to develop new products, but to sell these products in their existing markets. *Example: The development of the miniaturised Walkman for the consumer electronics market by Sony Corp KK*
	Geographical expansion	Geographical sales of product are expanded out of the company's existing spatial markets *Example: Castlemaine Toohey, the Australian brewer, entering the British beer market (via Allied Domecq) and marketing its XXXX lager to a new customer base*

While business strategy focuses on the organisation's existing product-markets, Figure 1.8 also illustrates the strategic choices arising out decisions at the level of corporate strategy – *vertical integration* and *diversification* – through which an organisation can change the scope of its activities.

Business strategy becomes international when a company is seeking to serve product-markets other than its indigenous local or national market, requiring it to sell products or services and manage operations which reach

Table 1.5 Strategic options – corporate strategy

	Strategic options	Product market implications
C O R P O R A T E S T R A T E G Y	*Vertical integration*	
	Forward integration	Scope of organisation expanded by including activities which bring the business closer to directly supplying the customer, e.g. a distributor acquiring a retail outlet. *Example: The establishment of overseas distribution companies by Nissan, the Japanese volume car producer, to market its products to individual national markets*
	Backward integration	Scope of organisation expanded by including activities which take the business closer to raw material supplies, e.g. distributor developing a manufacturing operation. *Example: British Gas, a gas distribution company, taking a stake in offshore gas field developments in the North Sea*
	Diversification	
	Related diversification	Organisation moves into new product-markets where it can employ existing competencies – knowledge, understanding and skills. *Example: Philip Morris, the American tobacco company, acquiring an existing company, Miller, in the US brewing industry, but substantially improving performance by applying its marketing expertise developed for the tobacco industry to brewing*
	Unrelated diversification	Organisation moves into new product-markets where new competencies are required in order to be an effective competitor. *Example: The UK-based company British American Tobacco buying an American financial services company, Farmers*

across national borders. Similarly, corporate strategy will have an international dimension to the extent that the overall scope of the organisation's activities are international and/or are influenced by international competition. Table 1.5 identifies the different strategic options available to a company wishing to extend the scope of its corporate activities.

In summary, business strategy is about achieving competitive advantage in the organisation's chosen product-market. This can be developed and/or maintained by using either same game or new game strategies. Further, the development of competitive advantage can be related to the range of business strategy options that the organisation can pursue. Since competitive advantage is product-market specific, options relating to scope – namely, vertical integration and diversification – cannot be considered as business strategy. They are not concerned with how an individual business may improve its competitive advantage within a product-market, but with how the corporation as a whole adds value to the business portfolio.

Functional strategy

The successful implementation of an organisation's international business strategy requires the key functional areas of the business – *marketing, finance, logistics, operations* and *human resource management* – to be effectively and efficiently organised in order to operationalise the strategy. The linkage between international business and functional strategies is illustrated in Figure 1.9. Functional or operational strategies refer to how the different activity areas of a business contribute to the overall business strategy. Ford of Europe, Illustration 1.1, has already provided an example of the inter-relationship between business and functional levels of strategy.

To reconcile the dilemmas between conflicting sets of needs, international businesses often operate with complex organisational structures seeking to integrate each of these key functional areas. Changes to the organisation's international business strategies may substantially increase the demands on management, and require significant changes to the resource disposition of a particular functional area. Equally, as new functional strategies evolve, the organisation's business strategy may be modified. Consequently, while the relationship between business and functional strategy is bi-directional, the key requirement is fit. Business and functional strategies must match, ensuring not only that the general thrust is appropriate, but that the overall strategic intent can be implemented.

Each of the functional areas, however configured, offers a potentially important contribution to the success or otherwise of the chosen business strategy. Some of the key aspects of each function which need to be both effectively and efficiently configured are briefly described below.

Figure 1.9 The relationship between business and functional strategy

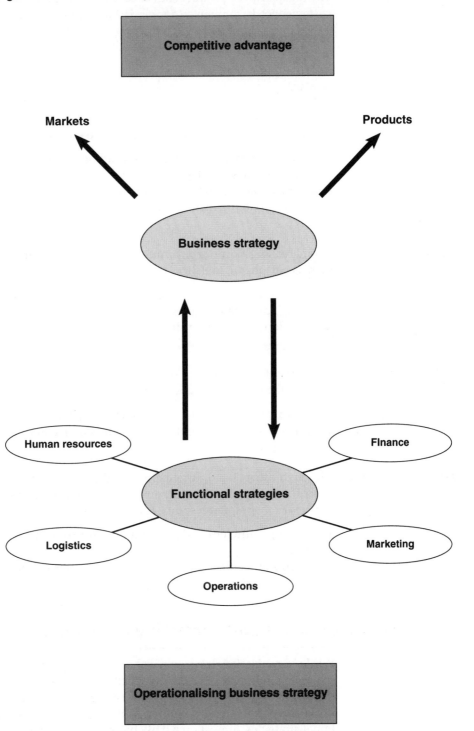

Marketing	The organisation's product and/or service offer should be matched effectively to customer needs, through an appropriate application of the marketing mix, namely:

- product
- price
- promotion
- place

Finance The finance function should be operated to ensure:

- appropriate means and levels of funding are available in order to fund the chosen business strategy;
- organisational controls and budgets are established to assist in the planning and control of financial resources.

Logistics An increasingly important function for many organisations and no longer seen as peripheral, logistics is concerned with:

- effective and efficient organisation and management of procurement, haulage and warehousing;
- provision of support systems.

Operations Delivery of the product/service offer in order to satisfy customer needs requires the operations function to ensure:

- the availability of sufficient productive capacity;
- the effective and efficient use of production facilities.

Human resources Although often stated, it remains true that this is often the most critical firm-specific resource if the implementation of a strategy is to be successful. Aspects of the human resource function include:

- ensuring sufficient well-trained and appropriately skilled personnel are available;
- effective and efficient processes and structures are developed for managing the organisation's human resources.

Business performance and corrective adjustments

While organisations may make the best laid plans, inevitably faced with a dynamic environment and firm-specific imperfections there will be the need to make constant adjustments to the organisation's strategy. The majority of these adjustments will be minor, representing the natural evolution of functional strategies, almost on a daily basis. Such changes will reflect the constant updating and adjustment as the organisation adapts in the face of external or internal contextual changes.

Provided that business performance is judged satisfactory, strategy can be expected to evolve on an incremental basis. If, however, business performance for whatever reason is judged less than satisfactory, the organisation will need to consider what corrective adjustments might need to be made. According to the work of Grinyer and Spender (1979), almost inevitably initial attention will be directed towards the implementation of the existing strategy, focusing at the functional level as shown in Figure 1.10. If the overall thrust of the strategy is correct, revisiting implementation is likely to bring about improved performance. If, however, there are more fundamental weaknesses in the strategic approach, it will be necessary to review the organisation's competitive strategy and how it competes in its chosen product-markets. Beyond corrections to the business strategy, corporate concerns arise. First, if corrections to business strategy do not prove successful there may be a need to look at organisational scope. Does the business 'fit' with the organisation to the extent that it may be viewed as a 'core' activity? If not, perhaps the organisation needs to divest itself of this area of its business. Alternatively, the activity may be judged too small at its current size and require further growth either by internal or external means to reach a critical mass which will enable it to compete with its rivals. Secondly, perhaps the corporate parenting style is inappropriate and should be changed. Does the corporate centre, for example, control the business too tightly? Alternatively, is the control ineffective?

As Figure 1.10 emphasises, inadequate performance is often an important trigger to changing elements in an organisation's strategy. Without, at this stage, discussing in detail how to measure business performance, Table 1.6 considers how performance at each level of strategy might be compared against (1) past performance; (2) competitors; and (3) within the corporate group by taking one business division against another in order to inform corrective adjustments.

Figure 1.10 The relationship between corporate, business and functional strategies and business performance

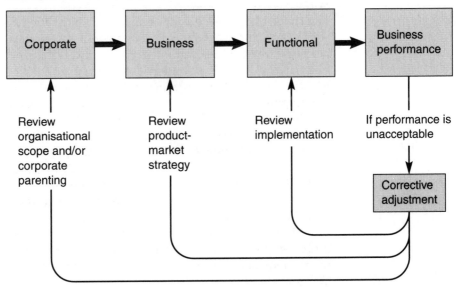

Table 1.6 *Review of business performance and adjustments to corporate, business and functional strategies*

Level of strategy	Corporate	Business	Functional
Review	Review overall corporate performance against: ● past performance ● other corporates	Review business performance against: ● past performance ● other businesses in the group ● competitors' businesses in the same product-market	Performance in each functional area against competitors in order to assess efficiency and effectiveness
Possible adjustments	Make adjustments to: ● organisational scope; and/or ● corporate parenting style	Make adjustments to product-market strategy in order to improve competitive position	Make adjustments as required to: ● marketing ● human resources ● operations ● logistics ● finance

While inadequate business performance does not itself result in modifications to an existing strategy, there is an increasing likelihood, the longer performance remains unsatisfactory, that adjustments to strategy at one or more levels will take place. The scale and scope of corrective adjustments not only differ at each of the three levels – corporate, business and functional – but the time frame is normally a critical enabling factor as to the level of change likely to be sought.

Summary

This chapter has considered the manner in which different disciplines and frameworks can contribute to the development of an understanding of international business strategy. The central tenet of the text is that an integrated approach to international business strategy is required to enable the various external, resource-based and process views to be incorporated into a holistic view.

Recognising that the nature of strategy can be considered in different ways, the chapter considers how the concept might be unpacked in terms of different levels: corporate, business and functional. Corporate strategy relates to issues of organisational scope and corporate parenting. Business strategy has a product-market focus and is concerned with whether organisations are able to develop and/or sustain the basis of competitive advantage. Considering how competitive advantage might be developed leads to discussion about 'same' and 'new' game strategies and the achievement of a 'virtuous' cycle of growth and development. Recognising the importance of looking to the future, emphasis is on taking a forward-looking view of an industry; developing the requisite core competences; and the need to consider market position. The importance of 'stretch' as well as 'fit' is also considered.

Strategy at the level of functions focuses on the implementation of business strategy through the areas of marketing, human resources, operations, logistics and finance. Each of these areas is critical to the effective and efficient implementation of an international strategy. If business performance falls short of expectations, it is likely that the organisation will first attempt to adjust its functional strategies before considering corrective adjustments in respect of the other levels of strategy.

Checklist

- Understanding international business strategy requires the reader to draw upon a number of different disciplines, bases and approaches to the subject.
- Three different approaches to international business strategy focus respectively on the external context, resource-based, and process issues.
- Each of the three main approaches to understanding international business strategy has a distinctive and important contribution to make.
- International business strategy is reflected in the spatial awareness, customer base, and scale and complexity of doing business.
- Organisational strategies can be considered in terms of four elements, namely: plan, position, perspective and process.
- Strategies are just as likely to be emergent as intended.
- The development of an organisation's strategy is normally incremental and evolutionary and only infrequently do major changes tend to occur.
- Corporate strategy is about 'adding value' through determining organisational scope and corporate parenting.
- Business strategy is concerned with developing and/or maintaining competitive advantage and relates to the organisation's product-markets.
- Competitive advantage may result from using either same or new game strategies.
- Companies should attempt to enter an upward rather than downward spiral in terms of how they compete.
- Linking future industry developments to core competences and market position can provide the basis of future competition.
- In assessing resource bases, 'stretch' is important together with 'fit'.
- Functional strategies are about the implementation of business strategy.
- Key business functions include marketing, human resources, operations, logistics and finance.
- Each functional area is critical to ensuring the effective and efficient implementation of the organisation's international business strategy.
- If business performance is judged unacceptable, corrective adjustments will be instigated, normally focusing initially on implementation.
- Only if inadequate business performance persists will attention turn to reviewing business and corporate strategies.

Danone SA

Introduction

Danone, which recently changed its name from BSN, ranks with Nestle and Unilever as one of the three leading European food manufacturing companies. Founded less than 30 years ago by its inspirational leader Antoine Riboud, the French company for many years focused on aggressive acquisitive expansion in Europe. According to Riboud 'in Europe our fundamental priority is, and will remain, gaining market share for our core products.' The company's strategy is to concentrate on the protection and development of its own extensive range of dairy, grocery, biscuit, beer and mineral water brands.

The next great challenge facing Danone is to share in the rapid expansion of markets in Eastern Europe and the Far East by establishing leading brands in those parts of the world. The strategy of rapid expansion in markets beyond Europe entails high expenditure and is open to considerable risks. Riboud's ambition for Danone to become a worldwide group also places considerable strain on management resources. If the company is not to stumble, strenuous efforts will be required to ensure that the rapid internationalisation programme does not depress business performance.

Vision and mindset

The company was formed in 1966 by the present chairman, Antoine Riboud, through the merger of two glass companies into Boussois-Souchon-Neuvesel (BSN). Having failed in an attempt to acquire the largest French glass manufacturer, St Gobain, in 1969, Riboud turned his attention to the food and drink sector. The first major move came a year later with the acquisition of the brewer Kronenbourg and Evian mineral water. In 1973 the present-day group started to take shape when BSN merged with the dairy concern Gervais Danone. By 1982, the last of the sheet glass businesses had been sold and non-food activities were confined to glass bottles, which are still part of the group today, representing about 10 per cent of total sales turnover.

Throughout the next decade the name BSN became recognised as an anachronism, although it was not until July 1994 that the change to Danone took place. 'The three letters that make up our name reflect its past more than its future. Unlike most of our major competitors, our name carries no reference to our core business, which is to feed as many people as possible around the world. On increasingly global markets where brands transcend national borders, this situation has become a burden,' said Mr Riboud.

By 1994, Riboud had been president of the company for some 28 years and was aged 75. He had publicly stated that he wished to continue in his present position for another five years, and hoped to see his son, Franck, succeed him. Riboud has proved to be a charismatic and almost omniscient figure, who frequently takes part in the operational decisions of the company. His ambition is to make the new corporate name, Danone, which is also the group's flagship brand in dairy products, the focus for steady expansion throughout the developing world.

Group strategy is firmly committed to further external expansion and the creation of a new international division has given the issue a high profile. This is divided into three business units, each covering all the group's products, with responsibility for operations outside Europe: one is responsible for Asia-Pacific; one for the Americas and Africa; and the third for exports. The challenge is to establish brand strength in these new markets on a par with existing operations. Outside Europe brand strength is less evident. Apart from the dairy brand Danone, the only worldwide brand is Evian – the top selling mineral water.

Corporate strategy

Danone's spectacular growth over the last 25 years has been fuelled by large branded acquisitions, including Gervais Danone and Bio (dairy), Lea & Perrins and Patzani (grocery), Belin and LU (biscuits), Kronenbourg and Kanterbrau (beer) and Evian and Volvic (mineral water). Riboud's unerring eye for a bargain is widely respected. He not only has the reputation of a mean buyer, but also has demonstrated considerable ability to orchestrate the post-acquisition integration of such purchases. These core skills facilitated the increasing momentum which characterised the growth of the group throughout the 1980s. Figure C1.1 charts sales growth through acquisition and brand development over a 10-year period, which came to an abrupt end in 1993.

Senior management are not focused solely on corporate acquisitions. Riboud believes that the key to competing more effectively in the food industry is a firm rein on costs of production, logistics and distribution. He is also convinced of the

Figure C1.1 Turnover record

(i) Ten year consolidated sales, 1984–93

Case Study 1

Figure C1.1 Turnover record

(ii) Year-on-year changes to consolidated sales, 1985–93

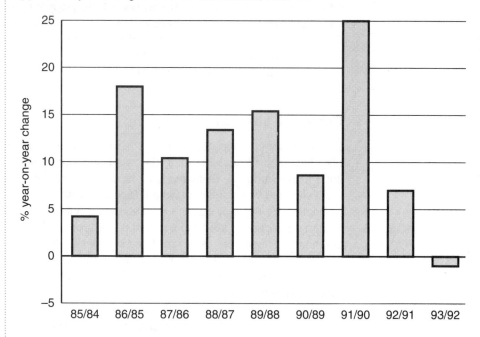

need for dynamic and efficient brand development and management. It is a well-established recipe that is now being applied to Danone's worldwide expansion: 'building on the same core principles which have served us so well in the past – leading market positions, robust brands, continuous innovation, flawless quality and production costs allowing us to offer attractive prices'.

In the particularly difficult sales environment encountered in 1993, Danone fully achieved its number one objective of holding onto existing share in all markets. Advertising expenditures were held at the levels of the previous year, although corporate policy prompted an increase in promotional outlays. Even so, there is still the suspicion in some quarters that the group could add even more value to its ongoing businesses. Figure C1.2 shows that over the last five years cumulative investments in subsidiaries exceeded year-on-year sales turnover increases. Generally, with a time lag, corporate investment has been rewarded with subsequent increases in sales growth. The Nabisco Europe biscuits purchase in 1989 is the exception to this rule: it was an extremely large investment that has clearly not performed.

Ever since Riboud took the crucial decision to fill glass bottles rather than look for new opportunities in packaging and containers, the shape of the group's portfolio of food and drink businesses has been in a state of flux. This has not precluded divestments as well as acquisitions. The disposal of Champagne Lanson, Pommery in 1990 was well timed, coming right at the top of the champagne price cycle. Table C1.1 highlights the key role played by head office in piecing together the jigsaw, as well as ensuring that such investments adopt group practices regarding quality assurance, staff flexibility and cost cutting. The level of activity and wide variety of strategic developments recorded in the table are typical of any given

Case Study 1

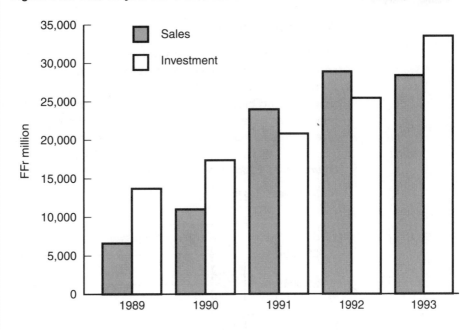

Figure C1.2 Year-on-year cumulative sales and investment in subsidiaries, 1989–93

Table C1.1 Acquisitions and divestments, 1993/94

Company	Country	Division	Nature of strategic development
European:			
Galbani	Italy	Dairy products	Increase in stake
Serdika	Bulgaria	Dairy products	Joint venture
Keretpest Plant	Hungary	Dairy products	Acquisition
Delta Dairy	Greece	Dairy products	Minority stake
B.E. International Food Ltd	United Kingdom	Grocery products	Minority stake
Vivagel	France	Grocery products	Acquisition
Aquas de Lanjarón	Spain	Mineral water	Acquisition
Volvic	France	Mineral water	Acquisition
SMDA (Mont Doré)	France	Mineral water	Acquisition
Seprosy	France	Containers	Divestment
Verreries de Masnieres	France	Containers	Merger
International:			
Britannia Brands	New Zealand, Singapore, Malaysia, Hong Kong	Asia-Pacific	Acquisition
Britannia Industries	India	Asia-Pacific	Increase in stake
Best Corporation	New Zealand	Asia-Pacific	Minority stake
Shanghai Dairy Corporation	China	Asia-Pacific	Joint venture
Delisle Foods Ltd	Canada	Americas-Africa	Acquisition

Source: Danone Annual Report, 1993

year, although the number of international acquisitions has increased.

Divisional activities

Traditionally Danone has organised itself around six divisions, which Figure C1.3 shows varied markedly in size in 1993: dairy products dominated with just one-third of sales turnover. A further third of turnover is shared equally between groceries and biscuits, while the remaining third is distributed evenly between beer, mineral water and containers. Given the high level of acquisitions and divestments taking place in any one year, year-on-year comparisons are to some

Figure C1.3 Divisional performance

(i) Divisional sales turnover, 1989–93

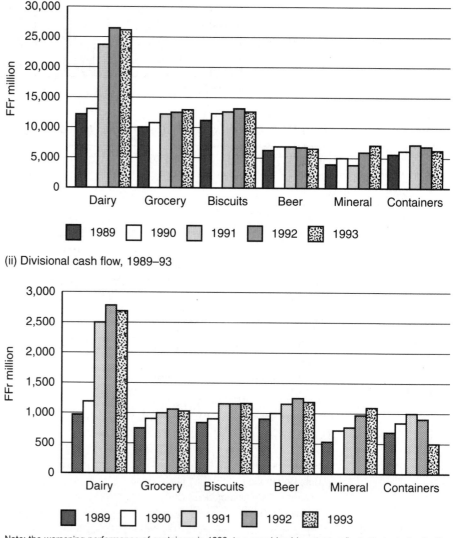

(ii) Divisional cash flow, 1989–93

Note: the worsening performance of containers in 1993, to a considerable extent, reflects the inclusion for the first time of loss-making associated companies and related restructuring costs.

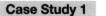

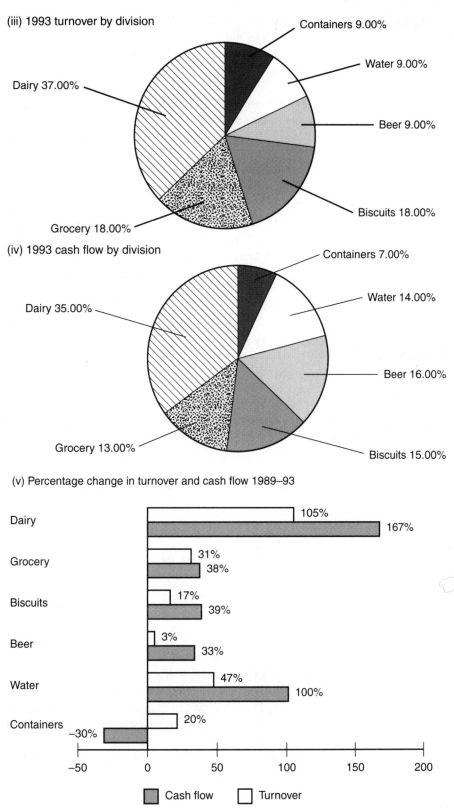

(iii) 1993 turnover by division

Containers 9.00%

Water 9.00%

Dairy 37.00%

Beer 9.00%

Biscuits 18.00%

Grocery 18.00%

(iv) 1993 cash flow by division

Containers 7.00%

Water 14.00%

Dairy 35.00%

Beer 16.00%

Grocery 13.00%

Biscuits 15.00%

(v) Percentage change in turnover and cash flow 1989–93

Dairy 105% 167%

Grocery 31% 38%

Biscuits 17% 39%

Beer 3% 33%

Water 47% 100%

Containers –30% 20%

–50 0 50 100 150 200

Cash flow   Turnover

39

extent problematic. Even so, 1993 saw sales curtailed in every division except mineral water – where the decline in continuing business was offset by additional turnover generated from the three acquisitions listed in Table C1.1.

Sales turnover trends differed widely from division to division over the five-year period 1989–93. As Figures C1.3 (i) and (v) show, in this period turnover of dairy products more than doubled from FFr12,627 to FFr25,898 (+105 per cent). By contrast, beer sales remain virtually unchanged at FFr6188 and FFr6353 (+3 per cent) respectively. Across the six divisions the average five-year growth rate was 43.5 per cent, which was only matched by mineral water. Groceries fell a little short of the average, while containers and biscuits only recorded around 20 per cent turnover growth over the period.

While group turnover fell 1 per cent overall between 1992 and 1993, the comparable fall in operating cash flow was 6 per cent. Moreover, Figure C1.3 (ii) shows that five out of the six divisions suffered a decline in operating cash flow. Two trends have developed recently in the relationship between food retailers and manufacturers, where downward pressure is being exerted on the cash and profit margins received by manufacturers. First, in order to improve their returns major European retailers are targeting branded high margin products for the development of own brands. Secondly, retailers are increasingly selecting smaller national companies as their own-brand producers, with the deliberate intention of eroding the market shares of the dominant players in each major food sector. Table C1.2 shows own-label market shares held by the major food retailers in each country.

Table C1.2 Growth in own-label food, 1980–95: percentage of total market accounted for by own-label products

Country	1980	1990	1995 (est)
Belgium	n.a	16	25
France	11	20	35
Germany	15	24	30
Italy	n.a.	5	10
The Netherlands	n.a.	24	30
United Kingdom	22	31	40

Source: Trade estimates

Private or own-label market penetration expanded rapidly between 1980 and 1990. This trend is estimated to have accelerated between 1990 and 1995. Own label offers a direct threat to Danone, and other manufacturers' brands. Pressure to utilise surplus capacity has prompted Danone to undertake limited own-label production. For the moment own-label volumes probably do not exceed 5 per cent of group turnover, although within biscuits they could be as high as 12 per cent. Table C1.3 shows the current price differentials between manufacturers' and own-label brands on three selected products being sold in both France and the United Kingdom.

Case Study 1

The growth of own label is inhibiting price increases and adding to the promotional expenses of manufacturers who seek to protect their brands. Many industry observers believe the growth of retailers' own-label products shows no signs of slowing. Pricing differentials between manufacturers' brands and own-label products look likely to fall further if, as seems likely, mainland European markets follow the United Kingdom's example and own label penetration increases.

Table C1.3 Comparison of price differentials between selected manufacturers' and own-label brands, France and the UK, 1993: percentage by which manufacturers' prices exceed those of own label

Country	Mineral water	Pasta	Sauces
France	41	48	41
United Kingdom	27	4	26

Figure C1.4 shows that no division of Danone was shielded from its competitors, with all food manufacturing businesses vulnerable to the growth of retailers' brands. The company is fighting to keep its market share positions by cutting prices and then cutting costs. The company has instigated a sweeping drive to cut costs over the last two years. This is all part of the ongoing rationalisation process directed towards offsetting the upward pressure on selling costs and the inability to raise prices. Reflecting on these pressures, it is possible to wonder whether Danone's product portfolio is too 1980s oriented, rather than looking to the consumers of the year 2000.

International division

The international division, created in 1994, is expected to grow rapidly through a combination of external and organic growth, although because of the lack of

Figure C1.4 Operating cash flow margin by divisions, 1989–93

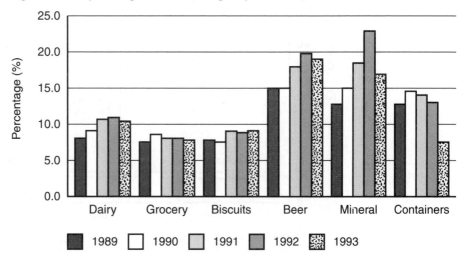

41

suitable acquisition opportunities the emphasis is likely to be on internal expansion and joint ventures. This is also because experience has taught Danone that local expertise is a vital ingredient of eventual success. In order to co-ordinate its Asian operations more effectively, a 'nerve centre' has been established in Singapore, which will control and promote expansion in the region, and ensure any potential synergies arising out of acquisitions are exploited. In addition to the Asia-Pacific grocery businesses of Britannia, Amoy and Best Foods (mainly biscuits and sauces), international operations comprise Danone's dairy operations in the USA, Mexico and Brazil, as well as Delisle in Canada. Even so, in 1993 the mature and highly competitive European market still accounted for 93 per cent of sales turnover and 95 per cent of operating cash flow (Figure C1.5).

Not only is group strategy fully committed to correct the geographical imbalance in sales turnover, but also to boost operating margins outside Europe. The inclusion of Britannia and some smaller acquisitions in Danone's results will raise international sales to around 10 per cent of turnover in 1994. Given, however, the lower margins and profitability, the cash generated by these business will be below the levels achieved in Europe. Comparisons with mature competitors, including Nestlé and Unilever who have had many years to develop their global food brands, are presented in Figure C1.6.

Danone needs much more time to develop its worldwide network of products and operations. As the international division matures, profits should rise as operating margins, estimated at around 6 per cent in 1994, start to respond positively

Figure C1.5 Sales turnover and cash flow

(i) Ten year regional sales record turnover (%)

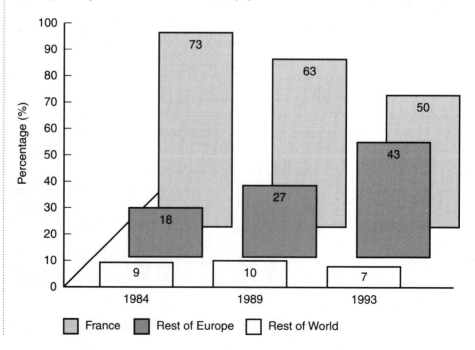

Case Study 1

Figure C1.5 Sales turnover and cash flow

(ii) Ten year regional record of operating cash flow (%)

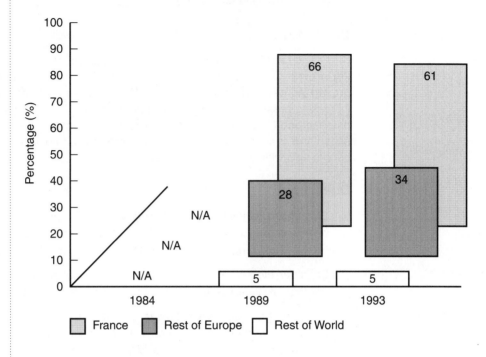

Figure C1.6 Major food manufacturers, rest of world (ROW) sales turnover, cash flow margin and group cash flow, 1993

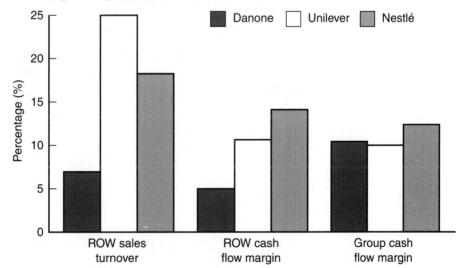

and the company increasingly achieves critical mass in a number of key markets, and exploits available synergies. Assuming sales turnover of FFr200 million by the year 2000 and an operating margin of 10 per cent, profits will rise to FFr20 million. Before this date the company is likely to rely predominately on its

43

European operations to sustain performance. If the performance in Europe can be maintained, in the longer term growth across the international division should be able to carry Danone forward.

Conclusion

Danone is facing a major challenge: how to sustain the virtuous circle of increasing growth and business performance. Against the context of slow volume growth across the food sector, its European operations are coming under increasing pressure from the growing power of retailers and the increasing cost of brand support. To manage these pressures the company is seeking to extend its scope and scale of operations, moving from a predominately European focus to becoming a truly worldwide competitor.

Questions

(1) *Distinguish between Danone's corporate and business strategies. What has been the role of Antoine Riboud in shaping the development of Danone? Review the strengths and weaknesses of this style of management.*

(2) *Consider the extent to which the company has changed its scope over the last thirty years and the methods of strategic development employed.*

(3) *Consider the company's business divisions. Are all divisions performing equally? Do you have any concerns about likely future performance? What strategic business options would you suggest the divisions might like to consider.*

(4) *How do Danone's geographical scope and business performance compare with those of other major food manufactures? What do these comparisons suggest in terms of Danone's future strategy?*

(5) *What do you see as the main challenges facing the company over the next three years in trying to achieve its stated corporate ambition of future international business development?*

Chapter 2

THE INTERNATIONALISATION PROCESS

Key learning objectives

To understand:

- the difference between 'pull' and 'push' factors
- the concept of discontinuity in moving away from a local/regional/national focus
- the external and internal triggers to cross-border entry
- how firm-specific factors may prevent or modify adaptation of external factors
- the application of the 'phase model' of international business development
- the importance of international financial management
- measures to assess international business performance

Context

As international trade and business links have increased in complexity, the strategic imperative facing firms of all sizes is responding to the twin pressures of increasing trade liberalisation and international competition. The increasing internationalisation of agriculture, manufacturing and services means that firms of all sizes may face competition from companies worldwide. To survive in such an international market, firms must choose between becoming one of the relatively few large competitors with the critical mass to service the whole market worldwide, or being a smaller-scale competitor focusing on one or a small number of domestic market niches.

Such competitive environments are typically industry specific. To survive in a given international industry, firms must have the strategic capability to recognise critical change factors and react rapidly. When establishing an

45

international market position, it is equally important to build an organisational form that delivers the performance required by the strategy. The structure of the chapter is as follows:

- *international business dynamics*
- *cross-border market entry decisions*
- *international business development*
- *international financial management*
- *measuring international business performance*

The chapter begins by looking at international business dynamics and asks (i) why is consolidation taking place among the leading players in many industries, and (ii) how can small and medium-sized companies compete internationally? This prompts consideration of why firms seek international business development. The triggers to the internationalisation process emphasise the dynamic interplay of external and internal factors. The organisation's external and internal contexts also shape the nature of the strategic response.

The phase model of international business development considers how the organisation is advanced in terms of international presence or absence. The phase model incorporates the spectrum between local, sub-national competitors at one end, and worldwide competitors at the other. For companies trading across borders, international financial management is a key area for attention. Effective and efficient financial management can contribute to overall business performance. The section on measuring international business performance examines the use of both financial indicators and the balanced scorecard. The chapter concludes with a summary and checklist. BMW, the German automobile manufacturer, is the case featured at the end of the chapter.

International business dynamics

International business dynamics reflect the changing international business environment and the organisational response of companies whose competitive strategies increasingly involve crossing national borders. As soon as at least one competitor gains from taking an international strategic stance competitive forces begin to change, with leading firms needing to respond. The dynamic nature of such responses inevitably results in increased international exposure, requiring the co-ordination of relationships with suppliers, distributors and customers across functions and geographical boundaries. Ultimately, such companies may seek to become worldwide players with international production and marketing operations, attempting to capture lower costs and higher brand awareness than is available to purely domestic competitors.

For these firms the world may be viewed as the home market. Competitors wishing to serve such worldwide product-markets have no choice but to internationalise their own operations. This does not mean that small and medium-sized firms should always seek to reach the necessary critical mass to serve a worldwide market. In practice most firms will never grow to the point where they become worldwide competitors, with cross-border production and marketing operations. Rather, such firms can seek to strengthen their competitive position by exploiting their unimportance and serving those parts of the market where the lack of a worldwide presence does not place them at a disadvantage.

A process of *bi-polarisation* is taking place in many industries worldwide, with a small number of large firms and a much larger number of smaller players competing for business. In such circumstances medium-sized firms, which may still dominate a particular national market, must make choices: either they must grow to become sufficiently large and capture critical mass, or they must aim to operate in those segments or niches of a market where being big is not essential to commercial success. The alternative is to sell the business before it is too late to another competitor who is also seeking to strengthen their competitive advantage by reaching the critical mass necessary to serve a wider international market.

Accompanying internationalisation is a change in the strategic perception of *how* you do business and *where* you do business. A home country orientation has major risks. First, a domestic market perspective prompts a lack of awareness and appreciation of the opportunities offered across borders. Secondly, arising out of this attitude is an increased vulnerability to international competition in the home market. This emphasises that no firm can persist in believing that international competition will not affect them on account of being small or because they are focused solely on their local market. All too frequently and within a comparatively short period, a local market may be regarded as part of the expanded home market of an international competitor.

All serious players within an industry must decide how to meet the competitive challenge of the internationalisation process. The bi-polarisation argument suggests that smaller firms must either occupy market niches which are too small to interest the largest firms, or they must increase in size. It is important to stress that niche markets do not necessarily mean local or national markets, and that successful niche players will often take an international perspective. As a result, not all niche players can be described as small in absolute terms.

Consequently, the terms 'large' and 'small' must be viewed in their industry-specific context. BMW AG, the luxury car maker featured in the case at the end of this chapter, is a small niche player in the context of the world's automotive industry. With less than 2 per cent of world car production, it is unquestionably small when compared to the broadly based volume competitors. In absolute terms, this specialist competitor was one of the 20 largest German companies in 1994.

Cross-border market entry decisions

Companies may be attracted to cross-border markets because of strong *pull* or *push* factors, or a combination of both. Pull factors are defined as factors which entice companies away from their existing local/national regional/national markets because of the perceived attractiveness of a cross-border market. The following list offers a number of factors which might be described as exerting a pull to companies moving into cross-border markets:

● a rapidly expanding market, which offers the prospect of an attractive level of sales;
● lower costs of production/supply, due to indigenous resource base (e.g. raw materials, labour) or because of easier regulatory climate; and
● higher levels of profitability when compared to existing markets.

Conversely, push factors arise out of perceived difficulties in a company's existing markets, and the opportunities to overcome these by moving into cross-border markets. Again, examples of push factors can be identified:

● market saturation in existing local market;
● increasing cost of production/supply due to rising input costs or increasingly difficult regulatory environment; and
● deteriorating levels of profitability.

Looking at pull and push factors in this way tends to suggest that the process of internationalisation is inherently a rational decision-making activity triggered primarily by forces external to the organisation. While this may be the case, in practice the organisation's internal context, as described by its vision/mindset and organisational dynamics, may be as, or even more, influential in its decision to internationalise. For example, the single-minded vision of an inspirational chief executive may be instrumental in taking a company international, even though its existing local/national market strategy is delivering good levels of business performance and there is the prospect of further sales growth. This was certainly the case with Honda and its decision to enter the US market. In this example, the company's founding partners, Honda and Fujisawa, spurred by ambition as much as any deduction, triggered entry to the American market (Illustration 1.2).

The relationship and interaction between an organisation's external and internal context provide an explanation of the internationalisation process. The development of an international business strategy, as described in Figure 2.1, is about explaining how an organisation leaves the loop of local/national business strategy and enters the loop of international business development. This model uses both external and internal triggers to explain the circumstances by which companies move from being local to international. Examining the components of the model in detail, the local business strategy loop describes the product-market options – *market penetration*, *product development*, *product extension* and *geographical expansion* – from which an established firm can choose.

The internationalisation process, illustrated by Figure 2.1, suggests that some organisations at least will arrive at a point in their history when they seek to break out of their local/national market. This cross-border process may be rationalised in terms of push or pull factors discussed earlier, but triggered by either external or internal factors, or a combination of both.

Figure 2.1 Developing an international business strategy

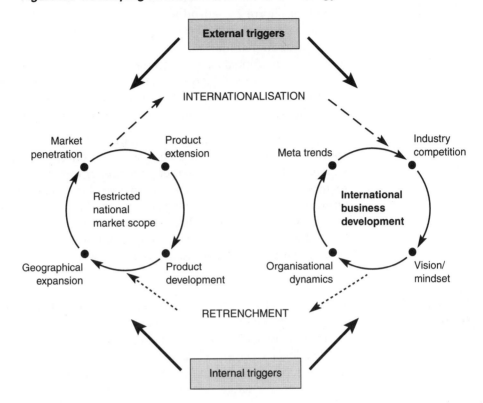

Four important observations can be made.

- Some companies may never attempt to enter cross-border markets and may continue to exist within a local/national business context, pursuing business development through strategies identified with the first loop of Figure 2.1 – product extension, product development, geographical expansion and market penetration – focused on their domestic market. Restricted geographical scope is the rule rather than the exception for many small and medium-sized enterprises (SMEs), many of whom continue to believe that their market is not threatened by international competition.

- The international loop of Figure 2.1 becomes the focus for those firms which do decide to pursue international business development. Consideration needs to be given to the informing role played by *meta trends, industry competition, vision/mindset* and *organisational dynamics*. Both meta trends (broad environmental factors) and industry competition describe the organisation's external context and the opportunities and threats it is trying to manage. Similarly, vision/mindset and organisational dynamics describe the organisation's internal context.

- If initial and subsequent development of the international business strategy is judged successful, further entry of cross-border markets and their development may be anticipated. Once the initial entry is affected, the organisation is faced with the same strategic options in growing the business in its newly entered markets as those described by the first loop of Figure 2.1 – product extension, product development, geographical expansion and market penetration – but this time in the context of an international market.

● If the international business strategy is judged a failure or conditions in the organisation's local/national market require it, a company may be forced to retrench and withdraw from cross-border markets, on either a temporary or what with hindsight proves to be a permanent basis.

The model underlying Figure 2.1 reflects the dynamics of the internationalisation process by allowing companies to enter international markets, to expand out of this initial market presence, or to retrench back to being solely focused on the local/regional/national market. The fundamental point to be appreciated is that, while changes to external and/or internal triggers explain *why* organisations seek to develop international business strategies, the external and internal contexts are also important in shaping the content or the *what* of the organisation's international business strategy.

External change factors

A change factor is classified as external where it relates to developments which are outside the organisation's control. External change factors relate to factors operating either at the meta level or at the level of industry competition.

Meta-level changes relate to the organisation's broad environment. This may be subdivided into *political/legal, economic, ecological, social* and *technological* triggers to change. Set against the broad context, *competitive forces* will operate at the level of the industry, reflecting the changing intensity of competition. Firm-specific external triggers relate either to a change in ownership of the organisation arising out of a *take-over/merger*, and/or to *shareholder pressure* which results in managerial changes, leading in turn to a change in strategy. Indeed a combination, rather than a single factor listed in Figure 2.2, may be responsible for a company breaking out of its local business strategy loop and beginning to internationalise.

For external factors to bring about change they must be interpreted by the organisation and acted on in a way which results in a company entering international markets. Often external triggers may have been present for a number of years but have not been acted upon because of the organisation's internal context. What causes these external triggers to lead to a change in strategy is likely to be internal triggers which enable a fundamental reappraisal of the organisation's strategy, and in this context result in the pursuit of international business development. Indeed, a company may exhibit a serious mismatch between the demands of its customers and its product/service offerings over a number of years before changes to its strategy are forthcoming.

Internal change factors

Internal change factors involve the complex realignment of the vision/mindset and organisational dynamics. One of the most potent internal triggers for change is the advent of an organisational crisis. Past evidence suggests that

Figure 2.2 External and internal triggers for change

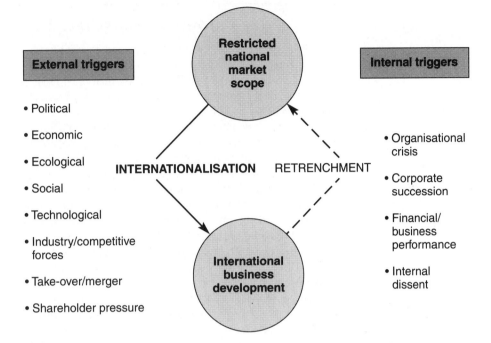

the reporting of poor financial performance, particularly in the Anglo-Saxon market economies, is often the trigger for increased shareholder pressure and the demand for a change in strategy or, which often amounts to the same thing, a change in the senior management of the company. In Germany, where the commercial banks are major stakeholders in many large companies, the role of ousting chief executives deemed to have failed is left to the supervisory board. Illustration 2.1 describes one of the most dramatic examples of this process in recent German business history.

Where significant changes to the senior personnel of a company take place this is often the trigger for a reappraisal of the organisation's business strategy and the decision to take new strategic directions. Such changes are often accompanied by changes to the organisation's structure, power and control. Equally, the perceived failure of the company's strategy may result in internal pressure for the removal of those senior managers deemed to be the architects of that strategy. Where both shareholder pressure (external) and managerial dissent (internal) are present, those responsible for the strategy may find it difficult to survive. Illustration 2.2, on the failure of the proposed merger between Volvo, the Swedish car producer, and Renault, the French motor vehicle manufacturer, provides a good example of the presence of both external and internal pressures bringing about a change in senior management and correspondingly in strategic direction.

Where shareholder pressure is not present, as in, say, a family business, the internal trigger for change may come through management succession, on for example the retirement of the founder of the company and/or a dominant chief

Illustration 2.1

Metallgesellschaft AG

Metallgesellschaft is a Frankfurt-based international metals, mining and industrials group. With an annual turnover of in the region of DM25 billion (£9.9 billion), the company operates some 250 subsidiaries. This structure reflects the strategy of Heinz Schimmelbusch, the chief executive of the Metallgesellchaft group from 1988 until the end of 1993.

During his stewardship, Schimmelbusch's strategy had been to reduce dependence on base metals by acquiring companies in other business areas, and in particular to develop the group as a provider of environmental services in Europe. The slow diffusion of strict environmental controls across Europe resulted in poor profitability from these businesses, exacerbating difficulties arising from falling metal prices. Confidence in Schimmelbusch was further weakened by the widespread perception that the company had used creative accounting techniques to enhance reported profits in 1991/92.

The events which finally led to Schimmelbusch's demise related to problems in the USA and Metallgesellschaft's trading subsidiary, MG Corp, which had experienced difficulties in its dealings in oil futures on the New York Mercantile Exchange. Metallgesellschaft was forced to seek assistance from its bankers in order to meet 'margin payments' – large cash calls arising out of its oil futures contracts – as the price of oil fell. Deutsche Bank and Dresdner Bank, two of Germany's largest banks and major shareholders of Metallgellschaft, provided the necessary liquidity to overcome the immediate crisis.

As the scale of Metallgesellschaft's problems became clear the supervisory board took action, complaining that the management had deliberately withheld information. Schimmelbusch and finance director Forster were sacked following a meeting of the supervisory board. A further four directors were either retired or demoted. Schimmelbusch was replaced by Kajo Neukirchen, who in the immediate aftermath announced that the group would refocus on its core business. As part of this strategy the sale of a number of subsidiaries to improve the cash flow of the group was anticipated.

The case of Metallgesellschaft illustrates how the supervisory board, under the control of the company's main bankers, removed almost the entire management team and installed a new chief executive. While the scale of the change was unprecedented, the case of Metallgesellschaft emphasises how, with the institutional shareholding structure of German companies, commercial banks who are both creditors and shareholders of companies are able to play a key role in removing an incumbent management team if this is deemed necessary.

Source: Based on reports appearing in the *Financial Times* between 18 and 22 December 1993, and 24 January 1994

---

executive. Once again, the incoming manager is unlikely to manage the business in exactly the same way as his or her predecessor and changes to strategy are likely to result. Alternatively, the founder of the company may have a clear vision of entering cross-border markets when starting the company with the result that a relatively small company trades in cross-border markets at a early stage of its development, while a more established competitor with a different set of organisational dynamics remains exclusively focused on local/national markets.

Illustration 2.2

The proposed merger of Volvo AB and Renault SA

In 1990 Volvo, the Swedish car producer, and Renault of France announced their agreement to form a major strategic alliance. The formation of the strategic alliance and the subsequent exchange of cross-shareholdings in 1991 was expected to be the prelude to a full merger at a later date.

A full merger of the two companies was proposed in 1993. In the end it did not take place. The merger was destroyed by the opposition of Volvo's shareholders and an internal management revolt. Volvo's shareholders found the terms being offered unacceptable, and also strongly criticised Pehr Gyllenhammar, the chairman who had led the group since 1971. Gyllenhammar's style of management had many critics and there was suspicion that the proposed merger had been crafted secretly between the chairman of Volvo and Renault with little attempt to inform other members of the board or senior management. Faced with widespread shareholder disaffection and a revolt of his senior staff, Pehr Gyllenhammar was forced to resign together with four other board members.

With the forced resignation of Gyllenhammar, Volvo's car operations faced an uncertain future. With its small domestic market and limited product range the company badly needed a partner as the world's car industry consolidated. At the same time, the aborted merger left both Volvo and Renault with difficulties in maintaining their existing alliance. Volvo's new management team would need to face these challenges and fashion a new strategic direction.

Source: Based on reports appearing in the *Financial Times* between 3 and 6 December 1993

These points serve to emphasise the importance of the internal context, which is strongly influenced by the nature of the organisation's corporate culture. The corporate culture of an organisation, which by its nature is difficult to define, describes the values, norms and behaviour of the organisation which either formally and/or informally govern how the collective organisation reacts to both routine and change events. Analysing corporate culture is an important area if the differing actions and reactions of various businesses are to be understood. Indeed, the existence of corporate culture explains why, when organisations are faced with the same external stimulus, they often react so differently.

In conclusion, an awareness of both the organisation's external and internal contexts is vital if the reasons for a company moving away from a purely local business strategy, or indeed being forced to retrench from international markets, are to be understood. Appreciation of this basic premise serves to emphasise that those commentators who look for solely external factors in explaining a firm's international business strategy are likely to reach erroneous conclusions as to the factors driving the internationalisation process at the level of the firm. A detailed examination of both external (Chapter 3) and internal triggers (Chapter 4) to the internationalisation process is undertaken in Part II.

International business development

The constantly changing dynamics of an organisation's external environment and the interplay with its internal context offer an explanation as to when and why organisations move out of a purely local/national business strategy. The same factors also explain the timing and the reasons organisations may develop out of an initial international market presence and expand their international presence until ultimately they become a worldwide competitor. The process is both dynamic and continuous, with four distinct market phases to international business development being identified, namely (i) *restricted national market scope*; (ii) *international market entry and development*; (iii) *international regional*; and (iv) *worldwide*. These four stages are illustrated by Figure 2.3. The process of moving from one stage to another is not, however, necessarily sequential.

Figure 2.3 The phase model of international business development

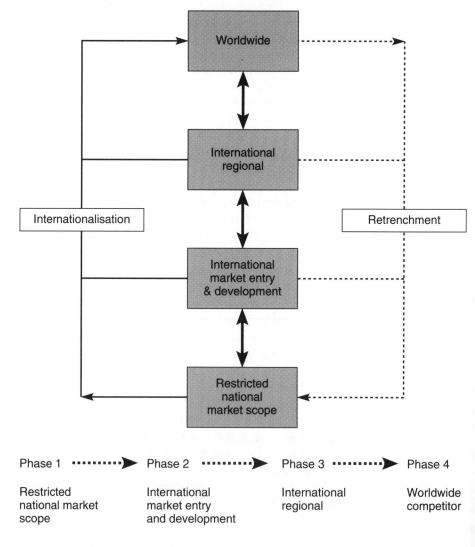

Starting with a purely *restricted national market scope* the organisation has no more than a local/national/regional market perspective and has no real involvement in cross-border sales, other than perhaps the occasional opportunistic export sales when short-term conditions are highly advantageous. The actual and intended thrust of the organisation continues to have a local orientation. As previously noted, many SMEs retain a domestic orientation and do not seek to break out of this restricted local market scope. Examining the likelihood of companies who employed up 200 staff engaging in exporting, Pera International (1993) sent some 4000 questionnaires to SMEs in France, Germany, Spain and the UK. While the responses varied by country, a considerable number of respondents did not consider themselves to be actively pursuing cross-border sales. Chapter 5 examines in detail whether restricted national market scope is a sustainable strategy in the face of increasing international competition in many sectors of the world economy.

International market entry and development, resulting in a cross-border presence in a single or small cluster of markets, may be considered the first phase of a company's international business development. Explanations of this discontinuity and the break with a purely local focus centre on the external and internal triggers to the internationalisation process introduced earlier. This is often a critical moment in the development of many firms, reflecting as it does a considerable increase not only in the the scope and complexity of the organisation but also in the level of business risk.

For many manufacturing organisations the initial entry to a cross-border market is likely to be on the basis of exports from the home country's base. This may be managed through a third-party distributor or agent. Alternatively, the organisation may set up its own sales company to direct sales and marketing in the international market. While the market scope has become international with both approaches, production remains local to the home market. Indeed, at this early stage exporting may be an additional function to the existing organisation, rather than part of the company's main thrust.

Sooner or later, if the organisation continues to expand its international market presence it is likely that it will consider setting up a cross-border production facility. Such a facility may be exclusively for the local market in which it is located, or serve a wider need, perhaps even sending output back to the company's country of origin. This move from exporting to cross-border production is likely to be a further discontinuity in developing the company's international presence. It also serves to emphasise that international business development is multi-dimensional and is not simply about marketing or production. These and other issues in respect of international market entry and development are examined in Chapter 6.

International regional business strategies are invariably focused on one of the three major economic trading areas of the world economy: North American Free Trade Area (NAFTA), European Union (EU) and East Asia/South Pacific. Organisations have three choices as to how they serve a regional market. In the first case, a company may be a *regional exporter* using a single production base. In the second case, the organisation's international regional strategy may be considered to comprise a series of country-based strategies, and termed *fragmented international regional*. The main benefit of operating in this manner is the ability to leverage organisational competences, which might include marketing, technology, and managerial capabilities. In the final case not only are organisational competences leveraged, but the organisation treats the region as a single entity and attempts to exploit regional interdependencies in order to achieve regional-scale economies. This is known as operating a *co-ordinated international regional strategy*. The development of international regional strategies is the subject of Chapter 7.

The *worldwide* competitor whose strategy encompasses all the major markets of the world is in the final phase of international business development. A key question is how the worldwide market place is to be served. At one end of the spectrum is the global exporter. This is a company who seeks to serve the world market from its home base, by exporting sales. Japanese car companies, including Honda, Nissan and Toyota, were global exporters at a relatively early stage of their business development. More recently, these companies have developed significant worldwide production facilities, responding to the threats of protectionism and changes to the relative costs of producing in alternative locations.

Worldwide competitors are faced with a range of organisational forms, and associated processes and cultures, when considering how to configure their global strategies. If the global exporter is at one end of the spectrum, then the multi-local organisation is at the other. Between these two extremes are other organisational forms, including the international company which in the past has been strongly favoured by US-based worldwide competitors. Each of these organisational forms has a number of relative strengths and weaknesses. Seeking to overcome the inherent weaknesses, Bartlett and Ghoshal (1989) emphasise the need to develop the transnational organisation. These and other issues associated with the development of worldwide competitors are examined in Chapter 8.

The internationalisation process is inherently dynamic and not uni-directional, as explained by the bi-directional arrows which form an integral part of Figure 2.3. The process is intuitive and/or rational, driven by external and/or internal change factors. To summarise, four key observations are made regarding the internationalisation process:

(1) Firms which move from one phase to another of international development may well at some stage in the future move backwards (as well as forwards), thereby readily changing the scope of their business strategy.
(2) While formally the model includes four phases, companies may miss one or more phases as they develop their international focus.
(3) The pace of change between phases is something highly specific to the particular organisation. In the past some companies, for example Japanese manufacturers, have succeeded in moving from a purely local focus to achieving a worldwide presence within a comparatively short period.
(4) The reasons for companies moving from one phase to another are multi-dimensional and cannot be explained by a single factor. It is normally a combination of external and internal factors.

In conclusion, the strategic imperatives of organisations at different stages of the phase model demonstrate marked differences. As a consequence, the strategic needs of organisations at each phase of the model – (i) restricted national market scope; (ii) international market entry and development; (iii) international regional; and (iv) worldwide – will be dealt with separately in Part III.

International financial management

A key business feature which affects international business performance is the extent to which organisations need to manage what are often complex monetary transactions across national boundaries. As a result of undertaking cross-border sales, an international business needs to move funds between different national currencies and tax regimes. While recognising that international financial management constitutes a major subject in its own right, the following topics have been selected to suggest some of the key areas requiring management attention:

● transaction exposure to foreign currency movements;
● translation of cross-border earnings, assets and liabilities; and
● international cash management.

Transaction exposure to foreign currency movements

Companies have a *transaction exposure* to the extent that current and future income or expenditure is affected by exchange rate movements. International businesses trading across a number of cross-border markets are often faced with having to manage complex permutations of foreign currencies. Very often such businesses may find themselves managing contradictory movements in exchange rates, which collectively can make a significant difference to their business performance.

As organisations move beyond the initial phase of international business development, complexities may well increase to the extent that production facilities may be configured on the basis of international, regional or worldwide market needs. While such strategies may increase exchange rate complexities, they may also counter the likely risks of adverse currency movements to the extent that production facilities are located within main regional currency zones focused on the US dollar, the German deutschmark and the Japanese yen. In this way, the dispersion of key value-adding facilities in line with consumption around the globe may be a deliberate strategy to counter individual currency movements. Illustration 2.3 indicates the extent to which one worldwide competitor, Swiss-based company Nestlé, experienced currency fluctuations in its 1993 accounting period by comparing sales in the company's local and reporting currencies (Swiss francs).

For a company reliant on an export strategy, using a 'home' production base involves particular risks. To emphasise this point, Illustration 2.4 examines the impact on the French company Le Creuset, the featured case in Chapter 6, of movements in the dollar exchange rate.

Illustration 2.3

Nestlé: sales to principal markets in 1993

Nestlé, the Swiss-registered food and drink manufacturer, had to manage movements across a wide range of foreign exchange currencies in 1993. Taking the company's 10 largest national markets by sales, profit levels compared with the previous year, as reported in the local currency, fluctuated from +0.3 per cent to +2308.6 per cent. When translated into the company's reporting currency, the performance varied between –13.7 per cent and +24.6 per cent.

Swiss francs (millions)		Differences 1993/92 (%)	
		Swiss francs	Local currency
USA	12,776	+8.2	+3.1
France	7051	–0.6	+1.0
Germany	6487	+1.7	+2.4
UK	3466	–7.6	+2.3
Japan	2878	+24.6	+3.2
Brazil	2795	+21.2	+2308.6
Italy	2737	+5.4	+29.2
Spain	1902	–13.7	+1.8
Mexico	1875	+8.1	+2.2
Canada	1122	–0.5	+0.3

Source: Nestlé Annual Report 1993, p 12

If the degree of transaction exposure is judged to be significant, the company may wish to reduce or eliminate this area of risk through the use of hedging. Hedging is a deliberate policy to reduce exposure to unforeseen movements in foreign exchange rates. In deciding whether it wishes to develop a hedging policy the organisation needs to do the following:

- Identify its net transaction exposure on a country-by-country basis, in order to assess which currencies are most influential in effecting business performance. In the case of worldwide competitors, as suggested above a significant amount of transaction exposure may be 'netted off' through the operation of subsidiaries located in different areas of the world. By contrast, as Illustration 2.4 suggests, the international exporter is much more vulnerable.
- Having assessed the degree of exposure, the organisation then needs to consider to what extent it wishes to hedge. It may decide to hedge all its future transactions or only a proportion.
- Finally, the organisation needs to choose the method by which it hedges. While there are different ways to undertake a policy of hedging, all involve entering

Illustration 2.4

Le Creuset SA – The effect of movements in the dollar exchange rates on reported profits

Le Creuset SA is a manufacturer of household goods, in particular cast iron cooking utensils, which it exports from its French plants. As an international company, with the majority of its sales in cross-border markets, Le Creuset is highly exposed to currency fluctuations. With all its production concentrated in France and profits reported in £ sterling, on account of its London stock exchange listing, the French franc and £ are the most important currencies for the company. This means that, while the cost of sales are in French francs, all sales need to be translated into sterling for the purposes of reporting profits.

As the USA is the company's third largest market, the US dollar is also a key currency. The following illustration shows what might have happened to the company's 1993 reported profits if the US dollar exchange rate moved by ±10 per cent against both the French franc and £ sterling.

Sensitivity to movements in the US $: FFr/US$ and US$/£

| | | 1993 Average 5.67/1.5 | | +10% 6.24/1.35 | | −10% 5.10/1.65 | |
	FFrm	US$m	£m	US$m	£m	US$m	£m
Turnover	–	15.3	10.2	15.3	11.3	15.3	9.3
Cost of sales	45.93	8.1	5.9	7.3	5.4	9.0	5.5
Other costs	–	5.5	3.6	5.5	4.1	5.5	3.3
Profits before tax	–	1.7	1.1	2.5	1.8	0.8	0.5

Notes: (1) US turnover based on 1993 accounts.
(2) Cost of sales assumed to be 53 per cent of turnover; all other costs relating to US sales assumed to occur in the US.

The table demonstrates that a 10 per cent appreciation of the US$ against the two European currencies would have increased Le Creuset's reported profits from its US operations by over 60 per cent in 1993 to £1.8m. Similarly, a 10 per cent fall in the dollar would reduce US profits by more than half. Clearly, movements in the dollar exchange rate are of considerable importance to Le Creuset's reported profits.

Source: The authors, based on Annual Report and accounts

into agreements regarding the rate at which future business transactions will be converted into another currency. Although not without a cost, hedging does in theory enable the risk of adverse foreign exchange movements to be managed. Foreign exchange contracts and currency options are two of the most popular methods of hedging. When adopting a hedging policy the company may use short-term instruments or decide to employ longer-term contracts. As Illustration 2.5 suggests, purchasing currencies too far in advance can lead to difficulties and indeed increase rather than decrease currency exposure.

Illustration 2.5

Japan Airlines (JAL)

Japan Airlines (JAL) indicated that it was likely to record currency losses of some yen 176 billion during its 1994 accounting year. These losses are a result of long-term forward currency buying contracts which the company entered into in 1985. Since entering into these contracts, which relate to the purchase of US dollars, the American currency has depreciated significantly against the yen.

JAL's forward buying of the US currency at predetermined rates reflects its annual bill, in excess of $1 billion, to pay for fuel and aircraft, both of which are priced in dollars. By comparison the company's sales revenues are predominately received in yen.

The company's decision to forward purchase dollars at rates determined up to 10 years in advance has proved to be costly in an era of floating exchange rates. As a result, company policy in respect of entering into new hedging contracts has changed. The policy is now to buy dollars on shorter and less risky contracts.

Source: The authors based on press reports.

In deciding its level of hedging, a company will often reveal organisational attitudes to risk, with some companies adopting much more comprehensive hedging policies than others.

The translation of cross-border earnings, assets and liabilities

In addition to the *transaction* effect of foreign exchange movements there is the question of how cross-border affiliates of an organisation *translate* their earnings, assets and liabilities into the parent company's reporting currency. For example, a German company's subsidiary operating in Australia and reporting its results in Australian dollars (A$) will need to have its performance translated into deutschmarks in order to allow the performance of the subsidiary to be consolidated in the parent company's accounts.

The principal question is at what rate of exchange business activities undertaken in a foreign currency will be translated into the reporting currency. In theory there are three choices, although in practice national accounting and legal frameworks may direct companies to a particular method. Nevertheless, in theory the choice lies between using:

- the actual (spot) rate of exchange at the balance sheet date, known as the *closing rate*;
- the *average rate* of exchange during the accounting period;
- the actual (spot) rate of exchange applying at the date of the transaction, often referred to as the *historical rate*.

The greater the proportion of the organisation's business conducted by foreign subsidiaries, the larger will be the influence of translation effects on the parent company's reported performance. By contrast, the company which is reliant on an export strategy is likely to have a much higher *transaction* than *translation* exposure.

Foreign currency translation will affect not only the profit and loss or income statement, but also the balance sheet. In broad terms, changes in the value of foreign assets and liabilities will influence the balance sheet, while the earnings performance of cross-border subsidiaries will affect the profit and loss or income statement.

The translation of cross-border business transactions is a complex area. A company's accounting policies on the subject can be found in the notes to the annual report and accounts, and this is inevitably the starting place for assessing how the company manages this aspect of its business. Illustration 2.6 considers aspects of Danone's policy in this area.

Illustration 2.6

Danone – Foreign currency translations and exchange rate sensitivity

'In general terms, balance sheet items are translated into French francs at the official year end closing rates; income statements are translated at the average exchange rate for the year for each currency.'

As a point of reference, detailed below is Danone's estimated exposure to all the major currencies in 1994. While the movement in the US$ is favourable, there is far greater exposure to adverse movements in the Italian lira and Spanish peseta.

Currency	Group exposure (%)	Average rate 1993	1994	1994/93	Impact[1]
French Franc	48.0	–	–	–	–
Lira	15.0	0.00359	0.000351	– 2.2	– 0.33
Peseta	9.0	0.0442	0.0416	– 5.9	– 0.53
US dollar	9.0	5.67	5.79	+ 2.1	+ 0.19
Deutschmark	6.0	3.42	0.165	+ 1.2	+ 0.07
Belgian Franc	6.0	0.163	0.165	+ 1.2	+ 0.07
£ Sterling	4.0	8.50	8.63	+ 1.5	+ 0.06
Other	3.0	–	–	–	–
Total	100.0				– 0.56

1. Impact is calculated by multiplying group exposure by 1994/93 currency change.

Overall in the first half of 1994 Danone has a negative currency sensitivity of – 0.56 per cent. This suggests that less than 1 per cent of the company's overall fall in sales during the year can be assigned to currency movements. The majority of this reduction results from the devaluation of the Spanish and Italian currencies against the French franc during the year.

Source: Based on Danone's Annual Report, 1993/94

Illustration 2.6 demonstrates the extent to which individual currencies can fluctuate, even over a 12-month period, making the point that in an era of floating exchange rates foreign currency translation has an important influence on reported business performance. Understanding the policies adopted by individual companies is not helped in some cases by the poor disclosure of foreign exchange transactions and translation of gains and losses. A brief description of some of the variations allowed in reporting foreign currency transactions using different national accounting frameworks can be found in Nobes (1993).

International cash management

The problems of managing the movement of funds in a complex international business are significant. International cash management seeks to optimise the movement of cash within the organisation, in order to minimise total requirements. This task is made more complicated by national restrictions/legal requirements, differing rates of inflation and fluctuations in exchange rates.

Every international business has to establish effective and efficient systems to manage its cash needs and ensure its international activities are funded appropriately. If its cross-border activities are being expanded and require additional funding, it will need to choose between the different methods of funding such developments. Conversely, where the organisation generates surplus funds from its cross-border operations, it will need to determine when and how these funds may be remitted back to the corporate parent.

The overall complexity of international cash management has increased in recent years as new forms of financial instruments have been developed and the speed of money transfer between geographically dispersed countries has increased. Today international cash management is increasingly a specialist corporate financial function in many of the larger international companies. The establishment of a specialist function recognises that careful cash and foreign exchange management may reduce working capital needs, keep financing costs to a minimum and minimise the effect of currency movements.

Larger international businesses are likely to give the following two areas of cash management particular attention:

- netting
- transfer pricing

Netting describes the procedures and processes whereby the movement of payments associated with the movement of, say, components and/or finished products between different parts of the same organisation are 'netted off'. This has a number of advantages, which include:

- a reduction in the number of cross-border financial transactions between subsidiaries, thereby reducing the overall administrative cost;
- a reduction in the number of occasions when foreign exchange conversion is taking place, thereby lowering the cost; and
- increased co-ordination and sharing of information between subsidiaries.

Bilateral netting describes the process of netting between the parent company and an individual subsidiary. In larger and more complex organisations, a process of multi-lateral netting involving more than two parties within the same company is likely to take place. Where this is the case it is likely to be co-ordinated from a central location, which may encompass activities worldwide, or in some companies relate to cash management on an international regional basis.

A transfer price is simply the rate at which a product/service is internally sold within the same organisation. By using *transfer pricing* an organisation can change the profile of where profits are made, and where tax liabilities fall. This may have advantages where the organisation is trading both in a high tax environment and operating in countries where taxes are appreciably lower. Clearly where this is the case there are advantages to increasing declared earnings in the low tax country, and conversely reducing earnings in the high tax economy. National governments have, in a number of cases, tried to limit the scope for using transfer pricing to engineer this outcome.

Even where the external context does not prevent the use of transfer pricing, the technique can lead to internal difficulties. In particular, the arbitrary use of transfer pricing may create problems in evaluating divisional performance by leading to profits in one country being artificially depressed, while advancing performance in another. This may adversely affect motivation in the subsidiary whose profits are being artificially depressed, unless alternative performance measures are also used.

The preceding discussion highlights the fact that international financial management is a crucial area for many organisations operating in cross-border markets. As a result, careful attention should be paid to what companies say in their annual reports in reviewing this area. Ultimately, the extent to which organisations successfully manage this whole area of their business can, and does, have a material effect on overall business performance.

Measuring international business performance

Forecasting and measuring the outcomes of a chosen international business strategy are important areas for management attention. Even where the impetus for developing a new international strategy may be largely intuitive, few companies are able to avoid taking major corrective adjustments if satisfactory business performance is not forthcoming. While key stakeholders may be prepared to accept less than satisfactory performance during the period when, say, a strategic presence in a new market is being developed, ultimately stakeholders are unlikely to have unlimited patience with a company management which fails to deliver promised performance. As witnessed earlier in Illustrations 2.1 and 2.2, poor business performance may assist in creating conditions when stakeholders take action to remove an organisation's senior management.

As discussed in Chapter 1, there is a strong linkage between an organisation's business strategy, the functional strategies necessary to implement the chosen strategy, and international business performance. An international business strategy describes the general competitive thrust of the organisation competing in its chosen product markets. The detailed implementation of the overall strategic thrust is developed through the key functional areas of the business – human resources, logistics, finance, marketing and operations. Functional strategies are thus concerned with the detailed implementation of business strategy. Both the appropriateness of the chosen business strategy within the business environment and the manner in which it is implemented will influence international business performance.

Earlier discussion in Chapter 1 emphasised that normally organisations, when faced with inadequate levels of business performance, will seek to adjust the manner in which the current strategy is being implemented before moving to review overall business strategy. By the very nature of the linkage between functional and business strategy, changes to functional strategies are likely to contribute to the evolution of business strategies. In effect, the system is dynamic and the changes in one component inevitably result in organisational learning and further adjustment to the other elements of strategy.

One question is how business performance is to be measured and judged. Traditionally, the response to this question has been to use financial performance measures as the basis of assessing the success or otherwise of the business strategy adopted. Justification for this arises out of the fact that, in the case of profit-making organisations, financial measures offer a quantification of business performance, enabling stakeholders to judge the success or otherwise of organisational strategies. In this context financial outcomes provide a *measure* rather than a *cause* of business performance. Managers know that if a strategy fails to lead to acceptable business performance, there will be a need to re-examine the justification for pursuing the strategy, or else a risk of alienating stakeholders who might instigate the managers' removal.

Financial performance measures, however, are not without their difficulties. Deciding which financial measures to use as a yardstick to assess business performance can prove problematic. In many countries the emphasis historically has been on the profitability or earnings performance of the organisation. The potential manipulation of reported earnings and other weaknesses in profit-based measures of performance have led to questioning of the appropriateness of such measures of business performance (see, for example, Ellis and Williams (1993), Chapter 10).

The response to the weaknesses in using profit as the basis of judging business performance has been twofold. One approach has been to consider alternative cash-based measures deemed more relevant, and not displaying the weaknesses inherent in profit-based measures of performance. Using cash as measure of business performance is the basis of the shareholder value approach, which has gained widespread acceptance in the USA. The basis of the approach is that only by increasing the cash value of the business will shareholders gain through increased dividend payments and/or an increase in the value of the shares.

Two years ago, Reebok undertook to transform itself from a powerful fitness shoe company, to a strategically driven global sports and fitness brand. Fundamental to this shift was our preoccupaton with long-term shareholder value. (Reebok International Ltd, 1993 Annual Report, p 25)

The cash-based measure of business performance emphasises that creating value requires actual and potential business performance to be measured in terms of the cash flow outcomes to a strategy rather than focusing exclusively on profits or earnings. This approach argues that an organisation's value and hence shareholders' returns will be enhanced if the international business strategy adopted creates sufficient additional cash flows, where these sums more than cover the financing cost of the strategy as shown by the cost of capital, thereby leaving the company with a greater value than it otherwise would have enjoyed. While the detailed calculation of a company's cash flow can be highly complex, it is helpful to recognise that a company's operating cash flow is heavily influenced by the sales revenue – price per unit times number of units sold – which it receives from selling its products or services and the costs of supplying the market. In combination with the amount of investment it needs to undertake to achieve sales, calculating both the trends in sales revenue and costs is important.

The extent to which individual business strategies create or destroy value can be illustrated by a simple example. Consider a small business enterprise which is moderately successful and is faced with three international strategic options: A, B and C. Option A is based on the business continuing with its current international strategies and selling into cross-border markets on an occasional basis, but with the company remaining primarily focused on the local/regional/national market. Figure 2.4 shows that over the next five years this option neither enhances nor destroys value. By contrast, option B is based on entering a new market, say, Japan and trying to establish a new sales base. In this case, Figure 2.4 suggests that value is destroyed because the additional financial rewards are insufficient to cover the costs of funding this strategy. As a result, this strategy should not be chosen as it detracts from the value of the existing business. Finally, option C is based on developing the company's embryonic sales in, say, the USA, through building a more substantial marketing base within that market over the next five years. In this case the financial benefit as illustrated by the business value created is well in excess of the cost of funding the strategy, and according to the shareholder value approach this should be the company's chosen course of action.

While the cash-based or shareholder value approach to measuring business performance is theoretically appealing, there are a number of practical difficulties when it is applied in practice. This includes how to forecast future outcomes and what is the appropriate cost of capital. There is also a view that as a technique it is more suited to assessing corporate rather than business strategy, given the difficulty of making the approach understood and relevant to all staff at all levels in the organisation. The shareholder value approach has also tended to be more popular in the Anglo-Saxon countries, where the predominant method of raising finance has centred on the issue of shares

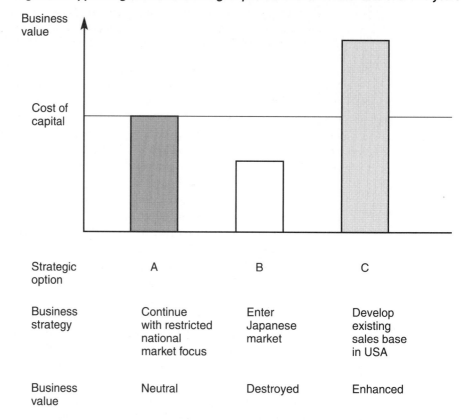

Figure 2.4 Appraising alternative strategic options: cash flow forecasts over five years

Strategic option	A	B	C
Business strategy	Continue with restricted national market focus	Enter Japanese market	Develop existing sales base in USA
Business value	Neutral	Destroyed	Enhanced

rather than dependence on the banking sector. Although there are signs that in countries such as Germany equity funding is likely to become more important in the future, for the present not all countries have such a strongly developed stock market as the USA and UK.

Rather than measuring business performance by using financial indicators some researchers have suggested using a wider range of performance measures (Kaplan and Norton, 1992). It is suggested that managers should assess those business areas which are the key drivers of financial performance. Given the relationship between business and functional strategies outlined in Chapter 1, this would suggest setting objectives and assessing the contribution which human resources, logistics, finance, marketing and operations make to the achievement of international performance outcomes. By setting milestones and assessing progress against each of the five functional areas listed in Figure 2.5, the overall business strategy is translated into specific areas in which a range of business performance indicators can be measured. Given that no one indicator is of paramount importance, it is helpful to develop a balanced scorecard of those measures that drive business performance.

In an international context the balanced scorecard has a number of attractions, not least because it offers a method of avoiding the problems created by, for example, transfer pricing, currency fluctuations and differences in national accounting standards. These and other aspects of international business render financial comparisons between competitors at best problematic, and at

Figure 2.5 Linking key functional drivers to international business performance

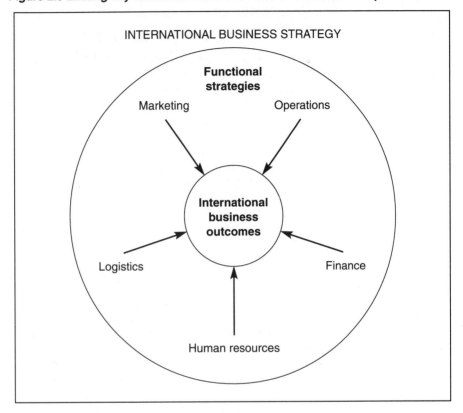

worst unhelpful. Illustration 2.7 shows how a company's reported financial performance can be markedly affected by some of these factors.

Developing a balance scorecard approach to assessing international business performance poses a number of challenges, not the least of which is to consider how to measure each key functional area and ensure what is being measured is both meaningful and relevant to overall business performance. This inevitably requires considerable skill and judgement, in order both to develop and assess a set of indicators appropriate for a given context. Drawing on Delbridge *et al.* (1994), a range of indicators are identified which might be used by a company supplying major components to the world automobile industry to construct a balanced scorecard:

- marketing
- human resources
- operations
- logistics
- finance.

Marketing
i.   levels of turnover achieved and trends in sales
ii. size and stability of contracts gained
iii. prices achieved, including levels of discounts required
iv. effectiveness of marketing function and operation of sales force

Illustration 2.7

Daimler Benz

Daimler Benz, the German-based automobile and aerospace manufacturer, has the primary strategic goal of becoming a global company. In pursuit of this aim Daimler Benz followed some 370 foreign companies which since 1991 have sought a listing on the New York stock exchange. The company's objective in taking this action was to gain access to the US capital market, and to break away from its more restrictive German legal and accounting base.

What shocked onlookers was not that Daimler Benz should seek to gain a US listing, but how complying with US accounting standards radically changed the company's reported profits. Using German standards the company's reported profit for the first half of 1993 was DM168 million. The same performance became a net loss of DM949 million, when the company complied with American General Accepted Accounting Principles (GAAP). More recently, for the same period in 1994 profit using German accounting standards was reported as DM462 million, compared to DM368 million under US GAAP.

The case of Daimler Benz has significantly changed the perception of stock market analysts as to the nature of German accounting. Prior to Daimler Benz gaining its US listing, the widespread belief was that German accounting standards were conservative, and tended to understate the level of business performance achieved.

A fundamental reason for the divergence of reported profit between in Germany and in the USA consists in the historical objectives of the accounting framework in each country. This primarily reflects the predominent method of financing companies. In the USA and UK companies have in the main sought equity finance. In other countries, including Germany, France and Japan, the link with the banking sector has been much stronger, and it is the banks who have provided the majority of funding. As a result, the accounting frameworks in these countries has placed less emphasis on the information needs of actual and potential shareholders. Rather, the objective has been to protect creditors and to minimise corporate tax payments. By contrast, the US and UK systems attempt to give shareholders a 'true and fair' view of the company's performance and financial position to shareholders.

While attempts have been under way for some 20 years to harmonise accounting standards, the different antecedents to national accounting bases suggest that differences will remain for many years between the way and level of reporting business performance.

Source: The authors

Human resources
i.   the stability of its workforce, including employee turnover
ii. comparison of age, length of service, qualifications/training and experience of workforce at all levels
iii. measurements of motivation and absenteeism
iv. levels of payment; terms and conditions

Operations
i.   measurement of capacity utilisation
ii. complexity of product and process design
iii. levels of productivity achieved

Logistics
i. procurement, in respect of price, quality and level of incoming defects
ii. supply chain inventories and rates of stock turnover for incoming materials (materials flow); work-in-progress (factory flow); and finished goods (shipment to customers)
iii.time in the supply chain for both incoming parts and finished products, including frequency and journey times to customers

Finance
i. balance and cost of equity and borrowings
ii. mix of short-term and longer-term borrowing; and between fixed and floating rates
iii. availability of cash and other reserves to fund strategic development

This list is not exhaustive, but does provide some guidance as to the areas which might be examined in each of the functional areas in order to assess comparative performance. If all areas are to be covered, then considerable data collection and evaluation will be required, which may be both time consuming and costly. Nevertheless, using the balanced scorecard approach does evaluate the actual performance drivers rather than using financial measures as a proxy.

In practice a mixture of the balanced scorecard approach and financial indicators is often employed, recognising the strengths and weaknesses of each. The extent to which inadequate performance, however defined, results in corrective adjustments depends very much on the organisation's internal context. Those organisations sensitive to the need to achieve international-class performance are likely to be much more proactive in assessing their performance and taking appropriate corrective actions where necessary. Unaware organisations, or those incapable of making any necessary changes, are likely either to be complacent about their relative performance or not be able to take effective action to improve the situation.

Summary

This chapter has explored the interaction between external and internal factors as an explanation of the internationalisation process at the level of the firm. This approach rejects a single dimensional focus as to why companies internationalise and the tendency to focus exclusively on either the external or internal context. Instead, the model of international business development presented offers a holistic approach to the internationalisation process recognising the contributions of, and complex interplay between, both sets of explanatory variables.

The dynamics of the internationalisation process have been a constant theme, together with the recognition that different organisations are at various stages of development. Rather than focusing on companies of one particular size, the informing frameworks presented in the chapter have wide applicability. The international phase model recognises that organisations will be at different phases of development, with some operating purely local strategies, while others are worldwide competitors.

International financial management is an important area for the international business to manage successfully. Adverse currency movements in particular can seriously affect reported performance. The need to measure international business performance resulted in a discussion between using financial indicators and the balanced scorecard approach. Both have merits, although equally both present difficulties. The extent to which organisations change their strategies in the face of poor performance depends on their internal context, with an increasing likelihood of corrective adjustments the longer, and wider, the gap is between expected and actual business outcomes.

Checklist

- Companies may be attracted to cross-border markets by either pull or push factors or a combination of both.
- The internationalisation of companies is explained by considering the organisation's external and internal context, and how these may act as triggers to change.
- The external context is comprised of meta trends and industry competition.
- The internal context comprises vision/mindset and organisational dynamics.
- Organisations may either increase or decrease their international business activities over time.
- Changes in the internal context are required for the strategic direction of the company to change fundamentally.
- The phase model offers a framework for examining different stages in the scope of a firm's international business activities.
- The phase model has four distinct stages of international business development, namely (i) restricted national market scope; (ii) international market entry and development; (iii) international regional; and (iv) worldwide competitors.
- International financial management is a key aspect in the success of the cross-border business, encompassing such areas as foreign exchange movements and international cash management.
- Measuring international business performance is an important requirement to enable the success or otherwise of a strategy to be evaluated.
- Business performance is influenced by the overall strategy and the manner in which it is implemented.
- Financial measures have traditionally been used to measure business performance.
- There is a tension regarding whether profit or cash-based measures are the best way to measure business performance.
- In an international context, financial measures are problematic given exchange rate movements and different national accounting bases.
- The balanced scorecard offers an alternative to financial-based approaches in measuring international business performance.
- Financial measures and the balanced scorecard may be viewed as complementary rather than competitive.

Case Study 2

Bayerische Motoren Werke (BMW) AG

Introduction

Bayerische Motoren Werke (BMW) AG, predominantly a maker of luxury motor cars, radically changed its configuration in 1994. In a bold strategic move for a company renowned for its conservative attitude to risk, the completion of its first American manufacturing plant represented a significant departure from BMW's long-established 'build local' policy. Likewise, by acquiring Rover with its specialised Land Rover range and Rover small car models, the company choose the short route to realising its long-term aim of expanding its core car-making business into new market segments.

Narrow product-market focus with broad geographic scope

BMW car sales had increased steadily in the 1980s. For the first time ever in 1992 it produced and sold more cars worldwide (595,000) than Mercedes-Benz (593,000), its traditional arch-rival in the luxury car market. Delivery of 535,492 cars in 1993 was a decrease of 9 per cent compared with the previous year's unusually high level. Even so, the company's share of the world automobile market in 1993 was only 1.6 per cent. However, in the luxury segment of the market, which annually accounts for some 5 million unit sales worldwide, every 10th newly registered car was a BMW.

With the downturn in the automobile industry in 1993, BMW's domestic and export volumes were below the all-time highs recorded in 1992. Over the 10-year period 1983–92 the company enjoyed strong and rising domestic sales volume, with Germany continuing to be the most important market for BMW. As the Chairman Pischestrieder explained, 'we are at home and shall continue to produce here.' Notwithstanding a 17 per cent decrease in domestic sales between 1992 and 1993, Figure C2.1 shows that again BMW sold more than 200,000 cars in its home market.

Figure C2.1 BMW automobile sales by volume ('000s of units sold), 1983–93

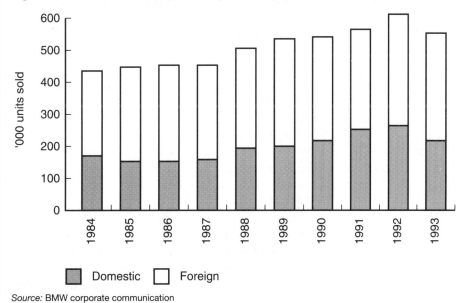

Source: BMW corporate communication

Case Study 2

For a number of years BMW's sales volume in the key North American market has been lacklustre. North America is the largest car market in the world, with sales to the luxury segment accounting for some 1.1 million new cars in 1992. The market has changed considerably since demand for BMWs last peaked at 96,000 new cars in 1986. Sales fell to a nadir of 53,343 units in 1991. Among the radical changes to take place were:

● downsizing to more economical models;
● significant Japanese penetration through very keen pricing of new up-market models – Honda's Acura, Nissan's Infinite and Toyota's Lexus – introduced in 1988;
● 10 per cent luxury tax on cars priced above $30,000 from January 1991 onwards.

BMW views the establishment of an American manufacturing base as critical to competing with the Japanese for the luxury US car market. The new US plant in South Carolina is expected to produce 75,000 cars annually from early 1996. It will supply both the American and international markets with a new and more affordable addition to the BMW range. With the upturn in the American economy, there was further growth in the US car market in 1993. Table C2.1 shows that BMW's annual sales rose by 19 per cent to 78,000 cars, thereby becoming the largest European importer to the USA .

Table C2.1 US Automobile sales, selected makes, January–December 1993

	Volume (units)	Volume change (%) 1993/92	Market share (%) Jan–Dec '92	Market share (%) Jan–Dec '93
US car sales	8,518,000	+3.7	100.0	100.0
Imports	1,844,000	−7.5	24.3	21.7
European makes	308,000	−6.9	4.0	3.6
US car sales by selected manufacturer				
BMW	78,000	+18.8	1.3	1.3
Mercedes-Benz	62,000	−2.2	0.8	0.7
Jaguar (Ford)	13,000	+46.7	0.1	0.1
Volkswagen/Audi	56,000	−35.8	1.1	0.7
Volvo	73,000	+7.4	0.8	0.9
Porsche	3,700	−9.4	0.0	0.0

Source: Financial Times, January 1994

With European manufacturers only selling around 260,000 luxury cars in the American market in 1993 (50 per cent fewer than in the mid-1980s), coupled with far fiercer price competition, it was becoming increasingly difficult to sustain a significant market presence from an industrial base in Germany. Labour costs of

Case Study 2

$24 per hour in Germany are the highest in the world. No productivity increases could possibly hope to absorb the effects of high labour costs and the low dollar exchange rate. Between 1986 and 1993 the US dollar lost about half its value against the deutschmark (DM), so that BMW would need to double its export prices to maintain sales revenue. As Figure C2.2 shows, in a depressed and highly competitive market this was not possible.

Figure C2.2 BMW automobile sales: value versus volume

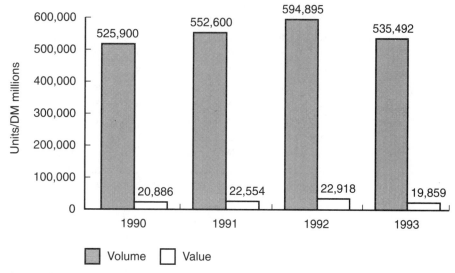

Source: BMW Annual Reports

As early as 1989, Eberhard von Kuenheim, then Executive Chairman of BMW, set the goal of increasing sales in the Americas, 'where based on our own standards, we are not yet sufficiently successful'. The building of a new administrative centre at a cost of $70 million in 1988 suggests that BMW had not abandoned its belief that better times were ahead. It was the culmination of 10 years of heavy investment in sales and distribution infrastructure in the USA. According to BMW's definition, success did not mean re-establishing the record sales of just under 100,000 cars sold in 1986, but surpassing this level. With production at the limits of capacity in Germany, it became inevitable to create additional capacity. As von Kuenheim explained, 'we needed new capacities, but where?'

Market pull or cost push?

Kuenheim explained that two results emerged in late 1989. The question as to whether car production outside Germany would be feasible had an affirmative answer. The list was quickly reduced to ten locations in three countries: USA, Mexico and Spain. The location decision depended on whether the market or costs were more important: 'should we set up shop in a promising market, which is bound to be hotly contested, as is surely the case in America, or should we become established in a low-wage country in order to minimise costs and to supply the world's markets from this base?'

Case Study 2

Initially Mexico and then, with the political and economic transformation in the former communist bloc in 1990, the former German Democratic Republic and Czechoslovakia were investigated thoroughly as low wage locations for a new BMW industrial development site, before being rejected. As von Kuenheim put it, 'products from Mexico are not highly regarded in our market segment. And production in the new Eastern German states held no incentives because rapid assimilation with Western Germany would have eaten away any low wage benefits without helping to tap into a new market.'

A market-related investment in America was finally announced on 23 June 1992. As then company chairman von Kuenheim remarked, 'those who are not successful in the USA are not likely to enjoy success elsewhere for much longer.' He added, 'the competitive conditions prevalent in America today will reach Europe in the next five to ten years. Even if some of our competitors harbour the delusion it won't happen to them: we decided it would be better to enter the lion's den than to wait for the lion to come to us.' The final choice of Spartanburg, South Carolina was not the cheapest location in terms of labour costs. It was, however, an optimal location as regards raw materials and components. Additionally, the wish to see BMW locate in South Carolina resulted in both state and federal governments helping to create the necessary conditions in the locality to meet the needs of BMW. They anticipated everything BMW wanted and mobilised $300 million in up-front subsidies, together with 20-year freeze on taxes, estimated to be worth a further $150 million.

From a strategic perspective, BMW considers that it is equally as important to make its presence felt in the market in terms of production as it is in terms of sales. Fears of 'fortress America' with the signing of the North American Free Trade Agreement (NAFTA), together with preferential treatment received by BMW as an 'insider' producer, also figured in such calculations. Not all commentators agree. Volkswagen (VW), Germany's largest volume car producer which shut down its loss-making American operations in 1987, supplies the US market from a plant in Mexico. With the new plant beginning to come on stream, many commentators remained to be convinced that the company could make a success of its new strategy. No European car company, much less one that built luxury cars, has ever successfully manufactured in the USA.

Operations and logistics

BMW intends to produce its more affordable model for about 30 per cent less than it would cost to produce in Germany. US labour costs are expected to reach a rate of $16 per hour by mid-1995. Each production associate will work some 1900 hours per annum, some 35 per cent longer than their German counterparts. Figure C2.3 shows that while labour accounts for about 20 per cent of costs, material costs, depreciation and transportation costs play a much more significant role per automobile than wage costs.

From the businesses that will relocate or expand to meet BMW's voracious appetite for components, South Carolina expects to gain an additional 2000 jobs. Like its Japanese counterparts, BMW has developed in Germany a 'shared destiny' with suppliers through long-term relationships. Many suppliers have become

Figure C2.3 Expense structure in terms of total value of production, 1993

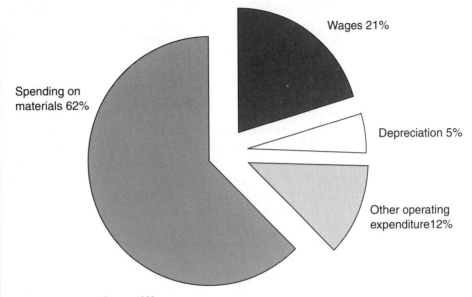

Wages 21%

Spending on materials 62%

Depreciation 5%

Other operating expenditure 12%

Source: BMW Annual Report, 1993

systems partners, participating directly in the process of development and pro-curement. It is expected that many of its existing suppliers will also move to South Carolina, although new relationships will also be forged with American firms.

Whether products or materials can be transported cost-efficiently is depen-dent on transport connections. An airport suitable for wide-bodied freighters was deemed imperative for the American site, for two reasons. First, air freighting of finished cars and spares to international markets reduces transit time. Secondly, air transport was also held to offer a reduced likelihood of goods being damaged in transit. From the outset, BMW's aim was to develop a linked production net-work serving an international market.

Von Kuenheim commented, 'our investigations have clearly shown that German companies which have invested in the USA in order to produce for the American market were much less successful than those firms which use the USA as a basis for supplying the world market. It would of course be possible to adapt certain beneficial features to the requirements of different markets, but not to adapt the overall product – because the basic concept has to be applicable to the international market.'

From the outset BMW has designed an international logistics network in such a way that the production site is an irrelevance as far as the customer is con-cerned. Sixteen national sales subsidiaries worldwide account for 90 per cent of all BMWs sold. The members of this highly efficient sales network all have direct computer links to manufacturing sites, so that all BMW car plants are sufficiently flexible to respond to consumers' individual demands. This is matched by a local approach to advertising and promotion, since the common worldwide marketing approach in the early 1980s proved unsuccessful.

By linking manufacturing and marketing, BMW's new US plant has the ability to make a completely different vehicle, albeit one based on a standard model, every time without incurring an unacceptable cost penalty. It is only the first of a global network of manufacturing sites that will preclude expansion in Germany. The company's new chairman, Pischestrieder, in late 1994 announced the intention to extend an assembly plant in South Africa and to set up an assembly operation in Mexico.

Organisational culture and human resources

American president of BMW, Al Kinzer, said that he needed to recruit production associates who could demonstrate the mental and physical skills required to build a self-directed work team manufacturing culture. Self-directed work teams would be utilised throughout the new US plant. Moreover, all associates will be trained in and perform a number of functions as well as taking responsibility for quality, efficiency and other measurements of performance.

Kinzer stated that 'we will offer an open manufacturing environment with no private offices, reserved parking or barriers that could inhibit communications. All associates – not workers – wear uniforms to show team unity, exhibit a quality image and project the product. Each day will begin with team meetings to keep all associates abreast of company and industry news that is vital to our goal of continuous quality improvement for our customers.' Methods of 'total quality management' were established throughout the organisation in 1993, at a time when senior managment were increasingly concerned about press reports which were critical of BMW's build quality.

Showing clear lessons learnt from other car manufacturers, Kinzer emphasised the need for the company 'to become known for its commitment to associates, customers and communities through the quality of the people it employs, the quality of the cars it produces and the quality involvement of all BMW associates in community services chosen and directed by associates.'

These points serve to emphasise the importance of its workforce to BMW. In its 1992 Annual Report the company stated, 'the above-average qualifications of the workforce are still the most important argument in favour of Germany as an industrial location.' Indeed, in the same year the company spent over Dm200 million on the training, upgrading and further education of its employees. Moving to the USA one of the company's basic requirements was to have access to a large, well-skilled labour force. South Carolina was able to convince the company that the labour force in the surrounding area was well motivated, mobile and that training programmes existed which could be supplemented by a company-specific vocational training scheme in accordance with the company's culture.

Throughout the organisation greater flexibility has been achieved by a continuing programme to develop different forms of organisation and management structures. Maintenance, material supply and quality control tasks were assigned to production groups. This allows all employees to develop creativity and responsibility, as well as to initiate improvements with organisation work sequences. Table C2.2 suggests that changes in production techniques have not necessarily resulted in increases in efficiency.

Speaking in June 1994, the new chairman Pischetsrieder said, 'the objective is to reduce the general level of costs by 20–30 per cent within two years, in the process building up a significant lead in productivity over the competition.' This is

Table C2.2 BMW's workforce, wage costs and expenditure on materials, 1989–93

	1989	1990	1991	1992	1993
No of employees	66,267	70,948	74,385	73,562	71,034
Wage costs (DM million)	4,833	5,313	5,823	6,387	6,245
Expenditure on materials (DM million)	15,280	15,749	17,427	18,542	17,368

to be achieved with more independence and responsibility in all divisions and reduced hierarchies at all plants. Whereas in 1990 there were six management layers between the plant manager and the shop floor, today this has been reduced to three layers. In order to improve the cost structure, all units are organised into cost and profit centres. The products and services of these units now compete with those of other suppliers. At the same time, they can offer their services to non-BMW customers.

At senior management level, BMW has developed over recent years a leaner management structure. The traditional, stultifying hierarchic structures are being removed, in order to encourage initiative, orientated to results and individual responsibility. There is now a well-developed regional structure, with responsibilities devolved to the regional management team. Teamwork is a guiding principle, not only within plants but also within senior management, where it can be expected to gain increasing prominence as BMW's global network develops.

Design and production

The completion of BMW's Munich research and development centre (RDC) in 1994, a 10-year phased project, is an important symbol of the company's commitment to create the organisational conditions and facilities for work of the future of the motor car. When designing the RDC the concept was to put all areas of vehicle development together, thereby enabling all the specialists working on new cars and their production technologies to be in close proximity to each other. Previously these functions had been carried out at 10 different sites scattered throughout Munich.

To develop and build a new model costs the company around £800–1000 million, and takes four to five years. While the RDC is to ensure the future becomes a reality at the earliest possible date, important strategic decisions have to be made concerning which projects to progress. Whatever decision is reached, new chairman Pischetsrieder believes that in order to improve product quality the design team 'must make it simpler to build'. As a result, BMW is seeking to ensure design and manufacuring work closer, with zero defects being the corporate aim.

Its rival Mercedes-Benz is at the final pre-production stage with its small car project, while the comparable BMW Z130 and E1 designs are only at the concept stage. Moreover, Mercedes-Benz has finalised an off-road vehicle design which will shortly be made in its new American plant in Alabama.

Table C2.3 shows that the Series 3 upper mid-range car dominates BMW's sales, with the Series 5 and 7 offering luxury performance cars. Series 3, 5 and 7

Case Study 2

Table C2.3 BMW Cars: production figures ('000s of units), 1986–93*

	1986	1987	1988	1989	1990	1991	1992	1993
Series 3	328	312	272	271	265	324	385	353
Series 5	93	76	163	202	212	184	173	150
Series 7	28	57	61	50	49	45	32	29
Total	449	445	496	523	526	553	590	532

*All figures rounded
Source: BMW Annual Reports

cars compete directly with Mercedes-Benz. The model range is constantly updated by each year adding new model variants and engines. The last full year of production of the current Series 7 was 1993, it having been first introduced in 1986. A new Series 7 car was introduced in late 1993. Recognising the trend towards smaller cars, reflecting an increasing environmental awareness and the problems of traffic congestion on the part of its customers, BMW introduced in 1993/94 a new three-door compact, a smaller and more affordable version of its 3-series saloon. While seeking to retain the brand image of luxury and quality, the Series 3 is in response to changing consumer tastes which are making conspicious consumption unfashionable. The new car is intended to attract former owners of the lapsed two-door version of the previous Series 3 and to compete with models such as the VW Golf and Ford Escort for sales.

Rover Group acquisition

Early in 1994 BMW acquired the Rover Group, the last remaining British volume producer of cars, for £800 million. In what was considered to be BMW's boldest strategic move to date, the company took the high-risk acquisitive route into the new market segments of off-road vehicles and small front wheel drive cars. The principle of maintaining a high level of autonomy within a common framework also applies to the Rover purchase. This is why BMW is committed to maintaining Rover as a separately managed British company. There will be no over-riding holding company, with the two companies being guided instead by joint committees made up of Rover and BMW representatives.

The two product ranges are an almost perfect match. While other car manufacturers are trying to build a world car, BMW (upper mid-range and luxury performance cars) and Rover (off-road vehicles and compact front wheel drive cars) build unique automobiles for a very specific and exclusive group of customers worldwide. Together BMW and Rover are able to offer exclusivity in a broad range of market segments, although there is overlap at the top of the Rover range with comparable BMW models. Chairman Pischetsrieder holds the view that 'the brand profiles of the Rover and BMW should not be "muddled" or "blurred" but rather made even more distinct and outstanding than before.'

No Rover cars will be sold through BMW dealerships, instead BMW intends to develop a worldwide dealer network for Rover. This is in line with Pischetsrieder's thinking of resisting short-term gain for the long term: 'the father of 90 per cent of mistakes is the urgency to take decisions. We must resist the temptation to make obvious decisions. We were successful in the past because we never decided to take the obvious decision.'

Sales of Land Rover off-road vehicles have risen dramatically in the US, with sales volumes in the six months to 30 June 1994 almost reaching the level achieved for the whole of 1993. Land Rover operates in one of the fastest growing segments of the world automobile market. Four out of ten vehicles sold in the USA are off-road vehicles, and BMW hopes that by joint use of sales channels the prominence of the brand will be greatly strengthened. Further benefits from joint purchasing are anticipated in the medium term. The increasing use of common parts and components, where these are not key to differentiating the brand, is a longer-term goal. Already BMW turbo diesels have been introduced into Land Rover off-road vehicles.

By continuing their co-operation with Honda and establishing a new relationship with BMW, Rover has a unique opportunity to develop a meaningful presence in the increasing important small car market. The Rover brand will become the focal point of small to medium-sized front wheel drive developments. In this way, BMW hopes to ensure a presence in this market segment without the danger of diluting its highly prized brand image. Pischetsrieder is adamant that 'there will be no smaller BMW than the 3-Series. You must not over-stretch the core brand values of BMW. A small BMW would not comply with the core BMW image that we have worked for twenty years to achieve.' It is intended that the new Series 3 is the smallest model that will carry the BMW badge.

Successful co-operation with Rover does not preclude change. Not only must both companies learn from one another, but they need to accept each other's ideas and cultural differences. It is far too early to say whether the expectations of both parties will be met. Difficult long-term decisions have to be made concerning the up-market end of Rover's range, which overlaps with BMW's products. Moreover, long-term collaboration with Honda is critical. Honda's technological expertise has led to the company supplying many key components critical to the production of Rover's front wheel drive cars. All the company's recent models are based on Japanese platforms. BMW does not possess front wheel drive technology, and it would be very expensive for Rover to develop its own design and development capability. Rover's most urgent need is to replace its smaller car range. All the signs suggest that Honda will cease to collaborate with Rover once its current agreements lapse.

Financial performance

Bayerische Motoren Werke (Bavarian Motor Works) is rightly named, with the German word 'Motoren' meaning engines. These are central to the company's automobile business, which forms the largest component of the group's sales as shown in Table C2.4. BMW's interests in aero-engines are not reflected in the table. The company entered into a joint venture with Rolls-Royce in 1990 and set up a separate company to produce engines for the civil aircraft market. Production of engines by the joint venture has yet to materialise, with 1995 being the expected date of the first sales. The BMW's origins as an aero-engine manufacturer nevertheless continue to be symbolised by the badge – a blue on white propeller – found on all of the company's automobile and motor cycle products.

As Table C2.4 shows, group turnover rose from DM27.2 billion in 1990 to DM31.2 billion in 1992, before retreating to DM29.0 billion in 1993.

Table C2.4 Net sales by product category, 1991–93, DM million

	1990	1991	1992	1993
Automobiles	20,886	22,554	22,918	19,859
Motorcycles	385	429	457	462
Leasing	1,925	2,374	2,884	3,442
Other [1]	3,983	4,478	4,978	5,253
Total	27,179	29,835	31,237	29,016

[1] Other sales are primarily from spare parts and accessories
Source: BMW Annual Reports

Table C2.5 shows that between 1990 and 1993 the company's profit from its normal business (operating profits plus interest paid/received, but before taxation) fell from DM1.66 billion to DM0.83 billion, having peaked in 1991 at DM1.75 billion. BMW along with Rover was one of only a handful of European producers which did not record losses in 1993.

Table C2.5 BMW Operating profit from normal business, 1989–93, DM million

	1989	1990	1991	1992	1993
Operating profit from normal business	1,561	1,664	1,752	1,477	832

Source: BMW Annual Reports

During the same period the company cash flow position had been strongly positive. Figure C2.4 shows that cash flow was in excess of DM2.3 billion for the period. As a result the company was able to spend around DM2 billion annually on investment and to claim that this sum was 'once again, financed completely from cash flow'. Nevertheless, with the purchase of Rover and the completion of a new plant in the US in 1994, BMW has increased its equity base by a further DM805 million.

Total assets employed have risen in annual increments of around DM2500 from Dm 20,689 in 1989 to DM30,295 in 1993 (Table C2.6). Reflecting the company's investment policy, fixed assets have risen from DM6.3 billion in 1989 to over DM7.1 billion during the same period.

Table C2.6 Total assets, 1989–93, DM million

	1990	1991	1992	1993
Total assets	22,501	25,405	27,504	30,295

Source: BMW Annual Reports

Case Study 2

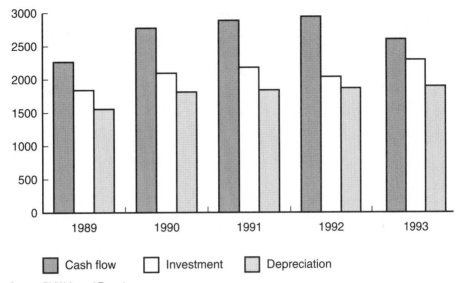

Figure C2.4 Cash flow, investment and depreciation, 1989–93, DM million

Cash flow ■   Investment □   Depreciation ▨

Source: BMW Annual Reports

Conclusions

In May 1993 Eberhard von Kuenheim, the long-standing Chairman of BMW, handed over the baton to Bernd Pischetsrieder. The new and youthful chairman was the champion of the move to the US and the purchase of Rover Group. It is on his shoulders that the future of BMW will rest. The most important question is whether BMW can turn itself from a maker of luxury cars based in Germany into a highly profitable international group manufacturing a broad range of exclusive automobiles.

Questions

(1) *Analyse BMW's sales, production and financial performance from the data in the case. What do you think are the challenges facing the company?*

(2) *Using Figure 2.2 critically appraise external triggers for change influencing BMW's future strategies.*

(3) *With further reference to Figure 2.2 critically evaluate the internal triggers to change.*

(4) *Consider the balance between external and internal triggers for change.*

(5) *Comment on BMW's logistics network, marketing, organisational culture and human resources. How are these functional strategies related to the company's business strategy?*

(6) *Comment on the acquisition of the Rover Group. Do you think BMW has made a wise strategic move?*

81

Part II

INTERNATIONAL STRATEGIC ANALYSIS

Chapter 3

EXTERNAL TRIGGERS TO THE INTERNATIONALISATION PROCESS

Key learning objectives

To understand:

- the emergence of the global triad and the inter-linkage of markets
- key economic and political drivers of the world economy
- the importance of lifestyle as both a barrier and contributor to the internationalisation process
- how technology facilitates the internationalisation process
- the relation between PEST, derivative trends and changes at the meta level
- contradictions between localisation and globalisation
- how to assess the forces for globalisation and localisation at the industry level
- bi-polarisation and the need to achieve a sustainable competitive position

Context

The major economies of the world and their trading systems are becoming increasingly integrated. This borderless world is centred on the interlinked economies of the Triad – Asia, Western Europe and North America – where growth in international trade is expected to outpace forecasted rises in world output. Alongside the growth in world trade, foreign direct investment continues to rise. The accelerating rate of growth in both trade and direct foreign investment reflects the increasingly international nature of both industry structures and the ownership of value-adding facilities.

Assessing the extent of the borderless world at an industry-specific level prompts consideration of the anticipated speed and response to changing external drivers. In all industries a tension exists between those factors driving an industry towards globalisation and those working in an opposite direction for localisation. By determining the size and direction of external drivers impacting on a particular industry, it is possible to determine the extent of the internationalisation process. The structure of the chapter is as follows:

> - *external triggers to the internationalisation process*
> - *meta-level developments in the world economy*
> - *PEST analysis*
> - *assessing the internationalisation of industries: globalisation v localisation*
> - *bi-polarisation*

The chapter opens by examining external triggers to the internationalisation process and the discontinuity experienced by firms as they pass from one stage to another of the international phase model. Operating at the highest level, meta trends set the broad context for external triggers affecting individual firms. These trends rarely offer a single message, but rather reflect the relative tensions between globalisation and localisation. Recognising and weighting these factors at the international industry level is important if their effect on specific industries is to be determined. It is also important to determine the tendency towards bi-polarisation – broad versus niche – within such industries. This will require an assessment of how a company can develop and maintain a sustainable competitive advantage. The chapter concludes with a summary and checklist. Following the checklist a case study on the world airline industry offers the reader the opportunity to apply a number of the frameworks introduced within the chapter.

External triggers to the internationalisation process

The essential message of the internationalisation process as described in Chapter 2 is that it is the outcome of *both* external and internal change triggers. Figure 3.1 summarises the international phase model depicted in Figure 2.1, emphasising the role of both external and internal triggers to change. In the current chapter the focus is on exploring in detail external triggers to change. It is also concerned with how these external triggers may create conditions when a discontinuity in the firm's international business development can occur. Figure 3.1 emphasises how external factors may result in a firm moving from its current phase to a new phase of international business development, subject to overcoming any organisational inertia. It should be remembered that the movement between stages of the phase model is bi-directional and that any discontinuity may result in firms increasing or reducing their international exposure.

Focusing on the external triggers to change, it is possible to show how these operate at different levels. At the highest or meta level, broad trends may be identified which collectively help to shape the competitive environment of the world economy. Trends at the meta level set the broad context. How these trends affect individual industries and their competitors requires further sector-specific analysis. Within such sectors it is important to determine how individual firms respond to bi-polarisation. As Figure 3.2 demonstrates, external triggers need to be analysed at the meta level to set the broad context, together with how they relate to individual industries and their competitors.

Figure 3.1 External and internal triggers to a stage change

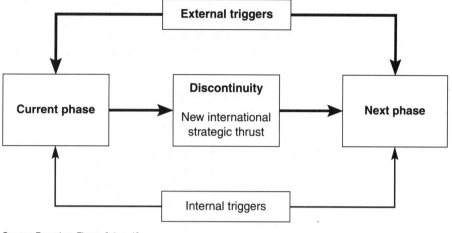

Source: Based on Figure 2.1, p 49

Figure 3.2 External triggers at the meta, industry and firm-specific levels

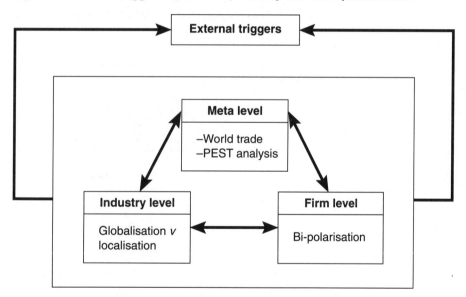

The bi-directional arrows between the components of Figure 3.2 serve to emphasise the inter-relatedness of external triggers at the meta, industry and firm-specific levels. Changes at the industry level influence and are influenced by respective changes at firm and meta level. Moreover, there are inevitable overlaps between the trinity of external triggers. Notwithstanding these practical difficulties, for expositional ease the three different levels are discussed in the sequence of moving from broad, through industry, to firm specific.

Meta-level developments in the world economy

Firms which shape flexible responses to the challenge of, and changes in, the world economy are most likely to succeed. This ability is predicated upon an appreciation of meta-level trends in the world economy, and in particular:

- the 'Triad'
- intra- or inter-block trade
- direct investment
- dynamic adjustments

The 'Triad'

The last decade has witnessed the emergence of three major international regional trading areas within the world economy: the European Union, Japan and the 'Tiger' economies of Asia and Pacific, and the North American Free Trade Area (Canada, Mexico and the USA). As Figure 3.3 shows, these three international regional trading areas account for one-fifth of the global population and almost four-fifths of the world output as measured by gross national product (GNP). It is within this so-called 'Triad' that currently most of the wealth of the world is created, consumed and traded. As a result more and more large companies have manufacturing/service divisions in Europe, Asia and North America – all three legs of the 'Triad' – where management do not necessarily think or act on national lines. In such an interlinked economy 'the nationality' of companies becomes an increasingly outdated concept, together

Figure 3.3 The 'Triad' and the world economy, 1991: percentage of world GNP; population in millions

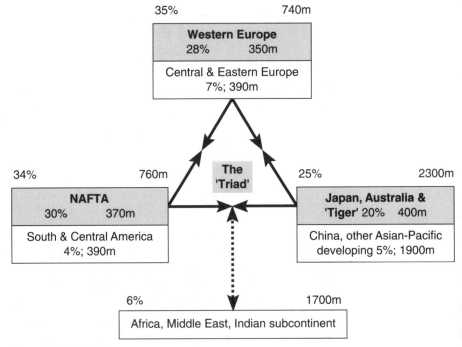

Source: IMF; World Bank

with the view that national governments can obstruct or impede the process of internationalisation through protectionist or exchange rate policies.

The changes taking place within the interlinked economy are something that companies ignore at their peril: it is a pressing issue. Statistics on import penetration for countries within the 'Triad' make this point clear. For the USA in 1970 imports represented 4.1 per cent of GNP. By 1980 the proportion had risen to 9.1 per cent and by 1990 it had further increased to over 18 per cent. During the same period Japan witnessed imports increasing from 10 to 13 per cent of GNP. Rising import penetration across the major industrial economies of the world not only underlines the interlinked nature of the 'Triad', but also emphasises that the main competitors for indigenous firms are increasingly likely to be foreign rather than domestic companies.

Illustration 3.1 explains the significance of GNP, as well as highlighting the exceptional growth forecasted for the Asia-Pacific international region. By 2001 it is anticipated that this region will have a GNP comparable with NAFTA and Western Europe. This is because the growth throughout the Asia-Pacific area has been exceptionally rapid, and this is expected to continue. Between 1991 and 2001, Japan, Australia and the 'Tiger' economies are forecast to grow by 68 per cent (more than twice the percentage rate of NAFTA and Western Europe), while China and the Asia-Pacific developing countries are expected to achieve a 126 per cent increase in GNP. As a result, while North America, Western Europe and Japan will remain important components of the world economy, the emerging 'Tiger' economies are likely to be increasingly significant.

Figure 3.4 shows the large absolute size of the three legs of the Triad, as

Figure 3.4 Forecast growth of world 'Triad' markets, 1991–2001: levels of GNP and estimated percentage changes over the period

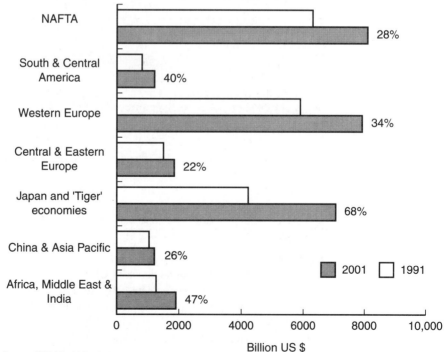

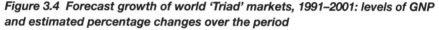

Source: IMF; World Bank

Illustration 3.1

Gross National Product (GNP)

GNP is a measure of the economic wealth of a country, based on the amount of goods and services that it produces. The higher a country's GNP, the greater the amount of goods and services produced by the economy. While difficulties arise in comparing data between countries, GNP is taken as the standard measure of the economic wealth of different countries. These difficulties reflect both the accuracy of each country's data and the means by which economic activity is translated into a common international currency, usually the US dollar, to enable aggregation and comparison. Statisticians seeking to use a common denominator have the choice of either translating the value of output using market exchange rates or seeking to adjust for the actual differences in price levels existing between countries.

Using market exchange rates expressed in constant 1991 US dollars, the table below presents worldwide GNP figures in 1991 and estimates for 2001. The projections will undoubtedly be revised over time, but these and other comparable estimates point to two conclusions: (i) the continued importance of NAFTA and Western Europe; and (ii) the increasingly significant role played by the Asia/Pacific economies.

GNP measure by constant market exchange rates (1991)

Country	1991 GNP 1991 US$bn	1991 % of total	1991 GNP per capita US$	1991/ 2001 Annual growth rate (%)	2001 GNP 1991 US$bn	2001 % of total
NAFTA	6,328	30.0	17,103	2.5	8,089	27.0
South & Central America	844	4.0	2,164	3.4	1,181	4.0
Americas	**7,172**	**34.0**	**9,435**	**2.7**	**9,280**	**31.0**
Western Europe	5,906	28.0	16,874	3.0	7,935	26.0
Central & Eastern Europe	1,477	7.0	3,780	2.0	1,800	6.0
Europe	**7,383**	**35.0**	**9,977**	**2.8**	**9,735**	**32.0**
Japan & 'Tigers'	4,219	20.0	10,547	5.3	7,069	24.0
China & other	1,054	5.0	555	8.5	2,384	8.0
Asia/Pacific	**5,273**	**25.0**	**2,293**	**6.0**	**9,453**	**32.0**
Africa, Middle East & India	1,266	6.0	744	3.4	1,546	5.0
Total	**21,094**	**100.0**	**3,835**	**3.6**	**30,014**	**100.0**

All figures rounded.

The economic wealth for each individual in the country, a measure of the standard of living, is found by dividing the country's GNP by its total population to give GNP per capita. The worldwide average in 1991 was just under $4000. Europe and North America enjoyed levels four times greater than this, with per capita consumption of around $17,000.

Source: The authors, based on IMF and World Bank

well as highlighting the large relative growth rates of emerging markets between 1991 and 2001. The term *emerging markets* encompasses a heterogeneous group of countries which need to be divided further in order to gain a better appreciation of the current stage and future growth potential of each. Illustration 3.2 clarifies what is meant by 'emerging' and considers how the markets may be clustered into sub-groups.

Trade liberalisation

The overall growth of the world economy and the emergence of newly international competitors, depicted in Figure 3.4, has been greatly facilitated by the successful conclusion of the Uruguay Round of the GATT trade talks, implemented with effect from 1 January 1995. In the face of a relatively slow-growing world economy and calls for trade protectionism, the successful outcome to the Uruguay Round has brought significant reductions in trade barriers on a number of fronts. First, agreement resulted in 'reciprocal and mutually advantageous arrangements' to make substantial cuts in tariffs on manufactured goods. It also effected the promise to bring a number of areas under the umbrella of the GATT framework, notably farm products, textiles and services. Further, much greater protection has been afforded to intellectual property rights at a time when this was causing tension between the industrialised and developing countries. Finally, the ability of countries to impose trade barriers unilaterally has been reduced through clarifying the conditions under which countries might choose to safeguard their own industries.

Looking to the twenty-first century, the interlinked economy is likely to grow faster. This is particularly clear from the estimates presented in Illustration 3.2. What the Uruguay Round signalled was a period of further trade liberalisation and an additional push to the development of an increasingly interlinked world economy. The confident prediction is that the growth of international trade is likely to continue to *exceed* the growth of world output. In short, international competition is increasing more quickly than output growth. For example, between 1950 and 1991 the volume of total world exports grew twelve times, while output only grew six times. Within this total, reflecting trade liberalisation, the volume of world exports of manufacturers grew 23 times, while output rose only eight times.

The shifting shares of world export trade reflect the dynamics of the world economy and the changing costs of producing in different locations. Not only do the newly emerging industrialising countries (NICs) of South East Asia enjoy the benefits of a low cost manufacturing base, but also they are characterised by an increasing well-educated and hard-working workforce who have the ambition to interlink with the Triad. Growth of the emerging economies of Asia is reflected in their increasing share of world trade in export of manufactured goods. In 1986 their share of world trade was 11.5 per cent, compared to 13.5 per cent for Japan. By 1995 the expectation is that the newly industrialising Asian economies will account for 19 per cent of world trade, while Japan will only account for 10 per cent (*Independent*, 31 January 1994).

Illustration 3.2

Emerging countries

The term 'emerging countries' has been defined by the International Finance Corporation (an affiliate of the World Bank) as those countries which have low or middle per capita incomes based on GNP. Almost 80 per cent of the world's population lives in those countries which fall under this definition, including as it does much of Latin America, South East Asia, China, the Indian sub-continent, Africa, the Middle East, the former Soviet Union, Eastern Europe and parts of Southern Europe.

These countries can be divided further into the following groups:

- the first tier of emerging countries: the newly industrialising countries (NICs) which are the most advanced in terms of their economic development and with relatively low economic and/or political risk, including Mexico, Brazil, Singapore and Malaysia;
- the second tier of emerging countries: these developing countries include China, Israel, Hungary and South Africa; and
- embryonic or submerged countries: those which have poor economic and social infrastructure, who are only at the first stage of development. Countries falling into this category include the Soviet Union, Morocco, Zimbabwe and Peru.

Those countries which constitute the first tier not only enjoy low labour costs, but have improving levels of education in their population and are increasingly gaining access to Western-style technology and capital.

Actual and forecast annual GNP growth rates for a number of emerging countries/regions compared to the EU and NAFTA, for the period 1991–2001, are shown below:

China	8.5
East Asia	7.6
South Asia	5.3
Africa, Middle East and Indian subcontinent	3.4
Central and Southern America	3.4
EU	3.0
NAFTA	2.5
Central & Eastern Europe	2.0
World	3.6

The average annual compounded growth rates, after adjustment for inflation, are consistently higher for the foreseeable future than the levels enjoyed in the recent past.

Source: The authors based on 'Emerging Markets', *Independent*, 29 October 1994, and Brookes (1994)

The development of the European Union and more recently NAFTA has resulted in the emergence of large unified international regional trading areas. The convergence of trading and investment requirements within these areas means that increasingly these trading blocs are being treated as single entities for the purposes of trade. Within these blocs the reduction or outright removal of trade restrictions not only brings the benefit of trade liberalisation, but also in the context of the world economy the increased competition results in further benefits for consumers. This makes the point that trade liberalisation has not only promoted the growth of inter-bloc trade, but also within in each trading area intra-bloc trade has also been encouraged. Intra-bloc trade will be encouraged to the extent that the trading bloc has common currency or culture characteristics, as discussed in Illustration 3.3.

Inter- or intra-bloc trade

The emergence of trading blocs raises the question of whether companies should focus on intra- or inter-bloc trade. Table 3.1 shows that, in respect of the EU over the period 1980 to 1992, intra-bloc trade of manufactured exports became more important, while the relative importance of inter-bloc trade (to the rest of the world) fell. This suggests that over the period EU countries became more inward looking. As a result, it is possible to describe EU trade over this period as becoming focused increasingly on its own international regional common market.

The interlinking of international competition through trade and foreign direct investment is illustrated by Figure 3.5. GATT estimates that by the year 2005 over four-fifths of all world merchandise trade flows will be within and between the elements of the 'Triad'. Intra-America trade flows will be the smallest of all the Triad groupings, with more external trade as opposed to internal trading. Intra-Europe trade will account for over one-third of world

Figure 3.5 Projected merchandise trade in US$ billion and as a percentage of world trade for the year 2005

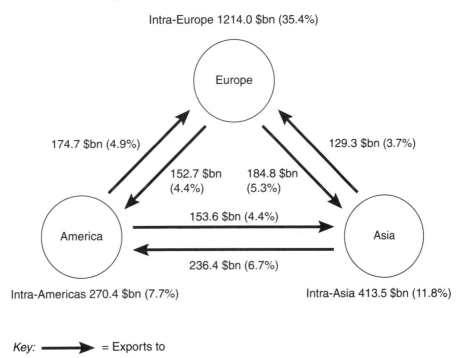

Intra-Europe 1214.0 $bn (35.4%)

Europe

174.7 $bn (4.9%)

129.3 $bn (3.7%)

152.7 $bn (4.4%)

184.8 $bn (5.3%)

America

Asia

153.6 $bn (4.4%)

236.4 $bn (6.7%)

Intra-Americas 270.4 $bn (7.7%)

Intra-Asia 413.5 $bn (11.8%)

Key: ⟶ = Exports to

Source: Adapted from GATT reports (1993)

Illustration 3.3

The 'Triad' markets – diversity or homogeneity?

The historical antecedents of the three 'Triad' markets and their present-day characteristics are very different. The USA has long enjoyed the benefits of a uniform mass market and single US dollar currency. These advantages have allowed many companies to enjoy the advantages of producing on a large scale without the difficulties and/or expense of cross-border currency transactions. Similarly, Japan, although a much smaller market than the USA, benefits from a single national culture, language and currency.

By comparison, the European Union (EU) is a community of nation states, each with its own powerful historical traditions and cultures. Within a comparatively small geographical area there are major differences in language, culture and heritage. Consequently, it is unlikely that Europe will ever achieve the same degree of market uniformity as either Japan or the USA. Similarly, the prevalence of individual national currencies means that the cross-border movement of goods and services is subject to the effect of exchange rate conversions. Recognising the transaction costs of moving from one currency base to another has led to the active discussion of the benefits of a single European currency. To many supporters of a closer EU, the achievement of a single European currency is a necessary condition to enable the emergence of a truly common market in Europe. The economic conditions required to be sustained in order that a single European currency could be achieved, however, would require the convergence of different national economic policies to an extent that to date has proved difficult to achieve. Until such time as this changes, companies wishing to trade between European nations will continue to need to take exchange rate movements into account when planning their European sales. Further, the linguistic and cultural diversity of European nations, established over many decades, will remain a distinctive element of the EU, even if convergence between different national markets continues.

Source: The authors

Table 3.1 Shares of world exports of manufacturers (%)

	1980	1986	1992
Intra-EU	24.1	22.9	26.1
Extra-EU	21.9	19.4	17.6
US	13.3	10.8	12.8
Japan	11.2	14.1	12.3
Rest of World	29.4	32.8	31.2

Source: Adapted from the *Financial Times*, 24 February 1994

trade, which is in line with current trade data showing the member states of the EU focusing their main trading in this regional market. By contrast, Europe will show a net deficit in trade with both North America and Asia. Asia will account for almost one-quarter of all traded merchandise, and show net trade surpluses with both Europe and North America. As Illustration 3.4 suggests no longer is the increased trade confined to manufacturing.

Illustration 3.4

Service sector internationalisation

In respect of the service sector, it is important to recognise that trade liberalisation is increasing cross-border competition for many industries. While in the past national barriers to entry across the service sector protected many producers from international competition and allowed inefficient national competitors to survive, this 'old' order is increasingly being threatened by cross-border competition. Nowhere has this been more so than in Europe, where national monopolies and/or regulatory control (e.g. Germany's tight control on shopping hours) have limited new entry to the market. Recent studies identified lower levels of productivity for a range of European service industries including airlines, banking, telecommunications and retailing. As a result, many of these sectors are now experiencing greater competition, most notably from US companies. The message would appear to be clear: services are likely to follow manufacturing in becoming increasingly subject to international competition.

Source: The authors

Japan's enormous trade imbalance with the rest of the world is likely to persist for the foreseeable future. Figure 3.6 details the changing trade balances for the world's electronics industry between 1987 and 1989 and estimates the position for 1995. European firms tend to be weakest in the world's most dynamic sectors, and the electronics trade imbalance is forecast to more than double over the period. The American imbalance also doubles from $7 billion to $18 billion. In 1995 Japan is projected to have a trade surplus in excess of $87 billion, while the growth of the 'Tiger' economies can be

Figure 3.6 Trade balance of world electronics industry: surplus/deficit in US$ billion

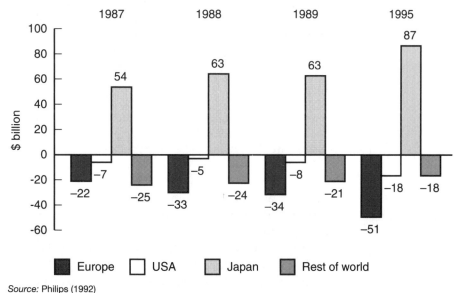

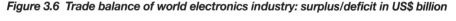

Source: Philips (1992)

inferred from the falling trade balance for the rest of the world. Overall these figures emphasise not only Japan's continuing trade imbalance, but also the continuing growth of the 'Tiger' economies subsumed within the figures for the rest of the world.

With the increasing movement of goods and more recently services within the world economy (see Illustration 3.4), imbalances between production and consumption in one region of the Triad will inevitably be corrected by trade flows to or from one or more of the other two elements of the Triad. For example, excess capacity (production capacity is greater than demand) in NAFTA may lead to producers seeking to sell into either Asia or the European Union. As a result, it becomes increasingly difficult for imbalances in any one region to exist for long without artificial barriers to trade or prohibitive transport costs. Further, the emergence of new competitors inevitably changes the balance between world supply and demand. For example, the European steel industry has experienced excess capacity in the early 1990s which has been exacerbated by the emergence of Eastern European competitors as the 'Iron Curtain' has been removed. Similarly, the emergence of new entrants to the petrochemical industry from the Middle East with direct access to feed stocks significantly increased competition in the market for basic chemicals.

Direct investment

World trade flows increasingly reflect the locational decisions of international competitors and not just the competitive position of indigenous nationally owned companies. A significant cause of foreign direct investment for German and Japan companies has been the effect of rising exchange rates which have made their exports relatively expensive. This has made German and Japanese products less competitive than similar product offers from the newly emerging countries who enjoy the benefits of lower exchange rates. Consequently, faced with such differences in the competitive bases of trade, many of the older industrialised countries are finding it hard to raise their productivity sufficiently to offset any intrinsic cost advantage brought about by the lower cost base of the emerging economies of the world. Both Germany and Japan face daunting challenges in this respect. At the end of 1992 Japan was a net owner of some $514 billion and Germany $300 billion of foreign assets. The perceived difficulties of Japan have promoted one commentator to write:

> never has an economy passed so quickly as Japan from non-industrialised backwater, through industrial giant, and now towards threatened industrial dinosaur – all in one generation. (Davies 1994, p 25)

Dynamic adjustments

The cases of Japan and Germany draw attention to the dynamics of the world economy and how success eventually brings attendant difficulties. Both countries for much of the post-war period have been well regarded as examples of successful international competitor nations. Now both face daunting structural challenges. The success of both countries has resulted in rising affluence which in turn has gradually eroded the respective cost bases, despite, for example, in

Germany's case significant fixed capital investment and expenditure on education and training. As a result the cost base for each country rose, a trend exacerbated by an appreciation in the currency rate for each nation. Ultimately, the product of both these forces has resulted in the home manufacturing base of each country becoming less and less competitive, until the point is reached that each is vulnerable to competition from lower cost locations.

The loss of export sales and employment will gradually result in corrective adjustments to the situation described, but only with the existence of considerable time lags. Thus a cycle of events is initiated based on (i) wage cost and (ii) currency movements which undermines the success of the previously rapidly growing economies, thereby enabling new countries to become the preferred production base. In this context protectionism slows the inevitable adjustment of companies and industries to the realities of the market place. In the final analysis, trade protection is unlikely to provide more than a temporary solution by offering an extended period to enable adjustment to take place. The paradox is that once adopted, a protection policy removes the competitive pressure to update and renew. As a result, when protection is removed the post-period adjustments may be much more dramatic.

The dynamics of the Triad world economy create instability and change, but there can be no such thing as absolute winners or losers. Winning becomes increasingly expensive as wages and currencies are adjusted upwards. Loser economies, by contrast, are able to rejuvenate in the long term since an unemployed workforce is available at reasonable cost and backed by a weak currency. Time lags to this process ensure that the adjustment process is slow, with changes in political, technological and social factors either reinforcing the economic adjustment process or retarding it.

PEST analysis

Developments within the world economy set the broad context for international business development. External triggers to these developments are usually clustered under three headings, namely:

- political and economic drivers
- social (lifestyle) changes
- technological developments

The factors listed are sometimes referred to as PEST analysis. They collectively provide an overall framework against which to consider developments at the meta level.

Political and economic drivers

Just as political forces have brought a liberalisation of world trade, so economic forces are responsible for many of the underlying dynamics of the world economy. A growing number of products and services are entering international markets, with countless companies undertaking international expansion, so that in many instances the norms of a national market become outdated.

Underlying cost differentials between countries may, as was previously noted, be exacerbated by movements in the exchange rates. The total cost of servicing a particular market from production located in one country rather than another must recognise all inputs into the production function. Consequently, differences in, say, labour costs may be insufficient to offset the costs of transport to a particular market. Neither is cost the only critical factor in the equation. For many products customers are not looking for low cost at the expense of quality. Illustration 3.5 describes the difficulties facing low cost component suppliers in India who wish to supply Western and Japanese motor vehicle producers.

Worldwide shifts in the economic location of many industries can be attributed to labour cost competitiveness. This is particularly true where labour costs form a significant part of total costs, and this advantage is not at the expense of productivity and an appropriate level of quality. Figure 3.7 shows differences in total labour costs per hour for three component products – seats, exhausts and brakes – sold to the world's automobile industry. Wage rates in both Germany and Japan are high, but when productivity is taken into account labour costs per unit in Japan are much lower. Conversely, labour costs per hour are the third lowest in the UK, but the second highest in relation to output (Figure 3.8).

Differences in Figure 3.8 not only reflect wage costs, but also many other factors including the level of the country's exchange rate. If a country enjoys a undervalued exchange rate, then its manufacturers are likely to benefit from improved export sales. If the country's exchange rate has a tendency to

Illustration 3.5

Indian car components industry

The Indian car components industry's main advantages as an equipment supplier are low labour cost and lax environmental controls. These factors, coupled with a long engineering tradition, make India a cost-effective country for hot and dirty operations (e.g. forging of heavy components) and the manufacture of components which require manual assembly (e.g. electrical components).

The country's disadvantages in the export market reflect the lack of an adequate industrial infrastructure and a reputation for poor quality. For the latter reason in particular, major Western and Japanese companies often decline to use Indian producers as original equipment manufacturers (OEMs): producers who supply the components which are incorporated into the manufacture of new cars. As a result, Indian companies are often reliant upon the spares market. Unfortunately, exporting low cost, low quality spares, sometimes at half the cost of OEMs, has tended to undermine the efforts of companies to supply original equipment.

The case of the Indian components industry serves to emphasise that low cost is an insufficient competitive base if it means poor productivity and inferior quality. What matters is how a company makes use of its low cost base.

Source: Based on Wegstyl (1994)

Figure 3.7 World component supplies, labour costs per hour (US$)

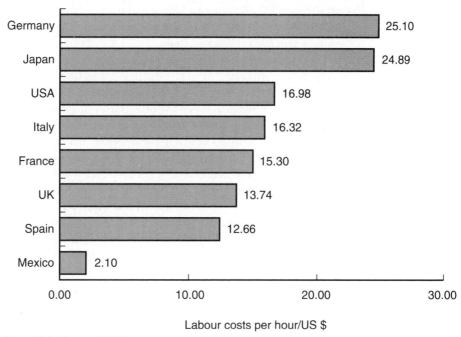

Labour costs per hour/US $

Source: Delbridge *et al.* (1994)

Figure 3.8 Index labour cost per unit of output (US$)

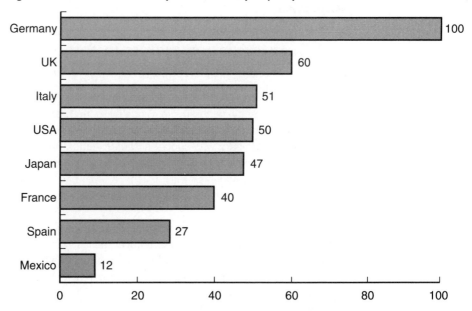

Source: Delbridge *et al.* (1994)

appreciate against competitor nations, then unless the cost of production can be reduced to offset the exchange rate rise, or the manufacturer supplies price insensitive markets, the country's exports are likely, in the long term, to be replaced by lower cost suppliers.

Faced with a continuing appreciation in the country's exchange rate, a company using its 'home' based production facilities as its source of supply to world markets faces uncomfortable choices. If the company wishes to continue to have an international exposure, it must either drive down costs to the point where any cost disadvantage is neutralised or decide to locate and/or increase production in cross-border locations. If the company is unwilling to take these steps, it is likely to find itself increasingly squeezed out of international markets and operating instead within a restricted national market scope. Unfortunately, this is unlikely to prove a sustainable strategy given the ability of cross-border producers to invade the company's home market, facilitated both by increased trade liberalisation and the lower cost of sales. The difficulties faced by many Japanese manufacturers derived from the continued appreciation of the yen are revealed in Illustration 3.6.

The location of low cost economic facilities is constantly changing. The rising star of the current decade may easily become vulnerable in the next as new competitors emerge. The inherent dynamics of the world economy ensure that competitive forces never stabilise to a steady state, but continuously bring forth new competitors, who are prepared to reward themselves less generously. Illustration 3.7 describes the emergence of a Korean car manufacturer and how its strategy of entering the US market is a direct threat to the dominance of the previous 'new order' Japanese producers.

Illustration 3.6

Yen appreciation results in components sourcing being transferred to a low cost location

The factory of Sanritsu Electric at Tokushima on the Southern Japanese island of Shikoku is currently standing idle. Since October 1993 the employees have been laid off. The factory which had supplied Sanyo Electric with consumer electronic products for 26 years was suddenly told in August that the company would no longer be ordering products from Tokushima. Production of compact disc, radio and cassette players which the Tokushima plant had previously supplied were to be sourced from Singapore. Two months later Sanritsu's Tokushima plant had run out of orders.

Sanritsu's problems are common among Japan's electronics manufacturers, reflecting the yen's sharp appreciation over the last year. As product prices fell and competition intensified, Japanese companies faced with higher costs had little alternative but to increasingly source products overseas to take advantage of lower labour costs.

Source: Based on Nakamoto (1994)

Illustration 3.7

Entry of Kia Motors of South Korea into the US car market

At the beginning of 1994, Kia Motors of South Korea entered the North American car market. Kia Motors' strategy was to replicate the policies of Japanese car producers in an earlier decade. In an attempt to establish its presence in an already highly competitive market, Kia Motors' strategy is to under-price its products, which are of similar quality to its competitors' and often include superior levels of standard equipment.

Greg Warner, executive vice-president of Kia Motors America, believes that a gap in the competitive US market has appeared at the bottom end. This has resulted from Japanese car producers increasing the price of their products in a response to a rise in the yen–dollar exchange rate. For example, the Kia Sephia is priced at $8495, while rival products such as the Toyota Corolla and Honda Civic have a lowest list price in excess of $12,000.

If Kia Motors succeeds it will replace Japanese models in the low price segments of the US car market. Recognising this threat, Japanese manufacturers are increasingly caught in the middle: unable to command premium prices from selling highly sought-after luxury motor cars; and equally unable to match the lower cost base of new entrants to the market.

Source: Based on Done (1994)

Social (lifestyle) changes

Social (lifestyle) changes exert a powerful influence on customer choice and the extent to which their requirements converge or diverge. Undoubtedly the world is becoming a smaller place, facilitated by major discontinuities which have both reduced the cost of international travel and enhanced communications. Satellite communications ensure that the mass media informs even isolated communities in many less developed countries about consumer products produced for the developed world. Faced with the apparent worldwide homogeneity of consumer preferences for a number of widely known products, it is unsurprising that many commentators, including Levitt (1983), should have emphasised the convergence of customer requirements.

While it is possible to point to a number of global products, including cameras, cassette players, jeans and soft drinks, it is also important to recognise continuing diversity. In many communities cultural and language identities pull in the opposite direction, offsetting at least in part the trend to convergence. Many nation-states have witnessed, for example, the emergence of separate groups who vocally demand that their differences to the rest of the country be recognised. Emphasising these tensions, Illustration 3.8 discusses the concept of the 'world car'.

Lifestyle trends need to be recognised as a critical external trigger, which may operate either to accelerate the convergence of the global economy, or continue to promote diversity.

101

Illustration 3.8

Nissan KK

Nissan is a major automobile company with manufacturing divisions in Japan, Europe and North America. The company's strategy is based on the need to penetrate successfully the three 'Triad' markets. Counterbalancing this need is the recognition that customers in each of the Triad markets and in some cases within sub-markets display vastly different sets of needs and preferences. Nissan believe that there is no universal 'world car' that will appeal on all continents. A major challenge facing the company is to design basic models which avoid pleasing the needs of none of the Triad markets, by trying to meet some of the needs of each.

Nissan has managed to halve the number of basic models required to cover the Triad markets and at the same time generate three-quarters of sales with cars designed for specific markets. Such optimisation has not been achieved by averaging across markets to reach a compromise design. Consumers do not want to purchase such a product. Instead, Nissan looks at the Triad region by region and identifies each market's dominant requirements. The company starts with what it calls a 'lead country' model in which cars are designed and tailored to the distinct needs of the dominant national markets. It is always lead country models that inform the basic design for different key markets.

Source: The authors

Technological developments

New technology – information, communication, travel and transport – both promotes changes at the meta level and facilitates the adoption of changes in other areas. Reference has already been made to developments in mass media broadcasting. Advances in satellite technology allow information to be transmitted around the world more quickly and cheaply, as well as enabling the emergence of pan-country media. In Europe the development of satellite broadcasting has already proved an important mechanism to overcome country-based restrictions on programme content and presentation.

Taking a broader perspective on communications technology, advances in computer science have resulted in a revolution. Developments in information technology have greatly facilitated the collation, analysis and transfer of data in ways which were previously not available. Consequently, the ability to co-ordinate activities from diffuse locations has risen. Equally, the application of information and communications technology to trading and financial systems has facilitated the movement of commerce by ensuring monetary flows can be much more easily managed by organisations. These developments in themselves have resulted in greater linkage between the major stock markets and financial systems of the world. They also offer new opportunities for companies wishing to finance their international operations. Illustration 3.9 details some of the developing technologies likely to play an increasingly significant role in the future.

Illustration 3.9

Developing technologies

Gene splicing

Key technology underlying biotechnology invented in the USA in the early 1970s. Likely to be increasingly significant for the pharmaceutical industry.

Magnetic resonance imaging (MRI)

Of major relevance to medical equipment industry, in which leading companies already produce MRI body scanners. Rapid advance in technology anticipated, with new machines showing not only images, but biochemical reactions inside the human body.

High-temperature superconductivity

Discovered in the 1980s. Current research and development activity is focused on exploiting new ceramic materials which lose all electrical resistance at workable temperatures.

Personal computers

Technological advances are continuing, with portable computers in particular experiencing rapid growth.

Neural networks

Primary application is to military and research purposes. More recently used in the industrial and financial sectors for pattern recognition and forecasting.

Communication satellites

Area of continuing growth and advancement.

Source: Adapted from 'Can Europe Compete?', *Financial Times*, 2 March 1994

Linking PEST and meta-level changes

Drawing together the political, economic, social and technological factors, these four fundamentals may be observed to drive a number of derivative trends which in turn may be clustered at the meta level. The linkages between these elements and the associated derivative and meta trends are illustrated in Figure 3.9. At the meta level the derivative trends result in four sets of inter-related changes: worldwide supply and demand; GNP and trade; consumer lifestyle; and diffusion of technology.

Trends at the meta level may be summarised as follows:

- *Worldwide supply and demand*: growing numbers of products and services are being traded internationally. With numerous countries of the 'Triad' taking part in international trade, it no longer makes sense to adopt a traditional view of local or domestic markets. While governments may persist in the belief that they can protect domestic markets, such a view should be resisted if further rapid decline is to be avoided.
- *Dynamic changes in GNP and trade*: each member of the 'Triad' needs to supplant that portion of the economic base which consists of stagnating or

Figure 3.9 *The relationship between PEST and meta trends*

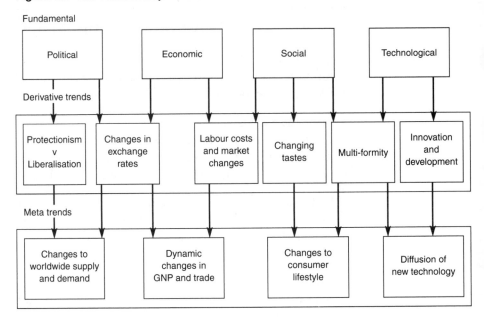

declining industries with vital and growing industrial activities. The dynamics of the 'Triad' ensure that countries are not engaged in a 'zero sum' struggle for economic survival. Provided that countries take the long-term opportunities offered for mutual enrichment, there should be no such thing as absolute losers and winners. Renewal is triggered primarily by exchange rate and labour cost adjustments.

- *Changes to consumer lifestyles*: changing and differing demands of consumers are increasing the multi-formity and dynamism of markets. Not only can the market no longer be approached in a standard way, but also product life cycles become shorter. The abundance of changes provides key challenges and opportunities.
- *Diffusion of new technology*: the fast proliferation of technical know-how generates successful products and services which meet the needs of dynamic and multi-form lifestyles. The downside is the high development costs. It is frequently necessary to recoup such costs through serving large international markets.

The inter-relationships between the four meta trends depicted in Figure 3.9 are self-evident. This is not coincidental, since they are the effect of the same causes. What is less clear is the impact of each trend at the meta level and the way in which these developments act as driving forces to far-reaching changes in management processes. Experience suggests that it is not particularly helpful to try to draw out such contextual issues at the meta level. Rather, it should be recognised that each of the PEST factors – political, economic, social and technological – will have a differential effect, depending upon the industry-specific context examined.

Assessing the internationalisation of industries: globalisation v localisation

If developments at the level of the industry are tending to converge on a worldwide basis the industry can be said to be *globalising*. In other words, from the perspective of competition the world needs to be treated as a single market. By contrast, *localisation* describes an industry where divergence at level of the local or national market is such that the world's industry is in effect made up of a collection of national industries. Competition is at a national rather than world level. Companies may compete in a number of these markets, but for some purposes at least they need to treat each market separately. Globalisation and localisation describe the extremes of a continuum, between which most industries will be located.

An important judgement before assessing the extent of globalisation/localisation is the need to consider how the boundaries to the industry might be drawn. Industries are about competition, and the boundaries to an industry should recognise and include competitive rivals offering products or services which are close substitutes for each other. In drawing industry boundaries the user's or customer's viewpoint must be paramount, even though traditionally many industries and their trade associations have taken a supply-side perspective. This prompts consideration of (i) the relationship between industries and markets; and (ii) whether a broad or narrow focus should be adopted when drawing industry boundaries.

Figure 3.10 provides four important insights into the relationship between industries and markets. First, it shows how industry definitions may be drawn by considering similar technologies, skills and processes. Secondly, the diagram suggests the need to consider competition from substitute products and services supplied by other industries. Thirdly, market entry from industry suppliers not currently supplying a particular segment can be considered and the degree of threat examined. Finally, where a market segment is exposed to convergence from two industries, a new industry, which is a hybrid of the previous separate industries, may emerge. The area of communications and in particular the emergence of multi-media offer examples of this outcome.

The cornerstone of market analysis is the ability to undertake segmentation of customer demands. Figure 3.10 shows three firms – A, B and C – in industry I which supply three different market segments. The challenge is to agree the basis on which the market segment – (i), (ii) or (iii) – is to be identified. While all three firms possess common technologies, processes and skills and have the potential to operate in all three segments, not all competitors choose to do so. This may be because they cannot supply a particular segment economically. Market segment (ii) appears to be the most competitive, with five companies supplying the market from two separate industries.

In the world airline industry case featured at the end of this chapter, relatively few national airlines are strongly represented in both intra-regional and inter-continental market segments. Even fewer airlines have recognised

Figure 3.10 Industries and markets

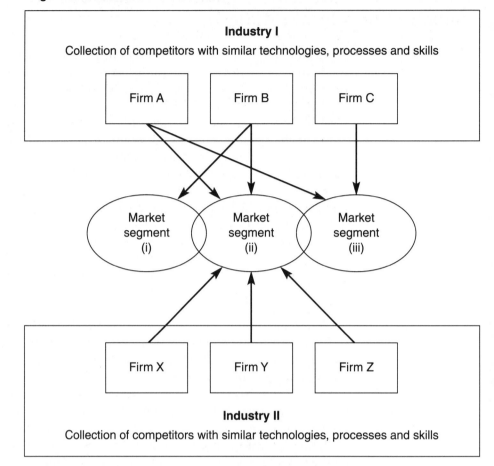

that the basis of competition in these segments is radically different. Any attempt to assess the extent to which an industry is moving towards globalisation or localisation must pay particular attention to how such boundaries should be drawn.

In order to assess actual and emerging trends at the industry level, an informing framework is required which can assist in determining the extent to which an industry is moving towards globalisation or localisation. The following framework, developed from Yip and Coundouriotis (1991), is presented to assist in this task. It identifies four sets of industry *drivers*. Drivers may be defined as those factors which set the direction of industry trends. The set of four drivers which need to be analysed in order to assess the potential for the industry's globalisation are as follows:

- Customers
- Cost
- Country
- Competition

The 'four Cs' or industry drivers identified above and illustrated in Figure 3.11 collectively determine the extent to which an industry is globalising.

Figure 3.11 Assessing the extent to which an industry is globalising

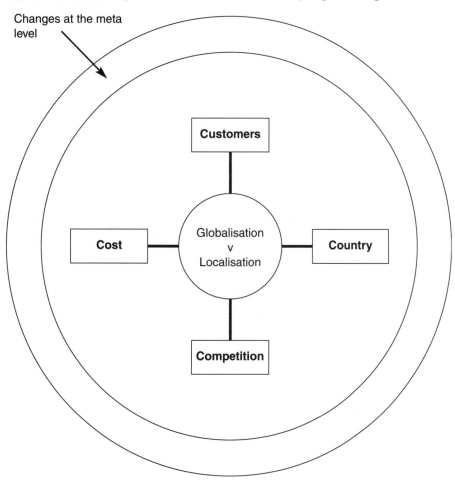

Customer drivers

Customer drivers focus on the market and the requirements of customers, distribution and the extent to which uniform marketing policies can be applied on a worldwide basis. Customer drivers can be sub-divided into three key components, namely:

- customer requirements
- distribution
- uniform marketing

Customer requirements

Reference has already been made earlier in the chapter to the fact that some products have achieved worldwide acceptance. Where consumer requirements converge to a common denominator it is possible for an industry to market standardised global products. Conversely, where local or national tastes differ it is unlikely that standardised products will achieve the same level of customer acceptance. Even within a single industry the standardisation of products can show marked variation. The food industry provides a good example. Some food products have gained increasing international acceptance and come close to conforming to the idea of a globalised standard product. Examples would include rice and pasta. Equally, however, there are many food products which have a much more localised appeal and do not cross national boundaries to any great extent. Examples would include sauces localised to a national market. Tomato ketchup in the UK is sweet, in France spicy and in the USA vinegary.

Distribution drivers

The role of distribution is often underestimated. The importance of different distribution channels and the presence or absence of different types of intermediaries varies enormously between nations. As a result, for many nations distribution channels need to be customised to ensure products are made available to purchasers. The extent of the challenge will depend upon customer push or pull. Customer push describes the situation where a producer attempts to 'push' products through the distribution channels in order to gain the attention of the customer. By contrast, customer pull describes the situation where demand from customers 'pulls' the product through the distribution channel.

The barriers that a national distribution system can present to the penetration of an important national market can be illustrated with reference to the Japanese market for consumer electronics. Former employees of the major Japanese electronics companies are encouraged on their retirement, usually at the age of 55, to set up retail outlets selling exclusively the products of their former employer. These so-called 'pop and mum' shops, which are in effect a tied outlet, are a major impediment to European and US companies penetrating the Japanese consumer electronics market.

Uniform marketing

The convergence of lifestyles referred to earlier opens up the possibility of using greater uniformity in the marketing approach in selling to different national markets. Development of satellite television is a feature of this trend. This contrasts markedly with the traditional approach of many international manufacturers, who have often sold the same product into different national markets using a variety of brand names. Rationalising brand names in order to develop a pan-national marketing strategy clearly has risks. Unilever, for example, uses a number of different brand names to sell the same soap powder across Europe. Its leading laundry detergents are variously sold as All, Omo, Persil, Presto, Skip and Via, depending on which national market is examined. By contrast, Mars, the US chocolate confectionery manufacturer, has spent considerable sums of money on changing the names of successful national brands – Raider to Twix in Germany; Marathon to Snickers in the UK; and Kal-Kan to Whiskas in the USA – in order to use a pan-national marketing approach.

Cost drivers   The principal cost drivers include:

- new product development
- scale economies
- transportation costs

New product development

The cost of research and development has risen steeply, as the technological sophistication of products increases, and competitive pressures require firms to introduce replacements to their existing product range within a shorter time. The escalating cost of research and development under these circumstances places huge resource demands on the firm. In many cases all but the very largest companies find such demands difficult to meet. As a result, the tendency is for new product development to encourage firms to become large. For example, within the European Union at the start of 1994 six volume car producers remained: Volkswagen, Fiat, Renault, Peugeot/ Citroën, and the European subsidiaries of the US companies Ford and General Motors. Despite almost all the smaller car producers having been absorbed, the expectation is that there would be at least one additional merger in the industry before long, leading to further rationalisation. A number of commentators draw attention to the heavy reliance of many European car manufacturers on European markets for sales. With a relatively limited sales base, it is difficult to see how such firms can meet future challenges from truly global car producers.

Scale economies

In common with new product development, the presence of scale economies encourages firms to achieve high volume sales in order to spread total costs and thereby reduce costs per unit. Under these circumstances, encouragement to globalisation reflects the need to achieve the necessary volume of sales in order to gain scale economies. Counterbalancing the argument in favour of scale is the employment of flexible manufacturing systems (FMS). Based on the use of computer robotics and flexible employment practices, FMS seeks to achieve a comparable cost base, but from producing a smaller volume. The relative balance between economies of scale increasing size of plants and by implication companies, and FMS having the opposite influence can be illustrated by reference to Table 3.2.

Table 3.2 The influence of scale economies and FMS on minimum efficient scale (MES)

World sales ($m)	MES output ($m)	Number of plants	Pressure to globalise
120	10	12	Decreased
120	20	6	Current position
120	40	3	Increased

Minimum efficient scale (MES) is defined as the smallest size required in order for a plant to achieve the minimum costs of production per unit. Below this scale of output costs per unit rise and further savings can be made by operating with a larger volume of output. Beyond MES no further significant cost reductions are to be expected. The shaded section of Table 3.2 represents the current industry position, with six plants worldwide each supplying one-sixth of global demand.

As MES increases from $20 million of output to $40 million, with total sales unchanged at $120 million the optimal number of plants capable of operating at MES falls from six to three. This is the worldwide economies of scale argument, and prompts concentration of production and increased pressure towards globalisation. Conversely, if technology leads to MES falling to $10 million output, the number of plants able to operate at minimum cost rises from six to twelve. Under these circumstances FMS can halt and even reverse the trend to increased globalisation.

Where FMS is important, the pressure to achieve scale economies can be offset and any industry movement towards globalisation will be restrained. Alternative technologies may play a similar role as FMS, by ensuring that high volume is not the only way of achieving low costs. A good example of this is the co-existence of integrated steel plants and mini mills in the steel industry. The traditional view for the production of basic steel is that volume is necessary to achieve high throughput for integrated blast furnaces and steel converters to be operated efficiently. This recipe has been adopted worldwide by leading steel makers over the last 30 years. Less well understood is that alternative technologies enable smaller steel makers to co-exist alongside larger competitors. Illustration 3.10 details how the benefits of mini mills in the steel industry have been able to neutralise the cost advantages of larger integrated plants.

Transport costs

The cost of transporting products is regarded often as a countervailing force to the trend towards globalisation. In particular, the costs of transporting low value bulky products (e.g. beer, bricks, building aggregates, cement, flour, etc.) have tended to ensure such industries remain localised. By contrast, transport costs in the case of high value to weight products, for example whisky, have not prevented the drinks industry becoming global. These two examples serve to emphasise the role of the value to weight ratio as a factor either assisting or preventing the onset of globalisation.

The general trend is for transport costs to fall and thereby to become less important in driving or restraining globalisation. Indeed, within the EU and NAFTA processes are at work to reduce restrictions on road transport between countries, thereby bringing transport costs down further (see case study on Frans Maas, Chapter 7).

Country drivers The principal country drivers include:

● trade policies
● technical standards
● cultural and regulatory barriers

Illustration 3.10

Nucor Inc

Nucor Inc, a US steel company, has a strategy of being a low cost producer of steel products. In pursuit of this strategy it has avoided the need to develop large integrated steel plants and has instead focused on installing mini mills. As their name suggests, these are relatively small-scale steel-making plants which are less capital and labour intensive, manufacturing a limited product range but highly flexible. They do not engage in the costly process of making steel from scratch, but rather melt down scrap metal. As a result of these differences the large-scale production and sales volume necessary to fully utilise a large integrated steel plant are not required in the case of mini mills.

By employing efficient labour practices in the operation of its mini mills, Nucor has been able to produce steel more cheaply than its larger American rivals. As a consequence, the company has been able to report healthy levels of profitability during a period when the large American steel makers have suffered poor earnings performance and rationalisation has been under way in the industry.

Nucor Inc reported profits of some $130 million in 1993, reflecting the company's ability to produce steel at $80 per tonne, three times below the costs achieved by the larger integrated producers in the USA.

Source: The authors

Trade policies

Despite previous comments made in respect of increasing trade liberalisation, some individual countries continue to have nationalistic trade policies. China, for example, remains outside of the GATT framework, which in any case is less complete for services than for manufacturing. Equally, while tariff barriers within the major economic trading blocs are being progressively eliminated, duty may remain on imported products from outside the trading bloc. Where tariff barriers continue to exist these can distort cost differentials and make local production, at least in the short term, competitive with imported products.

Technical standards

Differences in technical standards makes product standardisation more difficult to achieve. The configuration of domestic electrical power supply demonstrates market variation between, for example, France, the UK and the USA. Similarly, for food products local laws may set different requirements for what manufacturers are allowed to include as ingredients.

Increasingly international standards are converging following the Uruguay Round of the GATT talks and the work of the international standard-setting bodies. These developments potentially reduce the extent to which differences in technical standards are an impediment to international trade growth. Not all companies, however, have recognised the imperatives of adopting international standards in order to secure sales in cross-border markets. For instance, in the past US companies have paid little concern to international standards, believing that their large domestic market could be best served with products which met American standards. As import penetration to the US has grown this perspective becomes less sustainable, and the failure to adopt international standards leads to difficulties. For example, many US companies have failed to adopt the metric system of weights and measures now uniformly used throughout the world, preferring to remain with the US imperial system.

To the extent that technical standards converge, globalisation is encouraged, while conversely the continuance of nationally specific requirements encourages the continuance of localisation.

Cultural and institutional barriers

Cultural norms are often incorporated within the institutions of a country. For example, acceptable or unacceptable forms of advertising are likely to be informed by the cultural norms of the society and reflected in the controls on the country's media. Similarly, some business practices are considered unacceptable in some countries, but can be used without offence in other nations. To take one example, in pharmaceutical products the British and US markets are very different. In the US a very aggressive approach is used to advertise and market products, with individual firms often openly stating the superiority of their products over their rivals. By contrast, in the UK the marketing approach is more measured, and the use of aggressive sales policies is discouraged.

Competitive drivers

The final cluster of industry drivers can be sub-divided as follows:

● competitive interdependence
● new entry competition

Competitive interdependence

As firms broaden the geographical scope of their operations, national markets may become interlinked for the purposes of competition. When this happens, competitive strategies being pursued in different national markets become interdependent. Correspondingly, the attainment by a major competitor of such a position may place rivals at a disadvantage. Under these circumstances, competitors will need to decide whether they can remain localised and survive, or whether they need to increase their international scope and scale. The latter will be the case where increases in international scope offer significant benefits with respect to, say, sharing production, research and development or marketing costs.

The urgency with which companies may seek to broaden their geographic scope is at least partially explained by the competitive dynamics of an industry. Industry growth rates not only reflect cyclical patterns of demand, but also underlying secular trends. Industries tend to pass through phases of growth and maturity, before entering decline. As the pattern and length of each stage vary by industry, with periods of rejuvenated growth sometimes following an initial period of maturity, the strategic imperatives of competitors tend to change with the industry cycle.

In a maturing industry the emergence of an international competitor, enjoying the cost benefits from strategically interdependent markets, may mean that those rivals who wish to increase their international scope have limited choices and time to develop an international regional or worldwide strategy. For example, the rapid maturity of the food industry means that national firms need to consider whether they wish to refocus on defensible segments of their local market or become more international in scope.

For those food companies which wish to broaden their international scope, the importance of local brands and distribution channels in many market segments has inevitably required companies to develop a stronger market presence in many cross-border markets. As these markets themselves have tended to move beyond their growth phase, market entry and development from a newly established base are very difficult and costly, as sales have to be won from existing competitors. Correspondingly, companies may well choose a policy of acquisition in order to secure established brands and distribution channels. As national players are acquired by international companies, further competitive waves are created and companies wishing to increase their competitive scope aggressively seek additional acquisitions to fuel their growth. Hence the establishment of a single international competitor tends to alter the competitive dynamics of the industry, bringing further competitive actions and reactions. The outcome is that the globalisation process is accelerated. An illustration of this process is given in Illustration 3.11.

Illustration 3.11

Purchase of French ice-cream manufacturer, Ortiz-Miko SA

On 20 December 1993 Unilever, the major Anglo-Dutch international food and consumer goods company, announced it was acquiring the ice-cream business of Ortiz-Miko, the French frozen food manufacturer whose Miko brand accounts for a significant share of the French ice-cream market.

As a result of the purchase Unilever, which is the world's largest ice-cream producer, will become the market leader in France ahead of its international rival Nestlé of Switzerland. Other major international companies with a presence in the French ice-cream market include Mars and Grand Metropolitan. Unilever would continue to retain Ortiz-Miko's distribution network as part of its post-acquisition management of the purchase.

As a result of the Ortiz-Miko purchase, Unilever's penetration of the French market has increased significantly. By using a strategy of acquisition (external growth), the company has been able to develop its market position much more quickly than would ever be possible in such a mature market through the expansion of its existing business base (organic growth). Acquisition of Ortiz-Miko also prevented the company falling into the hands of a competitor, whose position would have been enhanced at the expense of Unilever.

Source: The authors, based on press reports

Entry of new competitors

The entry of new competitors to an industry may have a powerful influence on the balance between globalisation and localisation. As acknowledged when discussing trends at the meta level, the entry of new competitors can destabilise the existing industrial structure and change the competitive dynamics of the industry. For example, the entry of companies based in the newly industrialising nations of the world, which often enjoy lower cost structures, can have a profound effect on existing competitors. This has most certainly been the case in respect of many industries where competition has increasingly come from the 'Tiger' economies of South East Asia.

New competition may also reflect both increasing trade liberalisation and the application of new technologies and business practices to an industry. As country-based trade barriers reduce, the opportunity for cross-border entry increases. In such circumstances new entrants are likely to be those competitors which have adopted new technologies and/or developed more efficient systems of business operation. These points are perhaps most strongly illustrated by taking a number of service industries in a European context, as Illustration 3.12 demonstrates.

Illustration 3.12 shows how new entry competition can change the balance between globalisation and localisation within an industry. The entry of international competitors to domestic market places increases competitive pressure, and again in turn local players need to consider their response.

Illustration 3.12

European retailing

The 1980s and 1990s have witnessed cross-border entry across the retailing sectors of many European countries. This has surprised many observers who formerly considered retailing as an example of an industry that could be categorised as localised. For example, the entry of the US retailers Toys 'R' Us and Computerland has revolutionised two sectors of the formerly localised European industry. Similarly, cross-border entry by European-based companies into different national markets has also increased competition. For example, Aldi, Europe's largest discount grocery retailer, now operates in Germany, Austria, Netherlands, Belgium, Denmark, USA, France, UK and Poland. The company's entry into the UK has had profound effects on the existing competitive order, significantly weakening the competitive position of the existing industry leaders.

Source: The authors

Summary of industry drivers

An overall assessment of each of the factors listed above will need to be made in order to assess the likely extent to which the industry has globalised and/or whether trends are driving the industry in that direction. At two ends of a continuum will be globalisation and localisation. The conditions when an industry is either completely globalised or localised are described in Table 3.3.

Table 3.3 Globalisation versus localisation

Globalisation	Localisation
Market drivers • Customer requirements: homogeneous customer needs worldwide, enabling the industry to standardise products to all major markets. • Distribution: existence of a global distribution channel operating at a worldwide level. • Marketing: homogeneous nature of marketing mix allows common approach and brand names to be used to serve all major markets.	*Market drivers* • Customer requirements: heterogeneous customer needs, with strong local preferences. • Distribution: distribution channels are specific to a local market. • Marketing: key elements of the marketing mix need to managed on a local basis reflecting different brand names, market position, etc.
Cost drivers • New product development: significant research and development costs to be recouped. • Scale economies: economies of scale are highly significant and require volume output. • Transport costs: high value to weight ratio means that transport costs do not discourage centralised production on a worldwide basis.	*Cost drivers* • New product development: insignificant research and development costs. • Scale economies: any potential economies of scale can be achieved through servicing the local market. Small-scale producers are not at a significant cost disadvantage when compared to large rivals. • Transport costs: low value to weight ratio results in transport costs requiring demand to be met from locally based production units.
Country drivers • Trade policies: insignificant national trade barriers. • Technical standards: international technical standards accepted in all major markets. • Cultural and institutional norms: these are not an impediment to global marketing.	*Country drivers* • Trade policies: nationalistic trade policies prevent imported products being able to compete with locally produced goods. • Technical standards: divergence of national standards prevent product standardisation. • Cultural and institutional norms: these vary country by country.
Competitive drivers • Competitive interdependence: principal markets are strongly interlinked. Firms need to operate in all major markets. • Entry of new competitors: international competitors have entered the local market.	*Competitive drivers* • Competitive interdependence: product-market in one country does not affect the firm's competitive stance in another. • Entry of new competitors: entry has not taken place.
Summary Industry has globalised, requiring firms to operate on a worldwide basis in order to reduce costs and improve their competitive basis.	*Summary* Industry remains localised, with locally focused firms being able to compete on equal terms with companies with international scope and scale.

Convergence or divergence?

Recognising the dynamics of the process, the tensions between globalisation and localisation can be related to the idea of a pendulum. When the balance of forces moves in one direction or another, so the pressure towards either globalisation or localisation intensifies. As Figure 3.12 shows, subsequent changes may reinforce the direction of movement, or else partly or wholly reverse the process. The balance of forces is constantly changing, emphasising once again that change is a fundamental characteristic of the external context.

In practice, the majority of industries are neither fully globalised nor localised. Rather, some drivers will be pulling in one direction while others will be pulling a different way. Accordingly, it is helpful to employ Table 3.3 and map the extent to which each driver is exerting pressure in one direction or another. By its very nature this assessment is judgemental, and needs to take account of the current industry position and the extent to which the direction and force of individual drivers are projected to change over, say, a five-year period. Figure 3.13 takes the example of the electronics industry and considers the balance of forces influencing the direction of the industry over the next five years. It is particularly important to use 'narrow' industry definitions, to enable focus to be given to a sector, rather than covering different sectors which might be experiencing contrasting trends.

For the consumer electronics industry summarised in Figure 3.13, on balance the industry drivers are moving the industry to become more global. The key elements to this process would appear to be those related to the cost, customer and competitive drivers. By comparison, the forces favourable to localisation – distribution, trade policies and technical standards – are relatively weak. Not surprisingly the industry is already dominated by large international companies – e.g. Matsushita, Sony, Philips, Thomson, Hitachi – which are engaged in a fierce competitive battle across the three Triad markets.

*Figure 3.12 **The pendulum of change: convergence versus divergence***

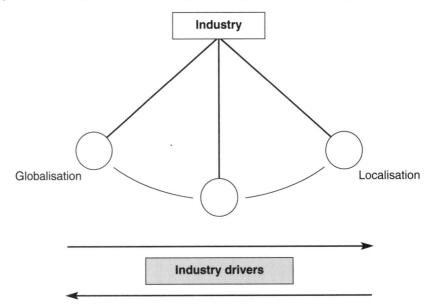

Figure 3.13 Summary of industry drivers for the consumer electronics industry over the next five years

Globalisation				Localisation		
High	Med	Low	**Industry drivers**	Low	Med	High
			Customer drivers			
	▨		Customer requirements			
			Distribution	▨		
		▨	Marketing			
			Cost drivers			
▨	▨	▨	New product development			
	▨		Scale economies			
	▨	▨	Transport costs			
			Country drivers			
			Trade policies	▨		
			Technical standards	▨		
			Cultural/regulatory barriers	▨		
			Competitive drivers			
▨	▨	▨	Competitive interdependence			
	▨	▨	Entry of new competitors			

High			**Overall**			

The overall assessment of the forces of globalisation/localisation requires considerable judgement concerning the relative importance of individual forces. It may be that one or two factors are of over-riding importance and these account for the predominant direction of the industry. This point emphasises that the process is not simply mechanistic, but is highly judgemental. Further, it is important not simply to focus on the present, but to consider how the forces are likely to influence the industry over, say, a three- to five-year period. Companies and their managers need to know not just what is happening today, but what will happen tomorrow, and to adjust their strategies accordingly. Periodically a review of industry drivers should be made to chart the progress of key trends.

Bi-polarisation

Recognising the inevitability of the globalisation process for many industries brings us back to the question of bi-polarisation. Bi-polarisation suggests that a company must either become a worldwide competitor with large critical mass or

117

seek to refocus on a product segment where the nature of the market demand and competitive independence enable the company to find a defendable niche. Such a segment may be found in the local market, but increasingly even narrowly focused competitors are becoming international. The relationship between product and geographical scope can be explored using Figure 3.14.

As Figure 3.14 illustrates, using the two dimensions of product and geography four competitive position can be identified, namely:

- *Local or national regional or national niche strategy*: competitive strategy is based on offering a narrow product range and operating with a restricted geographical focus.
- *Local or national regional or national broad-based strategy*: the organisation offers a broad product range, but focuses on supplying these to a restricted geographical market.
- *International niche strategy*: business strategy is based on a narrow product range, but one which is sold internationally.
- *International broad-based strategy*: operating in international markets, the organisation offers a broad product range.

The sustainability of each of the competitive positions identified in Figure 3.14 will be dependent upon a specific context and will reflect in particular the characteristics of *product demand* and *competitive interdependencies*. For instance, if the characteristics of demand reflect the needs of those customers who want

Figure 3.14 International competition and bi-polarisation

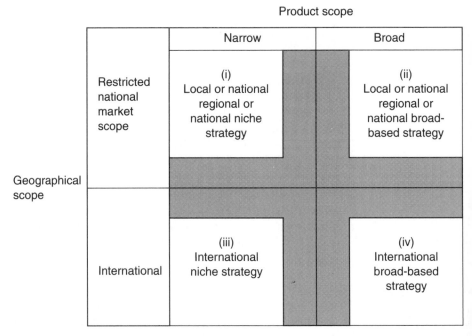

Key: ▨ = Zone of transition

a distinctive product or service offer, then a broadly based competitor may find these needs difficult to meet, suggesting that potentially a product-market niche exists. Equally, if competitive interdependencies are low between separate national markets, there may be little incentive to treat a cluster of national markets as a single entity for the purposes of supply in order to, say, gain economies of scale. By comparison, where competitive interdependence is high, the ability and costs of supplying the market economically are at least partially dependent on the organisation's ability to supply other national markets at the same time. Where this is the case the company supplying several national markets may well be able to share marketing and/or production costs across more than one country.

The application of the framework illustrated by Figure 3.14 to an individual industry needs to recognise both the *current* position of companies and the *dynamics* of the competitive process to enable an assessment of an organisation's competitive position. Used in this way, the framework looks at how competitive positions may have to be changed over time. Recognising the dynamics of industry environments and changing competitive strategies, Figure 3.14 is drawn with zones of transition between the different cells, indicating that in practice some companies will be attempting to transform their competitive position.

For a narrow local strategy to be sustainable, not only must the product-market be capable of being segmented and separated, but the ability to supply the market competitively should not be dependent on the need to supply other cross-border markets at the same time. In Europe there are a plethora of small local market brewers serving a spatially restricted area (local or national regional or national). Some of these companies, for example Grolsh NV which supplies premium beers to a specialist market throughout Europe, have progressed to operating with an international niche strategy by marketing their products in a number of cross-border markets.

For an international niche strategy to be feasible, a narrow product focus must be sustainable. In some industries this is not always possible. Take, for example, the world tyre market. Attempting to focus just on the speciality tyre market is not sustainable without at the same time being a broadly based volume tyre producer, once the high research and development costs associated with tyre development are recognised. By simply supplying the speciality market and having a narrow product focus, a tyre manufacturer would have insufficient sales volume to be able to recoup the research and development costs of bringing a new specialist product to the market.

Where the conditions for operating with a niche strategy are not met, a company will need to have a broader product focus. With a broad focus a company will seek to serve a number of different product-market segments. If competitive interdependence is low, then a company can develop a sustainable strategy by both being broad and having a restricted geographical scope. In judging whether this is the case the size of the local market has to be compared with the need to, for example, achieve economies of scale and recoup research and development costs. Alternatively, if competitive interdependence is high then a company will need to operate with an international scale of output.

If the dynamics of the external context are related to Figure 3.14, the extent to which individual competitive strategies may be available to a company can be discerned. Previous discussion has emphasised that in many instances two trends have been observed. In relation to product demand, in a number of sectors demand is becoming more homogeneous, thereby increasing the size of the available market. Similarly, in relation to competitive interdependence, increasingly companies in many industries are reorganising their production facilities, research and development spending and marketing efforts to reflect international rather than restricted geographical needs. This process is both driven by changes at the meta level and by the need to react to the competitive strategies of their main rivals.

Recognising the trends towards internationalisation in many industrial sectors suggests that the ability to operate with a restricted geographical scope in many industries is diminishing. To some degree, the factors leading to the internationalisation of industries are simply the extension of trends which in earlier periods meant that operating on a local area basis was insufficient and companies needed to become national in their geographcial scope. Now especially, broad-based competitors are finding that operating with only restricted geographical scope is not sufficient if they are to remain competitive. This conclusion explains why in many sectors there are no longer nationally owned competitors. National players who for one reason or another fail to recognise and meet the international challenge, or leave their response too late, will be forced to leave the industry, often by selling out to companies who are, or are in the process of developing as, international competitors. Further, as the linkages between the Triad become ever stronger, to operate successfully at an international level often requires a company to become a global player rather than simply focusing on one of the trading blocs which go to make up the Triad. In many industries an international regional focus – Asia, Europe or NAFTA – is no longer sufficient.

Competitors with a restricted geographical scope need to appreciate the dynamics of their industry and whether it is internationalising in order to make important strategic decisions. For example, if a broadly based competitor wishes to survive and prosper in a context where competitive interdependence is increasing, it has two choices. The company either seeks to become an *international player* or it must adopt a *segment retreat strategy*, whereby it refocuses and seeks to operate with, say, a national niche strategy. This is precisely the strategy adopted by Hotpoint, the case study featured in Chapter 5. Interestingly, as the earlier example of the world tyre industry shows, this may not be a sustainable strategy in the long term. Even where in the past such strategies have been sustainable, rising competitive interdependence is threatening nationally focused competitors who have traditionally had a narrow product focus. Increasingly organisations, whether they be narrow or broadly focused, need to compete internationally in order to remain competitive.

Individual company positions for a given industry may be mapped onto the framework described in order to gain an appreciation of the current strategic position of competitors. Figure 3.15 illustrates how this might be done by showing the position of four competitors in the chocolate confectionery industry.

Figure 3.15 The chocolate confectionery industry

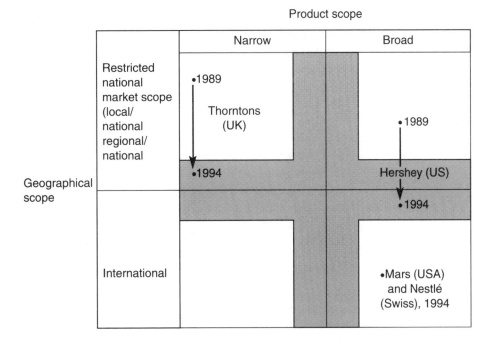

Key: ▓ = Zone of transition

The four companies' competitive positions may be described as follows:

- *Thorntons*: The company sells a range of distinctive and relatively expensive chocolates. It operates a predominately national niche strategy, although it has attempted to develop its international presence through acquiring a plant in Belgium to supply the French market. As a result the company is placed in a transition zone, indicating that it no longer has a wholly national focus.
- *Hershey*: The company has a broadly based strategy currently focused on the US market, where it is the largest producer of chocolate confectionery. The company decided in the early 1990s to develop an international presence by entering the Japanese and European markets. Strategy is changing from having a restricted geographical focus to becoming a truly international player. Currently, the company's international operations, are a relatively small part of its business, but expected to grow.
- *Mars/Nestlé*: These two companies operate with an unrestricted geographical scope, with a significant presence in both NAFTA and the EU and elsewhere in the world. Both sell broad product ranges and are clearly international competitors.

Diagnosing the potential for industry globalisation provides a dynamic perspective of anticipated changes in the importance of the 4 Cs: customer, cost, country and competitors. Where some globalisation drivers are weak,

121

there is room for a number of alternative competitive responses. Recognition of such strategic imperatives prompts consideration of the forces moving industries towards bi-polarisation and the need for companies to adopt a competitive response. Against this background the internal context of individual companies can be examined in order to judge which businesses are likely to be able to survive and prosper in the changing external context.

Summary

The present chapter has focused on the external context, beginning with developments at the meta level. The continuing development of the global Triad and the growth of international competition were key conclusions from the analysis undertaken. Driving developments at the meta level are political, economic, social and technological changes. These continue to have a differential effect according to the industry in question. At the industry level the key question was the extent to which globalisation or localisation was taking place. This in turn is dependent upon four factors – customers, cost, country and competitors – which collectively determine the pressure towards convergence or divergence at the industry level. Recognition of increasing convergence in respect of many industries raised the question of what strategies companies could pursue in order to survive. While in theory four industry positions are available, increased competitive interdependence is making a local focus less and less defensible for many industries. Consequently, even narrowly based competitors are needing to become international in their outlook. Whether they are able to effect such a transition or not raises the question of individual company resource bases and capabilities. Examining these questions and assessing a company's internal context are the subject of the following chapter.

Checklist

- The internationalisation process is the outcome of both external and internal triggers to change.
- The present chapter concentrates on external triggers to change.
- Developments in the world economy are leading to the emergence of a global Triad.
- The Triad comprises Europe, Japan and South East Asia, and North America.
- Growth of international trade is expected to exceed growth of output.
- Foreign direct investment has increased as (i) wage costs, and (ii) currency movements undermine the success of established industrial countries, notably Germany and Japan.

- Trade liberalisation has promoted not only the growth of inter-bloc trade, but also within each trading bloc intra-regional trade.
- Newly industrialising nations are entering world markets and destabilising the established economic order.
- Meta trends are driven by political, economic, social and technological changes.
- The extent of the globalisation of an industry is dependent on four sets of industry drivers: customers, cost, country and competition.
- Customer drivers can be sub-divided into customer requirements, distribution and uniform marketing.
- New product development, scale economies and transportation costs are the individual components of cost drivers.
- Trade policies, technical standards, and cultural and regulatory barriers collectively describe country drivers.
- Competitive interdependence and new entry are the key competitive drivers.
- Within any one industry, some industry drivers will favour globalisation, others localisation.
- An industry's position will reflect the balance of forces between drivers favouring globalisation and localisation.
- Bi-polarisation of companies reflects increasing international competition.
- As competitive interdependence increases, a local focus is more difficult to sustain.
- Increasingly survival requires a global focus.

World airline industry

Introduction

It is a watershed period for the world airline industry. In the four years to the end of 1993, airlines worldwide lost enough money to wipe out the accumulated gains of the previous 40 years. The impact of dramatic losses has prompted a major industry restructuring through mergers, acquisitions, alliances and exits. The big carriers are struggling against small, low cost airlines. By the end of the 1990s extensive consolidation and concentration of the world airline industry will have occurred. The long haul back to profitability will see many losers and only a few winners.

The US industry is emerging from an extended period of losses following deregulation. In Asia and Europe the process of deregulation is less complete, bringing the prospect of further changes. Competition will undoubtedly intensify and as in all situations some companies will survive and grow, while others will be absorbed into larger groupings or forced to exit the industry. Anticipating these changes and developing a strategy to succeed in such an increasingly competitive context is the challenge that senior managers in the industry are facing.

Current situation

The airline industry is highly cyclical, with demand closely linked to levels of economic activity. Economic recovery immediately prompts large increases in the demand for air travel, while the onset of recession curtails demand just as dramatically. With an approximate time lag of some 18–24 months before aircraft orders are delivered, there is normally an imbalance between capacity and demand throughout the economic cycle. During an upturn airlines immediately experience an increase in load factors and increasingly worry at missing out on rising sales and order more aircraft. When Europe followed the US into recession towards the end of the 1980s, demand fell as capacity rose. In consequence, airline yields and profits fell at a time when capital expenditure was at an all-time high. This vicious circle resulted in airlines suffering large cash outflows.

The effect of the Gulf War, in dramatically reducing passenger volumes and consequently yields, turned the outflow into a haemorrhage. Analysts forecast negative cash flows for the top 20 airlines in excess of $17 billion in 1991 and $16.5 billion in 1992. Excluding capital expenditure, Table C3.1 shows IATA members' net profit (after tax and interest but before dividends) in constant 1992 US dollars. The major discontinuity of the Gulf War resulted in the industry moving from just above break-even in 1989 to total losses of $2.7 billion in 1990. Total losses in the five years between 1990 and 1994 amounted to $13.5 billion.

The relationship between utilisation and profitability reflects the cost structures of the industry and the level of operational gearing. A company or industry is said to be highly operationally geared when its fixed costs form a significant proportion of total costs. As fixed costs are inescapable in the short term, a fall in revenue risks leaving fixed costs uncovered. As a consequence, for an industry which is highly operationally geared, a fall in revenue feeds directly through into bottom-line profitability and very quickly losses emerge. Similarly, moving in the opposite direction, an improvement in demand raising utilisation levels has a disproportionate effect on profits. The nature of operational gearing explains why airlines are prepared to discount seats so heavily in periods of recession in order to attract customers. With inescapable costs to be met, even a modest contribution to the recovery of overheads is attractive. The high operational gearing of the airline industry explains the volatility of the industry's earnings stream, which is quantified in Table C3.1.

Table C3.1 Industry net profit/(losses) in constant 1992 US dollars ($million)

	$million
1987	950
1988	1500
1989	150
1990	−2700
1991	−4000
1992	−4800
1993	−2000
1994 (forecast)	−450

Source: IATA

By 1995 overall traffic growth is forecast to outstrip industry capacity for the first time since the Gulf War. With global growth in supply and demand in balance, break-even load factors should be achievable throughout the industry. Since the onset of the recession, yield and load factors have been interchangeable, with intense price discounting to fill seats. With increasing demand it should be possible for airlines to stabilise load factors, and use the extra demand to reduce discounting in order to improve yields.

Yield represents average passenger revenues per kilometre (RPK) and is particularly sensitive to volume trends in premium passenger cabins. Only filling 70 Club Class seats on a 380-seat Boeing 747 flying across the Atlantic is sufficient for an airline to make a profit, with the 20 per cent of travellers flying business class contributing 50 per cent of airline revenue. In a low inflation, post-recessionary era, business travellers will continue to demand high quality service at the lowest prices. Moreover, there is uncertainty as to whether the business traveller will return in anything like the numbers the airlines had hoped. In the last decade business travel in the US fell from 40 to 20 per cent of all passengers, and a similar but accelerated trend is anticipated in Europe over the next five years.

Medium-term prospects for low yield leisure travel are projected to grow between 5.6 and 6.5 per cent per annum throughout the remainder of the 1990s. It is anticipated that the demand for air travel will outperform GNP growth by a factor of two. GNP growth will not be uniform throughout the world. As a consequence, growth rates in Asia-Pacific will be around 8 per cent a year, NAFTA growth rates will be 5–6 per cent, and Europe approximately 4 per cent per annum. Such geographical disparities will lead to marked changes between and within Triad markets, as is shown in Table C3.2. Other airline markets, including South America, Africa and the rest of the world, are generally relatively small by comparison.

Table C3.2 World airline markets (percentage of total revenue passenger kilometres)

Passenger flow	1992	2010	Percentage change
Intra-Asia-Pacific	6.6	8.5	+28.8%
Intra-Europe	8.4	8.2	−2.4%
Intra-NAFTA	22.2	18.2	−18.0%
Trans-Atlantic	6.8	6.0	−11.8%
Trans-Eurasia	10.4	12.1	+16.3%
Trans-Pacific	13.4	16.8	+25.4%
Others	32.2	30.2	−6.2%

Source: Boeing Aviation Survey, 1993

Deregulation

Much of the world's air traffic regime is still heavily regulated by national authorities using bi-lateral and multi-lateral agreements to control market access, restrict competition and fix high-yield fare prices. Deregulation describes the reduction and eventual removal of restrictions to competition. Beginning in the USA in 1978, the introduction of deregulation encouraged the entry of many low cost new entrants. As a result, airlines have entered and left the industry and much money has been lost within a relatively short time. US domestic yields have fallen by around one-third in real terms since their peak in 1981. The traumatic deregulation process has resulted in a two-tier structure of large efficient carriers and small efficient carriers. The remaining middle-ranking carriers, such as Braniff International, Eastern Airlines and Pan Am, gradually failed, while the ailing TransWorld Airlines (TWA) and Continental sold most of their transatlantic routes. In the process American, Delta and United have become the undisputed 'Big Three' American airlines.

The Big Three's share of US carriers' North Atlantic traffic rose from 30 per cent in 1990, to 45 per cent in 1991 and 70 per cent in 1992. Many American and European airlines have already been weakened as a result of a prolonged and intense North Atlantic price war. International passenger yields for North Atlantic services have fallen by about 30 per cent in real terms for European carriers. This compares with an 11 per cent fall over the same period for US airlines. The intense competition has resulted in yield and load factors showing a marked inverse relationship, as the price of air travel has been pushed down by competition. Only when there is a strong positive correlation between increased yields and load factors will profitability return. In 1993 real passenger yields on the

Case Study 3

North Atlantic routes fell by 2.5 per cent for US carriers, and a dramatic 9.2 per cent for European carriers.

Airline deregulation has spread from the USA to Europe with potentially far-reaching effects. EU deregulation policy from 1993 is intended to open up domestic and intra-European routes to more competition, although the extent to which fares will be reduced and competition will be increased may well be limited by runway landing slot availability and air traffic control capacity. Ultra-high European short haul yields are unlikely to be sustained at a typical $0.30 per RPK compared with a US domestic yield of around $0.08. Low cost new entrants, such as British Airways' Deutsche BA, are attracted by current high yields. The effect of this is to reduce yields for incumbents, even if the new entrants only have a very small share of the traffic on a particular route.

High costs are a structural problem for the majority of European carriers. The average large US airline has costs of around $0.09 per RPK compared with a European average of $0.20. While BA, with unit costs of $0.11 per RPK, is almost in line with US competitors, Lufthansa and Air France have operating costs of $0.20 and $0.24 respectively. The abject failure of Air France to introduce a modest cost restructuring package in 1993 suggests that many European flag carriers will not be able to adapt rapidly enough to meet the challenge. In a totally unregulated market it is doubtful if any of the European flag carriers, with the exception of BA and KLM, would survive for more than a couple of years. Virgin Airlines, which operates within a narrow and restricted range of key international routes, is also expected to remain competitive.

Asia-Pacific airlines, such as Cathay Pacific and Singapore Airlines, are by far the lowest cost international carriers. Along with BA they are also profitable. This contrasts markedly with other Asian carriers, notably the Japanese. Their two flag carriers, Japan Airlines and All Nippon, have high costs and huge debts. This fast growing market is less regulated than Europe, but more so than the US. The intra-Asian market is highly fragmented. Access to such a market is eagerly sought by the mega-carriers, with Cathay Pacific, Malaysian and Singapore Airlines occupying a pivotal role in the development of this lucrative part of the world market.

Industry recipes

Three major strategic recipes are being adopted by the major international carriers: competitive positioning through progressive expansion of worldwide route networks, customer-oriented focus, and unit cost control.

Competitive positioning strategies

Accepted wisdom points to a competitive positioning strategy based on good slot positions in a co-ordinated hub and spoke system – that is, flying passengers from feeder cities on the spokes of the system into a larger central hub, from where they are redirected onto a flight to their final destination. BA, for example, benefits from its strong presence at an excellent and well-defended hub, based on London Heathrow airport. 'Grandfather rights' regarding 38.5 per cent of all landing and take-off slots at probably the best connecting hub in the world allows BA to attain 20 per cent higher passenger yields than US rivals on the transatlantic route.

The hub and spoke systems have a number of advantages over point to point, direct linkages on international routes. The system is seen as the most efficient way in which to gain multiplier effects on the number of city pairs served, as well securing increased load factors and lower unit costs. However, growing congestion means that on some routes passengers spend as much time at the airport as in the air.

Many of the mergers, acquisitions and alliances in the industry have been brought about by attempts to consolidate and strengthen global route coverage. Apart from a rather loose relationship between Delta, Singapore and Swissair, the ownership alliance between BA, US Air and Quantas is the only one to have a broad geographical scope, serving five out of the six key geographical markets. The Alcazar alliance between four medium-sized European flag carriers – Austrian, KLM, SAS and Swissair – failed over the issue of choosing a US partner for the alliance.

Smaller, no-frills airlines, running highly intensive shuttle services on busy domestic routes between pairs of cities, are shunning the hub and spoke system. Staff are kept fully employed throughout the day, as opposed to peak periods when all flights have to converge on the hub at the same time. Not only are aircraft more fully utilised, but customers spend less time waiting around and fly direct to their destination. This has prompted BA to question the applicability of the hub and spoke concept for high yield, point to point flights in Europe. With the purchase of TAT in France, the expansion of Deutshe BA in Germany and the extension of its relationship with Bryman and Maersk in the UK, BA is creating a collection of low cost niche airlines across Europe.

Customer-oriented focus

A customer-oriented focus aimed at improving service quality and securing brand loyalty is being followed by all leading airlines. Until quite recently ownership of a computerised reservation system (CRS) was seen as a key marketing weapon. Their vast databases enable customers to access a complete travel service of flight, hotel and car reservations. From the airlines' perspective their main advantage is in the opportunities created for market segmentation, together with a yield management link which ensures that aircraft fly as full as possible at the highest possible fares.

The huge capital costs of setting up and operating these systems has forced major airlines to pool resources. The world is spanned by several interlinked and largely joint-owned networks. While ownership of a CRS network has ceased to be a significant source of competitive advantage, the yield management link is commercially important. Due to the high operational gearing of the industry and its marginal profitability, even a few extra passengers at a heavily discounted fare can push a particular flight from loss to profit. BA is acknowledged to possess a particularly effective yield management system which generates additional revenues amounting to $120 million per annum.

The main drawback of yield management is not immediately apparent. The

Case Study 3

deep discounting generated by such systems trying to fill the last few seats has set up expectations on the part of passengers that fares will be low and that they will continue to fall. In many respects yield management has destabilised the price structure of the industry. In turn, it has made the product largely commodity based and, to some degree, undermined any concept of branding.

Unit cost control

High cost continental European carriers can expect that competition will intensify and current high yields fall, if the process of deregulation in Europe follows the US model. Observers of the European industry confidently expect that there will be a further collapse of profitability as intense competition radically reduces prices. European governments are seeking to avoid economic reality by providing further subsidies to their loss-making flag carriers. EU competition policy means that such protection cannot go on for ever. Moreover, the scale of subsidy may be insufficient to eliminate huge debts or finance cost restructuring. For example, early in 1994 press reports suggested that Air France was seeking a capital injection of $1.4 billion, following an earlier sum of $250 million provided by the French government.

The high cost European carriers may for structural and cultural reasons not be able to reduce costs sufficiently far and fast to avoid substantial contraction and even corporate failure. Small to medium-sized flag carriers, including for example Alitalia and Iberia, are particularly vulnerable. Like their larger state-subsidised rivals they have sought to protect market positions rather than cut costs and compete. They have deferred judgement but not avoided it. The third phase of EU deregulation has arrived and the level of competition will increase sooner rather than later. Table C3.3 illustrates wage costs per employee as a percentage of revenue per employee.

Table C3.3 Wage costs per employee as a percentage of revenue per employee, 1992

	%
Iberia	51
Alitalia	46
Air France	44
Delta	41
American	39
Lufthansa	38
United	37
KLM	35
Quantas	32
BA	31
Southwest	30
Cathay	24
Singapore	24

Source: IATA (1993)

Competition in the US has been particularly pronounced following domestic deregulation in the 1980s. Both the presence of excess capacity and new competition from low cost, no-frills airlines has forced the larger carriers to respond by cutting prices. For example, US Air in late 1993, with already major losses, was forced to slash both business and leisure travel fares on internal routes by 50 per cent on an indefinite basis. Against this background, the larger companies have taken action to reduce their cost base in an effort to match the low cost carriers. The actions adopted have included reducing the number of employees, reforming inefficient working practices, deferring the delivery of new aircraft and withdrawing from some loss-making routes. As a result, the trend in earnings is improving, but most companies are still far away from achieving acceptable profit margins (see Table C3.4).

Table C3.4 Selected US Airlines – revenue passenger kilometres (RPK) and profitability

Company	RPK (bn)		Profits ($m)	
	1992	1993	1992	1993
America West	7	8	(132)	37
Delta Airlines	50	52	(601)	(226)
Northwest Airlines	37	36	(971)	(115)
Southwest Airlines	9	12	97	154
US Air	22	22	(601)	(349)

Source: Based on *Financial Times*, 15 February 1994, p 25

In Asia increased competition from carriers based outside the region has eroded the profitability of a number of regional airlines. US airlines in particular, seeking to offset difficulties in their domestic market, have increased their presence in Asian routes. As a consequence of this development and the emergence of new regional airlines, including Eva of Taiwan and Asiana of South Korea, competition has intensified. Beyond the immediate term, the region's airlines also recognise the likelihood of a higher cost base. This reflects the expected wage increases as the economies of the region grow more affluent and workers demand higher wage increases. As a result, Asian carriers face the prospect of an erosion of cost advantages they currently enjoy against US and European carriers.

New game strategies

Southwest is a fascinating airline which has come from nowhere to become the dominant short haul carrier on important city pair routes in the USA. It has grown rapidly and profitably by attacking short haul, high yield city pair routes with low fares and high frequencies. It provides frequent flights and a no-frills, one-class service with no pre-booking. A US Department of Transport survey reveals that routes on which Southwest fly have fares set at roughly half the level of routes where it does not compete. The low fare, high volume strategy has trounced rivals to the extent that it usually dominates any route on which it operates.

Case Study 3

The low costs flow from abandoning the hub and spoke systems adopted by large airlines, together with the costly CRS system. Costs are further reduced by operating only one aircraft type with high utilisation levels, coupled with speedy turnaround times. Hard-working, flexible, non-union staff receive similar wages to other airline staff, but are far fewer and more productive. As a result Southwest has costs per RPK of less than $0.07, compared with around $0.09 for other US airlines, and an average of $0.20 for European short haul carriers.

The lesson that customers want low fares and high frequencies on popular domestic routes is causing some airlines to reassess their strategy. First, Southwest's success supports the concern that premium traffic is unlikely to recover to former levels. From an offensive perspective it shows how low cost fares can expand overall demand in even a mature US domestic travel market. The low cost shuttle service of the non-union Continental Airlines, CALite, has also reported better than expected profits in 1993. In Europe, BA has started the process of turning short haul domestic and European services along lines which mimic the lower costs and lower fares strategy.

End game

The pace of change in the world airline industry is quickening. In Europe the Gulf War, heavy capital expenditure, fare discounts and loss of the key North Atlantic route have pushed most flag carriers into deep losses and heavy debt. US airlines accumulated crippling debts as a result of deregulation dramatically reducing yields. Recession has served to compound these problems. In Asia, Cathay Pacific, Malaysian Airlines and Singapore Airlines all found their earnings coming under pressure in 1993, blaming not only the recession, but also competitive forces and adverse currency movements. All Nippon posted its first losses for 22 years.

Table C3.5 shows the net debt as a percentage of turnover for some of the world's major airlines. Given the extent of the indebtedness of many of the airlines, it is difficult see how they will be able reduce debt by organic cash generation. Privatisation of airlines, including Air France, could offer a way to recapitalise some companies in Europe, provided that they get costs down quickly. Elsewhere, and particularly in the USA, a period of sustained profitability which would allow airlines to improve their balance sheets is difficult to foresee, at least in the current decade.

Conclusion

The world airline industry is changing. Most major airlines do not appear to be responding quickly enough to meet the competitive challenge. The expectation is that only a few 'big airlines' will emerge as worldwide mega-carriers. To survive and prosper the mega-carriers will have to meet the emerging challenge of small low cost entrants on high yield routes (i.e. routes with high passenger traffic). In these circumstances mega-carriers could find their profitability undermined by rapidly falling passenger levels (yields), outstripping the airlines' ability to reduce costs. It is a finely balanced argument as to which sector of the industry will win out.

Table C3.5 Net debt as a percentage of sales turnover, 1992

European-based carriers	%
Air France	−51
British Airways	−22
Iberia	−44
KLM	−82
Lufthansa	−30
USA-based carriers	
American	−58
Delta	−36
Southwest	−18
United	−22
Asia-based carriers	
All Nippon	−78
Cathay Pacific	−24
Japan Airlines	−94
Malaysian	−64
Singapore	+24

Questions

(1) *Undertake a PEST analysis for the world airline industry, and distil key meta trends.*

(2) *Using the 4 Cs framework, assess the extent of globalisation in the world airline industry in respect of (i) inter-continental (global); and (ii) intra-regional (e.g. Europe, USA, etc.) carriers.*

(3) *Explain the concept of operational gearing and the effect it has on pricing policies and earnings of companies in the industry. Support your answer with appropriate industry data.*

(4) *Using the concept of bi-polarity, identify winners and losers in the industry over the next five years.*

Chapter 4

INTERNAL TRIGGERS TO THE INTERNATIONALISATION PROCESS

Key learning objectives

To understand:

- how internal change leads to discontinuities in a firm's international business development

- the importance of vision and mindset in guiding the direction of international business development

- the importance of organisational dynamics

- how administrative heritage shapes and constrains organisational response

- that organisational change management revolves around creating a new mindset, building competences/capabilities and changing corporate culture

- that competitive advantage is developed from the way in which an organisation applies its resource capability

- the relationship between improved business performance and the management of change

Context

Industries and competitors differ markedly. Firms in the same industry commonly follow differing strategies regarding global market participation. These are typically driven by differing managerial beliefs about the sources of competitive advantage and the way in which organisations should be managed. In competitive battles successful strategies must be implemented in a manner which is judged to be effective ('doing the right things') and organisationally efficient ('doing things right'). Superior internal organisational ability to implement strategy is an important basis for long-term competitive advantage.

By focusing specifically on the internal context, attention is directed towards the tangible and intangible resources possessed by firms and how distinctive core skills and capabilities are developed. It is the ability to nurture and develop strategically relevant internal skills and capabilities that generates competitive advantage. Since such unique organisational characteristics are firm specific, any strategic responses to the internationalisation process will be constrained by, and dependent on, the firm's organisational dynamics. This chapter looks at a resource-based analysis of the internationalisation process by reviewing the following topics:

- *internal triggers to the internationalisation process*
- *shaping an international vision and mindset*
- *organisational dynamics*
- *managing organisational change*
- *assessing and changing corporate culture*
- *resource capability and competitive advantage*
- *managing organisational change to improve business performance*

The chapter begins by looking at the internal triggers to a stage change in the international business development of a firm. This leads to a review of the vision shaping the international nature of the business and the way a widely shared and understood mindset is moulded. Changing an organisation's internal context, as described by its mindset and organisational dynamics requires the implementation of change. Managing organisational change has three key components – *creating a shared mindset, building competences/capabilities* and *changing corporate values* – which collectively need to be shaped and integrated if improved business performance is to be achieved. An analysis of the organisation's existing corporate culture and the potential levers for changing the collective behaviour of the organisation is provided by considering the cultural web. How an organisation utilises its resource base is of critical importance if it is to develop a sustainable competitive advantage and achieve superior levels of business performance. The chapter concludes with a summary and checklist. A case study on Philips NV provides the opportunity to apply a number of the frameworks introduced in the chapter.

Internal triggers to the internationalisation process

Throughout the text the internationalisation process has been viewed as the outcome of both external and internal triggers to change. In Chapter 3 the focus was on external change triggers. In the present chapter attention is directed to internal triggers to change and how they may create conditions in which a discontinuity in the firm's international business development can occur. Figure 4.1 illustrates how internal factors may result in a firm moving from its current to a new phase of international business development. It is

Figure 4.1 Internal and external triggers to a stage change

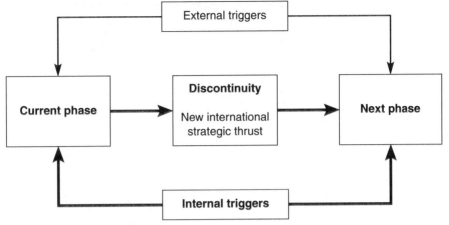

Source: Based on Figure 2.1, p 49

important to emphasise once again that the movement between stages of the phase model is bi-directional. As Figure 4.1 shows, any discontinuity may result in firms broadening or narrowing their international scope.

To appreciate how a discontinuity can occur, it is first necessary to define the components which describe an organisation's internal context. The internal context of an organisation is collectively described by two components: (i) vision/mindset; and (ii) organisational dynamics. The desired geographic scope of operations and strategic development is addressed by the firm's *vision*. The vision not only needs to be shaped, but also driven through the mindset of the organisation. A powerful vision, which is developed by senior management, and a widely shared mindset helps firms to embrace change by ensuring unity of purpose and common ownership of ideas.

By contrast, *organisational dynamics* is concerned with the people and processes which are vital to implementing any vision changes. This focuses on those bundles of skills and technologies in which an organisation is uniquely advantaged (core competence); its ability to adapt and innovate (organisational learning); and the resource inheritance of the firm (administrative heritage). Collectively, these three elements – *core competence, organisational learning* and *administrative heritage* – encapsulate the ability and willingness of the organisation to implement the vision.

Where there is a match between vision/mindset and organisational dynamics, the internal context may be described as balanced. Illustrating this relationship, Figure 4.2 emphasises the continuous relationship between the two elements. If the vision/mindset of senior management and the organisational dynamics are not aligned, then the mismatch between the two will generate forces for change which, depending on subsequent developments, will either be dampened or sustained. In order to understand internal triggers to an organisation's internal context, there is a need to appreciate *why* and *when* either the vision/mindset of senior management or organisational dynamics change, and *how* an initial change is dampened or sustained.

135

Figure 4.2 Internal triggers to change

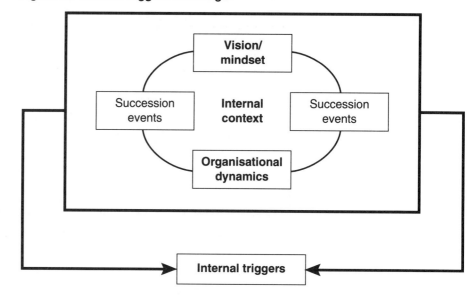

Change will be sustained when the other element of the internal context supports the initial change. Consequently, where both sets of factors – vision/mindset and organisational dynamics – are changing and moving in a single direction, the organisation may experience a fundamental change in international strategic direction. When these conditions are not met, the change is likely to be more limited. As a result of these tensions and the difficulties in overcoming the organisation's administrative heritage, the observed pattern of change for most companies is one of long periods of incremental change, interspersed with short periods of more dramatic shifts of strategy (Johnson, 1987; Pettigrew, 1985; Drucker, 1994).

Succession events

Changes to the vision/mindset of senior management most frequently take place when succession events occur at the top of organisations, leading to a change in chief executive. Succession events may occur against either a favourable or unfavourable context. In the former case they are likely to be planned events, for example the retirement of the current chief executive. By contrast, in times of difficulties the change in chief executive is likely to be unplanned and result from an organisational crisis. In the first instance, the change from one chief executive to another is likely to be a natural event enabling the transition to be more easily managed, while in the second instance the change may occur abruptly and be forced, with the incumbent resigning his or her post.

Where the organisational succession is a planned event against a favourable context for the organisation, the changes introduced by the new chief executive will result in one of two outcomes. First, the previous vision/mindset may be retained, with any changes to business strategy being minor. Correspondingly, the succession event is unlikely to result in a change in the phase of international business development to which the organisation is already committed. Alternatively, the newcomer may take the opportunity to reappraise the position of the business and implement a fundamental change in international business development. In these circumstances a major discontinuity is likely to occur in the international business development of the organisation.

When recruiting a new chief executive, the appointment panel is likely to take a view as to whether the new person needs to bring about a fundamental or incremental change in the international business direction. This judgement will colour both the search for, and the decision on, who to appoint as the next head of the organisation. Depending on circumstances, this may mean making an internal appointment or alternatively bringing in a 'new' person from outside the organisation. The judgement about which course of action should be adopted will need to recognise the realities of the organisation's dynamics and in particular the corporate culture. In some instances it may be inappropriate to consider external appointments, or the nature of the organisation's ownership, say in the case of a family business, may prevent this option being seriously considered.

Once a new leader has been appointed, they have the task of setting the vision for the organisation. On some occasions they may find the needs of the organisation are different to those that they had been led to believe, or the situation is very different to what was envisaged at their appointment. Equally, unless they are able to ensure their vision is shared and the organisational dynamics made supportive, any changes they attempt to bring about may be resisted. Even if there is general agreement as to the wisdom and direction of any change, the manner in which it is implemented can lead to difficulties. In the case of British Petroleum (Illustration 4.1), the planned changes were felt by many to be appropriate, but the style by which they were implemented was considered unacceptable by powerful groups in the organisation. This resulted in a new chief executive, who was expected to drive through the change programme in a more sensitive manner.

Often the replacement of a chief executive leads not only to a change in style, but also to a change in strategy, reflecting a different vision and mindset at the highest level in the organisation. For instance, the case of Volvo discussed in Illustration 2.2 offers an example of how the appointment of a new chief executive at a time of organisational crisis resulted in a change in the company's international business strategy. Again, an internal management revolt was instrumental in leading to the removal of the existing chief executive and the abandonment of his strategy of merging the car operations of Volvo and Renault into one company. Following his removal, the new chief executive and his management team focused their efforts on making Volvo a viable independent motor vehicle producer.

Illustration 4.1

British Petroleum

Robert Horton resigned as Chairman and Chief Executive of British Petroleum, a large international petroleum and chemical conglomerate, on 25 June 1992. Horton's resignation arose following pressure from fellow directors on the Board who believed there was a problem of personality rather than business strategy in the way the company was being run.

During his period of office Horton had launched Project 1990. This was an attempt to transform a sluggish, committee-driven company into one which was much more flexible and responsive, allowing managers to use their entrepreneurial talents. The actions implemented as part of Project 1990 had included:

- executive power of old managing directors being reduced;
- corporate centre reduced in size;
- number of employees reduced;
- greater enpowerment of individuals within the organisation;
- change of values, focusing on 'openness, care, teamwork and trust'.

Understandably, some of these actions produced resistance and bitterness. What, however, caused the senior non-executive directors to confront Horton and force his resignation were concerns about:

- the concentration of power in Horton's hands; and
- his style of management, which was seen to be arrogant and abrasive.

The directors were nevetherless 'unanimous' that the company needed to change and that a continuation of many elements of Horton's programme to bring this about was to be encouraged.

Source: The authors, based on press reports

A change of business strategy is almost certain to occur when an organisation is in a position of turnaround, which by its nature requires immediate and often drastic action. Illustration 4.2 gives a brief résumé of what constitutes a turnaround situation and a list of generic actions which may be applicable to attempting to rejuvenate a business.

In conclusion, depending on the organisational context a change in chief executive can result in either a continuation of existing strategies or significant changes in the strategic direction of the company. Where the outcome is the latter, this may well result in major discontinuities in the organisation's international business development. If this happens, the action of the new leadership will move the organisation from one phase to another phase of international business development. Alternatively, while the international scope of the business may not change, the way the organisation carries out its business may well be radically reshaped by a new incoming leader.

Illustration 4.2

> # Turnaround
>
> Although the magnitude of the difficulties and action required will vary on a case by case basis, *turnaround* describes a business situation where unless management takes significant action the business is in imminent danger of failure. Similarly, *sharpbend* has been used to describe a less serious business situation, but one where there is significant scope for business performance to be improved. Slatter (1984) provides an excellent assessment of the factors leading to turnaround situations and the generic actions that management can adopt. It should be noted that once it is in a turnaround position there is no guarantee that the business will survive. Many turnarounds fail and the firm either goes out of business or is taken over by a competitor.
>
> Almost inevitably management action in the face of potential business failure will require both *short-term corrective action* to stabilise the financial position of the company, and *longer-term action* to effect a substantial and sustained improvement in performance. As a result, most refocusing strategies cannot be implemented until a company's cash flow position has been improved, and it is not uncommon for short-term fire-fighting imperatives to be counterproductive for medium/long-term growth.
>
> The severity of any cash flow difficulties determines the selection of the most appropriate recovery strategy. Cost-reduction and revenue-increasing strategies all help to improve cash flow, although these sources, in the short term, are likely to contribute less than asset sales.
>
> Sustainable long-term recovery requires a refocusing of strategic direction in the light of internal resource availability and anticipated business opportunities. By fashioning competitive advantage, it should be feasible to effect a substantial and sustainable improvement in performance.
>
> *Source:* The authors and Slatter (1984)

Shaping an international vision and mindset

The nature of the spatial mindset adopted by senior executives has far-reaching consequences concerning the firm's geographical and competitive boundaries. Even in large international firms, senior managers are seldom 'equidistant' in their outlook. 'Domestic' (home country) and 'international' (everywhere else) distinctions may be implicit, if not explicit, in their strategic outlook. A domestic bias will be reinforced where Boards of Directors are chosen from nationals of the firm's country of origin. For such companies the challenge is to build an avowedly international mindset; while for many smaller companies the challenge is to adopt a less parochial mindset.

There is no one correct spatial mindset. Irrespective of firm size, the role of an international mindset is to promote a creative and innovative perspective. From an internal perspective, an important distinction can be made concerning whether geographical and competitive boundaries should be determined in a rational or intuitive manner. Herman (1988) contends that within the brain there are key tensions between left- and right-side thinking processes.

Illustration 4.3

National cultures: left-side versus right-side thinking

The issue of the predominance of either left- or right-side thinking has been considered in respect of national cultures and the manner in which managers who have grown up in these cultures think and act. Research by Fons Trompenaars, reported in Hampden-Turner (1990), presented managers with a series of questions designed to elicit the manner in which they thought. Trompenaars found that the USA was at one end of the spectrum, with emphasis on the responsibility of the individual and predominantly left-side thinking. As a result, business thinking in the USA tended to stress the need for analysis, the division of tasks into separable components, to be time oriented and the use of rational thinking processes. By contrast, at the other end of the spectrum was Singapore, where right-brain thinking was to the fore.

The bias in the USA to left-side thinking may suggest that American 'solutions' are not always appropriate in other cultural settings. Clearly, in operating in cross-border markets differences in national culture and the manner in which business is conducted can be a major consideration. It may also be an important element in whether to enter a market. Should, for example, an American company seek to enter the European market where cultural diversity may be less, or go for the more rapidly expanding markets of the Pacific Rim where cultural differences are much greater.

More recently, Trompenaars (1993) has emphasised that individualistic cultures, such as those predominating in the UK and USA, have a sequential view of time which places importance on short-term performance. By contrast, collective cultures with a synchronous view of time, including Germany and Japan, typically take a longer-term view when making business commitments.

Similarly, other reports have found significant differences between middle managers in Germany and the UK in respect of the 'whole' concept of management. German managers perceived themselves primarily as specialists whose power and authority were based upon their superior technical knowledge. As a result, German managers valued consistency and punctuality. By contrast, British managers relied less on technical knowledge and more on persuasion and networking to win support. They also tended to be more comfortable with uncertainty than their German counterparts. Equally, qualifications were more important in Germany than Britain. Arguably both nationalities could learn from each other: German managers in becoming more flexible, adaptive and innovative, and British managers in recognising the need to plan and improve their qualification base.

Source: The authors

The former is logical, analytical and fact based. The latter emphasises synthesis, integration and a holistic perspective. Left-side thinking places great faith in facts, while right-side thinking stresses opinions based on feelings.

National differences in left-side and right-side thinking are explored in Illustration 4.3.

In prescribing any firm's geographical and competitive boundaries, the vision needs to be constructed using the whole brain. All too often senior executives perceive left- and right-brain characteristics as mutually exclusive, and subscribe to 'rational' and 'intuitive' approaches respectively. Reference has already been made to the short-lived gains associated with rational 'same game' strategies (Table 1.2). Fresh and forward-looking views generated by right-side thinking processes are able to generate 'new game' strategies (Illustration 1.4). Even though left-brain thinking is unable to create new ways forward, such processes provide facts which help to trim away the excesses of creation. In this way the vision of the firm and its accompanying geographical and competitive boundaries can be founded on intuitive origins, but grounded in the hard realities of actuality.

Such a vision may take a narrow or broad-based competitive perspective. Numerous smaller firms have been successful because they choose to reject the prevailing wisdom concerning the need to adopt an international market perspective. By being selective in their choice of territory some companies, including Hotpoint, the case study featured in Chapter 5, have built organisational capabilities and successfully managed the dilemmas they faced in their traditional markets. Hotpoint has, to date, successfully resisted the siren call to internationalisation by forging close links with independent distributors in the UK national market, and by anticipating and influencing their needs with quality products at competitive prices. The choice of a restricted spatial mindset not only challenges prevailing industry orthodoxy in home appliances, it also demonstrates how the renewal process associated with internal changes can confer competitive advantage. Interestingly, as Illustration 4.4 shows, Whirlpool Corporation, the US home appliance manufacturer, has a very different vision of how it is seeking to compete.

Illustration 4.4

Whirlpool Corporation

Our Vision

Whirlpool, in its chosen lines of business, will grow with new opportunities and be the leader in an ever-changing global market. We will be driven by our commitment to continuous quality improvement and to exceeding all of our customers' expectations. We will gain competitive advantage through this, and by building on our existing strengths and developing new competencies. We will be market-driven, efficient and profitable. Our success will make Whirlpool a company that worldwide customers, employees and other stakeholders can depend on.

Source: Whirlpool Corporation Annual Report, 1993, p 1

The example of Whirlpool's vision (Illustration 4.4) indicates that a company may adopt a broader spatial mindset in order to reap significant benefits believed to accrue from the integration of pan-national production facilities. In these cases, expanding the geographical territory of a firm poses formidable organisational challenges. Moving across national boundaries requires the firm to address critical issues concerning the configuration and co-ordination of internal resources and to manage diversities of national culture. Capabilities need to be acquired or developed to deepen the knowledge of the organisation concerning new markets; to build new information networks; and to ensure that a new and more diverse set of people continue to work together.

In view of the fundamental implementation issues which surround these new ways of working across boundaries, it is not at all surprising that failure to shed the old mindset concerning the internal workings of the firm can jeopardise the change process. Illustration 4.5 provides two interesting examples of a changed mindset as shown by the experiences of two European

Illustration 4.5

The changing mindset of business managers

A business unit manager's view

In the first case the company's manufacturing, logistics and marketing functions have been reorganised on a pan-European basis, as opposed to being under the control of national subsidiaries. Whereas formerly the national subsidiary manufactured the full range of products sold into the national market, the change has resulted in the national subsidiary producing a much narrower product range. Similarly, the Chief Executive of the French company has now less autonomy in respect of marketing and logistics. 'In future we will still have a marketing function, but it will be driven much more from the centre, especially where pan-European marketing strategies are being devised. The worst thing is we will be completely dependent on warehouses in other countries – Belgium and Italy – for our stock. As a result, 'the centre will control this company. I will be left to run a shell.'

Transport manager's view

In the second case a transport manager is concerned that his existing skills have been made redundant by a change in company policy moving to contract distribution. 'What do I know about contract management? I can't even speak any foreign languages. How will I know what to do each day? How will the company judge whether I am performing well or not? . . . How will I be able to get on with my boss when he sits in a different country?'

Both the above cases illustrate how internal changes in the organisation need to bring about changes to the individual mindset, and indicate the current unease which both managers feel concerning the changes which have taken place.

Source: Based on Ernst and Young (1994)

managers reacting to significant changes in the way their organisation manages its business in Europe. Both of these cases reveal that mindset changes are required to foster a new strategic consensus and a new mode of functioning. Illustration 4.5 shows that in order for a vision of territorial expansion to be realised, a reframing of the mindset throughout the organisation needs to take place.

In summary, the spatial and competitive vision adopted by senior management must be articulated clearly and widely disseminated. Otherwise senior managers' visions are merely dreams. To be transformed into an effective mindset it must be widely shared throughout the organisation. While a powerful vision and a cohesive mindset may assist firms to embrace change, it is necessary to preserve order around change and change around order. Further, without the organisational dynamics supporting the vision/mindset of senior management the intending change is unlikely to be achieved.

Organisational dynamics

The second set of components forming the internal context of a firm at any point in time is described by the *organisational dynamics*. As Figure 4.3 illustrates, the organisational dynamics of a company are formed from three interrelated areas: *core competence, organisational learning* and *administrative heritage.*

Figure 4.3 Organisational dynamics

While each of the three components of a firm's organisational dynamics are in practice strongly inter-related, as emphasised by Figure 4.3, for expositional purposes they will be considered separately.

Core competence

Core competence refers to those aspects of the organisation in which it is uniquely advantaged over its competitive rivals. Hamel (1994) defines core competences as a bundle of constituent skills and technologies. The term competence is often used interchangeably with capability and can relate to both the corporate and business levels of strategic decision making. Illustration 4.6 provides an example of a corporate core competence that the organisation has succeeded in leveraging over a spectrum of businesses.

Illustration 4.6

> ## Core competence as a growth vector: Honda KK
>
> The success of Honda KK over the last 30 years can be attributed to its focus on small engine manufacture. By recognising that its core competence was small engine manufacturing, Honda transformed its organisational boundaries from motorcycles to cars, pumps and lawnmowers: all products where engines are a significant source of competitive advantage through their quality and reliability. The goal of an adaptive organisation is to ensure that core competences are linked to the most promising market opportunities. Had Honda decided that its core competence was in supplying motor cycles and related products, it would have overlooked a significant business opportunity in respect of lawnmowers.
>
> *Source:* Based on Snyder and Ebeling (1993)

It is, however, highly likely that some core competences relate to a specific business rather than to a corporate group. Three sets of core competences (see Hamel, 1994) can be defined:

- *market access:* skills which help to put the firm in close proximity to its customers;
- *integrity related:* allows a company to do things more quickly, flexibly or with a higher degree of reliability; and
- *functionally related:* invest in the firm's product/service to offer unique functionality.

Organisations need to protect, sustain and develop core competences in order to retain or enhance their competitive position. In some instances, organisations may need to develop new competences, emphasising their dynamic nature and characteristics.

Organisational
learning

Organisational learning reflects the ability of the organisation to continuously update itself and learn from its experiences. The extent to which organisational learning takes place can be related to the distinction between single and double loop learning. Single or 'first order' learning (Garratt, 1987) is about doing 'more of' or 'less of' already established routines. As a learning process, single loop learning is about reviewing performance against targets and taking corrective actions which do not fundamentally question the framework in which things are done. The very nature of single loop learning means that only low levels of organisational learning take place, and no real questioning of the established framework occurs.

By contrast, double loop or 'second order' learning questions the existing framework in which decisions take place, and brings to the fore assumptions about whether current routines and norms are appropriate. Second order learning questions the prevailing mindset, and tends to amplify rather than dampen change. It involves reframing underlying assumptions and is a process which is capable of producing innovation. This process is informed by wider trends associated with customer needs. Any organisation, in order to adapt to customer needs, will need to consider whether or not and/or when it is time to change its norms, expectations and actions.

Organisations engaging in second order learning will be able, providing they have appropriate networks to diffuse the new learning widely, to move forward constantly. Illustration 4.7 shows how one international company places a strong emphasis on being able to engage in this process.

Illustration 4.7

Organisational learning for change: Hewlett-Packard

Hewlett-Packard Inc is the second largest US computer company by turnover. By early 1994 it had become the world market leader in 'open system' minicomputers, computer printers and test and measurement equipment. In reaching this position the company had proved capable of recognising important external changes and reacting accordingly. The company has an excellent record of product innovation, as well as correctly anticipating and positioning itself to accommodate falling profit margins for the industry. As a consequence the company had progressively reduced its cost base. The company chief executive, Lew Platt, was far from complacent. He suggested that 'HP' stood for 'healthy paranoia', with managers being urged to be 'always looking over your shoulder at the competition, always thinking about the next move'. Further, in pointing to the failure of a number of previously dominant large US companies, Platt argued, 'the only real mistake they made was to keep doing whatever it was that had made them successful for a little too long.' Platt believed that 'the real secret is to build an organisation that isn't afraid to make changes while it is still successful, before change becomes imperative for survival.'

Source: Based on Kehoe (1994a)

Without second order learning, an organisation will find it difficult to renew itself and advance. Unfortunately, too many organisations which have demonstrated that they are primarily engaged in single loop learning realise all too late that they are in need of renewal. As the case of Hewlett-Packard in Illustration 4.7 demonstrates, the ability of an organisation to learn continuously can be a powerful source of competitive advantage.

In this context Pascale (1990) draws attention to the need for organisations to exhibit contention. Contention is defined as the need for organisations to question persistently the what, why and how of their strategy. Constructive conflict is a central component of contention and helps to maintain the balance between change and stability. As part of this process organisations should be aware of their own shortcomings and be able to accept self-criticism. If this is not tolerated or encouraged, the likelihood is that the organisation will not enter the second loop of learning.

Administrative heritage

Administrative heritage describes both the tangible and intangible inheritance of the organisation. Above all, administrative heritage recognises that organisations have a history which constrains their ability to adapt. In respect of physical assets the administrative heritage will reflect the configuration of assets the organisation has acquired over the years, reflecting the past history of the organisation. As Illustration 4.8 shows, such a configuration of assets may *not* be optimal in terms of current organisational needs. Nevertheless, the

Illustration 4.8

Administrative heritage: Minebea and SKF

Administrative heritage places unique constraints on competitive choices. In the ball bearings industry, existing plant locations and company history, rather than cost minimisation, have influenced international choice.

Minebea, the world's largest producer of miniature ball bearings, has pursued a focused low cost strategy. This has prompted the company to move production from Japan to other low cost locations in South East Asia. Initially a plant was established in Singapore, to be followed by a further production facility in Thailand. Despite labour costs in Singapore rising, the company decided to retain both plants, rather than concentrate production in Thailand. This decision reflected its committed investment and an established and skilled workforce in Singapore.

Likewise, SKF's locational decisions have been influenced by the company's administrative heritage. Within each region of the Triad, the company has focused production on specialised facilities. This strategy when introduced prompted widespread rationalisation. However, choice of plants to be closed and the resulting division of production between facilities was based less on cost optimisation and more on historical factors.

Source: Based on Collis (1991)

practicalities and costs of relocating key elements of the business may be prohibitive, emphasising that it is with the inherited asset base the organisation needs to work. Alongside the tangible assets of the organisation, administrative heritage also encompasses the intangible elements of the organisation as defined by its corporate culture.

In summary, a company's organisational dynamics comprise three components – core competence, organisational learning and administrative heritage – which collectively describe the ability and willingness of the organisation to implement the vision of senior management, and provide the resource basis by which the organisation can seek to sustain or develop enduring competitive advantage.

Managing organisational change

If there is an underlying structural mismatch between the organisation's business strategy and its external environment, the organisation will be faced with the need to manage successfully a *fundamental* as opposed to *incremental* organisational change.

> The incremental approach to change is effective when what you want is more of what you've already got. (Pascale, 1990, p 12)

Fundamental organisational change will by definition represent a major discontinuity with the past and require the organisation to transform the conduct of its business. By its nature the management of fundamental organisational change is almost invariably a long and time-consuming task with no guarantee of success. This is certainly the case for those organisations with an extensive administrative heritage. Nevertheless, overcoming inertia and resistance to change becomes unavoidable if an organisation's internal context no longer fits within its external environment.

A major explanation as to why an organisation's internal context may no longer fit with the external context is provided by examining the concept of corporate culture. The corporate culture of an organisation, which by its nature is difficult to define, expresses the values, norms and behaviour of the organisation. These formally and/or informally govern how the collective organisation reacts to both routine and change events, and hold in place the corporate mindset. Once established corporate cultures are particularly difficult to modify and change. As a result, it is not uncommon for an organisation to find that its corporate culture makes for difficulties or even prevents a change of external focus taking place.

Often an organisational crisis, frequently manifested in poor business performance, proves necessary before the conditions are created in which a change in corporate culture can be attempted. As noted earlier, this may well lead to the replacement of the current leadership who form the ruling elite within the organisation and who helped shape the prevailing strategic vision of the organisation. Frequently, the replacement of the existing management is a necessary condition for fundamental strategic change to be attempted. Unless those able to change strategy gain control, they will be powerless to influence change.

Having changed the senior management there is no guarantee that widespread organisational change will occur. There are many examples of organisations desperately trying to change, but finding themselves unable to do so. Not infrequently change can be attempted, but it proves impossible to implement and consolidate that change. Paradoxically, however, such attempts may help condition the organisation to a point where further attempts to bring about change can be successful. As noted earlier, if the organisation is in a situation of turnaround then the case for drastic change is often compelling.

The management of organisational change has to be focused around three key components, which collectively, if successfully achieved, should result in enhanced business performance. The three components that a change programme needs to influence are illustrated in Figure 4.4, namely:

- creating a shared mindset;
- building competences/capabilities;
- changing corporate culture;

which collectively lead to:

- improved business performance.

Figure 4.4 The components of organisational change

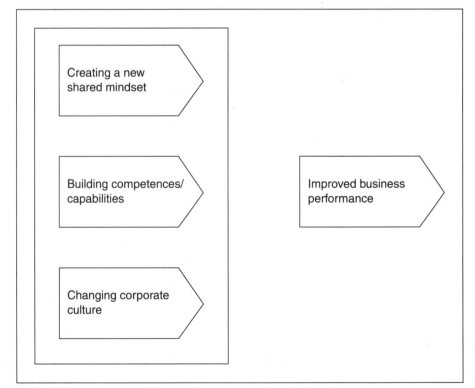

In this context it is important to recognise that it is frequently necessary to manage change to enable the competitive position of the business to be refocused. As a consequence, the management of change is not an option, but a fundamental need. Unfortunately, this is not always recognised when companies seek to change their product-market focus. The result is that such attempts all too often fail when the change programmes, which are a necessary part of changing the organisation's product-market focus, are either ignored or cannot be successfully implemented. As a consequence, the commitment and motivation necessary throughout the organisation to ensure success are missing.

In considering the change process, Lewin's (1951) model is frequently cited. Comprising three components – unfreezing, reconfiguring and refreezing – the model, depicted in Figure 4.5, encapsulates what each successful change programme needs to achieve. First, before any change can be attempted the existing ways of doing things have to be 'unfrozen'. Once this has been achieved, then a reconfiguration of the organisation can be attempted. Finally, to ensure the organisation does not regress to its previous ways of doing things, the new order must be secured by a process of 'refreezing'.

In seeking to manage organisational change it is important to diagnose and anticipate where the likely resistance to change will arise, and how it may be countered. Table 4.1 details potential sources of resistance to change and why they may arise.

Figure 4.5 Lewin's model of organisational change

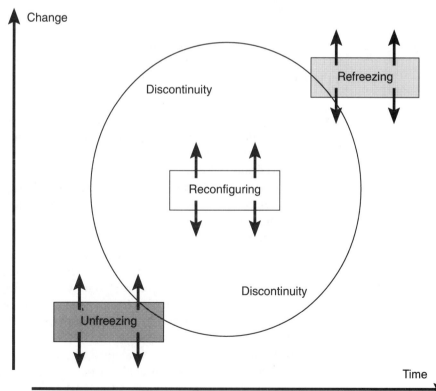

Source: Ellis and Williams (1993), p 275

149

Table 4.1 Resistance to change

Reasons why resistance to change may occur:

- *Personal self-interest:* individuals or groups within the organisation may fear that change will undermine their status, position and power in the organisation. Consequently, they may indulge in considerable 'political' behaviour to prevent the change or modify its effect to their advantage.

- *Lack of understanding and trust:* change is more likely to be resisted when there is little understanding of the reasons for the change and past behaviours have led to little trust between different groups inside the organisation. Where there is little understanding of the need to change and no trust, resistance may arise simply because different individuals and groups fear the worst based on past experiences.

- *Alternative assessment:* individuals and groups within the organisation may make different assessments of organisational needs based upon their information set and perspective. As a result, individuals and groups within the organisation may not share the same view of what needs to be done.

- *Individuals' fears and concerns:* organisational change may well result in new sets of behaviours and personal competences being required. Individuals and groups may fear that they do not possess these new requirements and are unable to develop them. Such individuals are likely to exhibit a low tolerance to change.

Source: Based on Kotter and Schlesinger (1979)

To counter resistance to change it is necessary to consider appropriate change strategies to be used either individually or collectively. Drawing on the work of Kotter and Schlesinger (1979), the following generic change strategies can be identified:

- *Education and communication:* this strategy focuses on the need to inform and communicate with all individuals and groups in the organisation in an attempt to develop understanding and trust. Without such information, individuals and groups within the organisation are unlikely to appreciate fully the need for organisational change. As a change strategy, education and communication is likely to be important when resistance occurs owing to lack of understanding and trust.
- *Participation and involvement:* in an attempt to overcome resistance the potential resisters to change are involved in the design and implementation of the new strategy. The potential advantage of this approach is that participation can lead to strong commitment to change on behalf of the individuals and groups involved in the change process. As a change strategy, however, it can be very time consuming and may result in poor solutions which reflect self-interest.
- *Negotiation and agreement:* this strategy seeks to overcome resistance through a negotiated outcome, allowing all parties to gain something from the proposed change. Unfortunately the costs of achieving a negotiated outcome in

terms of satisfying key stakeholders may become unacceptably high for the organisation, as one or more parties exploit their bargaining position.

- *Manipulation:* this is a highly 'political' strategy where individuals or groups are manipulated to achieve a particular outcome. It may be done through giving the impression of involving individuals in the decision-making process, when ultimately all that is desired is their endorsement. The strategy can be highly risky to the extent that if individuals believe they are 'being used', resistance may increase rather than decrease.
- *Coercion:* this relies upon the managers responsible for change bringing either explicit or implicit pressure to bear on individuals through the use of some form of threat. Although some managers use this approach success-fully, particularly when urgency is a major need, the strategy again runs the risk of leading to increased resistance over time as individuals and groups 'store' their grievances.

No single generic change strategy is entirely adequate. Resistance to change may arise from a multiplicity of causes, and require more than one change strategy. Further, time is a critical factor is so as far as some strategies take much longer to implement than others and the organisation may have immediate pressing needs. This may result in the parallel implementation of different change strategies, some which have immediate effects and others which take longer to achieve their goals. In deciding a way forward the following components to managing organisational change should be considered:

- an analysis of the organisation's current position, including its mindset, core competences/capabilities and corporate culture;
- assessment of what factors need to be changed in respect of the mindset, core competences/capabilities and corporate culture in order to achieve the desired outcomes;
- selection of a change strategy or strategies;
- implementation of the change strategy or strategies;
- evaluation and monitoring of outcomes.

The successful management of change will need to focus on the key element which underlies the organisational dynamics, namely creating a new shared mindset, building competences/capabilities and changing corporate culture, as depicted in Figure 4.4.

Creating a new shared mindset

Earlier discussion has emphasised the importance of the corporate mindset and the need for individuals within the organisation to share the vision of where it is seeking to go. The vision/mindset of an organisation is qualitative rather than quantitative and provides the overall direction in which the firm is seeking to progress. The new mindset describes the future direction in which the organisation wishes to move.

While the vision is often initially developed and promulgated by the chief executive and the senior management team, unless others in the organisation adopt the same mindset little in practice is likely to be achieved. If the mindset does become shared then it can be rightly described as the collective ambition of the organisation. The importance of achieving this shared mind-set explains why many chief executives, either personally or by detailing their senior subordinates, often spend considerable time talking to key stake-holders inside the organisation, for example middle and junior managers and operatives.

In order for employees to share the mindset and begin to take ownership of the change programme, it is imperative for senior management to communicate with the entire organisation, explaining the compelling reasons for change. It is important to establish why 'do nothing' is no longer a feasible option, and how the new vision must be seen as desirable and attainable. Each employee needs to understand what the business is trying to achieve and what is expected of him or her.

Building competences/ capabilities

Changing the corporate mindset is a necessary condition in order to allow the organisation to build or renew competences and capabilities enabling it to manage new industry/market challenges. As noted earlier, core competences and organisational learning are both potential sources of competitive advantage. The first is concerned with those aspects of the organisation in which it is uniquely advantaged over its competitive rivals (Illustration 4.6), while the second concerns the organisation being able to continuously update itself through innovation and organisational learning (Illustration 4.7). Unless new core competences are developed the organisation may well be unable to match the current and future competitive position of its rivals.

Changing corporate culture

Corporate culture strongly influences the collective behaviour of the organisation. If new behaviours are to be encouraged and achieved as part of the outcomes to the change process, then inevitably this will require a new or modified corporate culture. Hence changing corporate culture is likely to prove necessary if the new mindset is actually to be achieved. For example, the organisation may need to offer greater empowerment to its managers to enable them to use their initiative, as in the case of British Petroleum (Illustration 4.1), or to become more customer driven, as with IBM (Illustration 4.11). Similarly, the organisation's culture may need to become much more explicitly international. For these new behaviours to become the prevailing norm, the organisation's corporate culture will need to undergo change.

In practice, change often proves difficult. The development of an organisation's corporate culture takes place over a considerable period of time and is likely to have a long gestation. As a result, corporate culture can prove difficult to modify and this has often been the reason for change programmes failing to achieve their intended outcomes. For example, the Philips case study at the end of the chapter illustrates how the existing culture on which the organisation's past success had been built was an impediment to the development of a global strategy.

Improved business performance

Improved business performance is the outcome to the change process. Managers may well be set stretching business targets in order to prompt improved performance. Discussion in Chapter 2 considered how international business performance might be assessed using financial indicators and/or the balanced scorecard approach. If the latter approach is adopted operations may, for example, be required to reduce operating costs, while marketing is given the specific remit to increase the geographic coverage of sales or to improve market share in a particular market. Equally, the organisation may also adopt a superordinate goal, say to improve quality, which then becomes a major focus throughout the organisation.

Discussion at the end of Chapter 1 examined how unacceptable levels of business performance may help create the conditions in which an organisation's strategy is modified. As Grinyer and Spender (1979) suggest, corrective adjustments are likely to focus initially on implementation and seeking incremental rather than fundamental change. Ultimately if unacceptable levels of performance endure, then this is likely to trigger fundamental change as described by Illustration 4.9.

Illustration 4.9

Scandinavian Airlines System (SAS)

In the late 1970s Scandinavian Airlines Systems (SAS) found itself in severe financial crisis. All confidence had been lost in the incumbent Chairman Munkberg, who was replaced by Carlzon in late 1981. Carlzon set about the task of turning the company around with such drive and enthusiasm that SAS immediately returned to profit, even though worldwide losses for the airline industry were in excess of £16 billion a year.

During the 'first wave' of the turnaround a pronounced shift away from a technical/production focus to a market/service-oriented airline took place. This was matched with a new business concept in which the main emphasis was placed on the full fare paying business traveller. Carlzon replaced 13 out of 14 top executives as part of his effort to change organisational culture, as well as thinning out all management levels. The 10,000 front line staff were retrained, actively encouraged to question how resources were being currently employed, and motivated to implement over 140 service innovations.

In the mid-1980s Carlzon set about defining a new way forward to respond to a new series of challenges called the 'second wave', a period characterised by deregulation and the need for a creative response to an ever changing market environment (see Chapter 3, world airline industry). SAS sought to develop the business traveller aspect into a total service concept (including hotels, financial agency, car hire), as well as seeking co-operative agreements with other airlines. The failure of the Alcazar venture to be concluded effectively in 1993 ensured that SAS would not achieve their Chairman's goal 'to become one of the five (global airlines) in 1995'. Moreover, with business performance severely depressed by the difficult trading conditions of the early 1990s, the need to once again improve performance was apparent.

Source: The authors

The case of SAS also illustrates how the need to improve business performance can feed back and promote change in respect of the three components – creating a new shared mindset, building competences/capabilities and corporate culture – of managing organisational change, a compelling issue which will be returned to at the end of the chapter.

Assessing and changing corporate culture

Changing corporate culture is often one of the most difficult components of the change process to achieve. Corporate is to be distinguished from national culture, to the extent that the former is specific to the organisation, although the corporate culture of an individual company may be strongly influenced by a single national culture. Indeed, as companies develop an international perspective, often one of the most fundamental challenges is to change their predominantly national culture to one which is much more international in outlook. Periodically, a company's corporate culture may need to be reshaped to enable the company to achieve renewal and to develop a new basis for competitive advantage.

Before corporate culture can be changed the existing culture must be identified and understood. The concept of the *cultural web* (Johnson, 1992) is a powerful diagnostic tool for both recognising the different elements of corporate culture and helping to analyse culture as it relates to an individual organisation. The cultural web is illustrated in Figure 4.6. A major benefit of the cultural web is that it enables researchers and managers to surface the key components of corporate culture, rather than discussing the concept in terms of generalities. The cultural web also enables an assessment of the extent to which a company's culture has truly embraced the imperatives of the international market place.

At the centre of the cultural web is the *paradigm* or core values of the organisation, embodied in the corporate mindset. This describes the key elements of the organisation's core values and strategy, sometimes referred to as the *strategic recipe*. The organisation's strategic recipe or paradigm is held in place by the outer elements of the cultural web. These form a network of links and explain why changing the core values/corporate mindset of an organisation can be so difficult. Once established, each element of the cultural web tends to hold in place the existing corporate mindset, making change difficult to enact. Consequently, there is often a long conditioning process of 'unfreezing' the individual elements of the web as a necessary condition for major changes to the strategic recipe. Illustration 4.10 explains the concept of a paradigm in greater detail.

Reviewing the outer ring of the cultural web, each of the individual elements may be analysed, as illustrated by Table 4.2. This not only shows how the cultural web offers an important diagnostic tool for management, but also identifies the universal set from which to develop key elements of a change programme. What, for example, does the change programme require in order to succeed in terms of shifts in the power, structure, systems, myths and sto-

Figure 4.6 The cultural web

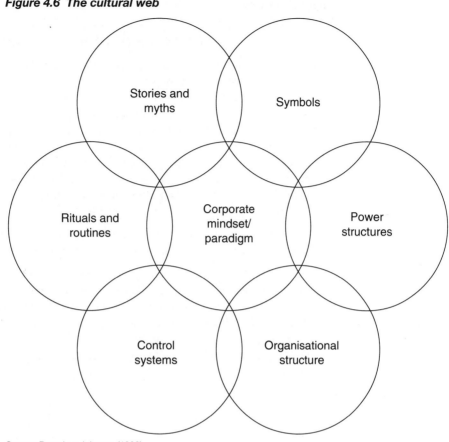

Source: Based on Johnson (1992)

ries and symbols in modifying the core values of the organisation? It is important in this context to recognise that changing formal systems and structures is
generally insufficient. Much of how an organisation functions is explained by
the informal systems, networks and relationships. Changing only the formal
systems and structures is likely to prove inadequate in bringing about the
desired change outcomes.

> Any halfway sensible organisational innovator knows that informal changes have
> to accompany formal ones, and often precede them . . . The truth is that the formal
> and informal aspects of an organisation are equally important and interdependent.
> (Lorenz, 1994, p. 11)

Recognising both the formal and informal aspects of an organisation, Table
4.2 considers the potential role of each component of the cultural web in
changing culture.

The power of the cultural web to generate important insights about how a
company's culture is changing or needs to be changed can be gleaned from
the case study of BMW. As the case study at the end of Chapter 2 demonstrates, the international focus of BMW has changed radically in the last few

Illustration 4.10

The concept of a paradigm

A paradigm is a set of beliefs or assumptions shared by the ruling elite or dominant coalition within a firm which shape the way the organisation sees itself and reacts to changes in its environment. Often operating at an unconscious level, the paradigm defines those values which are taken for granted by the organisation. For example, an organisation's paradigm may emphasise new product development, new market initiatives and flexibility of response, and eschew consolidation and stability. Equally, the company may have a strong 'home' market orientation, or conversely stress the international nature of its operations. As Stacey (1993) suggests, the paradigm is a lens through which the organisation looks at its external context and interprets what it sees.

> The problem with mindsets or paradigms is that we tend to see through them, and so the degree to which they filter our perception goes unrecognised. (Pascale, 1990, p 13)

As the paradigm encapsulates those values and beliefs held by the dominant power group within the organisation, it is difficult to challenge unless the authority of the group itself is coming under pressure, and the latter is prepared to countenance a revision. Normally a paradigm only evolves gradually over time, providing the means both to interpret external changes and to formulate action (Johnson, 1992).

Source: The authors

years. Not only has the company decided to establish production facilities in the USA, but in early 1994 it acquired the UK-based company, Rover Group. Table 4.3 illustrates how the cultural web can be used to disaggregate the organisational changes at BMW.

The importance of corporate culture is that it helps shape the organisation's response to any stimuli, and effectively restricts to a greater or lesser extent an organisation's response. Here lies the dilemma of corporate culture. In one respect corporate culture is critical in ensuring the cohesiveness of the organisation. Conversely, strong cultures tend to reinforce past values, making change difficult to achieve. Consequently, should an organisation need to make a substantial shift in its international business strategy this is likely to be achieved only if the corporate culture is able to support and facilitate the implementation of a change of direction.

If the 'old' culture remains, the successful implementation of a new international business strategy is likely to be threatened by resistance to change within the organisation. Indeed, the all-pervasive nature of culture means that simply pulling levers at one level of the organisation does not guarantee

Table 4.2 The elements of the cultural web

Component of the cultural web	Description	Role in changing culture
Stories and myths	Exerts a powerful influence on behaviour. Reflects what is seen as important. Describes the commonly held interpretation of important events and actions in the organisation's history, e.g. the reasons particular individuals succeeded or failed.	New stories need to be gen erated emphasising new pat terns of behaviour. e.g. reasons under the 'new' culture why a particular behaviour is rewarded; why some past behaviours are now strongly disapproved of.
Symbols	Powerful indicator of corporate culture, reflecting what the organisation sees as important.	Symbols of the 'old' culture need to be dismantled.
Power structures	Power can arise from a number of sources, e.g. individual or group's formal position in the organisation; expertise and resource base. Without power it is difficult, if not impossible, to influence corporate events. Alongside any formal power structure, informal networks may have a powerful influence.	Power is a fundamental requirement if a change to corporate culture is to be attempted. If those individuals with power are not persuaded of the need to change, then tacit or overt resistance to change is likely to result.
Organisational structure	Often reinforces the power dimension of culture. Structures may be very rigid or loose; functional or matrix. Establishes the reporting lines of different individuals or groups within the organisation.	Changing the structure and/ or reporting lines, can raise the importance of, or de-emphasise, different aspects of the business.
Control system	Reflects the degree of decentralisation/ centralisation; extent of formal/ informal controls. Key control systems indicate what process or aspects of performance are considered to be important.	Change nature/balance between formal and informal systems and extent of decentralisation/ centralisation. Ensure systems emphasise what performance is important and align reward system to encourage new behaviour.
Rituals and routines	Describe what patterns of behaviour have become established routines within the company.	New patterns of behaviour need to be established and accepted as the 'norm'. Managers can provide powerful role models in instituting new rituals and routines.

Table 4.3 Corporate mindset/paradigm changes at BMW: an appreciation of the cultural web framework

Component of the cultural web	Previous (pre-1992)	New and developing (post-1993)
Stories and myths	Long-established policy of building cars in Germany. Must win head-to-head battle with Mercedes-Benz, its traditional German arch-rival in luxury car market.	Need to have low cost production bases in, for example, USA and UK. Competitive battle is global; needs to be extended to beating the Japanese.
Symbols	Employees involved in development and planning scattered over 10 different buildings and offices in the Munich area.	Establishment of a single research and development centre to bring together all departments involved with new product and production work.
Power structures	Chairman: Eberhard von Kuenheim. Long-standing chairman, since January 1970.	Chairman: Bernd Pischetsrieder from May 1993. Young new chairman, champion of move to USA and purchase of Rover Group.
Organisational structure	Hierarchical, with many layers of management.	Flatter management structure with fewer levels.
Control system	Centralised and fragmented.	Greater devolution and integration.
Rituals and routines	Low risk, conservative attitude.	Emphasis on teamwork; greater individual responsibility and initiative; more tolerant of risk. Emphasis on results.
Corporate mindset/ paradigm	Global exporter of high quality luxury cars.	International producer of low and medium volume, high value motor vehicles.

diffusion of a 'new' culture throughout the organisation. Illustration 4.11 describes how IBM's 'old' culture in the 1990s led to a decline in the company's fortunes, and what the new chairman and chief executive has identified as needing to happen to the company culture in order for corporate renewal to take place. The case of IBM also illustrates that, for a radical change in culture to be contemplated, the ruling elite needs to be removed if they cannot significantly promote new ideas and behaviour.

Recognising the multi-dimensional nature of corporate culture as described by the cultural web explains why, when attempting to develop meaningful and lasting change programmes in an organisation, the need is to act on more than one aspect of the corporate culture. Even then, there is no guarantee that such a change programme will succeed. Generally speaking, changing culture takes time even when the organisation has been experiencing ongoing difficulties and a long-term conditioning process for change has been at work.

Illustration 4.11

IBM: A year of change

Early in 1993 Lou Gerstner was appointed Chairman and Chief Executive of International Business Machines (IBM), with the task of turning the business around. The formerly dominant computer giant had been overtaken by many of its competitors, and the high profit margins it had previously enjoyed on its mainframe computers were a thing of the past. Gerstner identified IBM's culture as the main cause of the company's heavy losses. He argued that the culture was too bureaucratic and that IBM had been 'too pre-occupied with our own view of the world'.

During the first 12 months of his appointment Gerstner set about changing the corporate culture, stating: 'we've got to become more nimble, entrepreneurial, focused, customer driven. We must become a principle-based company rather than a procedural-based company.' Gerstner's statement recognised that IBM's rule-bound culture prevented the company adapting more quickly to changes in the computer market. During his first year, Gerstner spent a great deal of time meeting many of the company's employees across the world, giving them this frank message as to what needed to be done.

Together with making statements about how the company needed to change, Gerstner also took a number of important actions, including:

- appointing outsiders to senior management positions and changing the roles of long-time IBM executives;
- eliminating IBM's executive management committee, formerly at the centre of power in the company and replacing it with a new corporate executive committee;
- slimming down the company's board of directors and changing its composition. During the year, 10 out of 19 members of the board retired.

While many New York analysts believed that Mr Gerstner had made a sound start to tackling IBM's problems, there was general recognition that much more work needed to be done before the company could be said to have a secure future. Indeed, many aspects of the future direction of IBM remained unclear.

Source: Based on Kehoe (1994b)

Changing corporate culture is not painless and there are likely to be winners and losers. Consequently, at least some of the 'old guard' are likely to prove resistant to change, and many of these individuals may be incapable of changing. The new management is likely to be faced with difficult human resource decisions to the extent that some individuals may need to leave the company, while others are moved sideways or retrained. Changing corporate culture is likely to prove difficult for both the organisation and particular individuals, but if the organisation needs to renew itself in order to rediscover its competitive edge then there is little choice. The organisation either changes or declines. Only by changing and rediscovering a basis of competitive advantage will the organisation be able to prosper.

Resource capability and competitive advantage

For companies to be able to survive and prosper in a dynamic international environment, they will need to be able to employ their resource capability in a way which enables the organisation to develop and sustain a competitive advantage. Durable competitive advantage is about the ability of a company to compete in its chosen product markets in a manner which leads to its achieving superior performance when compared to its competitors over a period of time. While competitive advantage is generally assessed from an external perspective, it is based upon the ability of an individual organisation to deploy its resource capability in a manner which is superior to its rivals.

Firms that define their competitive advantage in terms of their superiority in resource deployment are more often long-term winners. As Cronshaw *et al.* (1990) demonstrates, 'market positions can always be replicated by competitors, and what others can do cannot be profitable for long.' Rather, the ability of companies to craft a sustainable competitive advantage reflects how the organisation seeks to shape the five competitive dimensions (see Ellis and Williams, 1993) which it has at its disposal, namely:

- scope
- differentiation
- cost
- time
- linkages

These are illustrated in Figure 4.7.

Figure 4.7 *Creating competitive advantage*

ORGANISATION'S INTERNAL CONTEXT

Source: Ellis and Williams (1993), p 24

Taken together, these five competitive dimensions describe a firm's business strategy. The ability to develop and implement a business strategy is dependent upon the organisation's internal resource capability.

Scope

The first dimension, *scope*, reflects whether the company is seeking to be a narrow or broadly based competitor. This is a key consideration in relation to the resource requirements of an organisation. Companies operating across a number of market segments may be described as broadly based, while companies operating within a more limited focus may be described as having a narrowly based strategy.

The rationale for adopting a narrow focus is the ability to serve a small part of the total market in a superior manner to the broad-based competitor, thereby attracting sufficiently custom to make the strategy viable. For this to happen the size of the niche must be sufficient to offer the basis of economic supply, and sufficiently separable for the competitive offers of broadly based competitors to be unattractive to customers.

Differentiation

The second factor, *differentiation*, is often linked to the question of scope and reflects the firm's intention to be unique by some means within its chosen product-market. By adopting a strategy of differentiation, a company will be seeking to achieve a premium price for its products when compared to the undifferentiated offers of competitors. For this strategy to be worthwhile the additional price received must exceed the extra costs incurred in being unique. This requires the basis of the differentiation to be something that the company's customers want and are prepared to pay for.

Further, the basis of the differentiation must be sustainable, reflecting perhaps an established brand or technological feature which is difficult to replicate. To this end established product brands or business formats with associated customer goodwill, if effectively maintained by appropriate management action and reinvestment, can yield above average returns for their companies over the longer term. The basis of a company's differentiation and therefore customer appeal reflects the core competences of the organisation and its superiority in terms of, say, research and development or technological skills.

Cost

By contrast to differentiation, *cost* can equally assist in developing or sustaining competitive advantage. A low cost supplier is able to offer lower prices than its competitors, or maintain prices and enjoy higher profit margins. This can lead to the virtuous circle of improved profitability, additional reinvestment and further cost reductions. In an international context costs may be reduced by a variety of management actions including, for example, rationalising facilities, enabling production to be concentrated on a smaller number of sites. Equally, for some international industries economies of scale in purchasing, distribution and/or marketing are more critical than production economies, while in other industries spending on research and development is the key.

In practice companies cannot simply focus on cost and neglect differentiation, unless they are operating in commodity markets where quality is standardised and price is the only thing that matters. Even for products considered to be undifferentiated, such as basic steel, quality and delivery times will be important elements of the purchase decision. Hence managing the dilemma between quality (differentiation) and cost is likely to be a critical area for management attention.

Time-based competition

Recognition of the importance of time as an element of competitive advantage stems from the work of Stalk and Hout (1990), who refer to *time-based competition*. The ability to develop new products quickly from conception to market launch has been shown to be a key element of the competitive process for a number of technology-based industries. For example, in the past the ability of Japanese manufacturers to dramatically reduce new product development times and thereby constantly update their product range has been a source of competitive advantage over their European and US competitors in a number of industries. Unless competitors are able to match the speed of new product development, they are increasingly likely to discover that customers find their products outdated.

It may not only be a question of new product innovation. Earlier discussion on organisational capability stressed that this could provide the basis of competitive advantage to the extent that an organisation was able to be innovative and learn. Such innovation and learning may apply equally to the systems and the manner in which a company does business, as to the development of new products. Indeed, the concept of 'new game' strategies emphasises the benefit of finding new ways to compete. The essential point is that a company's ability to achieve the advantages of time-based competition is based upon its organisational capability and being ahead of the competition.

Competitive linkages

Finally, the position of an organisation within a total business system, and hence in relation to its supplier and purchasing companies, introduces the fifth dimension of competitive advantage: *competitive linkages*. The network of business relationships and how they are managed can be a major source of competitive advantage to the organisation. Conversely, if such relationships are poorly managed or neglected, then they can seriously undermine a company's competitive position. World motor vehicle assemblers are developing ever closer competitive linkages with key component suppliers, which are now undertaking tasks previously specified by the assemblers. Both parties have, or are in the process of adopting, just-in-time (JIT) systems of stock replenishment to improve stock control. The closeness of the relationship between motor vehicle assemblers and their suppliers can be an important factor in the latter's decision to operate in world markets. Certainly in the case of BMW, the decision to develop a production facility in the US has led to a number of German component companies deciding to locate in North America.

The five dimensions are not mutually exclusive and they are strongly inter-linked, as illustrated by Figure 4.7. Managers will need to recognise and reconcile tensions between, say, the extent of differentiation and cost. Baden-Fuller and Stopford (1992) have described these choices as the *dilemmas of seemingly irreconcilable opposites.* The key objective is to develop multiple sources of competitive advantage which are difficult or costly to replicate. Achieving this outcome means that the basis of the organisation's competitive advantage is deeply embedded in its vision/mindset and organisational dynamics, which by their very nature are difficult to replicate in other organisations. Illustration 4.12 shows how Benetton SpA achieved a sustainable competitive advantage by reconciling dilemmas encompassing both quality and cost.

Managing organisational change to improve business performance

If the organisation possesses a competitive advantage, it will be able to generate an above average performance. Conversely, weak performance is likely to result if the organisation is unable to use its resource base effectively and efficiently. Where performance is weak it can provide an important trigger to the management of change process, or indeed ensure that the momentum for change is sustained and renewed. In this way, measures of business performance provide important feedback to the three components of managing change, and may well ensure that either the need for a change programme is recognised or renewed efforts to drive change through the organisation are made.

Figure 4.8 offers a dynamic model the interaction between the elements of achieving change – creating a new shared mindset, building competences/capabilities and changing corporate culture – and business performance. This allows the element of time to be introduced. Organisational learning takes place over

Figure 4.8 *The dynamics between business performance and the management of change*

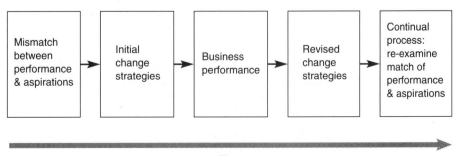

ORGANISATIONAL LEARNING

| Mismatch between performance & aspirations | → | Initial change strategies | → | Business performance | → | Revised change strategies | → | Continual process: re-examine match of performance & aspirations |

Time

Illustration 4.12

Benetton SpA

Intuitive decision making by Luciano Benetton, the founder and Chairman of the Italian family-owned clothing company, has enabled the firm to become the first truly global textile organisation. In less than 30 years the Italian clothing company has come from nowhere to sell its brightly coloured 'United Colors of Benetton' in more than 7000 shops in 100 countries. In the five years between 1989 and 1993, total sales turnover almost doubled from 1.5 to nearly 3.0 trillion lira, with a corresponding doubling of the net profit from 100 to 200 billion lira.

The firm's spectacular growth is underpinned by an iconoclastic marketing strategy, together with the ability to provide fashion at a price and quality accessible to young people. Benetton SpA pioneered techniques to produce high quality fashion garments with choices of varieties and colour at low cost. The firm only handles in house those aspects of manufacturing – mainly design, cutting, dyeing and packaging – that it considers crucial to maintain quality and cost efficiency. It has pioneered new lean methods of production (e.g. last minute dyeing in large quantities), new applications of information technology (e.g. reducing stock levels by linking electronic point of sale – EPOS – systems to facilities) and introduced new methods of product design (e.g. high technology cutting and packing).

Benetton views itself as a clothing services company rather than a retailer or manufacturer. A unique internal organisational system facilitates the pulling together of the production and distribution processes, with its products being sold through a franchised chain of retail outlets. A network of area agents links the whole operation together, finding investors for the shops and ensuring that the company's head office keeps in touch with changing customer tastes around the world. Throughout the organisation there are no long-term contracts with either its suppliers or sales outlets, but a strategic network linked with common strategic purposes and information sharing. It is a formula which many other organisations have sought and failed to achieve.

Viewed in this manner, Benetton's challenges sound less like those of a fashionable boutique and more like those of a large manufacturer of branded goods. Losing creativity is one of the biggest risks Benetton faces, particularly in devising a marketing campaign which will appeal to the next generation of young people who form its target market. The daunting prospect facing the second generation of the Benetton family in managing the business is how to stay ahead of the game; to retain its existing customers as well as attracting new ones and above all retain its competitive advantage.

To date the company has successfully managed a number of key dilemmas which relate to a clothing company. It has been able to market fashionable products to its chosen product-market, provide variety, and be highly responsive to often rapidly changing customer needs; but at the same time to do so at low cost. In other words, it has been able to recognise and manage many of the seemingly irreconcilable opposites inherent in achieving and sustaining competitive advantage in its chosen product-markets.

Source: Based on *The Economist*, April 1994

time as change programmes are revised following initial implementation. This suggests that while original elements of the intended strategy remain, much of the detail is likely to be emergent as the organisation learns through implementing the change programme.

The dynamic model of managing change provides a framework for considering the change needs of international businesses as they seek to manage phased change or to renew their position at a particular stage of international business development.

Summary

This chapter has explored an organisation's internal context and how this can bring about a change to the firm's international business strategy. Emphasis has been placed on the importance of vision and mindset at the highest level in the organisation for shaping change and on the role of organisational dynamics. Collectively, vision/mindset and organisational dynamics describe the organisation's internal context. Changing the internal context can prove problematic and the management of organisational change has three separable, but interrelated elements: namely, creating a new shared mindset, building competences/capabilities and changing corporate culture. The object of managing organisational change is to bring about an improvement of business performance. The ability to outperform rivals is dependent on the organisation's ability to develop and sustain competitive advantage, which is in turn a reflection of how the organisation applies its resource base. The interaction between the components of change and business performance offers a dynamic model which describes how both intended and emergent strategies shape further outcomes.

Checklist

- Organisations are typically driven by different managerial beliefs which influence international business strategy.
- Internal triggers to change can explain why organisations experience a major discontinuity in their business development.
- Changes to the senior management of the organisation can lead to profound discontinuities in the organisation's international business strategy.
- An organisation's internal context is described by its vision/mindset and organisational dynamics.
- The desired geographical scope of operations and the direction of international development are addressed by the firm's vision.
- The vision needs to embedded in the organisational mindset to be effective.
- The vision is the outcome of a combination of left- and right-brain thinking.

- Organisational dynamics comprise core competences, organisational learning and administrative heritage.

- Core competence describes those aspects of the organisation in which it is uniquely advantaged; organisational learning; the ability to adapt and innovate; and administrative heritage the resource inheritance of the firm.

- Managing organisational change comprises three key components – creating a new shared mindset, building competences/capabilities and changing corporate culture – and aims to improve business performance.

- Understanding an organisation's corporate culture can be assisted by the application of the cultural web framework.

- The cultural web offers a list of key areas to which action can be applied in seeking to change the prevailing paradigm or corporate mindset.

- Competitive advantage reflects how an organisation utilises its resource capability.

- Achieving competitive advantages involves managing the dilemmas of 'seemingly irreconcilable opposites'.

- The need to improve business performance provides an important feedback mechanism to the process of managing organisational change.

Case Study 4

Philips Electronics NV

Introduction

Philips Electronics NV (Philips) aims to become a world class quality electronics company by the end of 1995. It is a daunting challenge for a company which faced an unprecedented financial crisis in 1990, as a result of which the former president resigned. His successor, Jan Timmer, immediately instigated a world-wide restructuring and revitalisation programme to effect a lasting improvement in profitability. Known as 'Operation Centurion', the renewal blueprint is aimed at heightening cost, customer and quality awareness.

Operation Centurion is an ongoing, company-wide programme for change. Extensive restructuring was instigated at the outset, with many businesses sold and thousands of jobs shed. This was coupled with an extensive shake-up of the internal culture. This involved calling entrenched views and habits into question, changing working practices to raise productivity, and constantly improving quality awareness, customer orientation and cost consciousness. The Centurion pro-gramme, Mr Timmer said in April 1994, 'will not end . . . the company must be in a permanent state of change'.

Organisational structure

Founded in 1891 in Eindhoven, The Netherlands, Philips has grown from a small manufacturer of incandescent lamps into a company operating worldwide in the fields of lighting and electronics. Its early growth strategy was initially managed and financially controlled from Eindhoven, but in the early 1930s production had to be transferred to countries where it was commercially active, owing to the pro-tectionist world trading environment. This was the start of a 40-year period in which Philips thrived and expanded on a 'local for local basis': local factories making local products, for local markets, under local management control.

A matrix structure between product divisions and national organisations emerged as an organisational framework best suited to support the local for local concept from which Philips benefited for so long. Eindhoven's headquarters role was primarily twofold: first, to co-ordinate activities of the highly autonomous national organisations; and secondly, to act as referee and final arbiter in negotia-tions between product groups and national organisations. Even the relatively simple issue of setting a sales target was subject to complex negotiations, with fiercely independent national organisations often setting a higher target than the product groups.

As with all large sprawling organisations, the effectiveness of Philips' complex management structure owes much to the long-established core beliefs of its employees (Figure C4.1)

By the early 1970s the national structure and its supporting belief structure were becoming increasingly outdated in a world electronics industry dominated by global products, markets and competition. In particular, Philips had become vulnerable to competition from Japanese manufacturers who had built the sales volume necessary for investment in world-scale manufacturing and state of the

Figure C4.1 Accepted 'ancien' beliefs

- *Supremacy of national organisations:* perceived as the route to the top, with each Dutchperson normally undertaking at least one extended tour of duty.

- *Consensus and collective responsibility:* all senior executives being with Philips all their working life; internal transfers; intuitively knowing what can be done and what cannot be done.

- *Dual authority management:* found at all levels in the organisation, with both technical and commercial managers sharing decision making. Stems from the late 1890s when Anton Philips joined the firm as a salesman to complement his brother Gerrard's talent as an engineer.

- *Self-sufficiency:* belief that company is good at mastering new technologies, that its own technology alone is sufficient to create competitive edge.

- *Sales volume/market share:* internal performance scorecard.

Source: Business Week, 12 January 1972

art technology. While in theory Philips had the volume to match the Japanese in the automation of manufacturing and the rationalisation of products and sourcing, in practice this proved difficult to achieve.

The company's existing structure, based around powerful national subsidiaries, made it difficult to integrate and co-ordinate national operations into a cohesive global strategy. The company's national managers were strongly jealous of their autonomy, and had previously controlled both marketing and strategy. With their mindset focused on a single national market, individual managers were unable to perceive the global threat posed by the Japanese manufacturers.

Philips eventually came to terms with these difficulties and succeeded in closing many local factories and restructuring the remainder into large-scale international production centres (IPCs). Correspondingly, as the new large-scale factories – IPCs – produce for international markets, their activities extend well beyond the control of local management. Gradually, authority was regrouped in internationally structured core product divisions taking responsibility for worldwide product, production and profit policy. The gradual shift from national to international production centres, the tilting of the matrix structure in favour of the product divisions, and the more direct involvement at corporate headquarters represented a radical new organisational structure.

Apart from the organisational structural changes, there were also important changes in people's attitudes and beliefs that needed to be effected. The espoused changes in the 20-year period 1970–89 are illustrated in Figure C4.2.

Many senior managers in the once proud national organisations sought to stifle the structural and cultural changes outlined in Figure C4.2. Even if they recognised the need for a new global strategy and structure, their activities and beliefs were deeply rooted and entrenched in the 'ancien' regime. The espoused vision of successive chairmen had to contend with the entrenched 'Philips' way of doing business. It was like trying to fill a barrel that has holes in it. Moreover,

Figure C4.2 Changing belief structures

'Ancien' beliefs $\rightarrow$	Espoused 'new' beliefs
• *Supremacy of national organisation*	International product divisions: leaving once proud national organisations with little more than local distribution.
• *Consensus and collective responsibility*	Direct action and individual responsibility: a marked change in deeply rooted and entrenched beliefs.
• *Dual authority management*	Single general manager: replacement of dual system which operated since firm's inception.
• *Self-sufficiency*	Strategic alliances: recognition of high cost of R&D, and that technology alone is not sufficient to gain competitive edge.
• *Sales volume*	Profitability: no future without profits.

Source: Business Week, 12 January 1972

the non-productive internal battles undermined attempts to turn the organisation into an outward-looking, aggressive global competitor.

'While we debated our competitors acted and left us in the dust,' commented Jan Timmer. Philips continued throughout the 1980s to produce product margins which lagged far below those achieved in the 1960s. When in 1990 Philips posted record losses, shown in Table C4.1 – for a year in which a substantive upturn in performance was promised by senior management – a crisis of unprecedented enormity ensued. Radical measures in the form of Operation Centurion were taken to safeguard the survival of the company. Philips was clearly embroiled in a formidable race against time to prevent the future being overtaken by the legacy of its administrative past.

Operation Centurion, Phase I: Restructuring

Operation Centurion, launched in Autumn 1990, is a company-wide movement for change in order to improve profitability. The need to change was self-evident from the severe financial crisis facing the company, together with the accompanying changes in management at the highest level. Jan Timmer, the new Chairman, commented, 'the realisation that Philips, which many people regarded as a symbol of strength and enterprise, was vulnerable and might not last forever came as a great shock both inside and outside the company. Throughout the company a process of change has been set in motion which is becoming widely recognised under the name of Operation Centurion.'

Table C4.1 Philips Group – Ten-year performance history, 1984–93
(all amounts in billions of Dutch guilders (NLG) unless otherwise stated)

	1984	1985	1986	1987	1988	1989	1990	1991	1992	1993
Sales turnover	53.8	60.0	55.0	52.7	56.0	57.2	55.8	57.0	58.5	58.8
Operating profit	3.5	3.1	3.2	2.1	2.4	2.3	(2.4)	3.0	1.3	2.6
Operating profits as % of turnover	6.5	5.1	5.8	4.1	4.3	4.0	(4.3)	5.2	2.2	4.4
Total assets	54.5	52.9	50.6	50.0	52.8	55.0	51.6	48.7	48.8	46.3
Total sales/ total assets	0.98	1.13	1.09	1.05	1.06	1.04	1.08	1.17	1.20	1.27
% return on total assets	3.4	3.5	6.3	4.3	4.6	4.2	4.6	6.1	2.6	5.6
Employees ('000s)	344	346	344	337	310	305	273	240	252	239

Notes: Owing to factors including consolidations and divestments, the stated amounts year to year and corresponding ratios are not directly comparable for all years.

A senior executive believed that the change process begun by Operation Centurion could be best described by the characteristics outlined in Figure C4.3.

Figure C4.3 Key characteristics of Operation Centurion

- Turnaround management
- Changing the mindset
- External benchmarking
- No sacred cows (e.g. 'strategic' label)
- Decentralisation: accountability/personal contract
- Simplicity/efficiency/productivity (sales per head)
- Quality and custom driven
- Cost cutting and opportunity
- Internal communication: consensus building
- External communication: perform first/talk later

Operation Centurion was a blueprint for an intensive durable and ongoing process of change involving the whole of the Philips organisation. It is a radical and comprehensive process of change designed to succeed where previous restructuring changes had previous failed. From the outset Mr Dekker, Chairman of the Supervisory Board, recognised: 'the radical measures which are being taken to safeguard the continuity of the company weigh heavily on all employees in all sectors. We are conscious of the fact that individual hardship cannot always be avoided in these circumstances.'

Case Study 4

Within this movement for change two distinct phases were identified at the outset. An initial short-term restructuring phase was aimed at quickly closing the performance gap with competitors. This was to be achieved by streamlining sales organisations, closing factories, being more selective in product development, pruning product lines, intensifying and co-operative alliances. Major asset disposals and dramatic headcount reductions were envisaged. This was to be followed by a long-term 'Philips Quality Drive' charged with creating the mindset for the revitalisation phase of Centurion. All Philips' top 100 managers agreed upon this plan of action at its inaugural launch.

Similar visions with equally important milestones for orderly and speedy implementation had been offered by previous chairmen. The 1990 crisis was testimony to how they had failed to effect a lasting turnaround in the company's fortunes over the previous two decades. Notwithstanding some major portfolio changes, Operation Centurion did not envisage any major changes in organisational structure. International product divisions were to remain the corporate kingpins, with visible leadership instilling the skill and will to make previously espoused 'new' beliefs work. Between 1990 and 1993 Jan Timmer appointed eight new board members (only one appointment was Dutch), with two long-standing vice-presidents retiring.

From Jan Timmer's perspective the revitalisation process could only succeed if all employees showed a willingness to work differently, to listen better to others and to set their goals higher step by step. In his words: 'doing away with non-productive internal battles and learning to work towards a common goal. Mobilising the considerable talents of all our employees. Accepting that unless everybody becomes part of the change process, the company cannot optimise its profitability.' In short, involving everyone is the key to success.

In order to reach the heads and hearts of 240,000 employees spread over 52 countries and working in some 272 international production centres, a three-pronged communication process was instigated. First, a top-down cascade model of communication brought together 14,000 managers during weekend sessions in groups of 50 people. The first tier of meetings was primarily concerned with translating the vision of the change process into actions and targets for the product divisions and business groups. The second tier, involving more than 100 groups, was instigated to reach consensus and commitment for task-force issues which managers themselves believed were key drivers in the process of revitalisation. The taskforce clusters identified in Figure C4.4 were to be headed by a 'champion' with a proven involvement in the subject.

Secondly, a bottom-up communication flow arose from 'town meetings'. Every plant with in the Philips group organises discussion sessions between its personnel and the management about the change process in their own working environment. In this way, some 200,000 employees are involved. These communication efforts are not simply directed towards imparting information, but as a forum for working out plans for improvement. They are part of the ongoing activity of building an inherent change management capability.

Thirdly, two interactive satellite discussion days have been held for the whole of the European workforce. Taking place somewhat later than the two previous communication processes, 1992 and 1994 respectively, these events have

Figure C4.4 Operation Centurion: taskforce clusters

1. **Assets**
   - Stock management
   - Accounts receivable
   - Fixed assets

2. **Product**
   - R&D effectiveness
   - Miniaturisation
   - User interface
   - Software improvement/intelligent boxes
   - Purchasing/supplier base

3. **Marketing**
   - Customer first
   - Brand/channel management (USA)
   - Brand/channel management (rest of world)
   - Corporate image

4. **Strategy**
   - Strategic direction: software/services
   - Alliances/standards

5. **Governance**
   - Openness
   - Management skills
   - Shared values/corporate governance ('The Philips Way')

focused less on restructuring and more on the process of revitalisation. They have encompassed an interactive discussion on how to become more customer oriented and quality driven as an organisation. Group management have taken charge of all the taskforces through which these and other issues are addressed.

Speaking in January 1993, the President commented: 'the need and willingness to change is there. We are developing into a permanent learning mode; our goals have to be set higher and higher. We are certainly not underestimating this phenomenal task of changing corporate culture, but we should all be aware that it is a long-term processes as some companies – which went through similar exercises – have experienced and others will no doubt discover later.'

Operation Centurion, Phase II: Revitalisation

Management of change in any large organisation is not a quick-fix process. It is a long-term process on which the path to durable change and sustained improvements goes through several progressive phases. 'Philips Quality' creates the mindset for the revitalisation phase of Centurion. Nobody disagrees with quality principles. It is the gap between the rhetoric and everyday practice which holds back success. Philips' management believe that it takes time for quality to become self-sustaining. Shared visions and values, common principles, an integrating structure, skills, tools and techniques are all essential.

According to Jan Timmer, every Philips person must say 'Philips quality starts with me. I am the first to do so. I am chairman of the Corporate Quality Council, the top quality team which includes the Group Management Committee. It is our role to provide the vision and the leadership. We will have the lead in goal setting. We will conduct management audits of the Product Divisions, national organisations and corporate staff. We will monitor customers' satisfaction and employee morale. We will participate in quality training and act as ourselves. All management teams and every individual must make similar, specific commitments. Together we will delight our customers by doing the right things, the right way, the first time, all the time.'

To emphasise the company's commitment to quality, the Group Management Committee adopted a code of conduct, 'The Philips Way', listed in Figure C4.5, which identified five cornerstone corporate values.

Customer first is the route to securing customers by surpassing their expectations. Jan Timmer believes that 'customer-perceived quality of our products and services is what makes the customer buy. The customer is the final arbiter. Therefore the key to our recovery lies with the customer. Only when we satisfy our customers can we be profitable and continue to exist.' To encourage such a market-led perspective Philips has instigated a continuous customer monitoring feedback system. Moreover, benchmarking is undertaken to see how other world-class companies are responding to customer requirements.

Leadership provides the inspiration which enables individuals to give more and achieve more than they might otherwise have accomplished. 'Above all quality requires leadership. You must make a stand on quality. You must put some passion into it.' Timmer claimed that it is leadership that is needed to make things happen. These comments are borne out of the direct experience of a company that launched a quality initiative in 1983. On reflection, senior managers believed that too few of them had adopted quality as a way of life. Links between pockets of outstanding improvement were never built and a critical mass never materialised.

Figure C4.5 The Philips Way

• *customer first*	→ surpass customer expectations
• *demonstrate leadership*	→ inspire the passion for quality
• *value people as company's greatest asset*	→ respect for each other; teamwork
• *encourage entrepreneurial behaviour at all levels*	→ strive for excellence
• *achieve premium return on equity*	→ improve continuously

Our values say 'what's really important around here' and define 'the way we do things around here.' To make Philips a world-class quality company, we have to create a Philips Quality culture based on shared values.

Value people is concerned with empowered individuals working in teams to make Philips Quality happen. 'Quality is delivered by people, we are the essence of our organisation. Technology alone is not sufficient to gain the competitive edge. The difference lies in us, in our attitudes and actions, in how we relate to our customers and each other, in our willingness to take responsibility', stated Timmer. To this end a new company-wide performance appraisal system was introduced which seeks to put team success ahead of individual goals, and to provide mutual support in the service of common goals.

Encouraging entrepreneurial behaviour at all levels does not happen automatically. Changing customer needs and fierce competition makes continuous improvement necessary. 'To me, quality is a state of mind . . . the relentless pursuit of excellence of never being satisfied with what you do, how you do it and how quickly you do it,' commented Timmer. In short, continuous quality improvement requires an ongoing management commitment to a shared vision, together with an organisational structure supporting new goals and the goal-setting process.

A premium return on equity has not been achieved to date. In March 1994 Philips announced its first dividend payment since the extensive restructuring and revitalisation of Operation Centurion was set in motion in 1990. Analysts attributed the sharp move into the black to cost cutting and to a strong reduction in financing charges. There are still precious few signs that the Japanese onslaught on the European electronics industry has abated, that price margins can be restored to 1990s levels. Timmer stated, 'we hope the worst of the problems are behind us, that we have cautiously started on the road to recovery.'

Industry dynamics

Notwithstanding Philips' attempts to put its house in order through the implementation of Operation Centurion, all competitors in the field of consumer electronics are experiencing considerable trading difficulties and a dramatic fall in earnings. Under the pressure of intense global competition, consumer prices for televisions and video recorders fell by 20 and 30 percentage points respectively over the five-year period 1987 to 1992. The severity of the price erosion in consumer electronics was a setback for Philips' turnaround strategy, which necessitated a further attack on the cost base in 1992. It also resulted in a revenue shortfall of NLG1.6 billion, equivalent to almost 4 per cent of the company's total net sales (Figure C4.6).

Accompanying lower profits is the question of the company's cost base. Production of a 1 Mbit D-Ram silicon chip in Europe is 10 per cent more expensive than in the USA and 16 per cent more expensive than in Japan. For an 80C51 micro-controller and 5000 gate array, the comparable figures are 8 per cent (USA) and 15 per cent (Japan) and 8 per cent (USA) and 33 per cent (Japan) respectively. As these selective figures from the European Electronic Component Manufacturers Association (EEC MA) (April 1993) show, production costs are much higher in Europe compared with the other two main global production locations.

Finally, social costs create an enormous cost hurdle for all European firms. Table C4.2 shows striking differences in social systems and associated costs worldwide. In terms of working hours per year, wage costs per hour and social

Case Study 4

Figure C4.6 Price erosion in consumer electronics 1990–92
(millions of Dutch guilders)

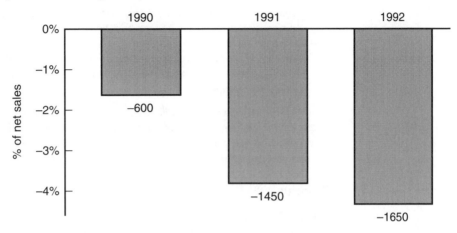

costs as a percentage of wages, Europe compares unfavourably with the two other Triad regions and the 'Tiger' economies of South East Asia. Moreover, in Europe any downsizing of the workforce carries major costs of employment protection and associated expenditure.

Table C4.2 Differences in social systems

	Europe	USA	Japan	SE Asia
Working hours per year				
– employees	1,460	1,750	1,850	1,800
– managers	1,610	1,850	1,900	1,900
Wage costs per hour	100	84	75	23
(Index: Europe = 100)				
Social costs as % of wage costs	40	30	20	27

Source: EEC MA

Against the background of a global competitive battle, it is of vital importance to restore European competitiveness. In short, Europe must resolve its dilemma: an expensive, protected European welfare society or an open economy with a cost and productivity structure which can stand the test of global competition.

Philips' roots lie in Europe, but as a company with worldwide operations we are able to compare the business climates in the various regions of the world. And we have to conclude that in the global battle that is being waged, Europe lags behind in competitiveness.

This serious finding is reflected in a growing level of unemployment, which in my view is Europe's highest priority issue.

175

Europe is facing a dilemma:

- either, it gives priority to the European way-of-life based on the European concept of the welfare state, but then we have to isolate ourselves from the world competition and that means: protectionism;
- or we go for free trade, but then we have to withstand the competition from the Far East and other dynamic regions of the world and that means that we have to adapt ourselves to their competitive standards, their way of working and their sense of urgency.

So Europe has to make choices and act very fast. Because one thing is for sure, the longer we wait, the more we will see vital competence centres disappear and the harder it will become to get back on the right track. (J D Timmer, extract from a speech to the Dutch Society of Chief Editors, 29 September 1993)

Conclusion

For Philips Electronics NV, the current embodiment of an ongoing process of change management is 'Operation Centurion'. This is an intensification of major efforts over the past decade to change the organisational structure and implement cultural change. Under Operation Centurion specific taskforces have been chosen to realise the firm's needs for restructuring (cost cutting to address the 'performance gap') and for revitalisation (building and enhancing strengths to address the 'opportunity gap'). Given the parlous state of the European electronics industry, it is taking all the running Philips can manage not to fall even further behind.

Questions

(1) *What was the basis of Philips' success for much of last 60 years? Why did this success and the accompanying culture make it difficult for the company to respond to the Japanese threat in the 1980s?*

(2) *How did the company need to change its strategy, structure and culture in order to respond to a new competitive environment?*

(3) *Discuss how Timmer attempted to communicate his vision throughout the company and develop a shared mindset.*

(4) *Compare the 'ancien beliefs' of the company versus the 'new beliefs' incorporated in Operation Centurion by using the cultural web (Figure 4.6)*

(5) *How did senior management attempt to emphasise the importance of quality throughout the organisation?*

(6) *To what extent is there evidence in the case of the company performance having improved? Can the company afford to sit back and be complacent?*

Part III

INTERNATIONAL BUSINESS DEVELOPMENT

Chapter 5

RESTRICTED NATIONAL MARKET SCOPE

Key learning objectives

To understand:

- the conditions under which restrictive national market scope offers the basis of a sustainable business strategy

- the distinction between local, national region, national and international strategies

- the role of product-market demand and competitive interdependencies in influencing the scope of business strategies

- how changing external dynamics may influence the success of strategies with restricted national market scope

- the link between competitive advantage and business performance

- what measure to use in assessing competitive advantage, in what market and over which competitors

- the importance of undertaking inter-market comparisons

- the role of benchmarking in assessing and developing performance improvement

Context

Business boundaries are influenced by changes in product-market demand and competitive interdependencies. This may result in a widening or narrowing of the product and/or geographical territory of firms and their competitors. The pressures and drivers for altering the boundaries of product and/or geographical coverage may be endogenous ('internal triggers') or exogenous ('external triggers'), with ambiguity surrounding which strategic direction will prove to be the most rewarding and for how long. Ambiguities will be most pronounced when discontinuities arise from product-market demand and competitive interdependencies which are working in different directions, with some forces favouring restricted scope and others calling into question the validity of restricted territory and product scope.

Restricted national market scope is feasible whenever product-market demand and competitive interdependence collectively enable firms to become or remain viable competitors within their national boundaries. The focus of this chapter is on the competitive viability of restricted product or territorial scope over time. The structure of the chapter is as follows:

- *restricted national market scope*
- *national market development over time*
- *sustainability of national strategies*
- *measuring competitive advantage*
- *inter-market comparisons*
- *benchmarking*

Emphasising the need to identify and assess key underlying trends in order to evaluate the sustainability of strategies employing restrictive geographical or product market scope, the chapter opens by raising generic issues of strategic scope over time and space. The success or otherwise of strategies of restricted national market scope requires business performance to be assessed in order to determine whether a competitive advantage has been developed and can be sustained. This in turn raises issues as to the appropriate measure of competitive advantage, in the context of what market it applies to and over whom. The limitations of only using national competitors as a basis of making such judgements results in the use of inter-market comparisons. Further, the importance of staying ahead of the competition argues for going outside a single industry and employing the techniques of benchmarking in order to achieve 'world class performance' of key processes. Finally, the chapter concludes with a summary and checklist. This is followed by a case study of Hotpoint which allows the reader to apply a number of the frameworks introduced in the chapter.

Restricted national market scope

Restricted national market scope is used to describe companies pursuing a strategy which is either national or sub-national in its market scope. The term applies to companies operating with a strategy which is focused on a single national market at most, and who do not seek to leverage (i) competences/ capabilities, and/or (ii) competitive interdependencies across different national markets. The critical issue to be examined is the long-term viability of companies operating with such a strategy. In short, what are the conditions for developing and sustaining a competitive advantage?

If restricted national market scope does provide the basis for a sustainable business strategy, then important implications follow. On the one hand, it means that companies which have achieved national dominance need not become overly concerned about developing an international presence. Quite simply, such companies are able to gain any product-market benefits or competitive interdependencies by operating on a national rather than international scale. Equally, international players competing across borders in the same market as indigenously owned national companies are at no advantage, as they are unable to achieve any greater resource leverage than that available to the domestically based competitor. These international companies are free to organise on the basis of having a series of autonomous national subsidiaries each operating to meet the needs of an individual national market, with little or no attempt to develop or exploit interdependencies or competences/capabilities across national markets.

If international competitors are able to leverage competences/capabilities and achieve greater resource leverage than that available to companies with a restricted national scope, then the latter will be forced to become international in their scope and seek to develop and exploit interdependencies. In such circumstances, if companies with restricted national market scope fail to develop

Figure 5.1 The phase model of international business development

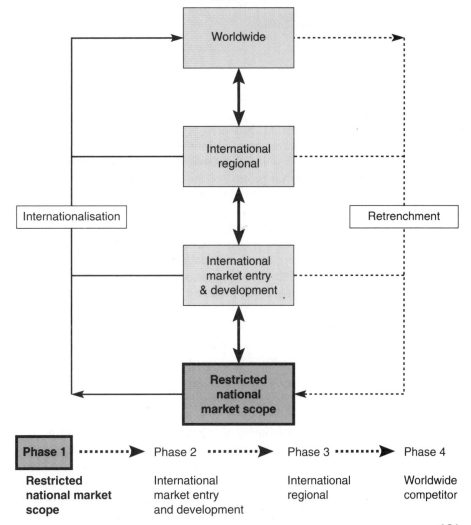

an international business strategy they will ultimately lose out to companies with a broader international outlook.

The current chapter seeks to explore the conditions under which a restricted national market strategy is sustainable, allowing organisations to remain at the first phase of international business development as shown by Figure 5.1.

In assessing whether organisations operating with a restricted national market scope have the basis of a sustainable competitive strategy, Figure 5.2 examines whether the current strategic posture of such organisations is stable or unstable. In making these assessments, the term *national scope* will be used to include the spectrum of local/national region/national market coverage.

Figure 5.2 International business development matrix

Internal context

		National	International
External context	National	Stable	Unstable
	International	Unstable	Stable

A national business strategy can be described as stable when both the external and internal contexts are supportive. Alternatively, national business strategies will be unstable when either the external context is unsupportive, or the internal context of the organisation is seeking to develop a more international focus. Under these circumstances the organisation will be facing pressures to reorientate itself and thereby move to a different phase of international business development.

In assessing issues of restricted strategic scope there is a need to consider both internal and external drivers, and how these collectively fashion the strategic imperatives. As assessment of these factors enables an organisation's current strategic posture to be assessed as well as the dynamics of the competitive environment. Exploring in further detail the external context (Chapter 3), the two necessary conditions for a national business strategy to prevail include:

(1) *product-market demand:* customer requirements in respect of the product are highly reflective of national tastes and preferences; and
(2) *competitive interdependence:* ability to supply the market competitively is not to be dependent on the need to supply other cross-border markets at the same time.

The internal context has been defined in Chapter 4 as including the relation between vision/mindset and organisational dynamics. Where both external and internal contexts are synchronised and in support of national scope, organisational strategy will be stable and focused on a restricted national market.

The first stage of business development, phase 1 in Figure 5.1, which describes national strategies can be sub-divided further as follows:

- *local:* strategic scope of the organisation is highly localised, usually based on a small local area;
- *national region:* scope includes a number of local markets, although coverage across the country is incomplete; and
- *national:* organisation seeks to cover the national market comprehensively.

The three categories of national scope – local, national region and national – form a continuum, encompassing organisations of all sizes and product-market coverage in respect of a single national market. Illustration 5.1 provides examples of (1) local, (2) national region and (3) national companies.

Illustration 5.1

(1) The local company (France)

The family-owned *boulangerie* is one of only two retail shops in the village of Chitnay, some 10 kilometres from the town of Blois in the Loire region of France. Such a small-scale family organisational unit typifies the 46,000 bread bakeries operating in France, where there is one bakery for every twelve hundred people. The structure of the industry has changed little over the last century, with local bakeries serving a very localised market. This is in marked contrast with other occidental countries, where consolidation has heralded the demise of the small bakery.

The French bread industry has resisted the call to replace local bakeries with a smaller number of larger regional bakeries, as has happened in many other countries. This is partly attributable to cultural differences in eating habits, where fresh bread is bought twice a day. It is reinforced by laws dating back to Napoleonic times which regulate opening hours, purity and price. Moreover, the bakers themselves try to resist all attempts by flour suppliers to deliver to a bakery outside the network of small bakeries.

Ultimately the position of the small local bakery will become less secure as new kinds of bread become accepted, with changes in the cultural habits promoted by large retailers who wish increase their market share of bread sales.

(2) The national region company (Nordwest Zeitung)

Local newspapers need to provide their readers with local news. Nordwest Zeitung is one of Germany's most successful newspaper groups. Formed in the aftermath of the Second World War, the strategic recipe from the outset was to tailor a common format to meet the special needs of local markets. Each main locality served by the newspaper has a front section exclusively devoted to news for the local community, while the other three sections are the same in all editions.

The zoning strategy encouraged further areal extension. A number of small local newspapers joined Nordwest Zeitung in a co-operative partnership. This enables Nordwest Zeitung to concentrate on the production and sale of the non-local sections of the paper to the partners, while the local partners focus on local

▶

news editing and distribution. Although some sections of Nordwest Zeitung marginally overlapped with other newspapers in the network, this has not been perceived to be a major problem because editors competed on the basis of the quality of the local content.

Nordwest Zeitung is also able to increase the overall size of advertising revenues. By acting as an advertising broker on behalf of all newspapers in the partnership, national/regional advertisers are able to choose the combination of publications in the partnership in which they wish to advertise. The network as a whole benefits from savings in overhead and direct costs in securing advertising revenues from agencies and customers who refuse to deal with small newspapers, while Nordwest Zeitung receives a mutually agreed commission for providing service to its partners.

(3) The national company (South African Breweries Limited)

South African Breweries Limited (SAB) holds a virtual monopoly position in the South African clear lager market. It is a significant player in a large market currently brewing 98 per cent of all the lager consumed in the domestic market, the 10th largest beer market in the world. SAB's net profits in the year to March 1994 reached 1.33 billion rand (£270 million) on sales of approximately 24 billion rand (£4800 million).

The national market for lager is effectively a series of regional markets, each served by a regional brewery. It is difficult to supply such a large market economically from a centralised production site, since savings on production costs tend to be overwhelmed by steeply rising transport costs associated with moving a low value bulky commodity over long distances. Instead an homogeneous national brand is supplied through a distribution network tied to regional breweries.

Sources: (1) Authors; (2) Ketelhohn (1993); (3) *The Economist*, 21 May 1994, pp 90–1

The size of national regions and national product-markets does show marked variation by individual nations. Comparing the UK and the USA, there are considerable differences in the geographical size, population and purchasing power of national regions and national markets. The terms should be interpreted with care and only used in relation to an individual market to describe a company's product-market scope relative to the national market. Indeed, in respect of very small countries local, national region and national markets may coalesce into one.

National market development over time

Within national markets the different categories identified in respect of strategic scope – local, national region and national – describe the three phases of business development. These are normally associated with individual companies becoming established and growing to the point that they emerge as national competitors. To understand the reasons and processes behind why companies change their local/national scope over time, three sets of questions need to be examined, namely:

- *Why* do companies, and often industries, move from being local to national over time?
- *What* are the implications for key business functions and processes?
- *How* do companies grow and develop over time?

The explanation of 'why' companies change their local/national strategies over time again focuses on the relationship between the external and internal context. Following the earlier line of discussion in relation to the international business development matrix, it is possible to derive a second matrix. This sub-divides phase 1 of a company's business development, enabling local, national region and national strategies to be delineated. Similarly, when the external and internal contexts are mutually supportive, there is no pressure for the strategic posture of the organisation to change. Alternatively, if the two are inconsistent the organisation is likely to change its strategic posture. Figure 5.3 illustrates the circumstances when a company's current strategy is likely to be unstable and subsequent changes to its scope occur.

Figure 5.3 Local/national strategy matrix

Internal context

		Local	National regional	National
External context	Local	Stable	Unstable	Unstable
	National regional	Unstable	Stable	Unstable
	National	Unstable	Unstable	Stable

Reviewing both the external and internal contexts, the key factors encouraging a movement away from local to national region and national strategies revolve around:

- *External*
  - product-market demand: greater homogeneity in customer tastes and preferences, e.g. branding – the acceptance of national brands rather than purely local ones;
  - competitive interdependence: the ability to supply local markets more competitively through becoming a national supplier, e.g. the ability to realise national economies of scale and scope and to pass these on to customers in the form of lower prices and/or improved quality.

185

● *Internal*
  – innovative vision/mindset of key internal managers, which when combined with succession events may result in a dramatic change to the organisation's strategic intent;
  – development of knowledge, competences/capabilities which the organisation finds it is able to exploit beyond its current market scope.

In the development of national markets, national regions offer an intermediate stage, although as Figure 5.3 implies, some industries do not progress beyond the point where companies are competitive with either a local or national regional strategy. Illustration 5.1, for example, has emphasised this point by discussing both the French bread industry and Nordwest Zeitung. Care should be taken when considering any firm or industry examples to the extent they may well be time specific, with the underlying dynamics of the competitive environment subsequently resulting in a new phase of business development.

The nature of the relationship between internal and external triggers for change is shown in Figure 5.4. It is important to remember that, while the external or internal context can trigger instability in a company's current strategic posture, unless ultimately both contexts are supportive either the change will not occur, or it will subsequently not be sustainable.

Figure 5.4 *Internal and external triggers to a discontinuity in business development*

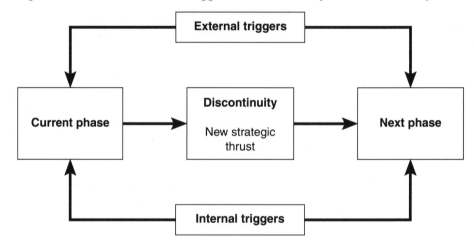

Extending an organisation's business scope from local to national region and then to national is likely to offer significant business challenges, reflecting the need to manage important discontinuities in key business functions and management processes. Traditional ways of dealing with key business functions may no longer be appropriate and new solutions must be found. Equally, the scale and scope of managerial needs will change, often requiring the managerial resources to be increased and reshaped. The specific needs will vary according to a number of factors, including the characteristics of the company, the nature of the product and the size of the product-market in which it is competing. Table 5.1 seeks to identify the broad areas of change as a firm and the industry of which it is part moves from a local to a national orientation.

Table 5.1 Key business discontinuities associated with the emergence of an industry dominated by companies operating with national strategies

Characteristic	Local strategy strategy	National regional	National strategy
Market coverage	Local	National region	National
Products	Local products or brands	Regional products or brands	National brands
Marketing	Likely to be relatively unsophisticated	May become increasingly important	For fast moving consumer goods (FMCG) may be highly developed
Human resources	Number of employees likely to be small	Depending on nature of business, number of employees may grow significantly	Likely to become an increasingly important area as the number of employees increases
Operations	Can be very simple, especially in relation to some service sectors	May lead to additional outlets or production facilities being established	Co-ordination and management needs can be expected to increase
Logistics	Relatively uncomplicated	Importance likely to increase	Increasing scale and scope are likely to result in increasing complexity
Finance	Capital requirement likely to be relatively low	Increasing capital requirement to fund working capital and/or increasing fixed asset base	Capital requirement to grow business into national player may be substantial
Number of competitors/ industry concentration	Many; fragmented industry	Number of competitors is reducing and industry has become more concentrated	Few; industry is concentrated

The question arises as to how companies move from having a local strategy to operating with a national strategy. Broadly speaking, companies may use one or both of two routes, namely internal (or organic) growth or external growth (acquisition). Illustration 5.2 compares and contrasts the benefits of internal or external growth. It should be noted that the industry context in some circumstances, notably in the case of an already mature market, means that companies seeking to establish a national presence may find organic growth difficult to achieve, as additional sales can only be made at the expense of existing competitors. It may be difficult to do this, or to satisfy the speed of development envisaged by the organisation. In such circumstances, external growth, despite its greater risks, may be more attractive than organic growth.

It should not be thought that the underlying dynamics of an industry always dictate that companies must compete on a national basis. There are a

Illustration 5.2

Internal growth

Context

Likely to be an option available to management when an industry is still growing, allowing new companies to enter the market, or where the industry is fragmented and not dominated by large companies.

Resource requirements

Organic growth requires the company to develop its own resource base. This can be a particular problem if the company is seeking to expand rapidly and/or resources are difficult to obtain. A key question is whether the company has appropriate managerial and financial resources to execute the strategy successfully.

Relative benefits and disadvantages

Strategy allows the company to pursue incremental growth and to learn from 'doing'. Risk is correspondingly easier to manage, and there is the option for the company to abandon the strategy before too many resources have been committed, and the decision is irreversible. A major disadvantage is that the speed of development may be slow, with initially low levels of market penetration. It can require many years before a company builds a significant presence in a new product or geographical market by using a strategy of organic growth.

External growth

Context

An attractive option to management wishing to enter a mature market which is already highly concentrated and dominated by a small number of sellers.

Resource requirements

By using external growth the acquirer is purchasing an established operation. The purchase of a new business brings no guarantees of the quality of the resources purchased. The purchased company may be highly successful with good quality management; alternatively, the acquired company may require drastic action to make the business viable. In the latter case, does the acquiring company have the necessary management and financial resources to do this?

Relative benefits and disadvantages

External growth provides the acquiring company with an immediate presence in the market. This benefit of speed is counterbalanced by risk. Once entered into acquisitions are not easily reversed, and certainly not without cost. Post-acquisition management is crucial if an acquired company is to be integrated successfully with an existing organisation.

Source: The authors

number of cases where the emergence of national players ultimately leaves gaps in the market for smaller companies to exploit. Perhaps one of the best examples to be found is the establishment of microbreweries in the USA, which is discussed in Illustration 5.3.

Illustration 5.3

US microbreweries

By the early 1980s American beers had gained the reputation of being dull and uninteresting. Almost without exception the beers were produced by major national producers. These companies produced a 'lager' type beer which was almost indistinguishable in taste from other competing products.

Against this background of virtually homogeneous products there began to emerge the so-called microbreweries. These were small local breweries aiming to produce uniquely flavoured products. By the early 1990s some 400 breweries were producing a variety of local beers in competition with the products traditionally made by the large companies. The products of the microbreweries were aimed at a particular market niche – customers seeking a distinctive-tasting beer – which had been virtually ignored by the large breweries in seeking to produce a product with as wide a customer appeal as possible. Although the market share of the microbreweries was small, in the region of 1 per cent, the larger breweries were concerned enough by the threat to start producing distinctive beers of their own alongside their traditional products.

Source: Based on *Financial Times*, 23 September 1993, p 13

The case of the US microbreweries illustrates that once a national industry has become concentrated opportunities may subsequently emerge for new entry to the market. Certainly, the emergence of the microbrewers emphasises the opportunities afforded where there is latent demand which has been overlooked or left unexploited by the industry incumbents.

How companies develop a local or national scope needs to be examined on a case by case basis to understand fully the richness of the individual business histories. Illustration 5.4 (overleaf) provides insights into how two food retailing companies, one in the UK and the other in the USA, have developed national strategies at a time when the industry is becoming increasingly concentrated.

The essential point to this discussion is that the industry dynamics need to be examined on a case by case basis to understand the underlying trends and the likely speed of any change. Nevertheless, four general observations can be made:

(1) Even where an industry progresses from a local to national and ultimately international focus, the speed of development between industries tends to show marked variations, with some industries progressing quickly and others more slowly.

Illustration 5.4

J Sainsbury plc and Wal-Mart Inc – Food retailing in the UK and USA

J Sainsbury plc and Wal-Mart Stores Inc are two of the largest food retailers in the UK and the USA respectively. Sainsbury's initial focus was on London and its surrounding metropolitan area. Subsequent expansion away from its original base was focused predominately on the southern counties of England. More recently the company has extended further its geographical coverage to some of the more peripheral regions of the UK, e.g. far South West, North East/Scotland, as it has pursued its ambition to become a truly national player. While the company's expansion from a local to a national player was based on organic growth, this process has contributed to an increasing concentration of the industry over the last 20 years as these large food superstores replaced local and regional retailers.

Similarly, Wal-Mart Stores Inc, US discount retailer, opened its first store in the Rogers, Arkansas in 1962. Between 1962 and 1974 the company established itself in Arkansas and adjacent states. More recently, during the years 1975–84 the company began to compete on a broader regional basis, using both organic and external growth to further its expansion plans. Since 1985, the company has pursued expansion plans to serve all areas of the United States. More recently Wal-Mart has broadened its product range include fresh food, in an attempt to become a cut-price full service supermarket.

Although the geographical size and scale of the UK and US markets are noticeably different, both Sainsbury's and Wal-Mart have moved towards operating national strategies over similar periods. In both instances external and internal factors have been responsible for the growth and development of each company. The two companies, Wal-Mart Stores and J Sainsbury, provide illustrations of organisations expanding when both the external context allowed and the internal context provided the vision and drive. In each case strong chief executives played important roles in the expansion: Sam Walton, the founder and long-standing chief executive at Wal-Mart, and Sir John Sainsbury, the chairman of the family-run company for much of its period of rapid growth.

Despite the similarities between the two companies, there are also important differences in their locational patterns and process. J Sainsbury provides a good example of a company which decided to pursue international expansion before it had exhausted its market opportunity within the UK. In 1983 Sainsbury's initially acquired a minority equity stake in Shaw's, a chain of supermarkets based in Massachusetts, USA. Following the purchase of an equity stake in the company, Sainsbury's acquired full control in 1987. Indeed, following the entry of international competitors into the British food retail market in the early 1990s, the company announced in 1994 that its further investment spending was to be more strongly focused on the USA, in order to achieve higher returns on the capital employed. By contrast, Wal-Mart formed a strategic alliance with Ito-Yokado to supply the company's own brands to the Japanese market.

This contrast between J Sainsbury and Wal-Mart raises an interesting question, which is at what stage of development does the company seek to become international, if at all? Does it wait until the home market offers few further growth opportunities, or does it seek to become international at a much earlier stage?

Leaving the development of a cross-border presence until the home market becomes saturated has attendant risks, notably that the time available to undertake incremental development and 'learn from doing' is reduced. Interestingly, J Sainsbury took a minority stake in Shaw's before purchasing the company outright, while Wal-Mart entered the Japanese market through a joint venture. The timing of both companies' cross-border moves has differed, but the strategies chosen in each case have initially limited the degree of risk and enabled the company to assess alternative cultures and business practices.

Source: The authors

(2) The process by which firms and their industry competitors progress from one stage of development to another can be attributable to both external and internal factors.

(3) As firms move from one stage of development to another the configuration and management of key business functions is likely to require marked change.

(4) The movement into cross-border markets may be triggered by both 'push' and 'pull' factors, suggesting that international market entry cannot be presumed to arise solely from a firm's reaction to the increasing saturation of its national market.

Sustainability of national strategies

In order to assess the sustainability of a national strategy, it is important to move beyond the present position and consider the underlying dynamic of the market in which the firm is competing. The future ability of firms with a national strategy to sustain their competitive position is dependent upon the existence of forces which reduce the necessity to be international and emphasise the advantages of localisation. The commonly accepted view is that the forces for change move from localisation to globalisation, do so only once, and then in the predictable direction of globalisation. What is often overlooked is that the underlying industry dynamics are just as likely in some circumstances to move competitive imperatives back to a much more local focus. Market convergence or divergence cannot be taken for granted, and to this end it is helpful to re-examine the idea of the pendulum introduced in Chapter 3 and reproduced in Figure 5.5.

As Figure 5.5 illustrates, if industry drivers are moving towards localisation then local/national strategies are likely to remain sustainable. Alternatively, if the dynamics of the industry are moving towards globalisation, the pursuit of a national strategy becomes more difficult. These observations mean that the industry drivers identified in Chapter 3 need to be revisited and assessed in the context of firm-specific strategies. The four principal industry drivers are:

- customers
- cost
- country
- competitors

Figure 5.5 The pendulum of change: convergence versus divergence

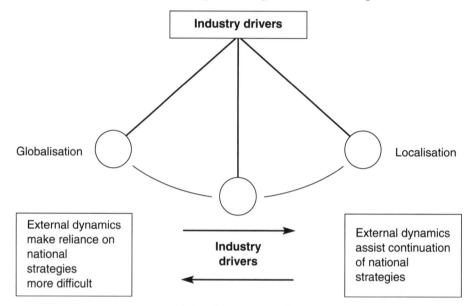

Each of these factors can be subdivided further to aid overall assessment. It is important to evaluate the extent to which each factor is driving the industry towards globalisation or localisation, as well as making an overall assessment. In seeking to undertake this task Figure 5.6 identifies the key elements of each of the four principal industry drivers and offers a framework for making an individual and overall assessment of the balance of external forces.

In applying the framework described by Figure 5.6 to evaluate past and future industry trends it may be helpful to assess the direction and strength of the drivers at different points in time. By such means it is often easier to understand how individual forces may have changed, or are likely to change, over time.

To make an overall assessment of the direction and strength of external forces, it is possible to group the individual industry drivers under two headings, namely:

- *product-market demand:* is the nature of product demand specific to the local/national market or are tastes and preferences sufficiently homogeneous for a number of markets to be treated as a single entity? In other words is the variety of customer demands across markets increasing or decreasing?
- *competitive interdependence:* are there significant cost benefits from supplying more than one market, enabling the cost of supplying any one market to be reduced? Equally, is the use of flexible manufacturing systems (FMS) and/or strategic alliances enabling a local/national supplier

to gain the same benefits in terms of costs that a pan-national producer is able to achieve?

Figure 5.6 The framework for identifying and assessing external industry drivers

Globalisation				Localisation		
High	Med	Low	**Industry drivers**	Low	Med	High
			Customer drivers			
			Customer requirements			
			Distribution			
			Marketing			
			Cost drivers			
			New product development			
			Scale economies			
			Transport costs			
			Country drivers			
			Trade policies			
			Technical standards			
			Cultural/regulatory barriers			
			Competitive drivers			
			Competitive interdependence			
			Entry of new competitors			

			Overall			

In assessing the external forces there is a risk that internal forces are ignored, or considered secondary. It is important in this context to restate the importance of internal forces. All too frequently it is the vision/mindset and organisational dynamics of one company which are instrumental in shaping forces at the industry level. The installation of a new management team with the vision of transforming a company, and subsequently the industry of which it is part, may result in fundamental changes to the competitive process. To incorporate a change of this nature into the framework presented in Figure 5.6 it is important to recognise that change for the individual firm arises out of its internal context (i.e. endogenous), but for all other firms in the industry the change is external (i.e. exogenous).

If there are significant benefits to be gained from pursuing an international strategy, the expectation is that once one competitor has moved in this direction then others will follow. Equally, if the pursuit of an international strategy is not sufficiently superior to the use of national strategies, as Saatchi and Saatchi found in trying to become a worldwide consulting company in the

1980s, then the company seeking to operate with this international scope will be forced to retrench at some stage.

The constantly changing nature of industry often means that at any one point there will be a range of companies pursuing a mix of strategies. Some may be in the process of becoming international players, while others remain focused firmly on the national market. This outcome is likely to occur when the forces between localisation and globalisation are finely balanced. In circumstances where there no over-riding forces pushing in one direction or another, it is quite feasible for an industry to be characterised by different companies using a mix of national and international strategies. Such a combination will remain only as long as the underlying dynamics of the industry are not pushing in one direction or the other. Illustration 5.5 explores some of the ambiguities about which strategic recipe will prevail in the European domestic electrical appliance industry, which is the subject of the case study at the end of this chapter.

Illustration 5.5

The European domestic electrical appliances industry

The European domestic electrical appliances (DEA) industry has experienced marked changes in the balance between forces of globalisation and localisation. Initially, going back to the 1960s, the industry in Europe was dominated by national players. These were independently owned or autonomous subsidiaries of larger groups. Each of these companies supplied products which were focused on the needs of a principal national market. For those companies which were the subsidiaries of larger groups little or no attempt was made to exploit the interdependencies in marketing or production between individual national markets.

During the 1970s and 1980s the industry experienced a period of consolidation and the emergence of a number of large competitors, including Electrolux. These companies attempted to use pan-national strategies in order to achieve a competitive advantage over the remaining national players. Practical difficulties surrounding commonality of parts and management of the supply chain meant that the anticipated advantages of scale were not necessarily achieved. As a result some national players were able to deliver superior performance by continuing to operate with a deliberately restricted market scope.

More recently, the ambitious expansion plans of some companies, notably Whirlpool, are reopening the question of whether companies need to be international in order to maintain a profitable market position in the industry. By harnessing new lean production techniques and pan-European logistics systems, some observers believe that Whirlpool may achieve the necessary resource leverage to gain a competitive advantage over the remaining national players.

At present the situation is confused, with different companies pursuing alternative business strategies. Some competitors are operating with a restrictive market scope, while others are attempting to develop a pan-national presence. It is an open question as to which strategy will win through in the end.

Source: The authors

Illustration 5.5 shows that ambiguity commonly surrounds the forces of globalisation and localisation, thereby requiring considerable judgement to be exercised in an overall assessment of industry dynamics. It is not always clear whether market convergence or divergence will take place, so that alternative strategies may co-exist in such circumstances. It is only where the dynamics are overwhelmingly at one end of the continuum that there is likely to be a clear set of outcomes. Even so, a major discontinuity may reverse the apparently emerging market dynamics. Unless and until this occurs, where the dynamics of the industry are unrelenting, the presence of a mixed economy of alternative strategies can only exist while underlying forces exert themselves.

Measuring competitive advantage

The judgement of whether a company's strategy of pursuing a restrictive market scope is able to sustain its current business posture is a question of whether it has achieved and can maintain a competitive advantage. If the company can do this it will have been able to demonstrate a propensity to organise and marshall its resources in such a way as to manage the imperatives of its external environment, including being able to match and surpass the performance of its competitors. This point emphasises that competitive advantage is a relative rather than absolute term, and one which has to be measured in relation to other companies.

In seeking to assess whether a company has a competitive advantage three key questions have to be addressed, namely:

- *how* is competitive advantage to be measured?
- *in what market* does the competitive advantage exist?
- *over whom* does the company have a competitive advantage?

Each question is fundamental to assessing whether a company has achieved and is likely to sustain its competitive advantage.

How is competitive advantage measured?

As competitive advantage is about achieving and sustaining superior business performance, it will be reflected in terms of either financial outcomes and/or the balanced scorecard (Chapter 2). The latter information set may not be in the public domain, so that external measurement of competitive advantage tends to be related to financial performance in some way. Within a national context, provided that all competitors are under a legal obligation to disclose their financial performance it is possible to assess this complex area.

Ellis and Williams (1993) provide a practical link between corporate and business strategies with financial analysis in a UK context, showing how companies with a competitive advantage will achieve a correspondingly greater level of operating profit and associated cash generation.

Deciding on appropriate measures of financial performance is an art rather than a science, with considerable judgement being required. All measures

195

require critical interpretation, with return on capital employed (ROCE) being one of the most frequently considered financial indicators. Illustration 5.6 outlines both the strengths and weaknesses of this performance measure, as well as showing how it can give practical insights into a firm's operating performance. If a company has a competitive advantage this should normally be reflected in its reported financial performance.

In what market does the competitive advantage exist?

The second task in assessing whether a company has a company advantage is to determine the product-market(s) in which it is competing. Experience from earlier analysis of the world airlines industry (Chapter 3) has demonstrated the critical importance attached to boundary definitions. This is not a technical issue of little importance, but a strategic imperative of the highest order. It is only by identifying the principal customers the firm is seeking to serve that realistic product-market boundaries can be drawn. Illustration 5.7 considers this point in relation to two companies in different segments of the food retailing industry in the UK, and shows how markedly different positioning strategies result in contrasting ROCE performance.

Over whom does the company have a competitive advantage?

By definition competitive advantage is a relative rather than absolute term, so that it is important to measure the performance of one company against another. Once the market(s) in which a company is operating have been defined, then there is a need to define competitors against which comparisons can be made. Where a market is dominated by national players, the temptation is to measure whether a company has a competitive advantage over companies employing local, national region or national strategies within the market. Such a myopic viewpoint can prove to be dangerous, if the barriers to competition between national territories are declining.

In these circumstances it is insufficient to measure a company's performance only against other national players. Rather, if the basis of competitive advantage is to be robust, comparisons must be made with competitors in other national markets, who may at some stage seek entry to the national market. Continuing the analysis of food retailing in the UK, Illustration 5.8 provides a good example of how being reliant on making national comparisons can be misleading.

To conclude, companies need to recognise that where the barriers to international competition are declining, as they are for many industries, they can only be confident in claiming a sustainable competitive advantage if they measure themselves against actual and potential international competitors. In such circumstances simple comparisons against national competitors are fundamentally flawed. Even if a competitive advantage currently exists in a particular market, it is important to determine that a national competitor is able to sustain its superior performance in the future

Illustration 5.6

Calculating return on capital employed (ROCE)

Return on capital employed (ROCE) is taken as an overall measure of business performance. As a financial ratio it measures the amount of trading profit a company is generating in relation to its capital employed. A higher ROCE suggests that a company is using its assets more effectively and efficiently, so that *normally* the higher the ROCE the better.

ROCE is calculated by combining two other financial ratios: net profit margin and asset turnover. Details of how these ratios are calculated are shown below:

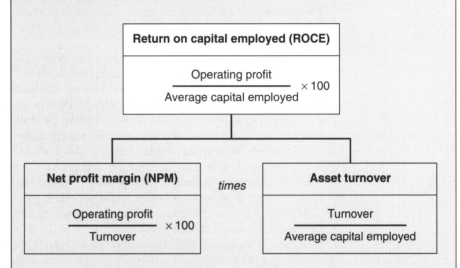

In making inter-company comparisons, how reliable and robust is ROCE as a measure of performance? In practice there are a number of potential weaknesses to using ROCE. The first point is that profit is subjective to the extent that accounting policies influence the reported figure. While this is less of a difficulty when comparing one company's performance over time, providing accounting policies have not been changed, it becomes more problematic when making inter-company comparisons.

Secondly, the amount of capital employed is based on historic values. A company which has recently replaced its capital equipment will have a higher amount of capital employed than one whose assets were acquired some time ago. Unless the profit margin more than offsets the larger denominator, the second company's ROCE will be higher, even though its capital assets may be close to becoming worn-out. In these and other circumstances ROCE can offer a misleading picture of performance. These points emphasise the need to check a company's report and accounts carefully to ensure that accounting policies are broadly similar, and the company's asset base has been regularly replaced. These and associated difficulties surrounding financial performance indicators are responsible for the growing interest in the balanced scorecard measures of competitive advantage.

Source: The authors

Illustration 5.7

J Sainsbury plc and Kwik Save plc

Both J Sainsbury and Kwik Save operate food retailing chains in the UK. Both companies consider that their principal business activities relate to food retailing. The market positioning and the strategies adopted by the two companies are markedly different.

J Sainsbury operates predominantly out-of-town food superstores costing sometimes in excess of £25 million per store to develop. Each store is expensively fitted out, and the store layout is considered an important aspect of the company's differentiated retail strategy. The company sells leading manufacturers' products and a high proportion of own-brand products of good quality. As a result of its perceived quality and good operating efficiencies, the company is able to achieve a high net profit margin.

By contrast, Kwik Save is a food discounter, selling predominantly manufacturers' brands on the basis of highly competitive prices. Its stores are smaller than those operated by J Sainsbury and only contain basic fixtures and fittings. Whereas Sainsbury's spends upwards of £25 million on developing a new store, Kwik Save's investment in a new store is likely to be in the region of £1 million, with property being rented and not owned by the company.

Sainsbury's seek to appeal to a broad spectrum of customers, including above-average income groups, offering a wide product range and combining elements of differentiation and low cost in its business strategy. By contrast, Kwik Save offers a predominantly low cost strategy focused on a limited product range.

Although there are differences in each company's customer base there is also a degree of overlap and shoppers can, and in some cases do, change their loyalties in favour of one company's rival. The two companies' principal activities are sufficiently similar to enable a comparison to be made along the lines suggested in Illustration 5.6.

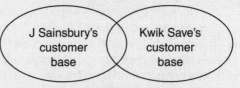

Food retailing industry

Comparing each company's financial performance is revealing. While its net profit margins are well below those of Sainsbury's, the lower level of capital employed means that Kwik Save's asset turnover is twice as high as that of its rival. Indeed, Kwik Save's ROCE is the highest of all companies operating in the UK food retailing sector.

	NPM	Asset turnover	ROCE
J Sainsbury (1991)	7.63	2.03	15.5
Kwik Save (1991)	5.51	4.11	22.6

Source: The authors and company reports

Illustration 5.8

UK food retailing

During the 1980s the leading food retailers in the UK enjoyed an unparalleled period of expansion and profitability. With rising consumer expenditure for much of the period and increasing competitive interdependencies, a number of companies, including J Sainsbury and Kwik Save, grew out from their national regions to become national players. While some industry observers feared saturation of the market, such concerns were dismissed as being premature by others who focused on the sector's proven ability to deliver above average performance.

The reality of the 1990s has provided a rude awakening for the national players. Not only did economic recession depress consumer expenditure, but the entry of foreign-owned retailers into the UK market added further pressure on the profit margins of the indigenous retailers. This resulted in a marked fall in ROCE. Food retailing in the UK, for so long seen as the preserve of national champions, suddenly, and for many unexpectedly, become an international industry.

Source: The authors

Inter-market comparisons

Competitive analysis is a particularly powerful tool when used within industries across national boundaries. Collecting data for the purposes of inter-market comparisons raises many issues not faced in a national setting (Ellis and Williams, 1993). Problems arise across the world where the fragmentation of language, systems and cultures makes for a wide divergence in how information is collected and presented. Differences in national accounting frameworks (Chapter 2), and the extent of disclosure in particular, cause problems when making comparisons.

Provided that these difficulties can be overcome, and in practice this is not easy, it is possible to advance the process of making inter-market comparisons. Alternatively, once again the balanced scorecard (Chapter 1) may offer a way forward. Comparisons between different markets offer the prospect of three areas of benefit, namely:

- assessment of the variations in financial performance between national markets and the prospect of market entry from international competitors;
- consideration of the extent to which trends evident in one market may ultimately affect or be applied to another market; and
- the evaluation of the extent to which the industry is internationalising, and the opportunity of national players to seek to position themselves accordingly.

*Variations in
financial
performance*

Although the relative lack of accounting harmonisation makes comparisons difficult and emphasises the need to handle numbers with care, inter-market comparisons can be revealing. This is particularly the case if any financial figures are treated as indicative and used as a first filter to see whether in general terms the market may be attractive to cross-border entry. Certainly, if the differences in financial outcomes are significant, and these cannot be explained by the variations in accounting frameworks, entry to a cross-border market is likely to merit further consideration. Illustration 5.9 provides comparative data on retail food margins in Germany and the UK, with the comparison suggesting why it was inadvisable for British retailers to look simply to national competitors in determining whether they had achieved competitive advantage.

Illustration 5.9

Retail food margins

In the early 1990s a considerable amount of work was carried out looking at the comparative food costs faced by customers in Germany and the UK. Research by KPMG Management Consulting found that a sample basket of supermarket groceries cost 12 per cent more before tax in the UK than in Germany. The sample basket contained 11 products, ranging from staple foodstuffs to higher value processed foods. The UK supermarket basket cost £26.36, while the German equivalent was £23.53. The division between retailer margin and manufacturers' selling price in each country was as follows:

	Germany	UK
Manufacturers' selling price	18.96 (80.6%)	19.17 (72.7%)
Retailers' margin	4.57 (19.4%)	7.19 (27.3%)
Total cost of shopping basket	23.53 (100.0%)	26.36 (100.0%)

In absolute terms the German retailers' margin is almost half that of its UK counterpart: £4.57 (19.4 per cent) as compared with £7.19 (27.3 per cent). This comparative analysis also destroyed the view that food costs in Britain were among the lowest in Europe and questioned whether UK food retailers had a competitive advantage when compared to German retailers.

Source: Based on 'Retail margins on food higher than in Germany', *Financial Times*, 10 May 1991

Market trends   While markets retain some degree of separation, there is the opportunity for cross-fertilisation between developments in one national market and another. Trends may emerge first in one market, but subsequently develop in many others. The USA, owing to its high level of GNP, can offer an indication for many product-markets of what might subsequently happen. This environmental sensing tends to be one of the significant advantages enjoyed by the international competitor. While developments in one market do not always 'cross over' into another market, it is important to keep a watching brief and to be able to respond accordingly. Similarly, business or product/service innovations introduced in one market can be readily cascaded, with or without modification, to other markets.

In a contestable market, where it is easy for firms to enter or exit, assessment of competitive advantage may be undertaken by firms not currently operating in the national market. Even where restricted national scope is an explicit choice made on the basis of an informed judgement, the ever present threat of entry from outside the market argues for constant vigilance. Illustration 5.10 demonstrates how entry can have a far-reaching impact on the strategies and performance of existing competitors. It also suggests that existing competitors need to have a clear view as to how their national strategy is to be defended, if they wish to continue to operate with their existing scope.

International-isation   By focusing on the current and past performance of competitors, inter-market comparisons may fail to identify potential changes such as those, depicted in Illustration 5.10. Inter-market comparisons measure what competitors have achieved rather than what could be achieved. Essentially they adopt a 'same game strategy process', in effect focusing on matching highest national market performance, often bringing at best incremental advantage, rather than stimulating new game thinking to surpass dramatically competitors' capabilities. There is a danger that management is encouraged to 'fight the last war' – developing the ability to match competitors as they compete today – rather than construct a competitive base for the future.

In this context the strategies of companies in other national markets, who may not currently be direct competitors, should be kept under review. This will enable such companies to be monitored to see whether they may subsequently become a threat, to the extent that they begin to change the basis on which the industry competes by developing international strategies which place at risk companies who continue to operate with a restricted national scope.

Illustration 5.10

UK food retailing under American 'entry' threat

A wave of American retailers with ambitious expansion plans is poised to enter the UK market, with implications for both the strategies and performance of existing retailers. This threatened retail attack is prompted by both push and pull factors. In part, this is attributable to fierce competition in the US market. Equally, the high retail margins in the UK look very attractive to outsiders. In short, there is a growing realisation that the time is ripe for an infusion of US price led, value for money, 'power' retailing.

Imminent entrants include K-Mart and Wal-Mart, the two biggest retailers in the US, who base their success on aggressive discounting. Both are widely believed to be undertaking feasibility studies for new warehouse club and discounting ventures. The entry of these retailers would follow in the wake of the opening in 1993 by another American company, Costco, of its first warehouse. Costco's entry broadened the already expanding discount market for food retailing which, following the entry of other cross-border competitors, namely Netto (Denmark) and Aldi (Germany), now accounts for some 10 per cent of total UK sales. In the face of this new entry competition, many existing competitors are having to operate with lower prices with far-reaching consequences to their former strategies of developing more expensive up-market stores.

Additional new entrants may well bring retail prices down further, and act as a catalyst to reshaping the industry. Already small to medium-sized supermarkets are being squeezed because they are unable either to offer the range found in the large outlets or match the low prices of existing discounters. Similarly, some of the weaker UK chains are finding the new competitive environment difficult. Undoubtedly any large-scale entry by US retailers will lead to casualties, with the main UK grocery chains not immune to such threats. Indeed, new restrictive planning agreements make it highly likely that further American entrants will use acquisition as the means of entry.

Source: The authors and *The Independent*, 31 January 1994

Whether from an outsider 'looking in' or an insider 'looking out' perspective, inter-market comparisons are particularly instructive in three ways, namely:

- *Vision shaping:* moving away from a parochial perspective to embrace wider issues and trends discernible from areal variations. To a large extent many companies find looking beyond their immediate market scope a major psychological barrier. This point becomes all the more powerful when it is recognised that numerically the majority of companies in virtually every economy tend to operate at the national or sub-national level.
- *Geographical and product scope:* highlight attractiveness of particular national markets (e.g. UK food retailing) and identify customer attitudes to product-market developments (e.g. emergence of greater price consciousness worldwide and threat to established brands in fast moving consumer goods industries in the mid-1990s).
- *Defendability of national territory:* restricted scope should be an explicit choice made on an informed basis, with views as to how national strategy (or sub-national strategy) can be defended.

Benchmarking

Benchmarking is a continuous search for and application of significantly better practices that lead to superior business performance. It has three key elements, namely:

- the identification and selection of world class performance in respect of key business areas/functions;
- an assessment of the processes which have generated the world class performance; and
- the task of seeking to apply such processes to the organisation itself.

The benchmarking process starts with competitive analysis to quantify performance gaps, but then proceeds to look beyond performance measures to provide a deep understanding of the processes and skills that give leading firms their competitive edge. The benchmarking process is a way of involving the organisation in looking at best practices outside the firm to determine both what is possible and how it is done. In its approach benchmarking can be related to the concept of the balanced scorecard to the extent that it seeks to identify the direct drivers of business performance, rather than to use financial outcomes as proxy.

Firms are enthusiastically embracing benchmarking as a means of continuously learning about process improvements that can be applied to their own organisation. Viewed in this way, the purpose of benchmarking is both to learn and to improve. By restricting studies solely to competitors the firm can at best hope to achieve competitive parity. Illustration 5.11 shows that to achieve competitive superiority benchmarking should not be limited to like organisations, since the purpose of the approach is to expose managers to new and superior ways about how to design and order their own processes. To this extent the process can be linked to the concept of double loop learning (Chapter 4) and help organisations to become more self-critical and develop as learning organisations.

The value of benchmarking lies in adapting business process improvements and best practices of organisations with process excellence. By undertaking such a systematic and continuous measurement process, the following advantages may accrue:

- *Stretch:* wide performance gaps occur within and across industries. Even among better performers within an industry, large functional and cross-functional performance gaps exist compared with best-in-class companies. The benchmarking process ensures that performance targets are set high enough to be stretching yet attainable.
- *Commitment:* through active participation in visits to other organisations' premises, managers can see superior operational practice at first hand and can convince themselves that the benchmarks which other companies achieve are valid and comparable.
- *Accountability:* comparison over time measures the rate at which continuous improvement is being achieved and is a powerful motivator for ensuring

Illustration 5.11

Xerox: Benchmarking as an operating philosophy

The current enthusiasm for benchmarking is generally credited to Xerox, which throughout the 1980s used the technique as a rigorous test of its strategy to confront and overcome the Japanese challenge to its dominance in the worldwide copier market. This broad-based counter-attack contained a new philosophy for quality and organisational effectiveness, as well as the goal of renewal through searching out whatever operational processes, practices and methods worked well and adopting them to the copier business. Xerox was among the first to appreciate that benchmarking could be applied to a wide range of processes. Earlier applications had restricted the analysis solely to manufacturing activity, with a preoccupation for measuring the performance gap with Japanese challengers. Xerox pioneered training and development programmes to ensure all employees knew about benchmarking and how it could enable competitive renewal. Moreover, Xerox was among the earliest adherents to recognise that benchmarking studies are free to search out excellent performance in an analogous process wherever it is found.

The most notable benchmarking activity outside of the industry involving involved sharing information with L.L. Bean, a household name in the American outdoor leisure business. Initial research uncovered that key functions performed in L.L. Bean's warehouse were similar to those undertaken by Xerox, in that the stock-picking and order-fulfilment process did not lend itself to expensive and automated handling systems. By observing at first hand how very basic handling processes were thought out and implemented, Xerox noted that L.L. Bean's productivity was three times higher than its own warehouse.

By transferring the data and findings to Xerox's warehouse and distribution system, significant improvements in operational performance were achieved. As a result of this and other benchmarking exercises throughout the organisation, the technique assisted Xerox to regain its leadership position in the copier business.

Source: Watson (1993)

the improvement. It can help to build commitment to gain knowledge about excellent performance in a comparable process.

● *change management:* an environment striving for excellence is established where change is expected and rewarded. Continuous performance improvement by adopting an outward-looking perspective to provide proven processes, practices and method to affect change. In this way organisational learning takes place.

Benchmarking becomes a rigorous part of the strategy process for many firms since it can be seen to assist in determining the root cause of the performance gap identified through comparative analysis. Benchmarking establishes how much a firm needs to improve in order to meet and surpass analogous processes in firms which perform them with outstanding results. Figure 5.7 shows that the benchmarking process involves seven steps:

Figure 5.7 The benchmarking process

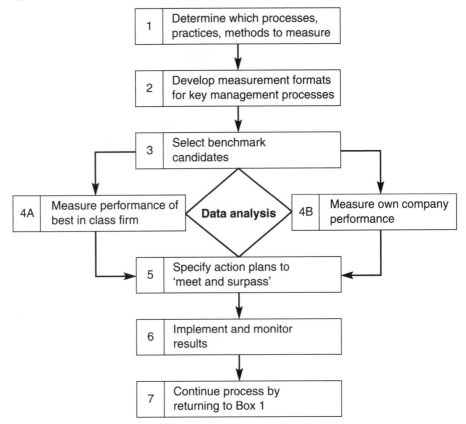

- *Step 1:* Focus should be on those core process issues that influence external customers' perception of the firm. These include purchasing, product/ process design, logistics/marketing, people management and the use of supporting procedures and systems.
- *Step 2:* Designing appropriate measures for selected key processes can be problematic. A trade-off may be necessary between what is feasible and what is desirable, with surrogate measures adopted.
- *Step 3:* Benchmarking should examine excellent performance in a directly comparable process, irrespective of the industry context in which it is found. It should not be restricted to direct competitors.
- *Step 4:* The magnitude of the performance gap is identified by comparing in detail the differential between how processes are performed in best-in-class firms with the benchmarking firm's performance.
- *Step 5:* The purpose of this step is to drive selected process improvements throughout the firm by applying the knowledge learnt as a result of the benchmarking activity. It is this search for excellence that creates the need for managed change.
- *Step 6:* Monitoring to ensure that a significant leap, as opposed to small incremental changes, is the outcome of doing things in a radically different way.

- *Step 7:* Identify opportunities for future benchmarking, to seek further opportunities for organisational learning.

Each of the seven steps contributes to the overall development of a 'gap analysis', which is used to identify the degree of performance differential between the best-in-class firm and the benchmarking firm. Gap analysis is key to identifying the performance level of excellence in a particular process relative to process performance in the benchmarking firm. The gap identifies the need for change by establishing quantitative measurements of relative process capabilities, as well as providing proven best practice necessary to effect change. Figure 5.8 shows how a gap analysis can be used to analyse process contributions affecting national market competitors over time.

Product/process design (process A) and logistics/marketing systems (process B) are depicted in Figure 5.8 as the two key processes that contribute directly and materially to the operation of a business in a particular industry. For illustrative purposes it is assumed that there are only two prime process candidates – A and B – although in practice the number of process candidates for benchmarking consideration will depend on the specific factors that drive a particular industry. It is also assumed that analogous processes across industry boundaries have been identified and measured. For further analytical convenience, the size and extent of the performance gap for the two prime processes over a five-year period is the same, with process A (product/process design) favouring the international competitor and process B (logistics/marketing systems) favouring the a national competitor. There is no net change in the performance gap over time.

The gap analysis arising from the benchmarking process depicted in Figure 5.8 yields important insights into the inherent capability of firms to operate at a national scale.

- First, in both examples it takes one competitor the entire five-year period to develop the process capabilities to match competition as it exists today. Such action will not close the gap. In view of the superiority of the respective processes adopted by competitors, at the end of the period the gap is even wider. It is not enough to set internally driven goals; its is vital to set targets based on external best practice.
- Secondly, failure to adopt external best practice processes will result in competitive decline. This may prompt mergers, acquisitions and alliances which seek to restore performance through internal transfer of process skills, or market withdrawal and ultimate death. Nature of outcomes is influenced heavily by awareness of competitors of trends in best practice process outcomes over the next five years.
- Thirdly, it is critical to study those key business processes that are vital to the success of the entire business. Within an industry context, incorrect specification will lead to erroneous views of the industry and its competitors' future. If the benchmarking activity had focused solely on either product/process design (process A) or logistics/marketing procedures and systems (process B), differing views concerning the supremacy of national players would have been expressed.

Figure 5.8 Benchmarking processes for national competitor over time

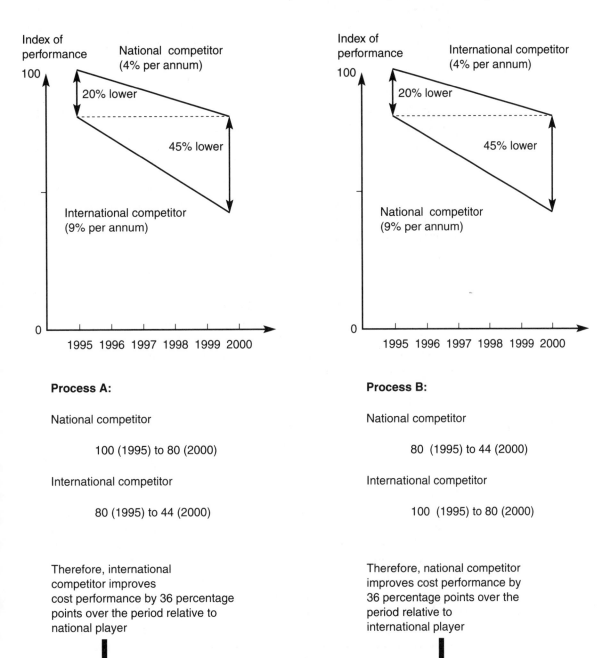

Process 'A' : Product/process design

Index of performance

100

National competitor (4% per annum)

20% lower

45% lower

International competitor (9% per annum)

1995 1996 1997 1998 1999 2000

Process 'B' : Logistics/marketing procedures and systems

Index of performance

100

International competitor (4% per annum)

20% lower

45% lower

National competitor (9% per annum)

1995 1996 1997 1998 1999 2000

Process A:

National competitor

    100 (1995) to 80 (2000)

International competitor

    80 (1995) to 44 (2000)

Therefore, international competitor improves cost performance by 36 percentage points over the period relative to national player

Process B:

National competitor

    80 (1995) to 44 (2000)

International competitor

    100 (1995) to 80 (2000)

Therefore, national competitor improves cost performance by 36 percentage points over the period relative to international player

No net change in performance

207

- Fourthly, the position of the national players is not unchanged because there is no net change in the performance gap. The product/process design issue (process A) will not go away for the national players, since the process performance differential will be worse in absolute terms over each of the next five years. It is imperative for the national competitor to set in train targeted action to close and surpass the performance gap (the same is true for the international competitor with respect to process B).
- Fifthly, within the same key processes there can be several successful managerial patterns. This is particularly the case where national and international competitors hold countervailing power with regard to equally important processes, such as product/process design (process A) and European logistics/marketing (process B). In such circumstances both national and international competitors can gain from partnership agreements.

The consequences of key process capabilities do not necessarily consist of performance gaps of equal and opposite scale for national and international competitors alike. The position of no net change in overall performance arising from two key processes is depicted for national and international competitors in diagrammatic format in Figure 5.9(i). In Figure 5.9(ii) different assumptions concerning the performance improvements attributable to the same two processes result in an outcome which over time favours the international competitor. In Figure 5.9(iii) these cost reductions are reversed, with the effect that the national player is favoured at the expense of the international player. In short, the defendability of a national strategy can only be determined by benchmarking performance against best-in-class international competitors.

Summary

The present chapter has examined the concept of restricted market scope and the conditions under which organisations operating with such a strategy may be able to compete effectively with larger international companies. Recognition of the inherent dynamics of the competitive process emphasised the need to monitor constantly and reassess when a strategy based on restricted market scope is appropriate. Businesses who fail to do this may continue with an inappropriate strategy long after the competitive environment has changed and there is need for reassessment.

The concept of competitive advantage was explored and the dangers in only using national market comparisons highlighted. Correspondingly, the need to use inter-market comparisons and benchmarking was affirmed, and the steps in carrying out the latter discussed. For those companies which believe the key industry drivers are pointing to the need to become international, the question arises as to how this might be done. The next chapter takes up this question and considers issues relating to entry and establishing an initial presence in international markets.

Figure 5.9 Benchmarking national competitor performance against best-in-class international competitor

(i) Competitive balance over a given time period

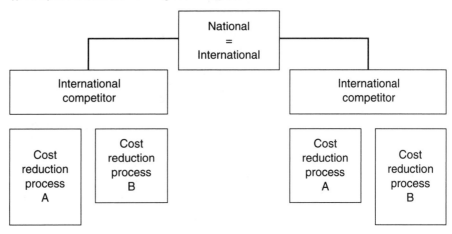

(ii) International competitor favoured over a given time period

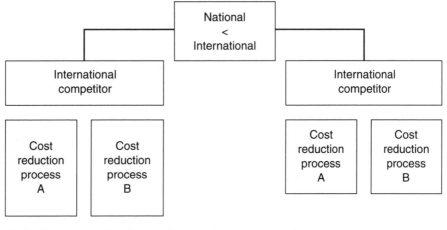

(iii) National competitor favoured over a given time period

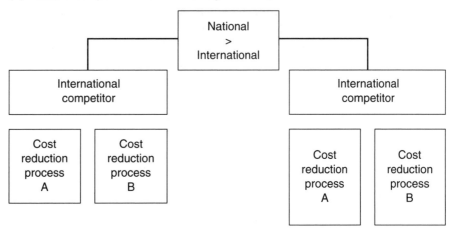

Checklist

- Restricted national market scope describes a business strategy based on serving a single national market.
- Numerically the majority of companies operate with a national or sub-national market scope.
- For a strategy of national market scope to be sustainable it must be able to offer the same or greater advantages than those available to an international competitor operating with pan-national strategies.
- External and internal forces will determine the scope of the organisation's strategy.
- Where external and internal forces are not in balance an organisation's strategy can be described as unstable.
- Restrictive national market scope can be sub-divided by companies operating with local, national region and national strategies.
- Some companies and industries are unlikely to progress beyond being organised on a local or national region basis.
- Moving from one stage of business development to another is likely to place significant demands on management to reshape key business functions and processes.
- Industry dynamics can result in a constant shifting between the sustainability of strategies based on restricted as opposed to international scope.
- A change in the external environment of competitors may result from a change of strategy by another competitor.
- Competitive advantage is a relative rather than absolute term raising questions about (i) how it is measured; (ii) in what market; and (iii) over whom.
- There are major dangers in only using other national competitors as a basis of claiming competitive advantage.
- The sustainability of a strategy of national market scope can only be confirmed by using the techniques of inter-market comparisons and benchmarking.
- Benchmarking is about (i) identifying world class performance; (ii) assessing the process which leads to this level of performance; and (iii) seeking to apply such a process to another organisation.
- Benchmarking can lead to significant organisational learning.

Hotpoint

Introduction

By limiting its geographical scope to a single country market, Hotpoint has emerged as the leading United Kingdom white goods manufacturer. The firm's commanding position in the national market is underlined by a 35 per cent market share for washing machines and dryers, coupled with 25 per cent of the dishwasher market, and a strong position in cooking appliances. Market dominance is such that its key brands – Hotpoint, Creda and Cannon – collectively accounted for 30 per cent of the UK market in 1994. This is two and a half times greater than the nearest market competitors, Electrolux, Maytag and Whirlpool, who have all acquired or established white goods businesses all over the world.

The fluctuating fortunes of national and international players are critically dependent on industry responses to the demand for customer variety (erodes benefit of economies of scale and pan-European market share) and new supply and distribution possibilities (enhances possibilities to integrate geographical businesses). With hindsight, supply and demand forces reduced market scope to national boundaries throughout most of the 1980s, with national players holding dominant market share in France (Thomson), Spain (Fagor) and UK (Hotpoint). Today, the defendability of a restricted national market strategy is far from secure, as major international players actively seek to develop the capability to operate effectively across borders as a unified entity.

Industry overview

The initial trigger to consolidation was the globalisation moves of the Italian white goods manufacturers in the 1960s, which captured around one-third of the European market by mass producing low cost well-designed appliances. During this period Zanussi, Ignis and Indesit established brand recognition and secured sizeable European market shares. German manufacturers, notably AEG, Bauknecht and Bosch-Siemen, also adopted an export strategy based on standard products aimed at the European market. With the exception of a few high quality niche producers (e.g. Neff and Miele), other small high cost volume producers like Hotpoint were doing badly in the face of these severe competitive pressures.

The once dominant export-based companies all found themselves swimming against the tide in the 1980s. The balance moved away from standardised mass production as consumers demanded greater variety and choice of models. The profits of Italian manufacturers Zanussi, Ignis and Indesit turned to losses and they were subsequently acquired by Electrolux, Philips (later Whirlpool) and Merloni respectively. Likewise the German producers, AEG and Bauknecht, experienced trading difficulties, and were acquired by Philips (Whirlpool) and Electrolux respectively. During this period several hundred small-scale producers exited the industry either through the business being sold or business failure. As Table C5.1 illustrates, the 'old' order was succeeded by a new elite of white goods manufacturers with contrasting strategic recipes.

One group of players – Hotpoint, Thomson and Fagor – sought to dominate their respective national markets. As Table C5.1 shows, their individual market share is much smaller than those of their international competitors. This small absolute total belies their respective national leadership, where they are outright brand leaders by a factor of between two and three over their nearest rival. The limited penetration of international brands in major national markets is an indication of the fragmentation of demand, as well as reflecting the fact that leading global players Electrolux and Whirlpool built their dominant European position by accumulating many small national shares. Despite its relatively small size, Hotpoint's performance throughout the 1980s can be regarded as particularly noteworthy, with the company achieving a remarkable turnaround to become the most profitable appliance manufacturer in Europe.

Another group of players – Electrolux, Bosch-Siemens, Whirlpool and Merloni – sought to satisfy varying consumer preferences throughout Europe. All have production facilities in more than one country, with long-term plans to become true customer-focused organisations. Throughout the 1980s these companies struggled to match the unified customer focus of the national producers, with many managers still running their businesses as disparate national entities, each with its own unique constraints and finite opportunities. Towards the end of the 1980s Whirlpool – the world's largest white goods manufacturer – spearheaded the challenge to integrate its European operations in such a way that the whole would be greater than the sum of its parts. This intervention has prompted further take-overs and co-operative deals.

Table C5.1 European market shares (%) of leading white goods manufacturers, 1986–94

	1986	1988	1990	1992	1994
Electrolux	16	22	18	23	29
Bosch-Siemens	8	11	13	15	16
Whirlpool	13	10	9	14	15
Merloni	3	7	8	9	10
Thomson	3	6	7	7	9
Miele	3	5	6	7	8
Hotpoint	4	5	6	6	6
Fagor	1	1	2	2	3

Source: Trade estimates with a ± two percentage points tolerance range. Figures exclude small domestic and hand-held appliances. Full ownership details are listed in Figure C5.1.

Electrolux has extended its leadership in the European white goods industry with a market share of 29 per cent in 1994, against 16 per cent for Bosch-Siemens, 15 per cent for Whirlpool and 10 per cent for Merloni. Table C5.1 also shows a 20 per cent increase between 1986 and 1990 in the four leading firms' market share which rose from 40 to 48 per cent, as compared with a 46 per cent increase between 1990 and 1994, which raised the collective market share of this group of companies to 70 per cent. There is a widening gap in the scale and scope of international versus national players. This quickening of the pace of market concentration poses new challenges for national market players, who lack the critical mass in both production and product development. As Figure C5.1 shows, both Hotpoint and Thompson have lost their independence. It remains to be seen whether far-reaching structural changes will break down national barriers and the ability of national champions like Hotpoint to sustain superior financial performance.

New supply opportunities for restricted scope

When Chaim Schrieber took a 37.5 per cent stake in Hotpoint in 1974 the company was on the verge of bankruptcy. Its reputation and market share were in sharp decline, with its numerous factories on short-time working. Moreover, Hotpoint produced a wide product range serving customers in many different segments in the UK and mainland Europe. There was no clear vision of the way forward, no shared mindset and worker morale was low. With almost missionary zeal Schreiber kick-started a wide range of initiatives to revitalise the organisation.

'Simplify' was Schreiber's rallying call to managers and workers alike. At a time when Italian imports were flooding the domestic market, Schreiber's first act was to sell Hotpoint's European distribution network. To remove further complexity he also sold its profitable small appliance business. Restricting market scope was a controversial means to an end. Both decisions released cash and management resources to focus on the priority issue facing Hotpoint in its restricted market territory in the UK: the need to match and eventually supersede the supply capability of leading Italian competitors, particularly Ignis and Zanussi.

Having simplified what the business was really about, Schreiber then devoted considerable energy to building an organisational capability to make fault-free appliances at low cost. At Schreiber's insistence, Hotpoint was the first European appliance manufacturer to implement a total quality improvement programme. This involved far more radical changes than simply posting charts on quality throughout the factories and setting stretching targets. To facilitate these and other changes required a change in organisational culture. There was to be no clocking on and off, piecework was abolished, and flexible rules of working introduced. An important symbol of the departure from the previous authoritarian regime was a shared dining room where workers and managers ate together.

The quest for quality brought further organisational changes. It prompted Schreiber, a very forceful personality, to make departments communicate with one another in an attempt to find new directions for progress. Departmental relationships were rebalanced to drive through the changes in after-sales service and product reliability. Rather than the after-sales function being a profit centre (whose performance increased with poorer quality levels), its departmental function was merged with production to provide a tighter feedback chain charged with ensuring faults were not repeated. By linking together in this way, after-sales service can also provide valuable information on customer desires for variety. This increased customer awareness not only facilitated two-way information flows with marketing, but also indicated how Hotpoint has found ways of linking together different organisational functions.

To rebuild market position new production facilities were commissioned in 1980. Building on six years of organisational learning under Schreiber's leadership, the

Figure C5.1 *The consolidation of the European white goods industry: 1980–94*

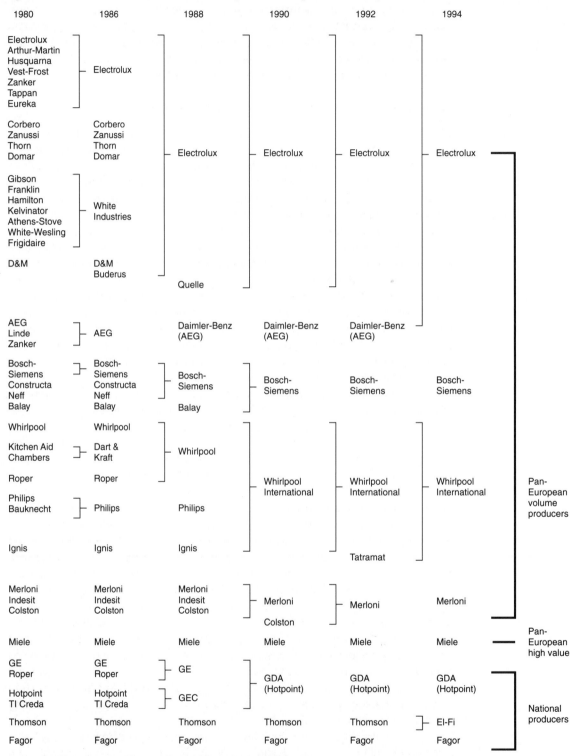

Source: Adapted and updated from the *Financial Times*, 24 June 1992, p 26

plant was designed to provide productive capacity that was different and better than its continental rivals. The difference lay in the plant being only about half the commonly believed optimal size of 1 million units a year operated by the market leaders. It was better to the extent that the plant was designed to harness numerous smaller process innovations to enable variety to be produced at lower cost. While cost reduction was a critically important driver of the investment decision, so too was the need to ensure greater quality to make more attractive products that would create fresh demand in an apparently mature market.

From the outset marketing was charged with developing a product range based on identified requirements of the customer. Rather than marketing selling what production had produced, marketing was made responsible for telling production what to make. This not only required production to learn more about markets and competition, but also allowed retailers to order models most in demand. Throughout this period Hotpoint invested heavily in a new distribution network to ensure stable pricing and increased market share and to roll back high levels of German and Italian imports. It was a basic tenet of Schreiber's philosophy that 'to be successful you have to have dealers to support you as much as the customer.'

Schreiber stood down as managing director of Hotpoint in 1982. His eight highly successful years at the helm were strongly formative in transforming Hotpoint into a company which restored both its reputation and market share in the UK. This was achieved by building new capabilities to deal with variety at low cost, and exploiting this capacity in a restricted geographical market.

Fragmented European market demand

While Hotpoint continued throughout the 1980s to restrict operations to the local geographical market, other competitors – notably Electrolux, Bosch-Siemens, Whirlpool and Merloni – operated plants in several countries and sought to secure a wide range of national markets. The greater the number of markets served the greater the challenge to co-ordinate effectively the needs of production, marketing, logistics and design. The complexity of serving a broad strategic territory in white goods on the demand side has in the past reflected three related factors: the growing demand for variety within national markets; increasing divergence of national preferences; and differing retail/distribution channels and structures.

With high levels of household ownership, the European demand for white goods is primarily for replacement purposes. Further, the durability of the product enables customers to some extent to defer replacement, by seeking to repair their existing equipment if they so choose. This pattern of customer choice was evident in the European recession of the late 1980s, and prompted a downturn in overall market demand between 1989 and 1994.

In a saturated market consumers, encouraged by producers, have demonstrated a propensity for product variety, with demand being influenced by fashion as much as basic need. The consequent proliferation of models per brand in recent years is most striking. It rose from one or two in 1974, to between four and six in 1984, and to around twenty in 1994. The need to deliver ever increasing variety to price-sensitive customers is particularly onerous, but it is a challenge all producers have to meet if sales growth is to be achieved.

A further challenge arises on account of the marked differences in consumer tastes across European national boundaries. These differences in consumer preferences for washing machines are probably more pronounced today than they were some twenty years ago. As Table C5.2 shows, consumer preferences vary from location to location throughout Europe. The demand for variety coupled with marked inter-country differences is not easily resolved by manufacturers, since the costs of complexity demanded by individual sub-markets can more than offset gains from having large production units each concentrating on the production of a single appliance for pan-European supply.

Table C5.2 Consumer preferences for washing machines in Europe

Feature	Country			
	France	**Germany**	**Italy**	**UK**
Loading	Top	Front	Front	Front
Spin speed	Medium	Fast	Slow	Medium
Filling	Cold	Cold	Cold	Hot

Source: Baden-Fuller and Stopford (1992), p 75

The lack of a homogeneous market for white goods is compounded by differences in retailing practices. With few exceptions, transnational buying groups have yet to emerge to affect European white goods retailing significantly. Powerful national retailers can favour nationally focused producers, which understand the buying habits and tastes of national consumers. As noted earlier in relation to 'mom and pop' shops for small electrical appliances in Japan (see Chapter 3), culturally based retailing practices and selling methods can lead to entry barriers which are not affected by regulatory changes. This example serves to emphasise that differences in retail practices and distribution structures can pose major challenges to a producer seeking to enter a national market, and may assist the continuing dominance of national producers.

In contrast to Hotpoint, which managed to grow both market share and profitability throughout the 1980s, most pan-European players were almost overwhelmed by the complexity of the challenges posed by the diversity of European markets. When Whirlpool acquired Philips' floundering white goods business for $1 billion in 1989, it immediately set about implementing a radical transformation designed to remove old regional fiefdoms and inadequate ways of satisfying customers in the European market. In seeking to achieve improved performance, Whirlpool had a different vision as to how pan-European producers should evolve. According to David Whitham, Chief Executive Officer (CEO) at Whirlpool:

> Our vision at Whirlpool is to integrate our geographical businesses wherever possible, so that most advanced expertise in any given area – whether it's refrigeration technology, financial reporting systems, or distribution strategy – isn't confined to one location or one division. We want to be able to take the best capabilities we have and leverage them in all of our operations worldwide.

Case Study 5

By 1994, the implementation of Whirlpool's vision had brought about a major transformation of how the company competed in Europe. This is shown in Figure C5.2.

Figure C5.2 Whirlpool Europe: pan-European white goods strategy

Production	→	Major drive to reduce costs and improve quality; regional manufacturing centres with facilities to ensure wide variety of models can be built on same basic production platform. Consolidation of suppliers into important dual sourcing partnerships.
Marketing	→	Three distinct pan-European brands: *Bauknecht* – products targeted at the upper end of the market; *Whirlpool* – fills the broad middle range; and *Ignis* – a price-orientated value brand. The 13 national sales offices rationalised into five regional organisations; key new targets are transnational buying groups.
Logistics	→	Improved logistics helping to streamline operations and reduce costs. Revamped distribution system, similar to the group's North American 'Quality Express', reducing delivery time, damage and costs.
Design	→	Produce new product features and styling dictated by European customer research; planned introduction of a number of major product designs between 1994 and 1997.

Today, Whirlpool is the front runner when it comes to implementing a pan-European strategy and leveraging global resources. It has a co-ordinated plan to operate effectively as a unified entity with the capability to meet the special needs of local markets. By entertaining a vision of how the challenges of diversity can be overcome, Whirlpool has thrown down a challenge to other European producers. It is a challenge which also requires a response from national champions such as Hotpoint.

Hotpoint's new strategic direction

In 1989 Hotpoint modified its strategic position when its UK owner General Electric Company plc (GEC) sold 50 per cent of the equity to the US white goods giant, General Electric Appliances, part of General Electric Inc. (GE). Following the sale, as Figure C5.1 shows, a new joint venture company, General Domestic Appliances (GDA), was established. As part of the change in ownership, Hotpoint gained free access to a flow of leading-edge technology and engineering best practices, which can only be supported by a producer with international scale. From GE's point of view its investment provides the company with a secure base in a leading European market, as well as the opportunity to sell into continental Europe. Whereas Hotpoint focused solely on the UK market in 1989, 6 years later sales to continental Europe comprise 6 per cent of turnover, with a further 2 per cent of sales going to Australasia.

217

Since 1991 day to day management of Hotpoint has been the executive responsibility of Bruce Enders, previously Vice-President of worldwide marketing and product management at GE Appliances. His appointment coincided with a marked slackening of Hotpoint sales, which prompted Enders to implement a substantial rationalisation programme. His target is to reorganise Hotpoint's eight UK factories so that they will each be producing upwards of 500,000 units per annum. At a minimum two of the eight factories are targeted to be closed and the facilities of the six remaining plants subjected to major upgrading. Additionally, a whole layer of management is to be removed from the service operation and two layers from production.

When Enders arrived at Hotpoint he found a comprehensive programme of efficiency enhancement already undergoing implementation. This will drastically reduce the number of component and material suppliers. Enders believes that both the efficiency and rationalisation programmes will be completed by 1994/95 and that even in an absolutely flat economy net margins should rise to 10 per cent in that year. This medium-term benefit can only be achieved at the cost of short-term pain, with the rationalisation of the production base incurring one-off restructuring costs.

In June 1992 Hotpoint announced its intention to link up in a limited alliance with Thomson of France and Fagor of Spain to form a integrated European Economic Interest Grouping (EEIG). The aims of the grouping are to pool research and development in commonly sourcing finished products to extend lines; and exchange ideas in design and manufacturing. 'The biggest deficiencies of the three partners come from the fact that we are doing a lot of the same things,' Enders explained. 'This [EEIG] is aimed at eliminating the duplication.'

The Italian washing machine manufacturer Ocean, a subsidiary of Elettrofinanziaria (ELFI), joined the EEIG at the beginning of 1993. With the arrival of Ocean (number four in the Italian market) the four companies' informal grouping had sales of approximately £2 billion. This ranks second in Europe, with 19.3 per cent of the market after Electrolux and AEG (acquired by the former in 1993) which achieved 29 per cent. The future creation of financial links between the four partners cannot be ruled out. On 21 January 1993, ELFI purchased Thomson Electromanger of France, increasing combined turnover to £1 billion, equivalent to some 9 per cent of the European white goods market.

Financial performance

Table C5.3 shows the dramatic impact Chaim Schreiber had on Hotpoint's performance. Under his leadership there was an almost fourfold increase in net profit margin from 2.3 to 8.9 per cent. Schreiber's restructuring of the company paved the way for achieving a 10.1 per cent profit margin over the five year period 1985–89. Brian Enders' stewardship coincided with the start of an economic recession in the UK, with the accompanying erosion of margins.

Table C5.3 Hotpoint's net profit margin, 1975–94

	1975–79	1980–84	1985–89	1990–94*
Operating profit/turnover (%)	2.3	8.9	10.1	7.5

* 1994 net profit margin estimated at 8.1 per cent

Case Study 5

By collating financial material abstracted from the segmental reporting of Hotpoint's competitors, Table C5.4 allows detailed comparisons over time of the financial performance of key players in the European white goods industry. All the figures have been converted into £ sterling to facilitate comparisons. It is clear that Whirlpool appears to be winning the head-to-head confrontation with Electrolux, whose continuing domination of the industry has been reinforced by its acquisition of companies which include AEG. The financial performance of AEG, another pre-dominately national player prior to its take-over by Electrolux, is noteworthy.

Table C5.4 European white goods industry: selected financial figures 1988–93, £ million.

	Electrolux	Whirlpool Europe	Bosch-Siemens[1]	AEG[2]	Hotpoint
Sales					
1988	–	N/A	1,434.5	N/A	291.1
1989	–	1,503.1	1,687.6	N/A	306.4
1990	3,164.7	1,351.1	2,321.2	463.1	551.2
1991	3,238.5	1,416.6	2,441.8	779.4	542.6
1992	3,405.1	1,511.4	2,668.5	885.5	533.5
1993	4,059.0	1,639.5	–	–	503.0
Margin					
1988	N/A	N/A	0.9	N/A	10.8
1989	4.7	N/A	1.0	N/A	10.1
1990	2.7	3.6	4.0	1.0	7.8
1991	2.4	3.3	4.7	2.3	6.9
1992	2.1	3.8	4.6	3.7	8.2
1993	1.9	5.4	–	–	6.3
Employees					
1988	75,371	10,520	16,524	N/A	6,106
1989	78,690	10,311	23,099	N/A	6,409
1990	77,517	7,811	22,821	9,056	11,938
1991	65,400	7,840	23,644	9,202	11,338
1992	60,180	7,802	23,563	8,702	10,612
1993	–	–	–	–	–
Total assets					
1988	2,703.1[3]	N/A	617.9	N/A	165.9
1989	3,168.0[3]	N/A	716.6	N/A	137.9
1990	3,226.8[3]	1,070.2	1,058.4	351.1	294.7
1991	3,076.3[3]	1,305.1	1,128.3	354.7	286.8
1992	3,651.3[3]	1,095.4	1,248.8	384.2	278.0
1993	–	1,195.9	–	–	280.0

Notes
1. Consolidated figures – includes small domestic appliances
2. Acquired by Electrolux in 1993
3. Interpolated figures

Source: Annual Reports; absolute figures converted into UK pounds (£) at mid-year rates

Case Study 5

Notwithstanding the severe price wars currently afflicting the European market, Hotpoint's margins are in line with Whirlpool International (USA), but well behind Maytag (USA). It has, however, taken considerable efforts by the company for Hotpoint's performance to be where it is. The anticipated net profit margin for 1990–94 is the lowest achieved for over a decade.

Table C5.5 provides fascinating inter-market comparisons. Ambiguity caused by changing industry dynamics not only prompts uncertainty as to the general level of industry performance, but also raises concerns surrounding which strategic direction will prove to be the most rewarding and for how long. In short, will Hotpoint's dominant position in the UK and concentrated manufacturing resource allow it to produce margins superior to its international peers?

Table C5.5 Industry comparisons – domestic appliance divisions, 1992

Company	Turnover £	Operating profit £	Operating margin (%)
Whirlpool (USA)	4,803	315.0	6.6
Electrolux (Sweden)	4,039	68.9	1.7
Matsushita (Japan)	3,900	204.0	5.2
General Electric (USA)	3,610	286.0	7.9
Bosch-Siemens (Germany)	2,669	122.8	4.6
Maytag (USA)	1,857	196.0	10.6
Hotpoint (UK)	534	44.0	8.2

Source: Annual Reports, segmental data; absolute figures converted in UK pounds (£) at mid-year rates

Conclusion

Choosing the strategic territory is an important decision facing any organisation. Whether the choice is made on either a limited or world scale, it may be modified in response to changes in both the internal and external contexts. It is the responsibility of business leaders to make carefully judged geographical and product-market choices, since inappropriate selections can be critical to an organisation's success.

Questions

(1) *Why do you think the number of competitors in the European industry have been reducing and concentration increasing?*

(2) *How did Schreiber change Hotpoint? What evidence is there in the case that the strategy of restricted national market scope adopted by Hotpoint has been successful?*

(3) *To what extent was the decision to sell 50 per cent of Hotpoint to the General Electric Company Inc in 1989 significant? What are the potential strategic benefits to Hotpoint of the sale?*

(4) *Compare and contrast the strategies of Hotpoint and Whirlpool. What are the management challenges inherent in the management of each company's strategies?*

(5) *Out of the three companies – Electrolux, Hotpoint and Whirlpool – which do you believe will be the most successful in the foreseeable future and why?*

Chapter 6

INTERNATIONAL MARKET ENTRY AND DEVELOPMENT

Key learning objectives

To understand:

- the inter-relationship between external and internal factors in shaping market entry and development strategies

- factors influencing country/market selection

- alternative methods of entering cross-border markets

- the need to configure and co-ordinate key business functions to effect the successful implementation of the chosen entry strategy

- how progressive corrective adjustments to market entry strategy result from inadequate business performance

- the reasons international market entry and development can fail

- market concentration versus market spreading

Context

If a company decides that it wants to pursue an international business strategy, then a decision has to be made concerning which cross-border markets are to be served. Equally important is the need to determine how to enter effectively and develop key international markets. In short, how should senior managers select a target market and decide on an appropriate entry mode for a specific product/service?

The appropriate market selection and entry strategy is potentially a complex decision, significantly influenced by the extent to which the internationalisation process has been triggered by changes in either external or internal factors. The underlying thrust of the change trigger will not only influence target market screening. It will also affect the choice and implementation of entry and development strategies. The structure of the chapter is as follows:

- *developing an international business strategy*
- *international market entry*
  - *market screening and selection*
  - *entry modes*
  - *implementation of chosen market entry mode*
  - *business performance*
- *reasons for the failure of international market entry strategies*
- *market concentration versus market spreading*

The chapter begins by looking at the overall role of external and internal change triggers in shaping market entry and development. After a review of these factors, specific attention is focused on which external and internal factors may influence market selection and entry modes. The role of external and internal forces in shaping the organisation's strategic thrust is emphasised, and a generic framework is provided which allows the organisation's market entry strategy to be disaggregated into four interdependent elements: (i) market screening and selection; (ii) entry mode; (iii) implementation of the entry strategy; and (iv) business performance.

Lack of business success may lead to withdrawal and retrenchment from an international market. Recognising this possibility prompts consideration of how different performance outcomes can lead to a re-examination of one or more elements of the chosen market entry and development strategy. Conversely, where the initial entry strategy is successful the organisation will be faced with the question of how it should further develop its international presence. Should a firm enter many markets, building up slowly in each (market spreading), or restrict expansion to a small number of selected countries (market concentration)? The chapter is concluded with a summary and checklist. A case study on Le Creuset SA offers the reader the opportunity to apply a number of the frameworks introduced in the chapter.

Developing an international business strategy

Companies seeking to develop an international business strategy will wish to build a permanent market position in their chosen international product-market. This contrasts with a transient concern in making occasional opportunistic sales to international markets, sometimes referred to as the sales approach (Root, 1987). Any intended movement away from a purely national business focus represents a fundamental shift in the business development of an organisation. No longer does the company have to concern itself only with its national market, but it now needs to look to wider horizons. In moving in this direction a company is entering the second stage of the phase model, as shown in Figure 6.1.

Figure 6.1 The phase model of international business development

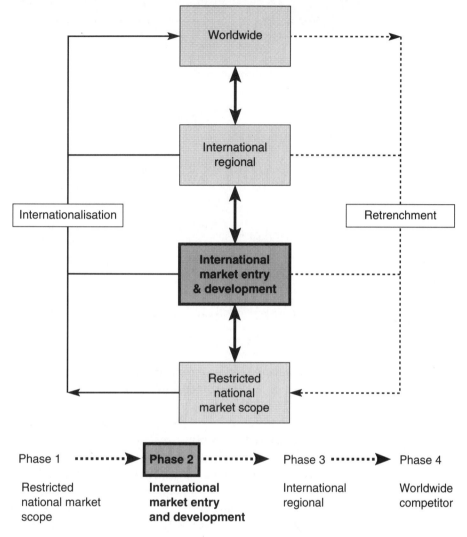

To understand what triggers such a change in the organisation's scope, it is necessary to return to fundamental drivers of the internationalisation process. Earlier discussion in Chapter 2 (see Figure 2.1) emphasised that the move away from a purely national focus would reflect external and/or internal triggers to change. Figure 6.2 summarises the earlier discussion by indicating that collectively changing external and internal factors will be responsible for the organisation seeking to develop an international business strategy, as well as informing the nature of the strategy pursued. Hence external and internal factors and how they change are central to explaining both the way organisations seek to develop international business strategies, and the nature of the strategy chosen.

Figure 6.2 Developing an international business strategy

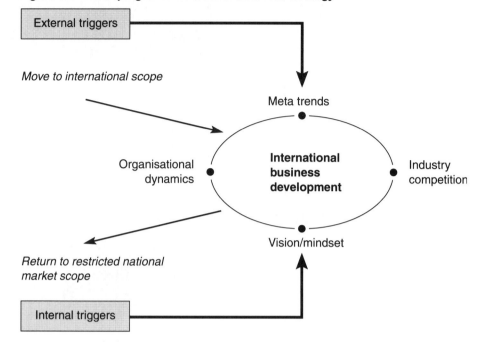

The nature of the organisation's strategic response may be described as *proactive* or *reactive* depending on which external or internal factors trigger international business development. The organisation may be considered proactive when it has a choice as to whether it wishes to expand internationally or remain with a restricted national focus. The development of many companies has, for example, been directed by visionary leaders whose appointment as the new chief executive has brought considerable change to the scale and scope of an organisation. Equally, for some companies the external context, which has been shaped by the competitive strategies of rivals, leaves them with no option but to seek to develop an international strategy. Table 6.1 identifies a range of external and internal factors and considers whether they lead to either a proactive or reactive strategic response.

In some circumstance the strategies of an organisation may reflect a combination of the above factors. This is the case with a number of US retailers, discussed in Illustration 6.1, who have recently entered international markets. Even so, careful analysis will normally reveal which is the dominant factor for a specified time. This should assist in determining whether overall a proactive or reactive factor has been the catalyst to market entry.

Table 6.1 External versus internal triggers to change: proactive or reactive?

	Internal	**External**
Proactive	● visionary leadership ● exploitation of core competences ● opportunity to realise competitive interdependencies	● cross-border market opportunities – growth and profits
Reactive	● current levels of business performance ● internal pressure from disaffected managers ● excess capacity	● saturation/decline of local/national market ● intensity of competition ● movement of key customers abroad ● entry by cross-border rivals to local/national market

Illustration 6.1

International expansion by US retailers

Throughout the 1970s and 1980s the majority of US retailers focused on their domestic market, which they believed was large enough to offer significant opportunities for growth. In the last few years, however, the number of retailers looking to expand across borders has increased considerably.

These developments are explained by both the extent of international opportunities and competition in the domestic market. US retailers are among the most innovative in the world, being at the forefront of developing new retail formats, including electronic shopping. The incentive to innovate is driven by the highly competitive nature of the US market, and the need to find an advantage over competitors. Competitive pressures have intensified in the last few years, as consumer spending has not grown to match increases in retail capacity. As a result, demand for many retail sectors has reached saturation point. In this context gaining sales inevitably means taking sales from another retailer, often a difficult and expensive task. Even those companies which find new innovations soon notice other companies copying their formats and methods, making any competitive advantage temporary.

Set against these factors, it is perhaps not surprising that so many large US retailers are looking outside their present market. In some cases retailers are attracted to entering Western Europe on the basis of cultural similarities, while in other cases the growth potential of Eastern Europe, Latin America or Asia is a strong draw. Equally, many companies have moved into Canada or Mexico, favouring the geographical proximity of those countries to the USA.

Source: Based on Tomkins (1994)

Regardless of the trigger to the internationalisation process, once an organisation has taken the decision to become international in its scope, external and internal factors will shape the chosen business strategy. The key external factors have already been discussed at length in Chapter 3 and include the broad *contextual* or *meta trends* – political, economic, social and technological – and *competition* at the level of the industry. Similarly, the organisation's internal context, discussed in depth in Chapter 4, comprises *vision/mindset* and *organisational dynamics* – core competences, organisational learning and administrative heritage. Collectively, external and internal factors will influence the organisation's market entry and development strategy.

Correspondingly, the market entry strategy which is chosen should be reflective of both the business opportunity and degree of competition (external factors) and the ambition and ability of the organisation to implement the chosen strategy (internal factors). The importance of the internal context emphasises that what actually happens in an organisation does not depend solely on rational considerations alone, but also reflects the organisational dynamics – the beliefs, values and culture embedded within the organisation. Conversely, external factors will help to describe both the business opportunities available within any international market and the degree of industry competition.

The balance between external and internal factors in determining market entry and development strategy is likely to be linked to the context in which the organisation finds itself. It is not surprising that the relative importance of each is rarely equal. In some circumstances external factors may be more important, alternatively on other occasions internal factors may dominate. While the relative importance of either external or internal factors in shaping a firm's international business strategy is dependent on the specific context and point in time, Figure 6.3 illustrates a generic framework of how each factor may influence and inform market entry and development strategies.

Regardless of the relative importance of different external and internal factors and the process by which decisions are taken, as Figure 6.3 illustrates, the selection and subsequent modification of the organisation's market entry strategy can be disaggregated into four components, namely:

- market screening and selection: the assessment of alternative cross-border market opportunities and choice of which market(s) to enter;
- choice of market entry strategy: decision on how to enter the market(s);
- implementation of market entry strategy: operationalisation of chosen strategy through the configuration and co-ordination of business functions; and
- business performance: assessment of outcomes and measurement against expected performance.

The model illustrated in Figure 6.3 is not prescriptive. It is highly dynamic allowing, say, the implementation of the chosen entry strategy to lead to modifications being made to the mode of entry. Business performance, especially where it does not meet expectations, will sooner or later result in corrective

Figure 6.3 Market entry and development strategies

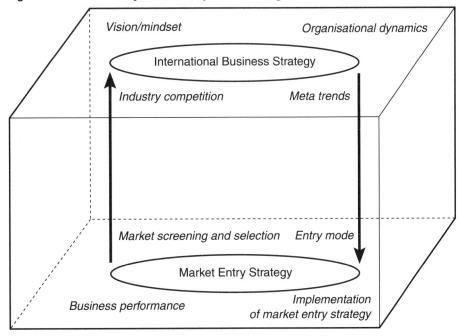

adjustments being made to the overall market entry and development strategy. The size and extent of any corrective adjustments are likely to reflect the degree to which business performance is at variance with what was expected and considered acceptable to the organisation. Initially any divergence between actual and expected performance is likely to focus on how the strategy is being implemented, but if inadequate performance continues, then progressively the other components of the market entry model will come under examination. As is shown later in the chapter, the organisation may ultimately question the basis on which it has selected the market for entry, and may even decide to withdraw.

The decision-making process by which the organisation chooses between different international markets and modes of entry is dependent on its context (external and internal), which is likely to change over time. At one end of the spectrum, some writers on international business and marketing strategies have suggested that the process is, or should be, highly rational and objective, being mainly influenced by the assessment of external factors. Alternatively, other commentators contend that the entry strategy chosen is much more likely to be influenced by internal factors, and in particular by the power elites within the organisation and their vision of the future direction of the organisation. In between these extremes is a continuum along which the relative importance of external as opposed internal factors changes. Correspondingly, Table 6.2 details the characteristics of two ends of the spectrum and identifies the inherent weaknesses of relying on one or other of the approaches.

Table 6.2 Alternative decision-making processes to choosing market entry strategies

External		Internal
	Characteristics	
Market entry and development strategy determined by external factors	*Overall decision*	Market entry and development strategy determined by internal factors
Strategy strongly influenced by external assessment of market and business opportunities, level of competition, etc.	*Key factors influencing the entry decision*	Strategy strongly influenced by power elites in the organisation who control overall direction of the organisation
Emphasis tends to be on a highly rational and planned approach	*Nature of the process*	Market selection and entry modes may be based on intuition rather than any 'hard' evidence; and/or personal preferences of chief executive/senior managers
	Potential weaknesses	
Over-emphasis on external factors may lead to neglect of internal context and in particular ability to implement externally determined strategy		Key decision-makers may have a 'dated' or inaccurate view of the external context, leading to the development of of an inappropriate strategy for the organisation

In practice, the determination of an organisation's market entry strategy is more likely to be influenced by a mix of external and internal forces. Almost inevitably if one set of factors is over-emphasised, at some stage in the future business performance will suffer and a more eclectic view will need to be taken. Often such paradigm changes are related to personal appointments at a senior management level and, as discussed earlier in Chapter 4, succession events are a major reason for a new strategic direction. It is for this reason that the nature and composition of the senior management team should always be monitored closely.

In short, it is important to discern which set of factors is helping to fashion market entry strategies. Solely internal or external factors are two polar extremes of a continuum. More frequently it is necessary to make a judgement as to whether internal or external factors are in the ascendancy, albeit mitigated by the other set of factors. Correspondingly, a detailed examination of market entry needs to give consideration to both set of factors.

International market entry

The need to make the right decision in respect of international market entry is emphasised by the likelihood of there being significant penalties if a wrong decision is made. Not only will there be the investment of management time and financial resources, but market entry failure may lead to shareholders experiencing a loss of confidence in the management of the company. Equally, for the organisation there is also the opportunity cost, as potentially better opportunities are forgone. Conversely, getting the decision right may help place the organisation on a higher growth path and result in shareholders giving greater support to the incumbent management.

The methods used to select markets and strategies vary. They range from highly sophisticated attempts to appraise markets to decisions based on the intuitive judgement of, say, the chairman of the company. This emphasises that the process is likely to be a mixture of rational-analytical judgements and highly subjective factors based on the organisation's internal context. Correspondingly, data collection prior to the entry decision being made can be substantial in some cases, but significantly limited in others. Illustration 6.2 describes how one company decided which new market to enter.

Illustration 6.2

Mappin & Webb opens first store in mainland Europe

Since the fall of the Berlin Wall the Czech Republic has become a much more attractive market, with consumers developing a taste for quality goods produced by the major industrial nations. One company which is hoping to take advantage of these developments is Mappin & Webb, the London-based up-market jeweller and luxury retail chain. In September 1993 its first European store outside the UK was opened in Prague, the capital city of the Czech Republic.

The new store located in the centre of Prague's Old Town represents a £2.5 million investment by the company and is targeting Czech consumers rather than the thousands of tourists who visit the city every summer. The expectation is that turnover would reach £2 million in the first year, and profits in the region of £150,000. Naim Attalah, chief executive of the group which owns Mappin & Webb, explained why the Czech Republic had been chosen by the company. 'I've got a good hunch about Prague. It's new, it's enterprising, people are making money.' Originally Mr Attalah had planned to open in Shanghai in order to take advantage of the emergence of China. He finally decided on Prague after 'wearing my feet out' wandering around the city one sweltering evening earlier in the summer, after attending the opera.

Source: Based on Boland (1994)

While the market entry model is presented as a four-stage sequence for ease of exposition, in practice the process is more likely to be one of constant adjustment and iteration as the different elements of the decision-making process are considered and reconsidered. Visually this can be illustrated by Figure 6.4 which shows how, for example, issues arising during the consideration of how a strategy is to be implemented may influence market selection; while expected performance may be an important factor in shaping the mode of entry.

The inter-relatedness of all elements of the market entry decision should be borne in mind when examining each of the four components below.

Figure 6.4 The inter-relationships between the elements of the market entry model

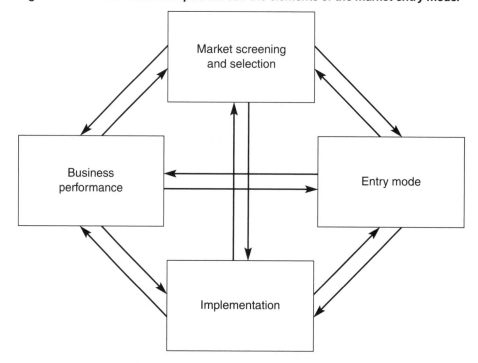

Market screening and selection

In the process of deciding to commit itself to developing a sustained international presence, management will need to focus on the task of market screening as a prelude to market selection. Market screening will include an assessment of both the general characteristics of the country:

- political and economic risks
- cultural diversity

and the specific nature of the product-market within any one country:

- product match
- size of market
- expected growth
- extent of competition
- scale of entry

   While in practice these two characteristics may be considered together, it is helpful to discuss them separately. Later in this chapter it is shown how these important variables are incorporated in a market selection grid.

Political and economic risks

There is widespread agreement that political instability is an important concern of senior managers contemplating cross-border market entry. It is not particularly easy, however, to reach a consensus as to what constitutes unacceptable political instability or how such instability can be predicted. Political risks may arise from wars and insurrection, governmental take-over of corporate assets, and discriminatory restrictions where entry involves acquiring existing companies and/or displacing national competitors.

   Political risk is not uniform. The extent of the political risk to a company will vary according to the country the company is seeking to enter. The degree of political risk is likely to be reflected in, or a reflection of, the underlying economic conditions of the nation. This in turn will be paralleled by the likely future movements in the exchange rate and the cost of, for example, securing finance for sales to the country. Factored into this equation are the underlying inflation and growth rates. Where the political economy of a nation gives rise to concern, any financing costs to be borne by the company will be increased correspondingly.

   Since financing rates reflect the expected future political economy of a country, selective financing rates may be used cautiously to indicate systematic political and economic risk. Table 6.3 shows selected forfaiting rates, with higher rates charged for greater perceived political and economic risk. Forfaiting describes the process whereby a third party, often a bank, purchases

Table 6.3 Selected fixed five-year forfaiting rates, June 1994

Brazil	13.50
Egypt	13.00
Czech Republic	11.50
Morocco	11.50
Mexico	10.50
Thailand	9.00
Malaysia	8.25
France	7.75
Germany	7.75

Source: Rates supplied by Banque Indosuez Aval, June 1994

the debt obligations of the exporter without having recourse to the seller. This provides an exporter with immediate cash once a bill of exchange or promissory note has been received. As a term, forfaiting originates from the fact that the exporter forfeits the right to future receivables in exchange for immediate payment. Table 6.3 shows that the political and economic risk associated with exports to Brazil and Egypt is almost double those associated with France and Germany.

Cultural diversity or convergence

An integral part of the assessment as to whether a country should become the focus of a company's international business development is cultural diversity or convergence. This is not only important in respect of the likely acceptance by customers of a product or business format, but also affects the perceptions of the company's management and in particular the attractiveness of cross-border locations for foreign nationals. This is not insignificant when organisations themselves are formed of managers who may possibly need to live and work abroad in order to operationalise the strategy. It also is a reminder that in practice subjective human judgements may be critical in making the final decision. Cultural factors will also encompass language, with a number of companies often preferring countries where English, the international business language, is strongly to the fore.

Below the broad contextual factors, country-specific considerations in respect of the product-market potential for the company's sales in an individual national market are important. Examination of these key factors will assist the firm in determining the order of entry into potential markets, assuming that it cannot and does not want to enter a large number of markets simultaneously. As revealed at the start of this section, five influential variables need to be reviewed.

Product match

The extent to which the company believes it can sell its current product-market offer into a new market or whether it needs to customise for a new market is often an important consideration. While tastes and lifestyles have tended to converge, often important differences between national markets remain. For example, chocolate confectionery is often instanced as a global industry, but in many markets national products remain significant. Further, the internationalisation of the industry is largely confined to countries which have a 'Western culture' and it has yet to incorporate countries, including Japan and other Asia-Pacific countries, where traditional cultures remain important. In Japan the more traditional markets for cakes, biscuits and Japanese-style snacks are more significant. Consequently, market entry to Japan may be less attractive to the major international chocolate confectionery companies, who market Western style products.

Even when the basic product requires little modification, considerable marketing effort may be needed to ensure the product or service gains acceptance. An established name in the company's national market is unlikely to be able to drive sales in a cross-border market until, for example, brand reputation has been established. Where product or service modification is required to match customers' needs in the international market, the company will have to consider the costs and benefits of doing this. Illustration 6.3 considers the extent to which one product with a highly successful record in the USA has been transferred to Europe.

Illustration 6.3

EuroDisney

In the year to 30 September 1993, EuroDisney experienced a net loss of FFr6.9 billion. The loss was a severe shock to investors who had expected that the theme park, located just outside of Paris, would be an outstanding success. This view was based to a large extent on the role Walt Disney Inc had in the venture. Many investors were convinced that Walt Disney's success in the USA, based on its proven management and marketing strengths, would ensure that EuroDisney, in which the company had a 49 per cent stake, could not fail.

Following losses in 1993 considerable debate took place as to whether the Disney concept was inappropriate for the European market, or whether the operation had just experienced bad luck since the theme park had opened in April 1992. Proponents of the latter view suggested that the economic recession in Europe, exacerbated by the strength of the French Franc, had caused short-term difficulties which could be overcome. Other commentators believed that the whole venture was misconceived, arguing that opening the park was a mistake.

Some commentators asked why build a theme park which included attractions such as artificial castles and simulated flights over Big Ben, in a continent where consumers could go and visit the real thing? Another concern was that, while EuroDisney seemed to be able to attract day visitors, consumers did not seem to perceive the park as the place to take their annual holiday.

Only when the European economies experience recovery and consumer spending begins to increase will the question of whether EuroDisney was misconceived be answered with confidence.

Source: Based on Skapinker and Ridding (1993)

Size of market and growth rates

The size of the potential opportunity afforded by a particular market is clearly an important consideration, as is the likelihood of a sustained overall growth of market sales. Companies may seek those markets which offer the greatest opportunity, knowing that if they can become established in such markets significant sales can be anticipated. Such markets may be considered to have particular strategic significance. Emphasising the inter-linkage between the elements of the entry mode, some companies may wish to consider part of the national market, in, say, the USA if resources do not enable the whole country to be covered at the outset, and choose to focus on a national region.

Estimating the size of the market and future growth requires that first the company defines clearly what its product-market is and then identifies the key drivers to demand. For some products there may be one or two clear drivers which help explain current levels of demand and provide the basis for forecasting future patterns of growth. Both the level and expected growth of GNP may be important for a number of products, although in each market there may specific characteristics which modify the demand functions found to exist for other countries.

Extent of competition

Competition is always a critical factor in considering market selection. An analysis of the company's products versus those of existing competitors will help in assessing the extent to which the organisation is likely to capture sales against the overall level of demand and market growth. This will also require an assessment of the nature of the competitive strategies used by incumbent firms, their size and likely reaction to the entry of a cross-border competitor to the market. In some circumstances, while the size and anticipated growth of the market may be attractive, the intensity of competition generated by incumbent suppliers may render entry to the market unattractive.

Scale of entry

Linked to the nature of the product-market and competition will be the scale of entry required. If the market is growing and the industry structure fragmented, with numerous small competitors, then entry may be possible on a modest level. Alternatively, if the market is mature and the industry structure has become concentrated, entry may need to be on a substantial scale in order to have any chance of success. Recognition of these factors in such circumstances is likely to influence the mode of entry and suggest, for example, that the acquisition of an incumbent competitor may offer the most appropriate entry mode.

A *market selection grid* may be used to assess systematically both general and product-specific factors outlined in the previous discussion. Table 6.4 is an example of a market selection grid used to assess countries for market entry. Irrespective of the intended scale of market screening, at some point the progressive application of the screening process will reduce the number of countries to be examined in detail to more manageable proportions. In the example shown in Table 6.4, Country D may be eliminated immediately from consideration on account of the fact that cultural diversity is considered unacceptable.

Among the three remaining countries – A, B and C – depicted in Table 6.4, values have been assigned to the five specific product-market factors previously discussed, since all of these countries merit examination on account of the broad contextual factors pertaining to each being declared acceptable. Where a specific factor is rated 5, the product-market is highly attractive with respect to this element of the selection criteria; while if the ranking is 1, the product-market is highly unattractive. Considerable judgement is required in determining what rating to assign to each factor in turn. While Country C may be eliminated on the basis of its low unweighted total score, Countries A and B with the same total score are more difficult to separate.

Table 6.4 Market selection grid

Contextual factors (U = unacceptable/ A = acceptable)	Country A	Country B	Country C	Country D
Political and economic risks	A	A	A	A
Cultural diversity	A	A	A	U
Specific product-market *(rank order)*				
Product match	5	5	2	–
Size of market	3	2	1	–
Expected growth	2	3	2	–
Extent of competition	2	1	2	–
Scale of entry	2	3	1	–
Unweighted total	14	14	8	–

In the application of the market selection grid not only is there the potential difficulty of assigning values to each of the factors, but also the question arises as to how each factor is to be weighted and an overall assessment reached. In Table 6.4 the values assigned to each factor have simply been aggregated and a judgement made on the basis of the unweighted total. This has resulted in two countries – A and B – apparently being equally as attractive from the point of view of market entry. It is very likely in such circumstances that subjective elements may knowingly or unknowingly play a part in the final selection of which market to entry. This may occur through the weighting frame incorporated in the market selection grid, with the basis for assigning relative weights to each of the factors being informed by the perceptions of key individuals. In particular, three likely biases to the final decision can be identified, namely:

● cognitive
● motivational
● unplanned

In the case of decisions based on *cognitive* bias, the decision-makers believe they are being objective, but either explicitly or implicitly rate one factor more highly than the others and the assessment of this factor determines the final decision. The desired outcome may be presented as the result of the objective assessment of all factors, although the underlying weights assigned to the key factors in the market selection grid are informed by individual prejudices. By contrast, *motivational* bias describes an outcome which is determined by the motivation of the decision-makers who ensure that the weighting frame used produces the outcome that they want. Again, while the decision may be presented as objective and the market selection grid used to justify the outcome, the process is very much determined by what the key individual(s) wish to achieve. Finally, and not infrequently, market entry selection may occur in an *unplanned* and random manner, and a seemingly most unlikely choice of market result. An example of such an outcome is described in Illustration 6.4.

The previous discussion highlights that, while market selection is often presented as a wholly rational-analytical process, inevitably a degree of subjectivity arises in making the final market selection. Indeed, as the case of roller bearing producer RHP Bearings demonstrates, the internal context can be very powerful.

When asked where RHP might open a new plant, initial discussion revolved around the pros and cons of Germany and the UK on dimensions such as access to customers, production costs and labour availability. However, Spain was raised as a distinct possibility because of its vibrant machine tool industry and because the commercial director's wife was Spanish. (A Bowkett, Chairman of RHP Bearings, personal interview, cited in Collis (1991), p 64)

Entry modes

Some elements pertinent to determining the mode of entry may well have been initially considered as part of the market selection process, not least an examination of the scale of entry required for the market. In practice, market selection and entry mode may therefore to some extent be considered collectively. Focusing on the entry mode, six factors are likely to inform the decision, namely:

- degree of control
- resource availability and extent of commitment
- degree of risk
- speed
- opportunities available
- expected return

Illustration 6.4

Bronnleys Ltd

Bronnleys is a traditional British soap manufacturer based in Northamptonshire, some 60 miles to the north of London. The company has three endorsements from the British Royal family and the majority of its sales are to the British market. Even so, the company is active in exporting, which accounts for approximately 30 per cent of total sales.

Using the market selection grid with five variables (ranked 1 to 5) and associated weights (weighting each variable between 1 and 10), thereby making the 250 points the maximum attainable score for any one country, the outcomes are presented in the figure below:

Germany	208
France	143
Italy	102
Singapore	93
USA	91
Switzerland	83
Netherlands	82
Spain	80
Portugal	72
Japan	66

While different analysts produce slightly different weighted scores, France and Germany – the company's top two markets – tend always to feature as the two most attractive export markets. The same cannot be said about the company's third most important market: Taiwan. This market does not feature in any of the rankings above, or any of the detailed analysis undertaken by the authors. In this country the organisation's success is largely down to the company's agent. Using a highly effective door-to-door salesforce, the company's agent has been able to achieve significant sales of the company's exclusive products. Interestingly, Taiwan is the only market where the company's product is sold on this basis. The company's success in Taiwan offers a good example of an unplanned and random choice of markets, based on an idiosyncratic approach by the now successful agent, who initially approached Bronnley's with an offer to sell their products.

Source: The authors

Alternative modes of entry will result in a different permutation of the above factors. An organisation will wish to consider which mode offers the best combination of factors to suit its needs and aspirations. The set of entry options that a company may wish to choose, ranging from export to investment modes, is presented in Table 6.5.

Table 6.5 Alternative modes of entry

Classification of entry modes
Export entry modes Methods of entry where the company's products are produced outside of the overseas market. *Indirect exporting* Uses middlemen who are located in the company's own national market, and are responsible for undertaking the exporting. *Direct exporting* Does not use home-country middlemen, but may employ middlemen based in the overseas market. Direct exporting can be sub-divided according to whether entry involves: (i) direct agent/distributor exporting – where middlemen in the overseas market are responsible for marketing the exported goods; or (ii) direct branch/sub-sidiary – where the company uses its own sales organisations in the overseas market. **Contractual entry modes** These may be described as non-equity associations between an international company (actual or emerging) and a legal entity in the overseas market, involving the transfer of knowledge, understanding and/or skills. *Licensing* An arrangement whereby the company is prepared to transfer to the overseas entity for a defined period the right to use its commercial/industrial property (e.g. technology knowledge, patent, etc.) in return for some form of compensation, usually a royalty payment. *Franchising* Franchising involves the right to use a business format in the overseas market in return for the franchiser receiving some form of payment. *Other* These include technical agreements, service contracts, contract manufacture and co-production agreements (e.g. own-label supply). **Investment entry modes** Entry modes under this heading involve ownership of production units in the overseas market, based on some form of equity investment. *Independent venture* These include overseas production facilities or outlets which are under the full owner-ship and control of the company selling into the overseas market. Such facilities may be newly developed, or acquired by taking over an existing operator in the market. *Joint venture* This mode of entry involves sharing the ownership and control of the overseas facilities or outlets with one or more local partners. *Source:* Based on Root (1987), pp 7–8

In reflecting on the alternative modes of entry there are important differences between manufacturing and service industries. By the very nature of their characteristics and the fact that many services are often produced at the point of consumption, export entry modes cannot be employed by many service industries. As a result, service companies wishing to enter international markets tend to use either contractual or investment entry modes. This point is of some relevance given the increasing internationalisation of many service sector companies. Six influential variables need to be reviewed in order to assess the most appropriate entry mode:

- degree of control
- resources available and extent of commitment
- level of risk
- speed
- opportunities available
- expected return

Degree of control

Broadly, the degree of control the organisation has over its sales in cross-border markets increases as it moves away from indirect exporting. Under either indirect exporting or direct exporting, using a direct agent or distributor the organisation's degree of control over its sales is limited. In both instances intermediaries are responsible for the distribution and the effective marketing of the company's (and other companies') products in the market place. While direct agents or distributors can be successful, they tend to be used where the anticipated volume of sales is relatively low. For larger sales volumes and/or greater control, organisations may move to using a direct branch or subsidiary through which to channel sales.

Compared with domestic sales, cross-border intermediaries typically reduce the net profit margin by around 50 per cent. On small volumes of discretionary sales this may be quite acceptable. As export volumes increase the potential loss of earnings to the company becomes more pronounced. In such circumstances the company may contemplate sizeable fixed investment in market infrastructure, so as to be able to secure a net profit margin similar to that enjoyed in its domestic market. For a manufacturing company the next stage beyond using direct agents is often to market its products using a direct branch or subsidiary.

In addition to gaining direct control of marketing and being able to set its own selling price, the company retains the large margin taken by the intermediary. The firm may also be better informed and responsive to market changes since it can directly monitor customer and sales responses. Where this method is used for manufactured goods being imported into the market, the direct subsidiary or branch will focus primarily on sales and marketing in the export market.

Resources available and extent of commitment

The organisation's commitment and vision may limit the entry options it wishes to consider. Investment entry modes are likely to require higher levels of capital investment than options focusing on either contractual or exporting strategies. Alongside the availability of financial resources, management time is both valuable and scarce. Limited managerial resources may persuade a company to go for entry modes which place relatively low demands on the company's existing management. Where the company's commitment and/or resource availability is low, export entry modes are likely to be favoured.

Level of risk

Some companies will be relatively risk adverse and wish to take a conservative view in making any commitments abroad. Often this will reflect the company's corporate culture. Where a company traditionally has taken a relatively careful approach to developing its business, it may be more inclined to take a gradualist approach. Alternatively, a company may decide that the time is right to make a major new commitment and be prepared to take significant risks, reflecting the vision of a new senior management team who do not feel constrained by the company's past. BMW's investment in the USA, discussed in Chapter 2, is a good example of such a discontinuity.

Speed

Speed can be a major consideration if, for example, an organisation realises its rivals have stolen an advantage. In such a situation the organisation may weight more highly those entry modes which offer the prospect of establishing a presence in the international market more quickly. Conversely, where competitive pressures are not so demanding the organisation may be prepared to take a longer-term view in developing its entry strategy. Consequently, the range of entry modes will not be so restricted.

Opportunities available

Entry modes may be limited by the opportunities available. For instance, the company may prefer an investment entry mode, but be unable to find suitable companies either to acquire or to develop a joint venture with. Lesser developed countries may, for instance, impose restrictions on inward investment, and require international companies to find a local partner to work with in setting up a production facility. Similarly, the company may wish to use a direct agent, but be forced to move to an alternative entry mode if it is unable to find an agent who it believes will effectively market its products.

Expected return

The objectives the organisation has in relation to its market entry will influence the entry mode selected. If its ambitions are modest with limited sales, then a relatively low cost option using indirect exporting may be preferred. Equally, if the company wishes to achieve a major presence in the market with a substantial level of sales it might, for example, establish an overseas subsidiary, which may strictly be too big an operation at the time of entry, but offer the prospect of meeting longer-term goals.

Choosing the appropriate entry mode is case specific. For any company it is highly dependent on both the value (where 1 is unattractive and 5 is highly attractive) and the weighting (between 1 and 10) given to the six market entry factors. The relative importance and thus the weight applied to each of the factors separately described will vary with the needs, the culture and the outcomes the organisation expects. Likewise the value ascribed to each factor requires considerable judgement. Table 6.6 provides a template to assess the weighted attractiveness of a given mode of entry, by identifying three entry options available to a company seeking international market entry. To operationalise the framework presented in Table 6.6, appropriate weights and values need to be imputed.

Table 6.6 Entry mode grid

Market entry		Entry option A		Entry option B		Entry option C	
Key factors	Weight (1–10) (1)	Value (1–5) (2)	Weighted score (1) × (2)	Value (1–5) (4)	Weighted score (1) × (4)	Value (1–5) (5)	Weighted score (1) × (5)
Degree of control							
Resource availability							
Level of risk							
Speed							
Expected return							
Opportunities available							
Total weighted score							
Rank order							

In similar markets different entry modes are likely to be selected, reflecting the individual weighting patterns adopted by the organisation. These will mirror the organisational dynamics and capture attitudes to risk and time scale preferences. Illustration 6.5 makes this point powerfully by highlighting two contrasting entry modes, used by the two leading Austrian banks, to establish banking networks in Central and Eastern Europe.

Illustration 6.5

Creditanstalt Bank

Since 1990 Creditanstalt, the Austrian-based banking group, has been committed to establishing a commercial banking network in Central and Eastern Europe. Creditanstalt anticipates that within the next three to five years they will have up to ten branches in the most important locations in each Central European country. This will be achieved by setting up their own branches, which takes between nine to twelve months from the moment the decision is made to establish a branch to the actual date of opening. Creditanstalt believes that its strategy allows the bank to have a uniform approach to its expansion and to control the process.

While Creditanstalt plans to open wholly owned subsidiaries which will each carry its name, its major Austrian competitor, Raiffeisen Zentralbank Österreich, is investing in existing local banks in the same countries. Raiffeisen's strategy of market entry through buying existing banks allows it immediate access to a local branch network. It remains to be seen in the medium term which of the two contrasting entry modes will result in superior business performance.

Source: Based on Troer (1994)

Together with determining the entry mode, the company will need to reflect on the tactics to facilitate entry to the market. This will be influenced strongly by the mode of entry, and whether, for example, the company is entering the market using an export or investment mode. Where the company is seeking to export to an international market it may, for example, plan to concentrate its resources on establishing a 'bridgehead' in the market, before seeking a higher volume of sales through extending its coverage of the market and/or increasing market penetration. Phasing entry to a market in this way, or focusing just on part of a large national market as might be the case with entry to the US market, may be highly attractive, especially for relatively small companies where there is a need to make the implementation more manageable and the expected outcome to the strategy more likely to be achieved.

Implementation of chosen market entry mode

Implementation of the market entry strategy will need to focus on the key functional areas, namely:

- marketing
- human resources
- operations
- logistics
- finance

Each of these functions will need to be configured and co-ordinated in order to ensure that they both effectively and efficiently support the chosen entry strategy. Importantly, unless this can be done then regardless of appropriate market selection and entry choices being made, the overall strategy is likely to be only partially successful at best.

Unless the previous stages to choosing a market entry strategy have taken sufficient cognisance of the internal context, any attempt to implement the strategy is likely to lead to difficulties. This point emphasises the fact that if the chosen strategy is at significant variance to the organisational dynamics, unless management intervention to change the internal context can be made effectively within the required time scale, difficulties will arise. In practice this is highly unlikely to occur. The characteristics of an organisation's dynamics – its beliefs, values, core competences, power structures, etc. – almost inevitably evolve slowly over time, suggesting that rapid change is often difficult to achieve.

A necessary condition for implementation to succeed is that sufficient managers and staff are committed to the organisation's international business development and that they are prepared to work to ensure the success of the company's market entry strategy. This emphasises the need for senior managers to move the organisation forward, but at the same time to ensure a sufficient match with the internal context. Total 'fit' is not what is required, and there needs to be 'stretch' as well as 'fit' in developing the strategy. As Hamel and Prahalad (1994) have suggested, simply emphasising fit is unlikely to mean that the organisation will be creative and able to encompass new challenges. Senior managers will need to judge the balance between 'stretch' and 'fit' to ensure that tensions between change and continuity can be successfully managed.

While the detail of each function and their co-ordination will vary according to the specific context and mode of entry chosen, each of the key business functions will need to be carefully configured and managed. Regardless of the entry mode selected, a number of generic tasks will have to be planned and implemented in order that the strategy has a good chance of success. How the key functions are configured to serve the new market may be expected to differ in important ways from the company's existing knowledge, understanding and experience. Many organisations can be daunted by these challenges, and third-party assistance may be sought to undertake a number of key tasks.

A third party, in the guise of a direct agent or joint venture partner, may carry out a number of the tasks listed below and/or offer local knowledge and expertise, thereby making more manageable the magnitude of the organisation's new learning. This emphasises one of the potential advantages of using these modes of entry. Similarly, if an existing going concern is taken over, then the company will inherit established functional structures and local knowledge, although their quality and the value are very dependent on the current health of the acquisition.

If a company is seeking to set up a cross-border organisation for the first time, it is more than likely that mistakes will be made. Indeed, the tests for the organisation may be how quickly it can learn; how critical are the mistakes made; and whether sufficient resources are available for corrective adjustments to be undertaken.

Marketing

The effective matching of the organisation's product/service offer to customers' needs has to be fashioned carefully in order to provide one of the necessary conditions for the successful implementation of the entry strategy. Key elements to an appropriate marketing strategy are likely to focus on the following:

- the initial target market for sales on which the organisation will concentrate. The organisation may, for instance, initially chose to focus on one area or national region; and/or one group of customers;
- whether product modifications will be necessary to secure cross-border sales, and the extent to which, for example, new or existing brands might be promoted;
- the developing of pricing strategy and structures, reflecting local demand, costs, competition and product positioning;
- determining the promotion and communication strategy; recognising and balancing the effectiveness of alternative media forms with the budgeted resources available.

Human resources

The 'people' element is central to the success of any strategy, and it will be necessary to ensure that staff at all levels of the organisation are committed to the entry strategy, and are prepared to contribute fully to its success. Some areas of specific attention which can be expected to contribute to the development of an effective human resources strategy include:

- the establishment of an appropriate management structure and associated reporting lines;
- the recruitment of skilled personnel, and/or development of members of the existing workforce/management, including where necessary provision of appropriate training, e.g. international selling skills, language training, cultural awareness programmes, etc.;
- the adjustment of personnel policies and procedures where this is appropriate, to accommodate prevalent local practices and/or differences in employment law found in the cross-border labour market.

Operations

The operations function will need to focus on ensuring output is available for sale in the international market. Differences will arise as to whether, for example, the product being sold is a good or service; products for export and domestic sales are being made in the same plant; the extent of product adaptation for the overseas market; and other characteristics of overseas market demand, including volume and seasonality. Specifically, the organisation will need to manage its operations to ensure that:

- international sales meet any local specifications, legal or otherwise;
- production is scheduled to meet international demand, while continuing to ensure the needs of the domestic market are also met.

Logistics

Increasing recognition of the importance of this once neglected function, indicates just how important logistics can be to the success of any business strategy. Accordingly, the logistics function will need to focus on:

- supply chain management, including procurement, transportation, distribution, stock control, etc.;
- the development of support systems, e.g. management information systems, systems of payment to suppliers and from distributors, agents, retailers, etc., as appropriate.

Finance

The finance function will need to manage any initial and ongoing investment costs associated with establishing the international operation; determine the basis on which income from cross-border sales is remitted back to the company; and ensure appropriate arrangements are in place for the transfer of funds across national borders. Some of the key components to the financial strategy are likely to include:

- how the establishment of the international operation is to be funded, e.g. internal resources, borrowings, additional share issue, etc.;
- establishing budgets for the international operation;
- arrangements for translating sales in the foreign currency into the organisation's reporting currency;
- terms on which products are sold in international markets;
- management of bad debts and credit control.

The key areas listed under each of the above functional areas are not designed to be exhaustive, but rather indicative of the range of tasks and associated complexities which have to be planned and managed successfully if an entry strategy is to have a good chance of success. Reflecting on the range of tasks, it is perhaps not surprising that many businesses find making a success of entry to a cross-border market so demanding and difficult. The Le Creuset case study at the end of this chapter gives important insights into these critical issues.

Business performance

Once the international market entry strategy has been implemented, attention will switch to monitoring performance. As part of the entry decision the company is likely to have considered what outcomes it anticipates from selling its products/services into the new market. Depending on the nature of the internal context, the anticipated performance may be articulated in terms of general aims or highly specific outcomes. Linked to these is likely to be some indication of the time scale against which a projected level of performance is expected to be achieved. Inevitably the setting of milestones for initial market entry is to a degree problematic, but successful business performance demands a reasonably close correlation between corporate aspirations and achieved outcomes.

Illustration 6.6

Thorntons plc

Thorntons plc, which has a majority of its shares owned by the founding family, is a major UK manufacturer and retailer of premium chocolates and confectionery. The company's niche strategy of selling up-market, high margin products in the UK has been highly successful. From its factory in Central England the company supplies some 497 shops located on high streets in the UK, with around 221 outlets being operated by franchisees.

In 1989 Thorntons made a bold initial entry into the European chocolate market. Acquisitions included Gartner Pralines NV, a speciality Belgium chocolate manufacturer for £1.7 million; together with the French confectioners Sogeca SA and La Société Nouvelle de Confiserie, for £7.7 million and £1 million respectively. This later purchase gave them 66 confectionery/ice-cream outlets trading under the 'Martial' brand name in France, through which output from its newly acquired Belgium factory could also be sold.

Unfortunately the attempted replication of the company's domestic niche strategy on mainland Europe was not successful. During each of the first three years the company's operations in France recorded significant losses, with the cumulative losses since entry totalling some £4.5 million. In 1992 a major reorganisation of the European management structure took place. This was followed in June 1993 with an announcement that the company was restructuring its European operations. Thorntons closed all but 20 of its French retail outlets, maintaining the most profitable stores in and around Paris and Ile de France. The reorganisation of its French subsidiary led to Thorntons' making a £7.6 million provision in its accounts to cover the anticipated costs of restructuring.

Thorntons' recent experience demonstrates the difficulties of implementing a successful market entry strategy. It also highlights the potential costs incurred when such ventures do not go according to plan. Currently, Thorntons is undertaking a feasibility study of entry and development with respect to the German market, where its products are currently being marketed on its behalf by Hussel GmbH.

Source: The authors

For a company entering an international market for the first time there will inevitably be a steep learning curve to be travelled. It is highly unlikely, given the nature and the scope of the elements that are required to ensure a successful entry strategy, that first time around the company will succeed in selecting and implementing a market entry strategy that does not need some subsequent correction. It is to be expected that adjustments to the entry strategy will take place after initial market entry. Most of the adjustments, provided that the overall thrust of the strategy and implementation are broadly correct, can be expected to be minor and constitute a refinement of the chosen strategy. Under some circumstances, however, a more fundamental review of the strategy will be required. Illustration 6.6 discusses how the chocolate maker Thorntons has been forced to reappraise its entry to the French market.

If actual performance does not match expectations once the initial phase of entry is past, or increased pressure on the company's domestic sales requires a re-examination of how long international losses can be sustained, corrective adjustments to the market entry strategy will need to be made. In the first instance, these are likely to focus on issues relating to implementation process, unless inadequate performance has been allowed to exist for a prolonged period and more fundamental action is required. If adjustments to the implementation strategy do not yield sufficient improvements in business performance then progressively, as Figure 6.5 illustrates, the other elements of the market entry decision are likely to be reappraised and adjustments made. This may prompt a re-examination of the entry mode and market selection, and ultimately, if improved performance of a sufficient order is not forthcoming, the company may well decide to withdraw from the market. At this point the organisation's options include a retreat to a restricted national market focus or seeking alternative overseas markets for expansion.

Figure 6.5 Corrective adjustments to the chosen market entry strategy

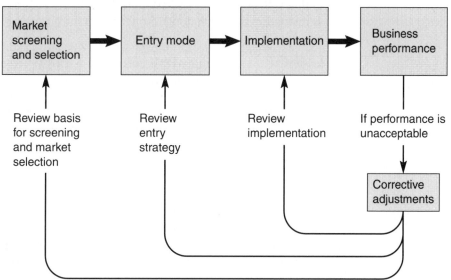

Important behavioural elements help to explain the adjustment process by which an incremental and progressive review of the key elements to market entry and selection takes place. Once a company has made the decision to enter an international market, then management is likely to have a vested interest in demonstrating the correctness of their decision. They are very unlikely, particularly early after the entry strategy has been executed, to admit that the wrong market was selected. Consequently, efforts will be made to make the strategy work, initially by focusing on the implementation process. Only after an acceptable period is attention likely to move to the earlier stages of the model and question the fundamental tenets in their selection of a particular target market. A potential exception to this statement is if the management team responsible for the entry decision are replaced and a new team of managers with little loyalty to the previous decision installed. Such a change may provoke a speedy review of the company's cross-border operations and possibly a fundamental change in strategy.

Reasons for the failure of international market entry strategies

Market entry and development strategies do not always succeed. As indicated earlier, for a company entering a cross-border market for the first time there are formidable obstacles to overcome before its strategy can be considered successful. While the rewards of a substantial growth of international sales may be attractive, the cost of failure may be just as great. The reasons for failure are many and may be complex, but include:

- inappropriate market screening and selection, and/or entry mode;
- the inability to implement a chosen strategy, reflecting an inappropriate balance between 'stretch' and 'fit';
- unforeseen events, affecting sales in the new market and/or the organisation's position in its domestic market which forces a reappraisal;
- retaliation by indigenous competitors, which undermine the entry strategy.

In extreme cases the circumstances may be such that the company is forced to retreat to operating with a restricted national scope. Where a restricted national scope no longer provides the basis of a sustainable competitive advantage, this may ultimately result in the organisation ceasing to trade or being sold to another competitor, unless another means can be found for extending the company's competitive scope through, for example, a strategic alliance. Certainly, for those industries becoming increasingly international there may be little option but to seek cross-border market entry. While success cannot be guaranteed, many companies see themselves as victims of their external environment and feel that they no longer have a choice other than to pursue international business development.

The importance of the failure to consolidate market entry is often that the organisation learns from its experience. Provided that the development of an international business strategy has not been left too late, the organisation may have the opportunity to try again. In order to adapt its strategy a company needs to know what to change and how. This can prove difficult, especially for many organisations which are inevitably inward looking and fail to use techniques such as benchmarking discussed earlier (see Chapter 5). The real danger is that the organisation does not make a serious attempt to analyse the reasons for failed market entry strategy and experiences further failure when it next attempts to develop an international business strategy. Whether the organisation is able to learn goes to the heart of the organisation's internal context and whether the company is a truly 'learning' organisation (see Chapter 4).

Market concentration versus market spreading

Implicit in the discussion so far has been the assumption that a company concentrates its efforts in entering a single market, and then, depending on whether it is successful, seeks further markets for international entry and development. While this assumption is valid for many companies, there will be occasions when a company simultaneously enters more than one market. This raises the question of whether a company should concentrate its efforts on a small number of markets, or spread itself across many.

Where a strategy of *market concentration* is pursued, the organisation will intentionally focus on a small number of key markets. In this context it is likely to develop a very strong involvement and competitive position before any attempt is made to enter new markets. This process has been likened to a 'cascade' to the extent that the organisation sequentially expands its presence in a number of international markets, but only after securing its position in the previous market entered. Using this strategy the company is likely to be reliant on a small number of international markets in which it builds a significant volume of sales. The overall strategy is based on the premise that the organisation has made optimal use of the market selection grid (see Table 6.4). One of the advantages of this strategy is that by concentrating on a relatively small number of markets, the company is able to limit the span of control necessary to manage its international development, thereby reducing the administrative complexities in dealing with a very large number of small markets.

By contrast, if the organisation adopts a strategy of *market spreading* it will seek to enter a large number of international markets, but only aim to achieve relatively low sales volumes in each. Sometimes referred to as a 'sprinkler' strategy, in this way the company is able rapidly to establish a broad international presence. Correspondingly the company's exposure to any one market is reduced, and fluctuations in the sales to one market are likely to be of minor importance. The large number of markets and relatively small volumes to each are likely to increase the complexities of administering the international sales and to raise the overhead cost. The company may in due course reorganise its infrastructure to cope with increased sales volumes in any one market.

The relative merits and demerits of both market concentration and spreading, together for some of the reasons of adopting each, are set out in Table 6.7.

Table 6.7 Market concentration versus market spreading

	Market concentration	Market spreading
Characteristics	Emphasis on a small number of markets, and on achieving high volume of sales to each	Emphasis on a large number of markets, with low level of sales to each market
Factors favouring adoption of the strategy		
(1) external	Necessary conditions for gaining high volumes are present, including level of potential demand and weak and/or fragmented competitors	Products in their early or late phase of the product life cycle.Difficult to gain high volume of sales to any one market, due to either low levels of demand or intensity of competition
(2) internal	Company prepared to concentrate significant resources on a small number of markets, and accept higher degree of dependence on key international markets	Company unwilling to over-commit to a single market, and wishes to spread risk of sales instability
Potential difficulties	Danger of concentrating on unattractive markets and/or impact of changing levels of economic activity in key markets	Unable to achieve significant presence in any one market, and loss of potential sales through spreading efforts too thinly

In practice, some companies may decide to use a combination of both market concentration and spreading strategies. They may decide for those markets judged to be strategically important to use entry modes which offer the prospect of achieving high volume of sales, while in the case of lower priority markets use low cost modes of entry. In this way the organisation aims to combine the best of both approaches.

It is important to note that any subsequent entry is likely to draw heavily on the organisation's learning and what it considers the optimal way of gaining entry to a market. As a result, companies will often use the same strategic recipe which has proved successful in one international context to secure entry to another market. In this way the previous practices of the company may provide important clues to likely future market entry strategies. This can be an important source of market intelligence for companies competing in intensely competitive arenas.

Summary

Triggered by external and/or internal change factors, market entry represents a major discontinuity for a company moving away from operating with a restricted national scope. Fashioning and executing a market entry strategy offer many challenges, and the organisation needs to manage the tension between continuity and change, if it is to secure a cross-border market and maintain its presence in its domestic market. To do this successfully the organisation must not only ensure a degree of fit with its organisational dynamics, but also recognise and manage the degree of stretch required to extend its competitive scope.

Business performance provides an important link in the process of entry and development, ensuring that there are constant adjustments where actual outcomes are judged unacceptable. Depending on the extent of any variance in expected performance and duration, corrective adjustments to one or more stages of the market entry process will occur progressively. International entry to a single market may focus on achieving a significant volume of sales as part of an overall strategy of market concentration, or alternatively only aim for modest levels of sales as the organisation focuses on market spreading.

Some organisations use a combination of market concentration and spreading in developing a sizeable international presence. Other organisations find entry and development fraught with difficulty so that entry to an international market may not be consolidated, but rather result in withdrawal and retrenchment to enable the company to focus exclusively on its domestic market. This emphasises that market entry and development strategies often entail significant risk and uncertainty as to the likelihood of their success.

Checklist

- A company will move to operating with an international scope due to external and/or internal triggers to change.
- The nature of external and internal factors collectively help to shape the market entry strategy.
- The balance of importance between external, as opposed to internal, factors in shaping entry strategies is highly situation specific.
- Developing a market entry strategy has four central elements: market screening and selection; entry mode; implementation; and business performance.
- Each of the elements of the entry process is interdependent, and rather than being a simple decision sequence the process is one of iteration and modification.
- Market screening has two elements: broad contextual factors relating to potential country selection; and specific factors relating to the product-market.

- Choosing a market to enter may be assisted by the use of a market selection grid.
- Although often presented as an objective assessment and decision, the choice of which market to enter is likely, knowingly or unknowingly, to be influenced by bias.
- Organisational dynamics must be recognised if an entry strategy is to be implemented successfully.
- There is considerable organisational learning associated with entry strategies and corrective adjustments to ensure business performance is acceptable are highly likely.
- Successful entry is not guaranteed and many companies fail, for a variety of reasons.
- If entry is judged a failure a company may switch its attention to alternative international markets, or decide to retrench and concentrate on its national market. This may not, however, be a long-term sustainable position.
- Companies may use a strategy of market concentration and/or market spreading when developing their international business strategy.
- Entry to further cross-border markets is likely to draw on the organisation's experience and learning in respect of previous cross-border entry.

Case Study 6

Le Creuset SA

Introduction

The South African born businessman Paul van Zuydam has revitalised the French cookware company Le Creuset since he acquired control in 1988. The company has traditionally concentrated on the manufacture and distribution of high quality cast iron cookware, but is now expanding through both organic growth and acquisitions into earthenware cookware, tableware and wine accessories. All products are manufactured at two production sites in France, with key export markets served by an international distribution network.

Background

The company was formed in 1924 to make cast iron cookware using traditional sand-moulding techniques. In 1957 the company acquired the Cousances foundry site in Eastern France with the purchase of its principal domestic competitor, Haut Fourneau et Fordenes de Cousances SA. As Table C6.1 shows, by the mid-1980s Le Creuset was operating with a high cost base and low operating profits. This led to the management at the time instigating a rationalisation programme. The Cousances foundry was closed in 1985, and the previous decision to undertake the enamelling of cast iron pans in the United States reversed.

Table C6.1 Le Creuset: Profit and loss 1984–93 (£ million)

	'Old management'				'New management'					
	1984	1985	1986	1987	1988	1989	1990	1991	1992	1993
Turnover	22.4	21.9	21.7	24.4	26.1	31.1	32.3	33.9	38.0	40.7
Cost of sales	14.7	14.6	14.5	15.8	15.3	17.5	18.0	18.6	19.8	21.4
Net operating expenses	6.4	6.5	5.5	6.6	8.2	10.1	10.4	11.0	13.3	14.9
Operating profits	1.6	0.7	1.6	2.0	2.7	3.5	3.8	4.3	4.9	4.4
Pre-tax profits	0.1	(0.7)	0.8	(0.4)	1.9	2.7	3.2	3.3	3.6	3.0

Source: Annual Reports

During this period Le Creuset suffered, like many family-controlled businesses, from under-investment in manufacturing plant, marketing and distribution. As Table C6.2 demonstrates, in the four years prior to 1988 capital expenditure was almost one-half of the annual depreciation charge, suggesting that the company was failing to maintain its capital base.

Case Study 6

Table C6.2 Le Creuset: capital expenditure and depreciation charge 1984–93 (£ million)

	'Old management'				'New management'					
	1984	1985	1986	1987	1988	1989	1990	1991	1992	1993
Capital expenditure	0.4	0.6	0.3	0.4	1.0	2.6	1.9	1.6	1.7	1.8
Depreciation	0.8	0.7	0.8	0.8	0.7	0.7	1.1	1.4	1.5	1.4
Capital expenditure as a % of depreciation	50	86	38	50	143	371	173	114	113	129

Source: Annual Reports

Acquisition of the company

In 1987, Paul van Zuydam – then Chairman and Chief Executive of the Prestige Group plc, the leading British cookware company – suggested to the executive committee of Prestige's parent company, Gallagher Limited, that they acquire the world-famous cast iron cookware manufacturer Le Creuset. After a year of indecision on Gallagher's part, van Zuydam decided to leave Prestige and acquire the ailing French firm himself. This has led to the unusual arrangement whereby a French-registered company is quoted on the UK stock exchange; its chairman operates from London; and all its manufacturing operations are based in France.

The post-1988 capital expenditure figures illustrate the importance placed by the new management team on increasing capital expenditure. Over the four years from 1987 around £7.1 million was spent on bringing the two manufacturing plants up to date. Following the decision to cease production and enamelling at Cousances, all cast iron products are now made and enamelled at the Fresnoy-Le-Grand plant. By contrast, the factory at Cousances has been dedicated to the manufacture of wine accessories, following substantial investment in a new plastic-moulding facility.

Traditionally Le Creuset sales have been dominated by cast iron cookware, but since Paul van Zuydam took over the range of houseware products has been extended. Product developments, including an earthenware range and Sabatier kitchen knives, are the work of a new product design team established since the company's take-over. Further, the Screwpull range of wine accessories was acquired from Hallen International Inc of the USA for US$6.5 million in 1991, with production being moved from Houston to Cousances. Le Creuset also distributes Weber barbecues and Zyliss kitchen tools for third parties.

Before the new management team took control there was little effective marketing of the company's products. One of van Zuydam's first priorities following his arrival was the purchase of The Kitchenware Merchants Limited, which had been Le Creuset's main UK distributor since 1960. This was the prelude to the setting up of a Le Creuset-owned distribution network worldwide to replace the previous

Case Study 6

arrangements, which included the use of independent agents in the USA and Japan. Le Creuset of America Inc and its former affiliate Schiller and Asmus Inc were legally merged into one distribution company in 1991, while Le Creuset Japan KK was set up to consolidate distribution in 1992. In 1993 Le Creuset bought a German distribution company Wolo GmbH (renamed Le Creuset Germany GmbH) to provide a distribution network for the German market.

Organisation and management

The current senior management team at Le Creuset is very experienced in the cookware/kitchen accessories sector. Paul van Zuydam is unquestionably the driving force behind the group. Not only does he occupy the roles of Chairman and Chief Executive, but he also owns 73.2 per cent of the issued shares. Table C6.3

Table C6.3 Le Creuset: Board of Directors, June 1994

Paul van Zuydam (57)
Chairman and Chief Executive. South African by birth, he has worked in the kitchenware market for over 25 years and was previously chairman and chief executive of the Prestige Group plc. Responsible for the overall strategy and direction of the company.

Ruddy Boussemart (39)
Managing Director for Manufacturing. French national who joined the Board in 1991, after being responsible for production for a number of years. Holds an engineering degree from a premier French university.

Jacques Buscaylet (58)
Group Finance Director. French national who joined Le Creuset in 1969 and became a director in 1989. Holds the French official accounting diploma and is a graduate in computer studies.

Stephen Marfleet (48)
Managing Director for Europe. Joined the Board in 1988 after working for Hilditch & Key as Managing Director. Previously worked with Paul van Zuydam at Prestige as Marketing Director.

Ian Puttock (71)
Non-executive director. Former Administrative Director who retired as an executive director at the end of 1993 on reaching his 70th birthday. A member of the 'new' management team who gained control of the company in 1988. Before joining Le Creuset he was Group Personnel and Administration Director at Prestige from which he retired in 1987.

Finn Schjorring (54)
President in North America. Joined Le Creuset in 1988 from Prestige where he was Chief Executive of European operations.

Tim Seymour (47)
Non-executive director. Chartered accountant and a director of Rea Brothers Limited, a London-based merchant bank. Became a director of Le Creuset in May 1988.

Michael Sworder
Managing Director for the UK and Ireland. Based in Andover, England, the headquarters of Kitchenware Merchants Limited. Has been associated with the company for some 13 years.

Source: Analysts' reports and Annual Report and accounts

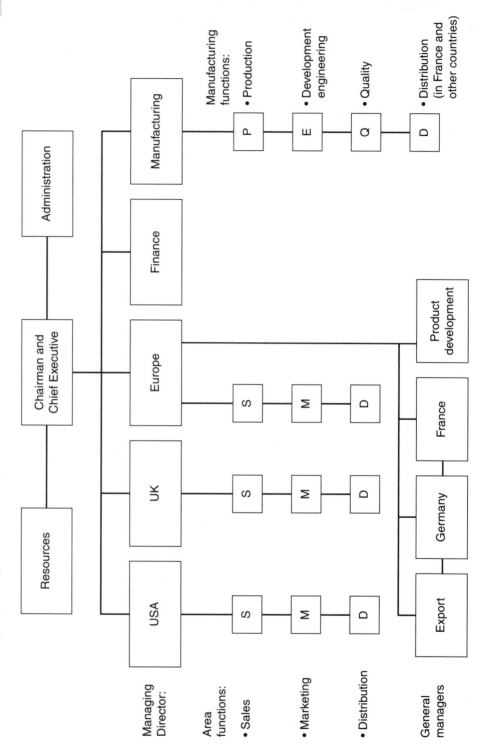

Figure C6.1 Le Creuset: group management structure, 1994

shows that four executive members of the Le Creuset Board of Directors previously worked together at Prestige. Many of the executive directors have held several different posts since 1987.

Important clues to the organisational dynamics of Le Creuset can be discerned from the organisational chart depicted in Figure C6.1. Both the UK and US markets, two of the company's principal export markets, are served by wholly owned distribution companies which each operate with their own managing director. Stephen Marfleet, who is a particularly influential member of the Board, has overall responsibility for the domestic French market and all other international markets. A team of four general managers reporting to Marfleet have particular responsibilities for France, Germany, Export and Product Development. All production is carried out in France and the heads of both the manufacturing and finance functions are French nationals.

Looking back to 1987 when Paul van Zuydam and his new team first took control of Le Creuset, it is apparent that the firm was very different from the company it is today. In the 1993 annual report the Chairman reviewed the period since he had taken control and indicated the direction in which the firm was expected to develop:

> Firstly, all our achievements since 1987 have been accomplished by an experienced and highly committed senior management team. This team has turned what was mainly a manufacturing orientated business into an international marketing led organisation with emphasis on professional, sales and distribution . . . In effecting this transformation, we have not by any means neglected the production and control aspects of the business. On the contrary emphasis has been placed on strengthening our financial control and investing in the latest appropriate computer technology. Very considerable investment has been made in production facilities . . .
>
> Strong sales and marketing departments have now been established in each of our major subsidiary companies in the USA, UK, France and Germany as well as our international export division and Japan . . .
>
> As a footnote, I am pleased to observe that all the changes that have taken place, which involved significant capital expenditure, have been funded internally from the Group's strong cash flow. (Extracts from the Chairman's Statement, Annual Report, 1993, pp 4–5)

Manufacturing process

Cast iron manufacture at Fresnoy-Le-Grand takes place through a four-stage production process: production of cast iron; casting; finishing; and enamelling. Each of these stages is illustrated and discussed in Figure C6.2.

Productivity at Fresnoy-Le Grand continues to be improved through an ongoing investment programme, although the current level of spending is below the level initially undertaken by the 'new' management team on gaining control of the company. Overall some £5 million was spent on reorganising and modernising the cast iron facilities at Fresnoy-Le-Grand between 1987 and 1993.

As a result of past investment, the cast iron production process is now more effective and cost efficient, with a substantial reduction in labour input over the last six years. The modernisation of the foundry was the first area to be tackled by new management. The installation of two Hamsburg casting machines, which became fully operational by the end of 1993, has automated the casting process and are six times more efficient than the labour-intensive process which has been

Case Study 6

Figure C6.2 Cast iron manufacturing process, Fresnoy-Le-Grand

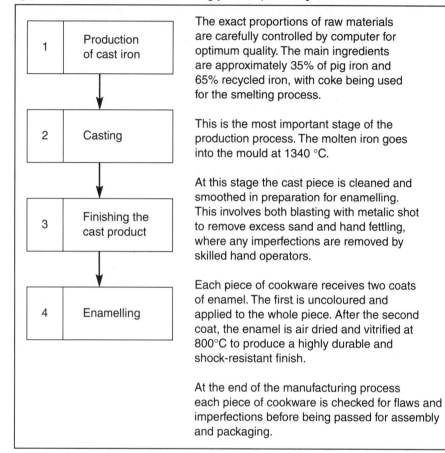

1	Production of cast iron	The exact proportions of raw materials are carefully controlled by computer for optimum quality. The main ingredients are approximately 35% of pig iron and 65% recycled iron, with coke being used for the smelting process.
2	Casting	This is the most important stage of the production process. The molten iron goes into the mould at 1340 °C.
3	Finishing the cast product	At this stage the cast piece is cleaned and smoothed in preparation for enamelling. This involves both blasting with metalic shot to remove excess sand and hand fettling, where any imperfections are removed by skilled hand operators.
4	Enamelling	Each piece of cookware receives two coats of enamel. The first is uncoloured and applied to the whole piece. After the second coat, the enamel is air dried and vitrified at 800°C to produce a highly durable and shock-resistant finish.

At the end of the manufacturing process each piece of cookware is checked for flaws and imperfections before being passed for assembly and packaging.

Source: Based on Annual Report, 1993

replaced. This was followed by the introduction of a Disamatic moulding unit, further reducing rejection rates. Equally, the enamelling stage has witnessed dramatic changes in recent years, with major capital expenditure to update and automate the enamelling process. Attention is now focused on how to reduce wastage rates further, as well as improving efficiency through conveyorisation and packaging for specific orders.

Cast iron production is sensitive to small increases in volume that can translate into large changes in profitability. Above a certain level, additional production can be made with little extra cost. Analysts estimated that in 1993 the Fresnoy-Le-Grand plant had 20–25 per cent excess capacity. Further assessment suggests that the newly modernised plant would not find it difficult to cope with volume increases of the order of 10 per cent per annum over the medium term (three years), translating into a 20 per cent increase in operating profit in each year.

Sales and profits by product and market

Le Creuset cast iron cookware has three outstanding aspects for which it is recognised: quality, durability and colour. The quality arises from stringent quality control checks at each stage of production and before dispatch. Quality control is

Case Study 6

assisted by the high specification regarding the thickness and weight of both the cast iron and enamelling, which also gives rise to the durability of the product. The brightness and depth of colour of Le Creuset's enamelled cast iron is the hallmark of the brand. Taken together, these three characteristics ensure a very up-market product that many consumers aspire to buy.

Having achieved very high levels of market penetration for cast iron cookware in France (70+ per cent) and the UK (80+ per cent), Le Creuset has not only sought to introduce its products to new markets, but also to widen its product range given that cast iron makes up only a small proportion of total cookware sales in any one market. Recognising that the non-stick frying pan tends to be the dominant cookware product, Le Creuset have introduced an aluminium enamelled frying pan positioned at the top of the market and a range of high quality earthenware products (which unlike cast iron can be used in a microwave and placed in a dishwasher). Distribution rights to another manufacturer's barbecues have been acquired and Le Creuset is also further developing its Screwpull range of wine accessories. Figure C6.3 provides a breakdown of the company's sales by principal product group. Casseroles are the top-selling cast iron product; barbecues, knives, kitchen tools and kettles are classified as kitchenware; and wine accessories are represented by the Screwpull range.

Figure C6.3 Le Creuset: sales by principal product group, 1993

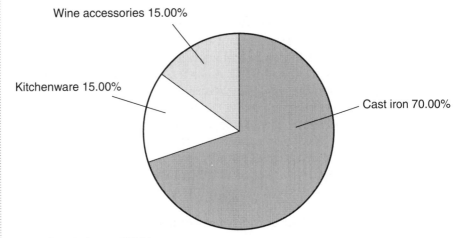

Source: Trade Estimates, 1993/94

Sales growth during the first half of the 1990s in the company's main markets has been affected by the overall levels of economic activity. Over this period the movement of the company's key markets into recession and their subsequent recovery have shown marked differences in timing and intensity. Consequently, sales growth by market has been affected not only by longer-term trends, but also by the phase reached in the economic cycle. Table C6.4 segments sales by geographical market and enables sales growth between 1990 and 1993 to be assessed.

259

Table C6.4 Le Creuset: sales by geographical market

Market	1990 £m	1990 %	1991 £m	1991 %	1992 £m	1992 %	1993 £m	1993 %
France	10.3	32	9.5	28	10.5	28	10.2	25
United Kingdom	10.5	33	10.6	31	11.0	29	11.5	28
USA	6.9	21	7.8	23	9.2	24	10.5	26
International	4.6	14	6.0	18	7.3	19	8.5	21
Total	32.3	100	33.9	100	38.0	100	40.7	100

Source: Annual Reports

As an international company, with the majority of its sales in international markets, Le Creuset is highly exposed to currency fluctuations. With all its production concentrated in France and profits reported in £ sterling, the French franc and £ are the most important currencies for the company. As the USA is the company's third largest market, the US dollar is also a key currency. Movements in these key currencies affect the translation of profits into the company's reporting currency, and the costs of producing in France. The difference in the company's reporting currency (£ sterling) and that of its production site (French francs) makes the interpretation of currency movements correspondingly more complex (see Illustration 2.4).

A lower French franc will reduce the cost of sales for cast iron cookware and improve gross profit margins across the world, but will reduce the value of sales to the French market when they are translated into sterling. Conversely, a rise in French francs will increase the cost of sales and reduce margins worldwide, but increase the value of sales to the French market in terms of the company's reporting currency. During 1993 the relative strength of the French franc adversely affected margins and undermined the company's export performance.

The level of economic activity together with currency fluctuations has affected the degree of profitability recorded in each geographical market. Group profits in 1993 were badly affected by recession in the French market, which resulted in a fall in sales and under-recovery of factory overheads.

Distribution and marketing

The importance of distribution channel control in key markets was established by Paul van Zuydam as a strategic imperative from the outset. Table C6.4 shows how in each key market from 1988 onwards there have been significant changes in the distribution of Le Creuset products. The objective to gain full control in the distribution of the company's products is not a one-off infrastructure investment, rather it represents a long-term ongoing investment with significant direct sales costs incurred by recruitment of sales representatives. Indeed, the development of its own distribution companies to serve national markets has significantly increased the company's fixed cost base. Nevertheless, Le Creuset is confident that the additional costs incurred are outweighed by the benefits which accrue from better

Case Study 6

control to the point of sale; improved communication with customers; and ability to exert greater influence on price and ensure it reinforces brand image.

Le Creuset's immediate marketing objective is to build each of the four parts of its worldwide sales – France, UK, USA and international – so that sales reach £12.5 million in each area. To achieve this aim, the international export division will need to achieve the fastest rate of growth. Stock market analysts believe there are opportunities to increase substantially US and export sales, as well as scope to add new products without increasing costs. Annual increases in sales of between 10 and 15 per cent should be achievable over the next three years. New market entry selection and development to meet this target are critical areas of management attention.

Since 1990 Paul van Zuydam has identified Germany, Japan and Scandinavia as strategically important export markets. The initial push was into Japan where Le Creuset Japan KK was established as a subsidiary to import and market cookware. The start-up costs were covered by a French government loan which need not be repaid if the venture fails. In 1993 Le Creuset made a further strategic acquisition so that the German market is now served by a wholly owned subsidiary located in the country. For the present the Scandinavian market continues to be served through agents.

One aspect of the company's operations which has not assisted the marketing effort has been the long delivery times in meeting customer orders. Orders for the USA take 2–3 months and those for the UK four weeks to fulfil. To compensate for this difficulty the company has traditionally held high levels of finished goods. Recognising the difficulties created, the company's intention is to move production and delivery onto a just-in-time basis in order to improve customer service and release funds for investment elsewhere in the business. Table C6.5 summarises Le Creuset's marketing objectives in relation to the company's main markets.

Manpower

Over the seven years in which Paul van Zuydam has been in control there has been a marked change in manpower deployment. As Table C6.6 shows, the number of employees engaged in sales, marketing and distribution has trebled, while at the same time the overall number of Le Creuset's employees has been reduced. The fall in production employees is indicative of concentrated attempts to reduce manufacturing costs and increase levels of efficiency.

The need for a structured salesforce in all key markets is amplified by widely differing market needs. There is little overlap in the top 10 products in the three key markets of France, UK and USA. There is a creative tension between national market needs and corporate brand image worldwide. In 1993 the marketing department was transferred from Paris to Fresnoy-Le-Grand in order to improve co-ordination with the technical and commercial departments. Conscious that product development and design are an integral part of the company's continuing competitiveness, a new design and product development team was established in 1992.

Table C6.5 Le Creuset: distribution channels and marketing objectives by key markets

France

1991 saw a major change in the distribution of Le Creuset's products with the development of direct delivery to large stores and hypermarkets throughout France. This not only raised direct distribution from 50 to 80 per cent of domestic sales, but required the building of a new warehouse at Fresnoy-Le-Grand from which Le Creuset can supply direct through its own salesforce. In 1993 the sales team was restructured and upgraded in order to reduce the number of reporting levels and increase efficiency. This was followed by investment during 1994 in information technology to improve data capture.

Germany

In 1993 Le Creuset acquired for £1 million a German distribution firm, thereby creating a Le Creuset sales and distribution company which became operative in 1994. Expectations are for sales of approximately £3.5 million in 1994 and £4.5 million in 1995. Sales are expected to be more even over the full product range, in contrast with other countries where cast iron accounts for 70 per cent of sales.

Japan

Le Creuset Japan KK has its own dedicated marketing and sales staff, serving over 80 department stores which display the company's products. In the first two full years of trading they achieved sales of £0.290 million (1992) and £0.296 million (1993). Le Creuset plans to support and invest in this strategically important market throughout 1994 and 1995, with the long-term aim of building a strong market presence in Japan.

UK

In 1988 Le Creuset acquired for £0.5 million its UK distributor, The Kitchenware Merchants (TKM), which also owns three retail outlets in England. In 1991 both the warehouse facility and the company's computerised sales system were upgraded. By 1993 the national sales team was approaching 20 full-time employees. Throughout 1993 fulfilment of orders delivered within ten days has been close to 98 per cent and this had been achieved with a substantial reduction in overall stocks. During 1994 TKM was renamed Le Creuset UK limited, to further strengthen brand image.

USA

Since 1988 Le Creuset has pursued two key distribution strategies: first, to work towards the medium-term goal of extending the range and nature of sales outlets from which customers could purchase the company's products; and secondly, to take significant steps to gaining greater control over its market coverage. From 1992 onwards a strong regional sales management structure has been installed, which in 1993 was supported by a reorganised marketing team. Customers are now served by a new infrastructure in which a third-party salesforce is being progressively replaced by employees of Le Creuset. Continued development of 'factory outlet' retail stores is also anticipated.

Others

Agency agreements with independent distributors have been established in some 20 countries. Almost half of the agreements are in Western Europe. Good progress has been made in establishing a worthwhile distribution channel in Scandinavia; while in 1993 new agreements were established to cover the Korean, Malaysian and Singapore markets. Less than 10 per cent of sales are booked by agents.

Conclusion

Le Creuset has developed its international business strategy significantly since the installation of the new management team in 1988. The company's development has focused on the rationalisation of its manufacturing facilities and associated cost reduction strategies, together with expenditure on distribution and marketing to build brand strength. Progress to date has been impressive, but

Table C6.6 Le Creuset: average number of employees, 1987–93

	1987	1988	1989	1990	1991	1992	1993
Production	554	523	473	473	457	418	401
Selling & distribution	62	102	123	153	178	185	192
Administration	64	75	91	66	67	62	64
Total	680	700	687	692	702	664	657
Sales per employee (£'000)	36.0	37.3	45.3	46.7	48.3	57.2	61.2
Change in sales per employee		+4%	+21%	+3%	+3%	+18%	+7%

major challenges remain if the company is to extend its international market presence. The extent of these challenges is made even more evident by the fact that in 1993 Le Creuset recorded its first fall in profits for six years.

Questions

(1) *Assess the extent to which external and/or internal factors have been responsible for shaping Le Creuset's international business strategy.*

(2) *Why do you think the company decided to enter the Japanese market? What rating would you give Japan as opposed to Germany when using the market selection grid to determine which market to enter? What conditions do you think are necessary for the company's success in the Japanese market?*

(3) *What different entry modes does Le Creuset use for its international markets and why? How would you use the entry mode grid to assess the alternative options?*

(4) *To what extent does Le Creuset employ a strategy of market concentration? What potential risks is the company exposed to?*

(5) *Identify the range of strategic options from which management can choose in shaping the company's future international business development. What are the respective challenges in pursuing each of these options? Which option do you think the company should follow and why?*

Chapter 7

INTERNATIONAL REGIONAL STRATEGIES

Key learning objectives

To understand:

- levels of economic integration

- the difference between exporter, fragmented and co-ordinated international regional strategies

- the role of external and internal triggers to developing an international regional strategy

- the benefits of operating with an international regional strategy

- the difficulties in managing the transition from fragmented to co-ordinated international regional strategies

- strategic options for national players who need to operate with regional scope and scale

- the need to co-ordinate and organise key business functions for a co-ordinated international regional strategy

Context

As economic integration proceeds in Europe and North America, and companies increasingly treat other economic regions of the world – Japan/Asia-Pacific and Latin America – as the focus for their business strategies, separate country markets are being brought together for the purpose of operating with a co-ordinated international regional strategy. In order to shape a co-ordinated international regional strategy, organisations have to manage discontinuities in terms of what has gone before, and what will follow. In recognising and examining these changes this chapter considers:

- *international regional strategy*
- *why do companies develop international regional strategies?*
- *strategic options for national players*
- *international regional co-ordination of key business functions*

International regional strategies represent a further phase of international business development, sandwiched midway between market entry and development and the use of worldwide strategies. At the outset the characteristics of both fragmented and co-ordinated international regional strategies are explored, and contrasted with one another. External and internal triggers are the key drivers in moving organisations to an international regional strategy, and each is considered in detail before examining how the interplay between the two sets of factors may result in organisational change.

Company-specific factors – vision/mindset and organisational dynamics – define how different organisations respond to the challenge of operating with international regional scope and scale. The strategic options available may differ significantly to the extent that the organisation is, or wishes to be, a broad-based or niche player. Implementing a co-ordinated international regional strategy brings to the fore how individual business functions are organised and co-ordinated on a regional basis. In particular, the balance between decisions centralised for the whole region and those remaining decentralised to national organisations is likely to change. Examples drawn from the European Union (EU) are used to illustrate how a number of companies are changing individual functions in response to the need to develop an international regional strategy. The chapter concludes with a summary and checklist. The case study used to illustrate many of the key issues introduced in the chapter considers how one company, Frans Maas NV, is responding to the need to develop an international regional strategy for the European freight transport market.

International regional strategy

International regional strategies are characterised by a focus on a given geographical area, with international market selection and entry no longer simply determined on a country by country basis. The distinguishing characteristic of an international regional business strategy is the recognition of the need to develop a network of closely 'interlinked' international markets. Such companies have not yet progressed to operating with worldwide global strategies, but as Figure 7.1 illustrates have moved beyond the initial phases of international business development.

Figure 7.1 The phase model of international business development

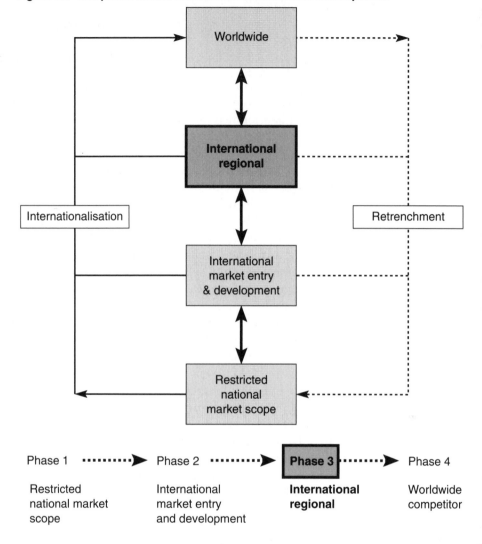

The development of interlinked international business strategies is receiving considerable attention at present as groups of countries are joining together for the purposes of economic integration. The two most notable examples are the continuing development and enlargement of the European Union (EU), and the emergence of the North American Free Trade Agreement (NAFTA). These developments have removed many of the former impediments to free trade between member states in two of the three 'Triad' regions. As Figure 7.2 illustrates, different forms of economic integration exist, of which the EU (Economic Union) and NAFTA (Free Trade Area) provide two examples.

Despite these trends towards the removal of many of the former impediments to cross-border trade, for those companies organising on a regional basis important differences between national markets remain to be accommodated. One important difference between NAFTA and the European Union is

Figure 7.2 Forms of economic integration

FEATURE	Free Trade Area	Customs Union	Common Market	Economic Union	Political Union
Removal of internal tariffs	X	X	X	X	X
Common external tariffs		X	X	X	X
Unrestricted movement of capital and labour			X	X	X
Convergence of economic policies				X	X
Political integration					X

that the former is dominated by a single unitary state (the USA) while the latter is a collection of national states with distinctive cultures, traditions and histories. As result, greater difficulty is often experienced developing an international regional strategy in a European as opposed to an American context. Illustration 7.1 describes some of the political and organisational difficulties encountered in developing an international regional strategy for the European defence industry in comparison to the USA.

In deciding if an organisation has entered the international regional phase of business development three conditions must be examined, namely:

(1) the extent to which the organisation operates with a regional market scope, applying and leveraging its accumulated knowledge and resources across borders;
(2) whether it operates international production facilities and/or has key value-adding activities located outside of its home country; and
(3) whether individual business functions are predominately organised and operated on the basis of the needs of the international region.

Using these three conditions it is possible to characterise different types of international regional strategies. As Table 7.1 illustrates, if only condition (1) is met the strategy is one of a *regional exporter.* If conditions (1) and (2) are met then the organisation is operating a *fragmented* international regional strategy. If all three conditions are met – (1), (2) and (3) – the organisation may be said to be operating a *co-ordinated* international regional strategy.

Illustration 7.1

The defence industry

The defence industry is facing a difficult period following the ending of the Cold War and a reduction in national defence spending. The generally slow response to the new business environment of the European industry can be contrasted to changes already taking place in the United States, where defence contractors are facing similar pressures. American companies have rationalised and regrouped as US government spending in constant prices has fallen from $120 billion in 1983 to $40 billion a decade later. By comparison, in Europe politicians and industrialists have shown their reluctance to sacrifice national independence and share accumulated knowledge. Britain, France and Germany in particular see their defence industries as vital security interests and status symbols.

As a result Europe continues to produce three main battle tanks and is developing three new combat aircraft. By contrast the US produces one main battle tank, and US companies are collaborating in developing a single new combat aircraft. With European firms predominantly organised as national players there is widespread fear that the attainment of economies of scale by US companies will enable them to undercut the prices of European defence contractors, forcing companies to be combined or even close down. Despite this threat some companies still believe that defence is essentially a national industry, and that they can survive by combining with any remaining independent companies of the same nationality. Other national players no longer believe such a strategy is feasible, arguing strongly that at the very least cross-border collaboration in weapons research and development is a necessity. Proponents of this view emphasise that it is no longer feasible to develop sophisticated weapons platforms for a single national market.

If lower operating costs are to be achieved as well as savings on R&D, duplicated facilities will need to be closed, which to date national governments have been reluctant to allow. In this respect the European industry faces impediments to change which the American industry does not.

If European governments and industrialists are not willing to be proactive in managing change, the likelihood is that declining defence spending and the threat of US companies undercutting European prices will ultimately mean that change is forced on national governments and companies.

Source: The authors based on Gray and Clark (1994)

While operating with regional scope, the exporter is likely to remain strongly focused on its home market, not as yet having managed the challenges of setting up core manufacturing or service operations in cross-border markets. Regional exporters normally retain their dependency on 'domestic' managers as they have yet to start the process of developing a truly international corporate culture.

Moving beyond an exporter strategy, the fragmented international regional strategy does involves companies operating with cross-border production and/or other key value-adding facilities. The strategy is fragmented as each

Table 7.1 Distinguishing different types of international regional strategy

Characteristics	International regional strategy		
	Exporter	Fragmented	Co-ordinated
(1) Regional scope; application and leverage of shared knowledge, etc.	Yes	Yes	Yes
(2) International production facilities/ key value-adding facilities	No	Yes	Yes
(3) Co-ordination of business functions on regional basis	No	No	Yes
Overall strategy	Supplies the region from its national production base, and has all key value-adding facilities located in its home country	Operates a series of country strategies. Little or no co-ordination between national markets served	Treats the region as a unified market and co-ordinates its business functions accordingly

country is essentially treated as a separate entity, with little or no attempt to leverage competitive interdependencies across national boundaries. The competitive advantages of operating with a fragmented international regional strategy tend to reflect the application and leverage of shared knowledge and competences across national boundaries. The nature of such firm-specific factors will vary, but might include knowledge and competences based on, say, technology, marketing or general management capabilities. The organisation size may also be a factor in the application of such competences to a single national market. Securitas AB, the Swedish international security company described in Illustration 7.2, is a good example of a company which operates with a fragmented international regional strategy.

Increasingly companies are recognising and seeking to exploit the similarities and interdependencies between each of the national markets in which they operate through developing a single strategy to cover a group of countries or economic region. Consequently, a co-ordinated international regional strategy is designed to meet regional, rather than simply national requirements. Accordingly, individual business functions are configured primarily on a regional base with, for example, production centres supplying the region and not just a national market. The Australian leisure company Flag International Limited, discussed in Illustration 7.3, provides a good example of a company which operates on an international regional basis, using a co-ordinated strategy.

Illustration 7.2

Securitas AB

Swedish-based Securitas is the leading security company in Europe, whose prin- cipal activities include operating guard services and alarm systems in eleven countries. The company offers security services consisting of guards and techni- cal systems to a wide range of customers. The company considers Europe as its natural area of expansion, having made acquisitions in many of the major national markets.

Until 1988 guard services and alarm systems in Sweden formed the core of Securitas' operations. On 1 January 1989, the company took its first steps to becoming an international company by making acquisitions in Norway, Denmark and Portugal. Since this initial phase of international business development Securitas has made further acquisitions, so that the company now has a major presence in Spain, Finland, France, Germany, Hungary, Switzerland and Austria.

The company's strategy of making acquisitions has been informed by the view that it expects the security industry in Europe to undergo rapid change with the emergence of a number of relatively large international enterprises, competing alongside local and national companies. Correspondingly, the company has since 1988 been using its experience and the knowledge accumulated from its origins in Sweden to assist its international business development. All branches are expected to subscribe to group beliefs concerning values, integrity and trust.

Securitas' organisational structure is based around a country manager, who has total responsibility for all business conducted in the national market. Using locally strong and independent managers, the company emphasises the virtues of operating with a decentralised organisational structure. While there are mech- anisms for exchanging knowledge, and the company has introduced recently a cross-border management training programme, the nature of the industry limits the exploitation of supply-side interdependencies. The company also believes that local management is an effective mechanism for implementing the neces- sary restructuring of new acquisitions in order that they fit with the overall philosophy and standards of the group.

While the company operates with a regional market scope, all business is organised around individual company strategies, so that it may be described as operating a fragmented international regional strategy.

Source: The authors based on Securitas Annual Reports, 1988–93

In the context of an ever changing competitive environment, the movement of an industry to organise on the basis of an economic region can have pro- found consequences for related industries. The complex competitive inter-relationships between industrial sectors can be expected to influence the evolution of both supplier and buyer industries through the existence of a range of competitive linkages. Examples of this tendency can be found by looking at many component or service industries dependent on one of the major manufacturing sectors where organisations are experiencing a shift to

Illustration 7.3

Flag International Limited

The Australian company Flag International Limited focuses almost exclusively on Australasia. Except for two hotels in London (UK) and San Diego (West Coast USA), the company's 450 independently owned and operated outlets are to be found in Australia, New Zealand and on the Pacific islands of Papua New Guinea, Fiji, Hawaii and Western Samoa. Alongside the company's regional market scope, it operates with broadly common marketing, operations and personnel policies.

An important element of the company's customer appeal to potential clients is being able to provide immediate information on bed availability for each outlet, even when the contact is through one of the company reservations centres or agents outside the region in which the organisation operates. In late 1994 the company rationalised its various national sales units in Europe into a pan-European network centred on Frankfurt, offering a toll-free reservation service throughout Europe.

The company's use of information technology is complemented by a strong marketing focus which includes:

- offering 'hotel pass vouchers' which are bought in advance and entitle customers to one night's accommodation with a discount to the standard room rate of an average 10 to 15% in any of the company's outlets;
- a standardised policy covering reservations;
- the use of 'Inn Club membership' issued free to customers and entitling the user to corporate rate discounts; and
- a frequent guest programme rewarding those Inn Club members who choose to stay with the company frequently.

The company's attractive and standardised marketing policies, coupled with a strong emphasis on consistent levels of service, has resulted in continued expansion in its chosen region.

Source: The authors

---

operating with an international regional strategy. The case study on Frans Maas NV at the end of the chapter provides a good example of this effect.

Why do companies develop international regional strategies?

An important question is: what factors trigger an organisation to begin the process of developing an international regional strategy? As with the initial process for an organisation to begin to develop an international business strategy, further phases of development, including the construction of an international regional strategy, will be driven by external and/or internal factors. Separately or together these factors will be responsible for the organisation breaking with its previous phase of development and seeking to formulate an international regional strategy. Inevitably this change is likely to result in a considerable discontinuity when compared with how the organisation has operated in the past. Figure 7.3 illustrates the discontinuity by showing that an organisation will need to break out of its previous phase of international business development and move to the next.

Figure 7.3 *The development of an international regional strategy*

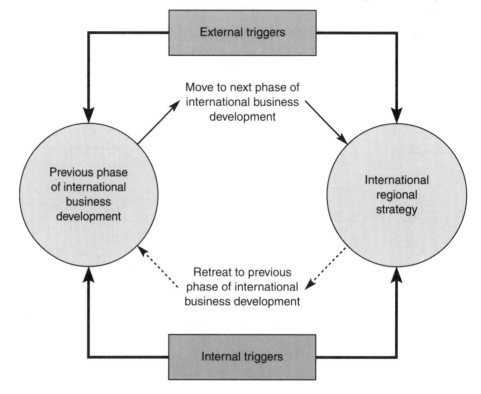

The external triggers to change will include both (i) *meta trends;* and (ii) changing *competitive forces* at the level of the industry. The interplay between these two sets of external triggers will influence the incentive and urgency for companies to develop an international regional strategy. Important *external triggers* include:

- the increasing opportunity for regional product/service standardisation;
- the emergence of cross-border customers and distributors;
- increasing competition emphasising the need to exploit competitive interdependencies;
- reducing product life cycles and the consequent need for faster decision making and implementation.

External triggers in themselves are unlikely to cause the organisation to move to an international regional strategy unless the internal context is at least compliant. Indeed under some circumstances the internal context may lead to the organisation developing an international regional strategy, irrespective of whether external factors are exerting a strong influence or not. The *internal triggers* which will be required to legitimise or initiate change will be an organisation's:

- vision/mindset; and
- organisational dynamics.

The intensity of these factors, the timing and the speed by which an organisation adopts an international regional strategy, will be situation specific. Each of the external and internal triggers will now be examined in detail, starting with the four external triggers.

Product/service standardisation

The convergence of customer preferences enables a number of previously separate national markets to be considered as one. As a result regional product standardisation becomes possible, reflecting the emergence of common consumer trends (external context) reinforced by the adoption of regional marketing strategies (internal context). While some elements of the product/service offer may continue to be customised for a single market, national differences will be accommodated with an overall policy of standardisation. This is frequently effected by allowing some elements of the marketing mix to be configured to reflect continuing national preferences and/or institutional differences (e.g. media buying and channels).

Emergence of cross-border customers and distributors

The movement to international regional strategies may be stimulated by the emergence of major cross-border businesses. Business falling into this category, operating either manufacturing or service outlets and a single strategy across the region, increasingly require common levels of product and service delivery to their network of sites. The demand for a common level of product or service by influential customers offering major contracts mitigates against sales by autonomous national subsidiaries whose product-market strategies may show significant variations.

Competitive interdependencies

If the organisation is able to develop a range of standardised regional products, then opportunities arise to exploit competitive interdependencies. Correspondingly, this will allow the organisation to configure its business functions in a way that treats the region as a single market, and to achieve economies of scale. The nature of these scale economies will vary, but they can be particularly significant in respect of production, logistics and marketing.

Standardised product ranges allow production capacity to be rationalised and concentrated on a few plants offering significant savings in operating expenses. In parallel the logistics function may be reconfigured to reduce the number of distribution centres offering significant savings in respect of the costs of stock holding, but also enabling the distribution centres retained to carry wider product ranges and/or offer additional customer services. Common product lines also open up the possibility of pan-regional promotional strategies using regional brands. At the same time increased volumes assist both the funding of and the subsequent recovery of research and development spending, which in many technology-driven industries can no longer be sustained on the basis of national market needs.

Shorter product life cycles requiring faster decision making

A collection of autonomous national subsidiaries rarely assists the development and introduction of new products. As competition reduces the length of product life cycles and time-based competition becomes an ever more important element of competitive advantage in many industries, companies need to have faster decision-making processes (see Chapter 4). Time-based competition requires that new products/services are brought to the market before rival offers, a process which is not assisted by the existence of powerful independent national subsidiaries, who each demand a part in the decision-making process in order to ensure local preferences are recognised. Unfortunately, the nature of the decision-making process in this context inevitably leads to protracted product development and the slow introduction of new products to the market. In today's competitive environments this potential loss of competitive edge can impinge upon business performance.

Despite the existence of strong external pressures to standardise products and exploit competitive interdependencies, there are some instances where the internal context may prejudice the development of an international regional strategy. Adoption of international business strategies cannot be deduced solely from external analysis, and it is important to recognise that the internal context is critical in determining whether the organisation is to be *reactive* in responding to external trends, or *proactive*, developing an international regional strategy before its rivals have embarked on a similar course and the external context means the organisation has no choice but to try and follow suit. Revisiting the two key internal drivers, the following observations can be made.

Vision/mindset

Previous discussion has emphasised the importance of vision in foreseeing and/or shaping events. Unless key decision-makers in the organisation have a clear vision that the organisation's future lies in the development of an international regional strategy and are able to inform and convince others in the company as to the value of their vision and mindset, then the organisation may be slow to see the need to change. Eventually, if the external context leaves no choice but for organisations to adopt an international regional strategy, a 'crisis' – for example, managerial or financial – may bring about change. Empirical evidence (e.g. Pettigrew, 1985; Johnson, 1987; Drucker, 1994), shows that many organisations tend to experience some form of 'crisis' intermittently which triggers a fundamental change in strategy.

Whether such a 'crisis' occurs in time to enable the organisation to recover and emerge stronger depends very much on the individual context the organisation is facing. At the other extreme, the organisation may be proactive in seeking to develop an international regional strategy, and gain significant 'first mover advantages' in developing such a strategy ahead of its rivals. This point emphasises that the need is not just to manage for today, but also for the future.

Organisational dynamics

The possession of core competences may prove to be the basis for an organisation to develop an international regional strategy. The application of core competences, together with acquired organisational learning from, say, previous international market entry, may offer the basis by which an organisation is able to leverage its shared knowledge and understanding in order to develop an international regional strategy. In such circumstances the impetus to develop beyond an earlier phase of international business development comes primarily from an internal rather than external perspective.

Recognising that the development of an international regional strategy or a change in the nature of how an international region is served represents a discontinuity, a necessary condition for success is normally the need to gain the agreement and commitment of a sufficient number of key individuals in the organisation. As an example of this need, Illustration 7.4 describes how one company, Unilever, carefully divided up managerial responsibilities in order to gain the support of senior managers to enable the organisation to move from a fragmented to a co-ordinated international regional strategy. That this was necessary emphasises the requirement to reassure national managers, who often perceive personal and operating disadvantages in integrating previously separate national organisations to develop a co-ordinated international regional strategy. If both senior and middle managers in each of the national organisations are not persuaded of the need to change and endeavour to make it work, then change can be effectively blocked as these layers of the organisation resist the new order. To support the new order the reward system can be refocused to encourage changed behaviours.

The case of Unilever, Illustration 7.4, also provides a good example of where both external and internal triggers to change were mutually supportive in leading to the development of a co-ordinated international regional strategy. External triggers to change were provided by the need to compete with Procter and Gamble, whose organisation, culture and systems put Unilever at a competitive disadvantage. Procter and Gamble, had already organised its detergents business on a pan-European basis, indicating that the intensity of competition was a necessary condition in exerting pressure on Unilever to change its strategy. External triggers were not, however, a sufficient condition to bring about change. This required alteration of the internal context, and in Unilever's case pressure came from many of the organisation's younger executives who realised change was inescapable. Only when the external and internal factors were brought together was the organisation able to move forward and undertake a radical reorganisation of its European detergent business.

Illustration 7.4

Lever Europe

In the 1990s the Anglo-Dutch company Unilever is working hard to transform its detergents activities from a confederation of largely autonomous national businesses into a co-ordinated international regional strategy. The changes, first suggested in 1988, were only agreed by both of the company's joint chairmen after many of the organisation's younger executives argued that change was inescapable.

As part of the overall strategy, Lever Europe has been created in order to treat Europe as a single market. The need to establish Lever Europe was particularly strong in detergents, where international standardisation was increasing. Since its establishment Lever Europe has reduced the differences in pack size and design features, reducing purchasing costs and paving the way for a pan-European communications strategy. By 1995 almost all the product range will be common across Europe. At the same time the company is rationalising and concentrating its production facilities. Whereas formerly each national plant produced the whole product range for a single geographical market, the number of plants is being reduced. In future some products will only be produced in one location for the whole European market. It is forecast that the company may reduce its annual operating costs by up to £250 million by rationalising its production facilities in this way.

Unilever's development of a European strategy for its detergents business requires its national operating companies to accept reduced autonomy over their traditional markets in exchange for a role in developing and executing a unified pan-European strategy. To achieve the commitment of each of the national organisations, the corporate centre of Unilever has had to strike a careful balance, by distributing among the operating companies new sets of responsibilities.

Unilever has linked to the new structures and strategy the reward system of its senior executives. Approximately two-thirds of the bonuses payable to executives is now determined by the company performance in Europe, rather than performance in one national market. The configuration of the reward system recognises that individual attitudes are extremely important in making the new organisation work. Changing attitudes and developing a shared mindset, emphasising the importance of the international region rather than the national market, is made even more demanding given the desire of the company to move quickly to a pan-European strategy.

Despite the overall move to a co-ordinated regional strategy, the company has left some elements of its human relations functions to be determined locally. These include industrial relations and wage bargaining, which the company firmly believes should remain the responsibility of local managers.

In making the changes described above, Unilever has been attempting to close the gap with its main rival, the US company Procter and Gamble, which has not been encumbered by a network of national subsidiaries in Europe. As a result of the competitive rivalry Unilever managers recognise the urgency of the situation, and the need to succeed. Jon Peterson, the Australian who heads Lever Europe, has been quoted as saying; 'Frankly, we haven't got the great luxury of time. This is survival stuff. We've got to act quickly.'

Source: Adapted from de Jonquieres (1991)

The case history of Unilever discussed in Illustration 7.4 demonstrates the role of both external and internal triggers in bringing about the development of a co-ordinated international regional strategy. In short, it will be necessary to consider both the external and internal contexts to assess whether the conditions exist for the organisation to attempt to manage a discontinuity in its international business strategy.

Strategic options for national players

Not all organisations will find it easy to respond to the need to move towards operating with an international regional strategy. Individual responses will depend very much on the organisation's specific context as described by external and internal factors. Attention will need to be focused on the nature and speed of the changes driving the internationalisation process, the existing structure of the industry, and the organisation's internal dynamics. In clarifying the strategic options available it is helpful to return to the discussion on *bi-polarisation* featured in Chapter 3. Discussion about bi-polarisation emphasised the need for organisations to find a basis on which they could compete as the nature of competition changed. Organisations could choose to position themselves as either a narrow or broad-based competitor, attempting to sell only to national markets or increasingly internationally.

Where important competitors and customers are organising across borders, the remaining national players are faced with the choice of either finding a defendable national niche or developing to a point where the company is itself operating with an international regional strategy. In practice, the extent to which one or both of these options is available to the organisation will depend on two interdependent factors: first, the external context, reflecting, for example, whether the business opportunity is available; and secondly the internal context, reflecting, for example, the organisation's dynamics.

What does need to be recognised is that not all national players will be able to develop an international regional strategy, as the underlying nature of the market place is unlikely to be able to support the volume of sales this would require. Equally, potential market niches may well have been occupied and aggressively developed by competitors who wish to become narrowly based international regional players. What is in theory possible and what may in practice be attainable may be very different for these and other reasons.

There will inevitably be a process of consolidation, whereby national players who are unable or unwilling to develop an international regional strategy or unable to find alternative markets, will be eliminated either by being acquired or through going into receivership. The market will become concentrated in the hands of a small number of larger firms. The natural outcome to this process is that the number of competitors serving the regional market is inevitably fewer than the number of national players they have absorbed or replaced. Figure 7.4 identifies the current market position of different competitors.

Figure 7.4 Product-market grid

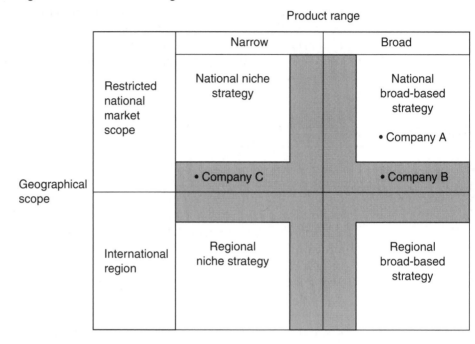

Key: ▨ = Zone of transition

Whether the current position of the three companies – A, B and C – located on the product-market grid in Figure 7.4 is sustainable depends upon whether the competitive environment is increasingly requiring the organisation to operate an international regional strategy rather than with a restricted national focus; and the extent to which product segments remain separable, enabling niche players to co-exist alongside broad-based competitors.

The extent to which the competitive environment requires companies to operate with an international regional strategy will, as discussed earlier, reflect the extent to which:

● there is a convergence of national preferences;
● important cross-border customers and distributors exist who require common products and services across a region;
● competitive interdependencies are increasing; and
● organisations need to respond to shorter product life cycles.

If narrow players are to prosper, they must be able to find product-markets which can be characterised by two key dimensions. First, markets must be sufficiently separable to enable differentiation to provide some protection from direct competition from broad-based competitors; and secondly, they must offer the prospect of economic supply, enabling the niche player to make acceptable returns.

Returning to the individual companies positioned on the product-market grid in Figure 7.4, only Company A has a restricted market scope. Two of the companies – B and C – are in transition to the extent that they have moved from being solely focused on a national market, although each has yet to operate with a truly international regional scope or scale. The strategic posture of each of these companies can be summarised as:

- *Company A:* A relatively small, broad-based national competitor who has yet to enter international markets and is wholly dependent on its national market.
- *Company B:* A medium-sized broad-based competitor who has entered a number of international markets, but is still largely dependent on its national market.
- *Company C:* A relatively small and narrowly focused competitor who has entered a number of international markets, but who like Company A has so far only moved away, to a limited extent, from its national market.

If customers or competitive moves now require companies to operate with an international regional strategy, what are the strategic options for the three national players? In general terms, each of the companies has the choice of *competing* and/or *collaborating* with competitors. Collaboration includes all options by which a company combines with another, including merger or acquisition, or the development of a strategic alliance.

The range of strategic options available to each of the three companies – A, B and C – when faced with an external environment increasingly requiring broad-based competitors to operate with a regional scope and scale, are detailed in Table 7.2.

To remain a broadly based supplier in an non-defensible national market, the company must extend its scope and scale. This need to exploit potentially both scope and scale on an international regional basis, requiring as it does the acquisition and/or leveraging of knowledge and resources across national boundaries, is particularly challenging.

To move from its current position the broad-based national competitor will need to use one or more of the following methods of development:

- internal or organic growth;
- merger or acquisition (external growth);
- joint venture;
- strategic alliances.

The extent to which an organisation can afford to take time in developing a regional presence or whether acquisition targets are plentiful and available will depend on the stage of development the industry has reached. If, for example, competitors have been developing international regional strategies for some time and many of the former independent national competitors have been acquired, then extending a company's market scope may be difficult by either growth path. Some of the generic issues in relation to context, resource requirements and relative benefits and disadvantages of using either internal (organic) or external growth in developing a business strategy have been previously discussed in Illustration 5.2.

Table 7.2 Strategic options for national players

Company	Strategic options	Strategic imperatives
A	(1) Do nothing (2) Develop broad-based regional strategy (3) Retreat to niche (4) Withdraw	Cease trading Extend competitive scope and configure business functions for regional market Refocus business on market niche Sell business to competitor and exit from the industry
B	(1) Do nothing (2) Retreat to national niche (3) Withdraw	Cease trading Find national niche on which to refocus the business Sell business to competitor and exit from the industry
C	(1) Do nothing	(i) For the present, depending on the characteristics of the niche, may be able to continue to develop its international presence at its own pace (ii) Could become vulnerable to competition from broad-based supplier offering standardised regional products and/or niche player developing an international regional strategy

Joint ventures may assist the speed of development by enabling local knowledge and additional resources to assist expansion into a single country. The disadvantages are that joint ventures can lead to difficulties in the development of a regional strategy, given the need to adopt a broadly uniform approach for all national markets within a region. Not all joint venture partners will necessarily easily agree to a change strategy. This may lead to a desire to 'buy out' the partner and assume full control of the operation. Similarly, while strategic alliances based on co-operation with other predominantly national players to form a pan-regional organisation in theory offer many benefits, often in practice they offer only a partial solution to the need to operate with an international regional strategy. For example, as discussed in Illustration 7.2, co-operation between European defence contractors may enable common weapons systems to be developed, but may not result in a rationalisation of facilities. Hence when compared to US defence contractors, European companies may remain at a distinct disadvantage.

Where national players with non-defensible boundaries realise too late that they need to develop a regional presence, two strategic options remain. They can either decide to leave the industry or retreat back to a niche where operating with an international regional strategy may not be necessary. If the company is forced to withdraw from a market, the most likely means of doing this is to relinquish its independence and be absorbed by a company which is better placed to develop an international regional strategy. The process whereby national players are acquired by pan-regional competitors will itself advance and intensify the degree of competition faced by the remaining national players. To this extent once the process has begun, the company with an emerging international regional strategy may be able to achieve a virtuous circle of lower costs and improved profitability, leading to price reduction and further sales growth. By comparison, for the remaining national players increased competition is likely to erode margins and accelerate withdrawal from the market or force collaboration.

If the company is unable to develop an international regional strategy but is equally unwilling to withdraw from the market, then it must seek to move from being a broad-based player to one operating in a niche. This presupposes that it is confident in the first instance that the characteristics of its chosen market segment are sufficiently differentiated to offer some prospect that it will not face competition from standardised regional products, or from niche players benefiting from successfully operating with an international regional strategy. If the latter is the case, the company will not be able to continuing to operate with only national scope and scale. Similarly, if the research and development costs necessary to fund its next generation of products can only be resourced from the volumes generated by operating as a broad-based competitor, then retreating to a particular market segment, often known as a segment retreat strategy, is not a viable long-term option.

Similar considerations will also apply to niche players operating with an international regional strategy. These companies must be able to fund product replacements and reduce the extent to which they are in direct competition with larger, and inevitably more powerful, broad-based competitors. One company attempting to operate in this way with an international niche strategy is DAF Trucks NV, discussed in Illustration 7.5.

Assuming the development of a broad-based international regional strategy is not feasible with the resources available and/or within the time scales necessary, a company faces two options. The company can either withdraw from the market, preferably by selling itself as a 'going concern' to a company extending its regional presence and wishing to make acquisitions in order to complete its international regional network; or again seek to retreat to a market segment where operating with a national strategy still offers the basis of sustaining a competitive advantage. The strategies available to Companies A and B if they are to avoid closing down or being absorbed are shown in Figure 7.5.

Illustration 7.5

DAF Trucks NV

DAF Trucks NV was formed on 2 March 1993 having acquired, with the help of external funding by the Dutch national and Flemish regional governments, many of the assets of the old DAF Group which had been placed into receivership.

The company's core operations are primarily concerned with the development, production, sale and after-sales servicing of medium and heavy trucks. Production of medium and heavy trucks is carried out in Eindhoven (the Netherlands), where the emphasis is on the assembly of trucks and the production of engines, while the company's second plant Westerlo (Belgium) makes axles and cabs.

The newly formed company's strategy is directed to remaining independent, focusing on the European market. The company has its own sales subsidiaries in the Netherlands, Belgium/Luxembourg, France, Germany, the United Kingdom, Switzerland and Italy.

The company has a modern product range which it believes will enable development costs in the first few years of its formation to be kept to a low level. It also recognises that its relatively low volume, especially at the heavy end of the market, does not justify its developing key components. Engines of over 500 hp are, for example, sourced from Cummins, the US engine manufacturer, while DAF Trucks concentrates its resources on developing engines for its smaller vehicles.

The company operates with a build-to-order policy, only putting into production those vehicles which have actually been sold. As this means the number of units produced per week depends entirely on sales, the company needs to operate with a high degree of flexibility to ensure production is efficient. Together with a flexible production process, the company is continuing its policy of standardisation through reducing the number of separate parts across its product range.

While DAF Trucks achieved almost 6 per cent of the Western European market for vehicles of over 6 tonnes gross vehicle weight in 1993, it is faced by competition from a number of larger broad-based suppliers in Europe, which includes Mercedes-Benz, Renault, Scania and Volvo Truck. With its lower volumes and the continuing rise of development costs across the industry, it remains to be seen whether DAF Trucks can operate with a narrow product range and demonstrate that it has a defendable international regional niche strategy. This point is made even more evident when it is realised that the number of independent European manufacturers of heavy trucks has fallen from 40 in 1965, to 20 in 1980 and to only 10 in 1990.

Source: Based on Annual Report 1993 and industry sources

For Company C, there is the opportunity of continuing with its current strategy, assuming that the market niche in which it operates is not undergoing transition and requiring companies to operate with an international regional strategy. Increasingly, however, even if a company is able to identify such a niche successful and distance itself from broad-based companies operating with a regional strategy, competitive forces are requiring the company to

Figure 7.5 Product-market options available for Companies A and B in the face of the need to operate with a regional strategy in their existing markets

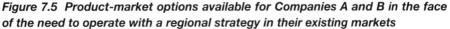

Product range

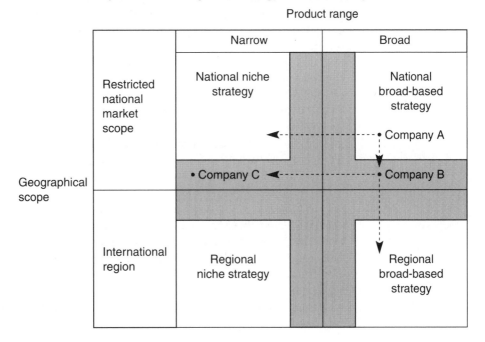

Key: ▨ = Zone of transition

extend its competitive scope and develop an international regional strategy. Indeed, some former national niche players have been proactive in developing international regional strategies, reflecting their vision and corporate ambition. Where these companies have succeeded, the external pressures on rival national niche players which continue to operate with a restricted national scope will increase.

Company C must also be careful that as technologies develop it does not become vulnerable to broad-based regional competitors able to 'customise' their standard products to meet the demand characteristics of its market niche. If the niche is no longer defensible the company may either seek alternative niches, or on rare occasions take the decision to turn itself into a broad-based competitor.

The previous discussion highlights that in the face of developing competitive trends national players may face uncomfortable choices. Even those companies who have begun the internationalisation process may have left it too late, and be unable to develop an international regional strategy in time to be able to match competitive rivals. This emphasises that when an industry is evolving to a point where an international regional strategy is a necessary condition for survival, those organisations which have the vision to craft, and the organisational dynamics to implement, an appropriate strategy before industry-wide developments reduce the chance of success will be in the strongest position. This serves to stress the need to be proactive and anticipate, rather than simply react to events.

International regional co-ordination of key business functions

The development of a co-ordinated international regional strategy can be expected to pose a considerable challenge for an organisation. While the nature and extent of such challenges will differ according to the specific context, significant discontinuities are likely to occur in the manner in which the organisation carries out its business. For some companies there will be the challenge of completing market coverage of the region, as well developing a single strategy to cover all national markets. In other cases where the company has already achieved regional coverage, but has yet to co-ordinate its strategy across the region, the need will be to manage the transition from a fragmented regional strategy to one which is co-ordinated.

The transition from a group of autonomous national subsidiaries operating fragmented strategies to the development of a co-ordinated regional strategy is likely to change the balance between the number and range of tasks which are centralised to a regional hub, and those decentralised to national operations. In respect of the balance of decision making between regional centre and country, complete centralisation and decentralisation represent the extremes of a continuum. Where there is no co-ordination between national subsidiaries the situation may be described as complete decentralisation, whereas if national organisations do not exist the co-ordination of business functions is completely centralised. Moving between these two points, as Figure 7.6 illustrates, the extent to which operations are co-ordinated on an international regional basis will vary.

*Figure 7.6 **Centralisation versus decentralisation of key business functions***

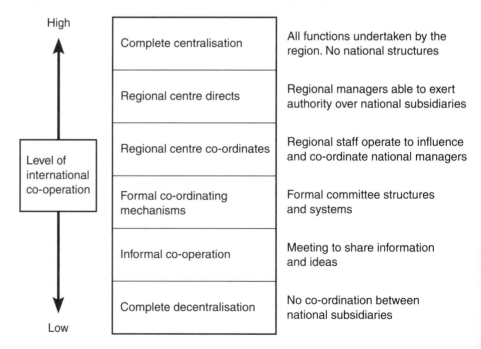

Complete centralisation	All functions undertaken by the region. No national structures
Regional centre directs	Regional managers able to exert authority over national subsidiaries
Regional centre co-ordinates	Regional staff operate to influence and co-ordinate national managers
Formal co-ordinating mechanisms	Formal committee structures and systems
Informal co-operation	Meeting to share information and ideas
Complete decentralisation	No co-ordination between national subsidiaries

The overall aim of a co-ordinated international regional strategy will be to standardise the principal product or service components, enabling a significant degree of standardisation across the region in order to reduce costs. Without such standardisation cost savings in respect of, for example, marketing, operations and logistics are unlikely to be realised. While individual functional variations may need to be accommodated, especially in managing the transition to a co-ordinated regional strategy, the objective will be to ensure that the core of the organisation's strategy is configured to enable the region to be treated as a single market. One frequently expressed concern accompanying the development of a co-ordinated international regional strategy is that contact with the national market will become diluted, and differences in national preferences be overlooked. The organisation will need to be aware of this danger and take steps to minimise the likelihood of that situation occurring.

The key tasks in respect of each functional area will now be reviewed, namely:

- marketing
- human resources
- operations
- logistics
- finance

Marketing

The marketing function will be needed to support and indeed reinforce the overall business strategy, but also may be required to recognise and accommodate a degree of 'customisation' to take account of differences between national markets. The organisation's response to such differences is likely to focus on the 'tactical' rather than strategic configuration to the elements of the marketing mix, thereby allowing the company's offer to be sensitive to local market preferences. Important considerations in respect of each of the elements of the marketing mix include:

- *Product:* catering for national preferences within the context of product standardisation. The extent to which the company continues to promote local rather than regional brands is often an important element in this respect. Where separate brand names have been established over time these may continue, although the product itself is virtually identical between markets. Alternatively, the organisation may decide to replace a local brand name in order to promote a pan-regional brand, enabling the adoption of, for example, a single promotion strategy.
- *Place:* the organisation will seek to gain market coverage of all markets considered to be strategically important within the region, and where necessary take steps to extend its presence where gaps exist in the organisation's scope using whatever means it considers appropriate, e.g. organic growth, acquisitions, etc.
- *Promotion:* the increasing development of satellite broadcasting and pan-national newspapers emphasises the extent to which, for many products,

the necessary conditions for a regional communication strategy are emerging. While national differences between alternative forms of the media remain, not least because of state control of the media in some countries, the ability to use a single medium to cover a number of national markets is increasing. In some cases elements of the communications strategy may remain focused on the national market, depending on institutional differences and where local brands are promoted.

- *Price:* while arguably the most sensitive of the marketing decisions to local needs, pricing policies will need to prevent parallel imports eroding price differentials between national markets. Price discrimination will only be sustainable where customer preferences are sufficiently distinct and markets can be kept separate. Otherwise, price levels are likely to move to a point where price differentials between markets reflect the actual differences in doing business in individual countries. As trade barriers between nations decline, the tendency is for national pricing policies to converge to a single pricing structure. Illustration 7.6 discusses how price differentials are being eroded following the liberalisation of the European insurance market.

Illustration 7.6

The European insurance market

The introduction of new rules on cross-border trade in the European market will lead to an erosion of the current price differentials between national markets.

The implementation of the European Union's 'framework directives' marks the final stage in the liberalisation of the insurance market. The directives: (1) allow companies to sell policies anywhere in Europe based on the regulations in their domestic market; and (2) remove the need to submit cross-border policies to local offices for approval.

The overall effect of these changes will be to increase competition and undermine the position of a number of national players in those national markets which have been more heavily protected. In the middle of 1994, before these rules changed, similar policies could cost a consumer in Portugal three times the amount he or she would pay in France.

While differences in the incidence of claims, legal disparities, local tax regimes and cultural factors will mean that a truly single market will not happen immediately, the long-term possibility of insurance companies penetrating each other's markets has become a real threat. Companies in some of the previously more protected markets, in particular, fear competition from cross-border entrants using direct telephone sales to market new policies, a marketing strategy which has already proved successful in some deregulated national markets. Using a direct sales strategy the new entrant is likely to have a significantly lower cost base than existing competitors whose structures have grown up in a protected environment.

Source: Based on Lapper (1994)

As Illustration 7.6 shows, while pricing for many services in previously separate and protected markets will not necessarily converge immediately, long-term price differentials which are not justified by underlying cost differences are likely to disappear as cross-border entrants invade any market where prices are unjustifiably too high.

Human resources

The management of the people resource has a central role in the development of a co-ordinated international regional strategy. As the organisation will need to undergo a transformation, moving from one set of structures and processes to another, a primary need will be to 'manage change' successfully. While the extent to which the management of change can be successfully accomplished will depend on the specific situation, generic issues arise in terms of companies developing both an international regional scope and a co-ordinated strategy.

If the organisation needs to extend its regional scope as well as develop a co-ordinated international regional strategy, some of the key considerations of the human resource function are likely to arise out of:

● the need to establish a corporate presence in additional national markets. This may be achieved through organic growth and/or the acquisition and integration of formerly independent national companies within the group. In the latter case post-acquisition management will have to ensure corporate cultures and policies 'fit' with the overall group philosophy and policies;
● extending organisational structures and process to encompass the wider scope and large scale of activity;
● the understanding and amendment of policies and procedures to deal, for the organisation, with new employment practices and legal requirements arising out of operating in additional national markets.

For a company moving from operating with a series of country-based strategies to a single unified approach to the region the emphasis is likely to be on:

● gaining acceptance and support for the need to change organisational structures and decision-making processes;
● changing the organisational culture and associated structures so that each country is no longer the focus of many major decisions, which are now to be decided on a regional basis; at the same time ensuring that company reporting structures and decision-making processes are configured so that national requirements are not ignored or forgotten;
● managing the changes arising from the overall business strategy in respect of the number of and/or skills required of employees, including, for example, the closure and/or movement of facilities to new locations with the region;
● deciding which matters will continue to be decentralised to national organisations to be determined locally;
● ensuring reward systems support new behaviours and encourage commitment to the strategy.

Changing organisational culture, which is often necessary in adopting a co-ordinated international regional strategy, is never easy. As the cultural web, introduced in Chapter 4 emphasised, many factors hold in place an organisation's existing strategic recipe. Consequently, a prior conditioning process is generally required for change to be self-generated. If the change is to be sustained and consolidated it needs to be supported by the majority, if not all, of the elements which form an organisation's cultural web, namely organisational and power structures, symbols and routines and control systems. Listing these elements indicates just how many factors need to be effectively managed if the transition to an international regional strategy is to succeed.

Even where there has been a lengthy period of consensus building, managing the transition from operating with powerful national subsidiaries to an international regional strategy is unlikely to proceed without any difficulties. Illustration 7.7 describes how the diversified American company, 3M, reorganised its European operations in the 1990s. The company's international regional strategy involved establishing 19 European Business Centres to cover the European market. Despite the company's having prepared the way through a programme of consensus building over a number of years, it openly admitted to some 'rough edges' when its new strategy was implemented.

Operations

The company will need to organise its production facilities for a single regional market, rather than duplicating facilities for each market. For a company extending its regional coverage, it may be able to build or acquire plants which are strategically located for the region, and thus avoid an unnecessary duplication of facilities. By contrast, organisations which have traditionally operated with a fragmented international regional strategy are likely to find themselves with too many plants for their future requirements, many of which may be either inappropriately located to support a co-ordinated international regional strategy and/or of insufficient size to meet the needs of the market as a whole. As a consequence the necessity of moving to a regional strategy will result in a major review and rationalisation of production facilities in order to achieve the cost savings which can be gained by concentrating production on a relatively small number of sites. Production facilities retained will need in large measure to meet the total regional demand, and offer the necessary production economies in order to achieve cost savings.

Another aspect of many companies' operations is the continuous attempt to reduce the input costs to the production process. Centralised purchasing on a pan-regional basis can offer significant cost savings to a corporate group. One example of a company seeking to make savings in this respect is the US-based company PepsiCo, discussed in Illustration 7.8.

PepsiCo has recognised that where there are related businesses many common products and services are purchased separately by autonomous business units. Consequently, as Illustration 7.8 describes, increasingly companies have an opportunity to combine the buying power of each of the separate business units within the corporate group in order to realise even greater savings on procurement.

Illustration 7.7

European reorganisation: the case of Minnesota Mining and Manufacturing (3M)

Minnesota Mining and Manufacturing (3M) is a diversified US company with extensive operations in Europe. In the early 1990s it decided to reorganise its European organisation along the following lines. First, 3M shifted most of the key strategic and operational responsibilities away from national subsidiaries to 19 centralised product divisions, known as European Business Centres (EBCs), each with a Europe-wide responsibility. The location of EBCs has been determined on 'where it made most sense' and they are spread over five countries: Belgium, Britain, France, Germany and Italy. This policy has minimised the need for costly and disruptive staff relocations across Europe. Location of EBCs was also helped by the fact that the company's production base had been previously developed to serve the whole region. Secondly, support facilities, including staff development, logistics, information technology and finance, have been concentrated away from the smaller countries, allowing, for example, the Nordic, Iberian and Central Europe regions to be combined to form one area.

The company has retained country managers for most of its geographical markets. The retention of these posts is designed to ensure that the company is appropriately represented in each country and that there is sufficient 'local' power to persuade EBCs that they need to continue to respond to national differences. The company has also given local managers both national and European marketing responsibilities in an attempt to ensure contact with national markets is not lost.

The reorganisation was facilitated by a long period of consensus building which had been under way since the early 1980s, helping the changes to take place quickly. There was also a growing consensus in the company that change was necessary. Nevertheless, some people have found the changes 'uncomfortable' and have needed to be helped. Individual responses partly reflect personal characteristics and experience, but often also national cultures. Managers from relatively authoritarian cultures have tended to find the greater autonomy unsettling.

To assist the change process the company has used 'team building' and other change processes. Nevertheless, some 'rough edges' experienced to date with the reorganisation continue to need attention, including:

- clarification of new procedures following the shift of responsibilities from countries to businesses;
- commonality within businesses in respect of recruitment, remuneration and other personnel practices;
- the development of a narrow focus by individual businesses reducing the amount of related selling, something which was not a problem with the previous country-based organisational structure.

The company believes that these difficulties can be overcome, and that 3M has sufficient organisational flexibility to adapt to the new challenges.

Source: Based on Lorenz (1993)

Illustration 7.8

PepsiCo

The US company PepsiCo is a major provider of beverages and snacks and an operator of restaurant businesses. It has operated traditionally with very autonomous, decentralised divisions, with a culture which gives managers a strong incentive to be entrepreneurial and grow their individual business.

In September 1994 the company announced that it was centralising the purchase of materials for its rapidly expanding but separate European businesses, in order to save up to $100 million per annum in operating expenses. Savings of this magnitude represented 5 per cent of the company's total costs of $2 billion.

Common items of purchase had been identified by the heads of major constituent businesses including Pepsi-Co, Pizza Hut and KFC (previously Kentucky Fried Chicken). Likely savings are anticipated in respect of TV advertising, sugar, spices, cooking oil, flour and packaging materials. For example, Pizza Hut buys an enormous quantity of cardboard for its boxes, while Pepsi-Cola buys cardboard for soft drinks trays.

If the newly adopted purchasing procedures are successful in Europe, the company intends to cascade the policy to other regions, including North and South America and Asia-Pacific, where it has a strong presence.

Source: Based on press reports

Logistics

For manufacturing industry, concentrating production on key locations within the region will inevitably increase demands on the logistics function. Unless the organisation's supply chain can be configured to ensure appropriate levels of customer service without excessive stockholdings being held in each national market, many of the cost savings from, say, concentrating production are likely to be lost. As a consequence, the development of pan-regional strategies by manufacturers will require a careful consideration of the organisation's logistics strategy.

Organisations have the choice of either managing the key operations of haulage, warehousing and provision of support systems through the company's own distribution function, or contracting these services out to a third party. Further, increasingly manufacturers are not just expecting the logistics function to support production facilities, but considering it as an important element of their cost reduction strategies and as part of the means by which customer service can be improved. The achievement of these aims is leading major companies to reconfigure their distribution functions to enhance their competitive advantage. For companies operating as a regional exporter, there is the opportunity to concentrate their distribution facilities on a single location to serve the whole region. As a result, a single distribution site replaces individual national distribution centres, and enables the organisation to move from (i) to (ii) as illustrated in Figure 7.7. Alternatively, for companies operating a co-ordinated international regional strategy a more complex pattern of distribution may emerge, as shown in Figure 7.7 (iii).

Figure 7.7 Changing patterns of distribution for international regions

(i) Logistics functions organised on a country by country basis

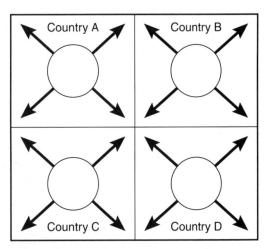

(ii) Development of a pan-regional logistics function for a regional exporter

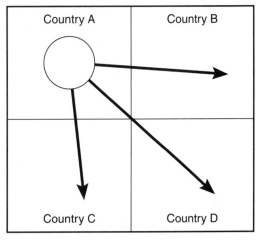

(iii) Development of a pan-regional logistics function for a co-ordinated international regional strategy

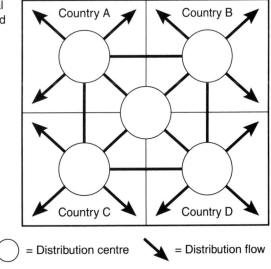

Key: ◯ = Distribution centre ➘ = Distribution flow

One company which has decided to concentrate its distribution using the principles illustrated in Figure 7.7 (iii) is the American company Nike. Nike's strategy of centralising its distribution networks on a single hub in both the USA and Europe is discussed in Illustration 7.9.

Illustration 7.9

Nike

The US company Nike is a major manufacturer of sports shoes and clothing, marketing its products throughout Europe. The company has depended traditionally on national or local warehouses to supply retailers. In a highly competitive industry it is now seeking to replace more than 20 national and local warehouses with a single new European distribution centre located in Belgium. The decision to concentrate its logistics function in this way follows the company's earlier experience in centralising its US distribution on a single 'hub' in Memphis.

By concentrating its warehousing and delivery in this way, Nike aims to reduce stock levels by avoiding duplication. The company will also be able to ensure a wider range of products is stocked in its central warehouse, helping to avoid 'stock-out' situations.

Source: The authors

The requirements of major client companies such as Nike are placing new demands on the logistics function. Traditionally concentrating on haulage, in-house logistics functions or third-party companies are having to extend their range of services and associated competences in order to meet these new demands. In Europe, for example, while in-house logistics still dominate, there are an increasing number of companies which have contracted out their logistics functions to a third party. Logistics companies wishing to gain this business need not just to provide haulage facilities, but to operate warehouses and offer appropriate information technology systems. Consequently, logistics companies which wish to serve clients operating with a co-ordinated international regional strategy are increasingly required themselves to operate with a regional scope.

Finance

The development of an international regional strategy will again raise the question as to which aspects of the finance function will be centralised to be co-ordinated on a regional basis and which will remain to be determined by local companies. Key treasury functions, including foreign exchange, medium- and long-term funding, where these have not previously been centralised, will almost inevitably be undertaken on a regional basis. Whether some treasury functions, including the raising of short-term finance, may continue to be managed on a national basis is highly company specific.

Other areas of change following the adoption of an international regional strategy include:

- removal of responsibility for major production and distribution centres from national companies so that these now report to, and are controlled by, the regional centre. These changes are likely to increase the complexity of intra-company funds transfer as production centres may invoice the national organisation in a different currency to the one used locally for sales;
- the transfer to the regional centre of a range of budgets formerly held by the national organisation, which might include advertising, procurement of major capital and revenue items, etc. The transfer of procurement, of at least major items, can be expected to lead to a reduction in the number of transactions the national organisation engages in with suppliers, as major areas of procurement are centralised and dealt with on a regional basis. Correspondingly the level and range of work undertaken by the finance function of the national organisation are reduced;
- changes of reporting lines, in order to provide data to the regional centre responsible for the product grouping, as well as to the national organisation, to monitor performance and, where appropriate, take corrective action.

Summary

This chapter has focused on what constitutes an international regional strategy and the conditions under which organisations seek to utilise this approach for the purposes of their international business development. The differences with an approach based on exporting and the distinction between fragmented and co-ordinated international regional strategies have been articulated, together with how external and internal triggers may act to bring about a change in strategy. Some of the potential difficulties in managing the transition of an organisation to a co-ordinated international regional strategy have been investigated, emphasising the practical difficulties of implementing new ways of organisational working.

For national players and organisations at an earlier stage of international business development, the recognition of the need to move to operating with an international regional strategy can result in significant organisational challenges. Equally, the realisation that not all national players can become regional players inevitably means that many companies will at some stage cease to remain as independent competitors. National players in an external context in which rivals are developing international regional strategies will be faced with difficult strategic choices.

Moving to a co-ordinated international regional strategy is likely to have a profound effect on how the individual business functions are configured and operated. The scope and level of decision making in respect of individual national organisations can be expected to change, with many more decisions being determined on the basis of the overall needs of the region. Consequently, the balance of power between the regional organisation and national operations is likely to undergo marked change.

A fundamental question in relation to the phase model of business development is whether international regional strategies represent an intermediate phase of transition with organisations aspiring to operate with a worldwide strategy, or whether operating with an international regional strategy is a sustainable basis for competing in an industry for the foreseeable future. While there is no universal answer to this question, in some circumstances industries characterised by companies operating with an international regional strategy may well be in transition to becoming dominated by worldwide competitors; in other instances there may be little or no incentive to develop beyond operating with an international regional focus.

Checklist

- The development of an international regional strategy represents the third phase of an organisation's business development.
- Regional economic integration is increasing, not least because of the emergence of NAFTA and the EU.
- There are a number of significant differences between forms of economic integration, which range from a free trade area to political union.
- An international regional exporter seeks to serve the region from its home production base and has yet to locate production and/or other key value-adding facilities in cross-border markets.
- The fragmented international regional strategy is based on serving the international region using a series of autonomous country-based strategies.
- A co-ordinated international regional strategy seeks to integrate and organise business strategy and its associated functions for the region as a whole.
- External and internal triggers are responsible for organisations adopting an international regional strategy.
- External factors in themselves are not sufficient to bring about change, the internal context must be receptive.
- Companies currently operating with a restricted national market scope may need to develop international regional scale and scope.
- Different opportunities and challenges may exist according to whether the organisation wishes to be a broad-based or niche player.
- Movement to a co-ordinated international regional strategy is likely to represent a discontinuity and present a number of challenges in the management of change.
- The balance of responsibility between regional and national organisations is likely to change, in favour of the former, with the implementation of a co-ordinated international regional strategy.
- Within the context of a co-ordinated international regional strategy some elements of individual business functions may continue to be determined on the basis of national market preferences.
- In developing a co-ordinated international regional strategy care must be taken not to lose contact with national market needs.

Frans Maas Groep NV

Introduction

Originally a road haulage company and later a forwarding agent, Frans Maas Groep NV is increasingly switching its operational focus to the field of integrated logistics services. Frans Maas is one of the few technology-driven forwarders with a truly international character. It is aiming to become one of the main European freight forwarders, primarily in the road transport sector. The company has built up its own European network comprising over 180 branches in 15 countries. This is reflected in the geographical breakdown of its 1993 sales, namely: European Union (EU) 88 per cent, other Europe 8 per cent, North America 2 per cent, and rest of the world 2 per cent.

The liberalisation of European transport markets on 1 January 1993 will over the following five years result in the ending of all existing bi-lateral and multi-lateral quotas that restrict intra-community distribution patterns. Already regulatory changes affecting customs and VAT clearance have resulted in high value cross-border administration business being lost by the forwarders. The disappearance of a number of protective measures dominating local trading conditions had also led to sizeable rate reductions. All these developments are transforming a once mature slow growth market into a fast moving highly competitive arena. Frans Maas has been developing new distribution patterns and forms of service in order to survive the rationalisation of the industry and the shakeout of less efficient firms expected over the next few years.

History

Frans Maas was formed in 1890 in the village of Venlo, The Netherlands, as a transportation company. In the subsequent 100 years, the family-owned road haulage company grew and developed into a specialist cross-border freight forwarder. The forwarding operations comprise the collecting and distribution of general cargo consignments throughout Europe via scheduled services, principally by road, but also by sea and air. In recent years around 75 per cent of road haulage activities have been mainly carried out using rented vehicles, attached to the company's owned fleet of trailers, which number in the region of 1700.

Enlarging its European network and filling in the blank spots became a key priority after 1987, when the need to adapt to anticipated changes in the internal borders of the EU first became apparent. Table C7.1 shows that the most important acquisitions took place in 1989 and the first half of 1990, with additional sales of NLG 251 million (Netherlands guilders) – equivalent to almost 50 per cent of existing turnover – being added to the company. This necessitated successive issues of convertible loan bonds in 1990 and 1991, a financing option facilitated by the 1985 decision to become a public company.

Table C7.1 Network consolidation, 1989–94

Consolidated as in	Company acquired	Country	Interest %	Net sales NLG m	Number of employees
1989	Spendinova A/S	Denmark	67	5	12
1989	Agence Maritiem Bauzin	France	100	6	18
1989	Weich Spedition	Germany	100	5	70
1989	Transped	Portugal	75	4	30
1989	Italexpress	France	100	20	100
1989	B.V.T Transport	Netherlands	100	90	165
1989	Roadspeed International	UK and Ireland	75	18	110
1990	Hunold Spedition	Germany	100	23	165
1990	Stewi	Germany	100	3	19
1990	Clement et Cie	France	65	77	275
1991	Freightmasius AB	Sweden	100	N/A	N/A
1991	Frans Maas Norge A/S	Norway	100	N/A	N/A
1992	Gerum and Furm Spedition	Germany	80	N/A	N/A
1992	Amsped GmbH	Germany	100	N/A	N/A
1993	Lito FM	Spain	51	N/A	N/A

Recognising that the abolition of border restrictions and documentation affects one of the principal reasons for the existence of European freight forwarders, Frans Maas has targeted logistics services as a key area of development in meeting the competitive challenge of the 1990s. This strategy takes account of the changes initiated on 1 January 1993 leading to a deregulated transport industry and greater price competition in the general haulage sectors of the market, where potential suppliers are plentiful and the service offer is difficult to differentiate. Price competition in the mid-1990s has been exacerbated by the low levels of economic activity encountered across Europe.

Frans Maas' concentration on logistics services will continue to encompass forwarding operations. Logistics services cover all aspects of the flow of goods from supplier via manufacturers to end-user or retailer. These services can be subdivided into materials management (just-in-time delivery from supplier to manufacturer), materials handling (services including storage, packing, sorting and labelling) and distribution (complex systems to meet end-user requirements, including forwarding). As the company seeks to transform itself from a traditional freight forwarder into a pan-European provider of logistics services, the company

Case Study 7

will only carry out the transport function if and in so far as this supports the group's primary activities.

The emphasis in broadening the range of activities is designed to move away from the commodity end of the transportation business and to focus on services with a higher value added. To facilitate the management of its increasingly complex operations, Logimax, a computer-controlled information and goods management system developed by Frans Maas, was introduced in 1990. This superseded the previous system used, the Frans Maas Tracking System (FMTS).

Structure

The Frans Maas Groep consists of three main business areas: network services, logistics services, and specialist freight associated with garment transportation. As shown in Figure C7.1, network services made up around 80 per cent of the stated net sales generated by the company in 1993. To achieve this level of sales, Frans Maas operates 15,000 liner services between its warehouses, and services 30,000 clients, of which 75 per cent can be regarded as regular customers (with the largest 18 accounts representing less than 10 per cent of turnover). Between 1992 and 1993 a distinct deterioration of trading conditions is discernible, reflecting both lower volume and lower rates which characterise a highly competitive general transportation market.

Figure C7.1 also shows that some 5 per cent of net sales turnover is generated by dedicated logistics services through the Logimax system, although this figure arguably undervalues the importance of logistics services. Turnover for logistics services only relates to the direct fee income from Logimax, and excludes the value of sales booked to network services which arise from providing dedicated distribution services. If both sources of turnover are aggregated, analysts estimate that the proportion of net sales arising from logistics services is around 20

Figure C7.1 Net sales and employment trends, 1992–93

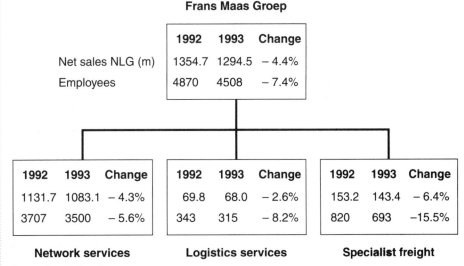

Frans Maas Groep

	1992	1993	Change
Net sales NLG (m)	1354.7	1294.5	− 4.4%
Employees	4870	4508	− 7.4%

1992	1993	Change
1131.7	1083.1	− 4.3%
3707	3500	− 5.6%

Network services

1992	1993	Change
69.8	68.0	− 2.6%
343	315	− 8.2%

Logistics services

1992	1993	Change
153.2	143.4	− 6.4%
820	693	−15.5%

Specialist freight

Source: Annual Reports

297

per cent. This leaves 65 per cent of turnover being generated from network services (freight forwarding), with a further 15 per cent attributable to specialised garment services.

Vision

In consequence of the dismantling of internal borders, Europe is emerging as a major testing ground for new patterns of distribution and services. Such developments require large infrastructure investments as well as initiative to leverage expertise in flexible logistics systems. These developments suggest that the market will be able to accommodate at most 5 to 10 large transport companies operating on a European-wide scale. Besides these large broad-based regional players, a number of smaller firms – probably specialising in specific products or geographical areas – will remain active.

In a bid to win a position among this limited group of international forwarders, Frans Maas has pursued an active acquisition policy so that it can currently offer a large and integrated network of branches across Europe. The company's strategic aims for the end of the millennium are as follows:

- optimise and expand the EU distribution network to include Eastern Europe;
- using intercontinental joint ventures provide outreach to network services outside Europe;
- grow the logistics services based on an overall forwarding concept, particularly by helping clients to find tailor-made solutions to their cross-border logistics problems;
- support these activities with appropriate information technology developments and investment; and finally
- to stress profit growth rather than increasing sales or market share as the key performance indicator.

Distribution network

Streamlining international freight flows by means of an integrated distribution network – effectively a hub and spoke system in which a fine mesh network connects 15 European countries with one another – requires comprehensive geographical coverage matched by a sufficiently high level of activity to enable optimal levels of utilisation to be achieved. Building an appropriate European network (both organically and through acquisitions) takes time and money. To ensure that the network system is more than just collecting and distributing groupage consignments, it is vitally important to ensure a homogeneous service provision at all branches.

As Chairman Dr J van Oijen has remarked, 'increased computerisation within Network Services has led to all branches having a uniform and standardised organisational structure. This is necessary, because groupage freight has a specific meaning for Frans Maas: collecting orders regionally, which are then regrouped for international transport along scheduled routes from country to country, from Frans Maas branch to Frans Maas branch, to be regrouped regionally with the customer.'

Case Study 7

To ensure that services are flexible and client oriented, the network is structured on a regional basis. It is the job of the warehouse manager to regroup every order and make them ready for one of the time-tabled inter-country scheduled services. Turnaround times agreed with the customer have to be met, as well as ensuring that trailers are loaded to maximum capacity. It is for this reason that expansion and optimisation of the European network remain top priorities, with specific adjustments being made to match the overall level of economic activity (Table C7.2).

Table C7.2 European road freight transport: trends in national and international traffic, tonnes per kilometre

	Growth rate 1989/88	Growth rate 1990/89	Growth rate 1991/90
National	−3.8	−2.8	−2.2
International	−9.1	−1.4	9.7

In Eastern Europe Frans Maas had tried to supplement its network by working with small flexible companies. The strategy of the company is aimed at gradually expanding the network to cover the whole of Eastern Europe. Coverage of the Polish market is through a subsidiary of the Clement et Cie Group in Lodz, while in late 1994 negotiations were concluded to a take a minority shareholding in the Promexim company based in Warsaw. Service level is an important factor in the selection of partners, as customers place a premium on forwarders meeting three key requirements: reliability, flexibility and punctuality.

Attention has also been focused on setting up strategic alliances to increase the volume of goods flowing through the distribution network. In this connection the alliance between the Dutch national airline, KLM, and Frans Maas was extended in 1992 by way of a jointly incorporated European Feeder and Distribution Network BV (EFDN). By linking the KLM road carriage network with that of Frans Maas, it is intended to create a fine meshed network with a high service frequency for air freight consignments in Europe. The system is to be implemented in stages. In addition to the existing services in France, Sweden and Austria were added in 1993. The Frans Maas office in Switzerland has also been involved in EFDN activities since 1994.

The co-operation agreement outlined in Figure C7.2 with the largest US trucker, Yellow Freight Systems Inc, to build a door-to-door groupage service between Europe and America became fully operational in 1993. YFM – Direct (Y[ellow] F[rans] M[aas] – Direct) provides a seamless merger of the two networks, offering outreach facilities for the customer who wants to deal with one single service supplier. The consolidation of European groupage shipments takes place at three dedicated nodes in the Frans Maas network: Rotterdam (The Netherlands); Great Yarmouth (UK) and Gothenburg (Sweden). All shipments pass through one of these nodes for transhipment to the adjoining network. The two systems share a dedicated computer system which shows within a few seconds both the price for the entire door-to-door trajectory and when the shipment will be received.

Figure C7.2 Frans Maas joint ventures

'One stop shipping'

The EFDN and YFM co-operative agreements show how the need to search for new ways and services continues to play an important and innovative role in organisational thinking.

A previous attempt to forge intercontinental linkages with Sealand-Logistics GmbH failed. Learning from this mistake, several potential partners were identified and analysed. According to one company executive, potential collaborators were assessed to ensure 'the culture, the objectives and the needs of the partner had to be more or less identical to those of Frans Maas.'

As the chairman Dr van Oijen remarked: 'It was not an easy thing to bring two large companies under one common denominator.' Listed below are some of the obstacles that had to be overcome in order to develop one common door-to-door concept:

- In Europe the price for carrying the parcel is determined by a means of a weight/volume ratio (m^3). In America this is done mainly by means of specific product groups.
- The price of sea freight parcels is usually established by volume.
- In America they do not work with kilograms but with pounds, and in the case of tons, there is a distinction between short tons, long tons and metric tons.
- In Europe people are used to working with several currencies. In America there is only one.

In many aspects it is relatively easy to expand distribution networks; the real challenge is to integrate them in an effective and efficient manner. All these different aspects had to be brought under one common denominator to arrive at an integrated door-to-door solution.

Frans Maas' strategic alliances, together with its existing network, show a company well positioned to benefit from a revival of European trade. The turnover of EFDN and YFM – Direct shows a steady growth which contributes to the use of the entire European network. Moreover, the new services enjoy higher rates than those applying to intra-European shipments. Analysts estimate that the gross margin on European services amounts to 30 per cent, while YFM and EFDN reach 40 per cent.

Contract services

Frans Maas is widely recognised as one of the market leaders in the area of contract logistics, providing premium inventory management and customised

Case Study 7

delivery services tailored to an individual client's needs. The real benefit for the customer is that, without having to arrange their own distribution and storage, fixed costs become variable and investment in fixed assets can be avoided. The present corporate trend of concentrating on core business activities and the subsequent externalisation of logistic services represents a significant business opportunity for Frans Maas.

Contract logistics provides a business solution to those companies who no longer wish to carry out these functions themselves, and at the same time through the application of advanced concepts and technologies offers the client company greater cost control. When Rank Xerox first took on Frans Maas as its sole distributor of inbound components in Europe, buffer stocks ranged from 10 to 40 days. Today there are no buffer stocks for just-in-time parts; while for other components there is a maximum of 10 days. Inventory levels, which used to run at 90 days, now average some 15 days. At the start of the contract the aim was to keep transport costs down to the previous level. In the event Rank Xerox reported a 40 per cent reduction in distribution costs.

In 1993 Frans Maas was awarded the logistics contract for AutoEuropa (the Ford/VW joint venture to develop a new 'mini' van), which is based in Portugal. The contract requires the development of a pan-European logistics operation involving the management of a central warehouse, collection from suppliers and delivery to production lines on a just-in-time basis. Each element of the project involves substantial time and manpower resources. The AutoEuropa contract will take around 15 months of project development time, with a further 12 months to become fully operational.

Given the present scale of Frans Maas' logistics services business (Figure C7.1), only one major contract can be dealt with a year. As a result, the company is still heavily committed to its core overland transportation business. Smaller projects by volume and nature, but requiring logistics services support, are grouped in the network services division (for example, SKF and Nintendo). Correspondingly, the turnover and cost division between logistics services and network services will always be arbitrary owing to this interaction.

Strategic investments

In preparation for the elimination of internal borders within the EU, Frans Maas has undertaken a substantial programme of strategic investments. Not surprisingly, Table C7.3 shows that between 1987 and 1992 net investments exceeded annual depreciation. This was to facilitate growth of the European distribution network coupled with further expansion in computerisation and communications infrastructure. Investment levels were curtailed heavily in 1993 (effectively limited to a level which was lower than depreciation), as cash flows declined from NLG74.4 million in 1992 to NLG38.6 million in 1993.

Table C7.3 Cash flow, net investment and depreciation, 1987–93 (NLG million)

	1987	1988	1989	1990	1991	1992	1993
Cash flow	30.9	39.0	49.9	61.9	69.5	74.4	38.6
Net investment	20.4	58.0	50.9	59.3	84.5	83.7	35.0
Depreciation	15.2	18.9	21.6	30.4	33.3	37.1	39.9

During the five year period between 1988 and 1992, 'other operating costs' increased by NLG88.3 million to NLG146.9 million (Table C7.5), reflecting the start-up of new logistics projects. Stabilisation at around the NLG140–150 million level is likely, provided that the size of the contract logistics division remains largely unchanged. The establishment of new logistics services requires high IT and telecommunications costs, currently of the order of NLG30 million per annum and likely to increase further.

Personnel

Table C7.4 reflects the European character of Frans Maas in a number of ways. In 1993 almost two-thirds of all staff were employed outside The Netherlands, as compared with almost half some 10 years earlier. The fall in the staff employed in The Netherlands, from 1724 in 1992 to 1504 in 1993, is solely attributable to the 200 redundancies arising from inter-company settlements being replaced by a new computer system. This will achieve cost savings of around NLG13 million over the next two years.

Table C7.4 Number of employees[1]

	1987	1988	1989	1990	1991	1992	1993
Number of employees (EU)	2397	2814	3635	4459	4779	4680	4335
Number of employees in Netherlands	1029	1218	1467	1610	1760	1724	1504
Netherlands % of total	42.9	43.3	40.3	36.1	36.8	36.8	34.6

Note: 1. Mid-year average; not year end as depicted in Figure C7.1

The optimisation of the European network offers opportunities to reduce the number of warehouses, since there is no need to have customs-forwarding terminals at either side of the border anywhere within the EU. Some 400 jobs in customs forwarding were lost in 1993, and it is not inconceivable that there is scope for this to come down by another 350 in 1994.

Financial results

As Table C7.5 shows, 1993 was a difficult year for the Frans Maas Groep NV. It was a year dominated by adjustments to new market circumstances, the unfavourable economic climate within Europe and the tougher competitive environment in the freight forwarding industry. Although Frans Maas repeatedly gave profit warnings in 1993, they did not specify the extent of the deterioration after intra-EU border controls were lifted on 1 January 1993.

Table C7.5 Financial performance, 1987–93 (NLG million)

Profit and loss	1987	1988	1989	1990	1991	1992	1993
Sales	496.5	585.3	811.5	1106.9	1263.0	1354.7	1294.5
Other revenue	2.9	4.7	3.6	10.3	3.1	7.9	8.4
Transport costs	(275.8)	(329.4)	(472.6)	(653.8)	(742.9)	(791.8)	(810.0)
Gross profit	223.6	260.6	342.5	463.4	523.2	570.8	492.9
Wages	(128.5)	(145.7)	(189.7)	(261.1)	(297.7)	(319.9)	(300.2)
Other costs	(49.9)	(58.8)	(80.4)	(114.0)	(128.7)	(146.9)	(136.6)
Depreciation	(15.2)	(18.9)	(21.6)	(30.4)	(33.3)	(37.1)	(39.9)
Operating profit	30.0	37.2	50.9	57.9	63.5	66.9	16.2
Financial charges	(2.8)	(3.2)	(3.8)	(5.2)	(7.5)	(9.7)	(14.0)
Tax and other charges	(12.4)	(13.8)	(20.5)	(22.4)	(20.5)	(20.7)	(4.9)
Net profit	14.8	20.2	26.6	30.3	35.5	36.5	(2.7)
Ratios							
Gross profit margin	45.0	44.3	42.2	41.6	41.4	42.1	38.1
Operating profit margin	6.1	6.4	6.3	5.2	5.0	4.9	1.3
Net profit to sales	3.0	3.4	3.3	2.7	2.8	2.7	(0.3)

In the 1993 Annual Report Frans Maas management notes that 'the disappearance of a number of protective measures in a number of markets has had the consequence that a large number of suppliers try to maintain or expand their market share by means of price reductions. This has taken the results in our branch of the industry to a low and companies have closed down regularly. Restructuring the forwarding industry and reducing the number of suppliers combined with a rearrangement of the market seems, therefore to be inevitable.'

Challenges facing carriers

The current state of the European transportation market can probably be best described as imbalance between excess supply of 'hardware' (trucks and warehouses) and strong demand for 'software' (value-added transport services). In these circumstances operators are simultaneously trying to gain market share, develop logistics products and dramatically reduce their cost structure. More specifically, in the aftermath of 1 January 1993 the following changes in competition and logistics management can be identified:

● The removal of internal barriers across Europe and the ensuing elimination of the customs handling business will have an abrupt impact on earnings in 1993 and 1994. For Frans Maas, the abandonment of customs activities led to an extraordinary restructuring charge of NLG10 million in 1992. It also resulted in an NLG60 million reduction in turnover in 1993, and an estimated fall in net profits of NLG15 million.

● In anticipation of the emergence of a single European market many local transport groups invested heavily. The returns on these costly expansion programmes have generally been poor, while the financial conditions of many of the major operators have deteriorated at a time when they are also struggling to integrate newly acquired subsidiaries.

● One result of the creation of a single market has been the removal of restrictions on permits allowing hauliers to operate throughout the EU. Many countries had maintained highly restrictive licensing arrangements, but now companies are allowed to make as many international journeys as they want between member states.

● Major pan-European groups (e.g. Danzas, Schenker-Rhenus, Nedlloyd and Kuhne & Nagel) are fighting for market share in order to generate sufficient throughput into their transport networks. Frans Maas has bucked the industry trend by increasing its volume throughput. Growth in volume terms has been achieved at the cost of lower prices in 1993.

Table C7.6 Sales of largest transport companies in EU, 1992 (US dollars millions except where indicated)

Rank	Company (country of incorporation)	Total sales	Transport sales	Operating profit	Employees ('000)	Sales per employee (US$'000s)
1	Danzas AG (CH)	6,980	6,988	42.2	16.2	431
2	Schenker-Rhenus AG (D)	12,503	4,652	182.0	34.6	361
3	Nedlloyd (NL)	3,499	3,372	32.0	21.7	161
4	Kuhne & Nagel AG (CH)	3,260	3,260	63.9	9.1	358
5	Ocean Group plc (UK)	2,108	2,052	56.2	11.7	180
6	LEP Group plc (UK)	2,172	1,986	38.6	10.1	215
7	NFC plc (UK)	2,544	1,493	134.0	33.8	75
8	Thyssen-Haniel GmbH (D)	9,763	1,288	166.0	28.7	340
9	TDG plc (UK)	834	834	59.8	10.8	77
10	Bilspedition (S)	1,960	823	n/a	11.1	177
11	Frans Maas (NL)	705	705	30.0	4.9	144

Notes:
1. All information based on annual report and converted into US dollars, where appropriate, using 1992 exchange rates. NFC transport sales based on best estimates.
2. Rank order based on transport sales.
3. Tranport sales include all forms of transport and not just road.
4. Countries of incorporation: CH = Switzerland; D = Germany; NL = Netherlands; UK = United Kingdom; and S = Sweden.
5. All figures rounded.

Outlook

A great many suppliers are active in European transport markets. Smaller companies focus primarily on the physical haulage operation, while the large companies also offer related logistics services. As Table C7.6 shows, Frans Maas is at best a medium-sized player. In comparing the various companies, it should be borne in mind that Frans Maas concentrates on the road transport market. Other companies focus on more limited or, at the other extreme, worldwide markets, and/or cover a wide range of transport modes, including sea and air freight activities.

By focusing solely on road transport-related turnover, Table C7.7 demonstrates the low level of market concentration accounted for by the 11 largest forwarding companies. The 11 largest companies account for only around 20 per cent of the total European road haulage market. The highly fragmented structure of European road haulage is a factor driving and shaping the intensely competitive battle currently under way. An outcome of this process is that the level of industry concentration is likely to rise significantly beyond current levels.

Table C7.7 Total sales and market share of the 11 largest companies in the European road freight transport industry, 1992

Rank	Company	1992 Sales (US$m)	Market share
1	Danzas AG	5,486	5.7
2	Schenker-Rhenus AG	2,666	2.8
3	Nedlloyd	2,004	2.1
4	LEP Group plc	1,986	2.0
5	Ocean Group plc	1,872	1.9
6	NFC plc	1,493	1.6
7	Kuhne & Nagel AG	1,034	1.1
8	TDG plc	834	0.9
9	Bilspedition	823	0.9
10	Thyssen-Haniel GmbH	753	0.8
11	Frans Maas	705	0.7
	Others	75,993	79.5
Total market sales		95,588	100.0

Source: Based on companies' annual accounts and converted into US dollars at 1992 exchange rates; NFC sales estimated.

In the medium term Group Transport 2000 Plus, a committee set up by the EU, has forecast that road haulage will not only undergo very strong growth, but will also win market share from other transport modes. Table C7.8 shows that transport volume in Europe (domestic plus international) is expected to increase by 51 per cent between 1990 and 2010, with the strongest increase expected from road transport.

Table C7.8 Transport growth, 1990–2010 (tonnes per km)

Transport mode	Total growth rates (%)
Rail transport	–4.0
Road haulage	+74.0
Inland shipping	+8.0
Total	+51.0

Further deregulation will lead to ongoing intense competition. From 1 January 1994 Germany has abolished *feste Frachtkosten* (fixed freight rates) which limited any discounts to a maximum of 30 per cent. Under the new deregulated pricing structure, price competition with Germany and The Netherlands should intensify. From the same date, the number of cabotage authorisations (picking up cargo en route between two destinations in different countries) will go up from 18,530 to 30,000. This allocation will increase by 30 per cent per year from 1995, with the aim of achieving full liberalisation in July 1998. This agreement has only been reached at the expense of allowing some EU members to impose levies on all domestic and foreign firms using their motorways.

Germany, Belgium, The Netherlands, Denmark and Luxembourg have all announced that they will charge nearly £1000 a year per vehicle for a permit to use their roads from January 1995. The immediate effect for haulage companies will be additional costs, which in the face of intense competition are likely to prove difficult to recover through increased prices.

Conclusions

The current trading environment is affecting volumes, which puts even greater pressure on rates. The low degree of consolidation and further deregulation could ensure that rates pressure continues unabated until 1995. The strength of Frans Maas lies in the company's solid management and strong infrastructure investment. When these factors are combined with the expected strong growth in intra-European trade forecast in the medium term, the European aspirations of Frans Maas may become a real possibility.

Questions

(1) *What effect has the removal of internal custom barriers within the EU had on the road haulage industry and Frans Maas in particular?*

(2) *What phase of international business development do you think Frans Maas has reached and why?*

(3) *Consider the business performance of Frans Maas and its different divisions. What is your judgement about the company's business performance?*

(4) *What are the competitive threats that Frans Maas is facing, and who are its main competitors?*

(5) *Identify Frans Maas' business strategies. Which of its businesses is it trying to grow and why? How do you think the company will be competitively positioned five years from now?*

Chapter 8

WORLDWIDE COMPETITORS

Key learning objectives

To understand:

- the need for worldwide competitors to configure product, geography, people and processes for global competitive advantage

- what advantages the global competitor may achieve over international regional or national players

- the potential benefits of operating international strategic alliances

- an understanding of the different organisational forms and their relative strengths and weaknesses

- what a transnational organisation is and its distinguishing characteristics

Context

The distinguishing characteristic of the worldwide competitor is the recognition of the need to find a balance between a responsive and flexible local approach and effective global co-ordination. Virtually no company has achieved a satisfactory solution to date, although a few have crafted flexible local and central management capabilities and attempted to link them in such a way as to partially allow the company 'to think globally and act locally'. Any attempt to globalise is faced with problematic strategic spatial imperatives, together with practical implementation challenges which demand a fundamental change in international business practice.

For most worldwide companies it is the development of transnational organisational capabilities that is the key to building long-term success. Current and aspiring global companies need to achieve both integration and autonomy while fostering and developing organisational learning and knowledge transfer. Having the structures and culture which enable knowledge transfer from one country to another can provide a key source of advantage for worldwide competitors, together with changing the ways companies compete across borders. Organising for worldwide effectiveness must take account of both strategic and structural imperatives and their interdependencies. The focus of the chapter is as follows:

- *developing a global strategy*
- *global strategic assessment and competitive moves*
- *international strategic alliances*
- *organisational forms for worldwide competitors*
- *reconciling the irreconcilable: the search for the transnational company*

Grappling with the organisational complexity generated by both product and geography prompts initial consideration of how the worldwide business should be run to ensure an appropriate product/service in each global market. This prompts consideration of how to develop an appropriate global vision. Implementation will take several forms, with international companies from the three main international business regions – North America, Western Europe and Japan – tending to have differing organisational structures and facing differing globalisation challenges. Making globally competitive and/or co-operative moves prompts consideration of the relative strengths and weaknesses of national and worldwide competitors. For the worldwide competitor the recurring theme of how to manage the tension between product and geographical perspectives is examined through looking at a number of different organisational forms. The penultimate section considers how organising for worldwide effectiveness requires the development of resource inter-dependencies and responsibilities among organisational units, and how these can be integrated into a highly leveraged transnational organisation. The chapter concludes with a case study on SKF AB, which allows the frameworks developed in the chapter to be applied.

Developing a global strategy

Figure 8.1 shows that worldwide strategies represent the final stage of the phase model. Two common threads characterise the emergence of the worldwide competitor. First, such organisations have progressed beyond operating with an international regional scope and look to achieve global market coverage. Product/service sourcing is characterised by the determination to play 'global chess' to take advantage of lowest national factor costs and/or expertise. A further distinguishing characteristic is the desire to tailor the organisation of the individual business along the three dimensions of product, geography and people/processes.

To manage the global business on an integrated worldwide basis it is necessary to reshape the organisation along three dimensions – product, geography and people/process – in order to exploit global competitive advantage. As depicted in Figure 8.2, the global player has the opportunity to integrate and co-ordinate business functions across multiple regions/countries and draw on

Figure 8.1 The phase model and worldwide strategies

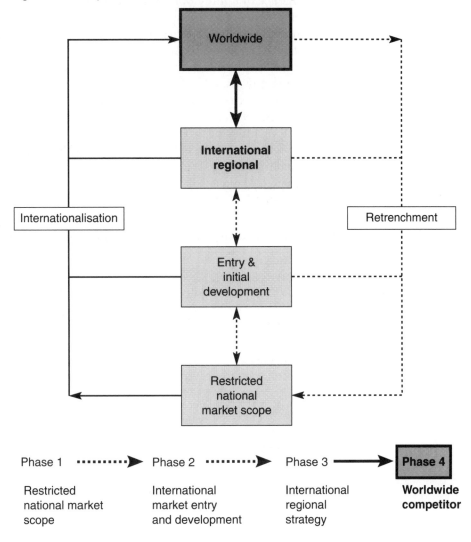

people/processes in a fashion unmatched by a business operating at an earlier stage of international business development. In order to do this successfully, the worldwide competitor needs to examine carefully its organisational structure, systems and values. While the extent of integration required varies by industry and specific company, global integration contrasts markedly with the 'multi-local' approach in which companies set up company affiliates that design, produce and market products or services on a country by country basis.

Some of the most pertinent external factors encouraging the emergence and subsequent development of worldwide competitors across a range of industries were discussed in Chapter 3. Among the factors discussed, the following have been perhaps the most influential:

- emergence of a more open trading environment reflecting the continued development of multi-lateral trading agreements;
- falling transport costs reflecting both containerisation and the operation of large bulk carriers, and deregulation in respect of air transport;
- emergence of new technologies which increasingly demand global scale in order to recover and fund new product and process research and development;
- increased international trade and communication assisting the convergence of customer preferences;
- the opportunity of producers both to 'customise' core products to meet local preferences and benefit from global-scale efficiencies by adopting flexible manufacturing systems; and
- the growth of global customers, demanding common product sourcing and quality standards for all plants regardless of geographical location.

Figure 8.2 Developing and/or reshaping the worldwide competitor

Product	Geography	People and processes	Global strategy
• Configure product/ service operations in order to:	• Achieve geographical coverage in order to encompass strategically important countries as determined by:	• Develop people and process in order to:	
(a) supply chosen market segments	(a) current and future sales potential	(a) achieve a global vision/mindset	
(b) achieve economies of scale	(b) the need to match competitors	(b) leverage cross-unit skills and competences worldwide	
(c) avoid unnecessary duplication of resources	(c) have access to low factor costs and/or expertise	(c) ensure strong co-ordinating and linking mechanisms between organisational sub-units	

When defining the appropriate scope and scale of a business, the way in which competitors and customers have decided to organise themselves and their future strategic intentions is a useful litmus test. Any assessment of how organisations can be developed to capture global competitive advantages will also need to focus on:

- vision/mindset; and
- organisational dynamics

Vision/mindset   The emergence of many worldwide competitors have reflected the driving force of visionary leaders who are able to instil their vision in the corporate mindset. In many cases a visionary leader either anticipates future changes in the external context, or helps to shape the future external context in ways which mean that rivals are at a disadvantage unless they themselves can operate on a global scale and achieve a comparable cost basis.

The emergence of visionary leaders may be a major catalyst in an organisation's breaking out of its existing stage of international business development and seeking to become a worldwide competitor. The vision of the leader is not sufficient to enable the organisation to seek to transform itself from an earlier phase of international business development. It is also necessary that the existing mindset or paradigm of the organisation can be changed successfully, and that a world mindset is developed.

To ensure that a world vision will be realised, a reframing of the mindsets of managers and employees throughout the organisation will need to take place. Reframing a mindset in this way represents a significant discontinuity, but one which is necessary if a new strategic thrust and a new mode of functioning are to be achieved. Realisation of a truly world vision normally requires five important components about the way an organisation does its business to be in place. Figure 8.3 depicts the five key world mindset imperatives, recognising that while they are separable they collectively fashion the spatial mindset.

Ultimately to develop into a truly worldwide competitor, all five elements of the international mindset need to be acquired by the company. Many companies, whether aspiring and/or existing worldwide competitors, will not

Figure 8.3 The world vision/mindset

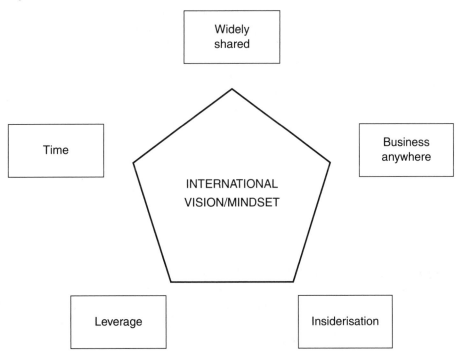

necessarily have developed fully all the characteristics. The achievement of a truly world mindset is thus an aspirational goal for many organisations, involving as it does the following components:

- *Widely shared.* The organisational challenges of managing across boundaries needs to be articulated clearly and widely shared throughout the organisation. It is not sufficient to focus purely on a vision of what the firm could and should be doing. Equally essential is the need to foster organisational cohesiveness concerning the new mindset; in short, a widely shared viewpoint which is more concerned with how you do business, as opposed to where you do business.

- *Business anywhere.* Where a worldwide competitor has its headquarters should be transparent to individual markets and the needs of local customers. Rather than being concerned with the question of which functions should be centralised or decentralised, it is vital that the organisational communications and logistics network is sufficiently efficient and effective to permit business anywhere.

- *Insiderisation.* The concept of international mindset resists any attempt to replicate domestic organisational systems in new cross-border territories. An insiderisation view requires an organisation to develop an equidistant view concerning the wants and needs of customers, and to adopt organisational systems to respond to local needs. Equally, the business should be managed from either where key business skills are present and/or the most strategically important country.

- *Leverage.* Making progress to becoming a worldwide competitor requires fundamental organisational innovation where the whole shared belief is greater than the sum of the parts. This necessitates creating a system of shared values across the company's operations, enabling a collective mindset to replace more nationally focused views previously held.

- *Time.* Building shared values takes time. All firms attempting to manage businesses across boundaries must establish organisational priorities and measure progress. They need to establish a baseline of where they stand in relation to their vision, and flesh out balanced scorecard directives which clarify and amplify the vision.

The extent to which an organisation has developed a global mindset can be quantified by completing Table 8.1. Companies which have reached the point that for each characteristic they are, or wish to develop as, a worldwide competitor should be assigned a value of 4, while companies whose focus remains on a restrictive national market focus should be given a value of 1.

Organisation dynamics

The organisation dynamics hold in place the existing mindset. Both emerging and established worldwide competitors will periodically need to undergo 'organisational renewal' in order to sustain their organisational capability and meet new challenges. For the *emerging* worldwide competitor this will mean ensuring it can develop to meet the global challenge, while for the *established*

Table 8.1 Assessing the extent to which an organisation has developed a world mindset

Characteristic	Restricted national market scope	Initial entry and development	Co-ordinated international regional	Worldwide competitor
Widely shared				
Business anywhere				
Insiderisation				
Leverage				
Time				
Total				

Notes: Values to be assigned: Restricted national market scope 1; initial market entry and development 2; co-ordinated international regional 3; and worldwide competitor 4.

worldwide competitor the focus will need to be on continuous improvement in order to sustain and improve itself in the context of a dynamic environment.

In all organisations the established mindset tends to be deeply embedded in the organisation and prove difficult to change. Paradoxically, this is likely to make the need to change the mindset periodically even stronger. If the previous mindset is no longer appropriate, the failure to overcome such organisational inertia and to commence the process of organisational renewal may place the organisation at risk. To avoid this outcome organisations need to seek constant renewal. In effect, organisational renewal becomes a journey without a destination, a process of continuously reshaping and reprioritising global mindset imperatives.

Global strategic assessment and competitive moves

Assessment of the position of rivals and the likely competitive moves an organisation might adopt are important in both revealing competitive strength and identifying possible strategic options. To undertake both of these inter-related tasks the key components – product, geography, people and processes – which build on the informing framework discussed in Figure 8.2 need to be examined in a specific context. This can be done by examining the following list of questions in order to establish the extent to which competitors need to operate, either now or in the future, with global scope and scale:

● *Product*

a. Identify market segments chosen: to what extent does the organisation have a narrow as opposed to broad product focus? Can the chosen segments be served by standardised global products, or do local preferences require local products?

b. Assess how far economies of scale are present: to what extent does the organisation have to be a national, international regional or worldwide competitor in order to achieve an efficient scale of operation?

c. To what extent is it necessary to concentrate, for example, R&D and/or production facilities in order to achieve efficient scale?

● *Geography*

a. How necessary is it for companies to have achieved coverage of all strategically important markets as determined by their current and/or future sales potential?

b. How important is it to match the market coverage of competitive rivals?

c. To what extent is it critical to have access to low factor cost locations, and/or countries which have a pool of key skills and expertise?

● *People and processes*

a. How many of the companies in the industry operate with a global vision/mindset? Are those with a global vision aggressively pursuing this goal?

b. To what extent is it necessary to leverage key skills and competences on a worldwide basis? To what extent do these skills and competences – e.g. marketing, technical, managerial capabilities, etc. – offer the basis of global competitive advantage?

c. Are strong co-ordinating and linking mechanisms between organisational sub-units important for competitive presence, or can cross-border subsidiaries be left to operate as independent entities?

The assessment of the three dimensions – product, geography, people and processes – will enable the current competitive position of companies in an industry and their international business strategies to be identified. How the key areas identified above can be used in practice is illustrated by taking three companies operating in the world chocolate confectionery industry.

The three companies – Thorntons (UK), Hershey (US) and Nestlé (Switzerland) – have been chosen to illustrate aspects of the framework developed. Table 8.2 begins the process of competitive assessment by examining global market coverage and the extent to which companies are represented in the both the 'Triad' markets and the emerging countries/regions of the world.

Table 8.3 undertakes a similar exercise to establish the geographical location of key value-adding facilities, e.g. R&D, manufacturing plant, corporate headquarters, etc.

Further aspects of the three key dimensions can be examined by plotting competitors according to their characteristics in relation to each other. Figure 8.4 provides an illustration of how this might be done, by a selecting three factors which assist in distinguishing between the three chocolate companies.

Once data collection has been completed and the framework applied, it will be possible to reach an overall assessment of both the external context and the nature of the companies operating in the industry, see Illustration 8.1.

Table 8.2 Assessing global market coverage

Company	EU	Japan	NAFTA	Asian 'Tigers'	Eastern Europe	Latin America	Rest of World
Thorntons	UK and France						
Hershey	Germany	Joint venture	USA				
Nestlé	All markets	All markets	All markets	All markets	All markets	All markets	All markets

Table 8.3 Location of key value-adding activities

Company	EU	Japan	NAFTA	Asian 'Tigers'	Eastern Europe	Latin America	Rest of World
Thorntons	Manufactures in UK and Belgium						
Hershey	Manufactures in Germany	Joint venture	Home country; major facilities				
Nestlé	Corporate HQ in Switzerland; production facilities in most countries		All key markets	All key markets	All key markets	Almost full coverage	All key markets

Once the strategic assessment of the industry and its constituent companies has been made, it is possible to examine a number of key questions in respect of future competitive developments, namely:

- To what extent is it important both now or for the future to operate with global market coverage and scale?
- Are there competitive niches into which companies which are unlikely to develop as worldwide competitors can locate in order to survive?
- To what extent are the competitive strategies of individual companies realistic and sustainable?

In answering these questions it is important to assess what competitive levers existing global competitors may employ against companies which are either national players or have an international regional presence. Together with any superiority arising out of, for example, the achievement of global economies of scale and the leverage of global brands, worldwide competitors may seek to adopt the following tactics.

Figure 8.4 Assessing product-market competitors

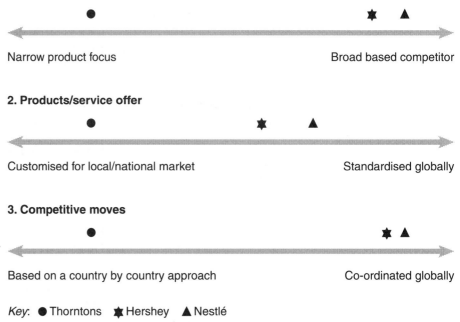

1. Product-market segments

Narrow product focus   Broad based competitor

2. Products/service offer

Customised for local/national market   Standardised globally

3. Competitive moves

Based on a country by country approach   Co-ordinated globally

Key: ● Thorntons   ★ Hershey   ▲ Nestlé

Illustration 8.1

World chocolate confectionery industry: overall assessment of chosen companies

Thorntons
Limited market coverage. Focused primarily on the UK and French markets with production facilities in the UK and Belgium. Essentially a niche player selling speciality chocolates which does not have a global ambition (Illustration 6.6).

Hershey
Very strong presence in the North American market. Recent joint venture to enter Japan. Weak in the EU. Ambition to develop greater market coverage.

Nestlé
Extensive world coverage. Has continued to acquire national players in order to strengthen its global network. Production facilities in most strategically important countries. Development of global brands; but also recognises the need to meet local tastes in many countries. Overall strategy informed by corporate centre, e.g. acquisitions, but considerable local autonomy (Illustration 8.4).

Cross-subsidisation of countries	Global competitors may, because of their huge size and corresponding resource availability, choose to cross-subsidise entry to a market and the competitive tactics employed to expand their market presence. Indigenous national players will correspondingly suffer disproportionately from such tactics to the extent that they are primarily dependent on a single 'home' market.

The same tactic may be employed against a large competitor which is dependent on specific markets and does not have the same market coverage to match that of the global competitor. In these circumstances the global competitor may attack its rival, knowing that it can do this successfully because of its competitor's lack of global market coverage.

Globally co-ordinated moves	Beyond the tactics chosen for a single national market, the global competitor may chose to operate with a co-ordinated strategy, which other worldwide competitors operating with a fragmented country by country strategy find difficult to counter. The global competitor may thus launch a new set of competitive moves simultaneously across a number of markets, to which an unco-ordinated worldwide competitor is likely to find the greatest difficulty in achieving a co-ordinated response.

The intrinsic advantages of the global competitor in many contexts, together with the option of employing globally integrated strategic moves, places such companies at a major advantage unless there are distinct benefits of operating with a more restricted scope and smaller scale.

In assessing how different rivals in the same industry may compete, the following three options will be considered, namely:

- price competition
- non-price competition
- co-operation/collaboration, including acquisition

Price competition

Where a global competitor is facing a smaller and relatively weak national player, it may choose price as a competitive weapon. The global competitor may consider that by aggressively attacking its smaller competitor the latter will be weakened to a point where it is forced to leave the industry. Where both competitors operate globally, the outcome of price competition between global competitors is likely to be much more uncertain and expensive to both parties. As a result, outbreaks of price competition tend to signal periods of discontinuity and imbalance, as characterised by excess capacity and/or the emergence of a new and aggressive entrants who are, for example, attempting to develop as worldwide competitors.

Non-price competition

The use of non-price competition tends to be a less direct way of competing, and is to some extent 'hidden'. Nevertheless, the use of, for example, advertising and promotions to support products can be expensive and again place smaller, less powerful competitors at a disadvantage. As a result, where companies are increasingly finding themselves disadvantaged in competition with global players, they are likely to differentiate their product/service offer in ways which may offer the prospect of not directly competing with their large competitors.

Co-operation/collaboration

Instead of competing, competitive rivals may seek co-operation/collaboration in different aspects of their business. For this to happen a number of conditions must be met, including mutual need. Indeed, in one sense the acquisition of one company by another represents the final form of collaboration to the extent to which the company giving up its independence no longer believes it can survive on its own. In many cases this is the outcome of the competitive process between large and small: global versus national.

Companies wishing not be acquired or forced out of business in the face of global competition will need to match their rivals in terms of scope and scale. This inevitably will means growing beyond their existing phase of international business development, using either their own resources through organic and/or external growth, or by co-operating/collaborating with other competitors. The different methods of corporate growth will also be of interest to existing worldwide competitors which are seeking to complete the gaps in their global network.

Few companies have universal world coverage and most, owing to their origins and subsequent development, are stronger in one or more international regions of the world. For these companies one of the major challenges is to continue to extend their geographical coverage in order to encompass countries/regions of the world where they have relatively little exposure. Further, the attraction of potential cross-border locations for organisations is constantly changing as political and economic factors change, especially as they affect emerging nations. Indeed, the early 1990s saw a widespread opening up of many emerging countries as previously employed protectionist measures were abandoned and governments sought to encourage foreign investment.

Entry to these countries had previously been denied or made unattractive to worldwide organisations. Among the countries which have become more 'open' many are highly attractive, reflecting as they do the prospect of rapid economic growth and development. As Chapter 3 suggested, many of the so-called 'emerging' countries are forecast to enjoy rates of economic growth far in excess of those expected to be achieved in the Western world. One of the most popular of the newly emerging economies as a destination for foreign investment is China, discussed in Illustration 8.2.

While existing worldwide competitors attempt to complete their global network, the ability of national and regional players to compete continues to come under pressure. As worldwide competitors grow stronger such companies have an even greater gap to make up if they are to match the size and resource base of the largest companies in their industry. In this context international strategic alliances offer many attractions and on this topic attention is now focused.

Illustration 8.2

Establishing production facilities for the Chinese market

The emergence of China from its previously highly regulated political and economic system has offered many worldwide competitors a major new, but underdeveloped market, which presents huge opportunities for the future. In both worldwide industrial products and branded consumer goods the country is at a very early stage of development.

Since China opened its markets to foreign investment in 1979, worldwide competitors have been attracted by opportunities arising from the country's 1.2 billion population. Many of these companies have established joint ventures with local companies in order to gain access to this huge market. Each of the major companies which have entered the Chinese market see the country as a vital element in their attempts to gain global dominance. Unilever, for example, expects current sales of $200 million a year to rise to $1.5 billion by 1999.

Entering the Chinese market and establishing new production facilities pose considerable problems even for large and well-resourced companies who have established brands and/or production technology. First, establishing a joint venture can be a long drawn-out process. For example, it took Nestlé some 13 years before it was able to establish its first joint venture in the production of powdered milk. Secondly, even bringing international brands to China does not stop local producers improving their own products and competing strongly on price. More important, however, are the problems which confront worldwide competitors in respect of the country's infrastructure and economic development. Not only does the country's geographical scale pose major logistical problems, but the transportation system is ill fitted to meeting the needs of national distribution. For example, it can take three weeks to ship finished goods the 1000 km from Shanghai to Beijing. Similarly, for television advertising, adverts have to be made abroad and sent to some 300 individual broadcast stations. It can also take up to six months to get a price increase approved by officials.

Given the country's recent emergence from a very different political and economic system, companies also face shortages of manpower, including managerial staff. Overcoming this shortage requires a heavy investment in training and development. Production workers in particular need to become familiar with and able to operate high technology plant very much more advanced than that found in much of Chinese industry.

All of these factors and others mean that companies investing in China do not anticipate much of a return on their investment in the short term. Any monies currently being generated are almost inevitably reabsorbed in further developing operations in the country. Equally, political and economic risks remain in doing business in China. Balanced against this, the potential of the size of the market means that in the long term few companies can risk not having a presence in the country.

> If you waited until the risks in China were lower then you would simply be too late.
> (Mr A Lenstra, Chairman of Unilever China)

Source: The authors, based on press reports

International strategic alliances

International strategic alliances have been used increasingly as companies recognise the need to develop as a worldwide competitor and/or survive by operating with less than global scale and scope. By seeking to develop a strategic alliance the organisation is signalling its wish to *collaborate* rather than *compete* with another organisation. Such collaboration can manifest itself in different ways, and organisations may find themselves collaborating in some aspects of their business and competing in others.

The motives for strategic alliances vary, but include the desire to:

- facilitate access to knowledge, expertise and skills possessed by other organisations in order to balance organisational capabilities/competences;
- achieve entry to new geographical markets; and
- spread financial risk.

Access to knowledge, expertise and skills possessed by another organisation

This factor has been a key driver to the formation of many international strategic alliances. For the formation of a strategic alliance to be of interest to both parties, each must possess a different configuration of core competences and resources, so that each party has something that the other desires. Further, given the context of each company, the opportunity to develop an international strategic alliance must offer as least an attractive option as independently developing or acquiring the missing competence or resource base. Indeed, many organisations seek to develop an international strategic alliance as it is not feasible to develop their own competence, owing to, for example, an inadequate resource base. Illustration 8.3 discusses the reasons for the Japanese company Honda and the British company Rover developing their international strategic alliance in the 1980s.

Access to new geographical markets

Access to new geographical markets was an important factor as far as Honda was concerned in developing its international strategic alliance with Rover, described in Illustration 8.3. This example emphasises that strategic alliances may enable an organisation to gain access to an established distribution network relatively quickly and cheaply. Additionally, for many emerging countries governments may require worldwide competitors to establish joint ventures with local companies as a precondition for allowing entry to the market.

Financial risk

Companies may enter international strategic alliances as a way of spreading the financial risk of entering a new geographical market where there is perceived to be a substantial economic or political risk; and/or developing new technologies. In such circumstances organisations may have a mutual benefit in working together rather than competing.

The nature of an international strategic alliance varies and, following Faulkner (1995), it is possible to identify three generic types, namely:

Illustration 8.3

Honda and Rover

The two car companies Honda and Rover began developing their international strategic alliance in 1978. At the time both companies were of similar size in terms of total sales, though Honda was profit making and Rover was registering losses.

Honda was interested in gaining access to the European market, while Rover was struggling to re-establish itself after a period of restructuring and government support. The likelihood of a change of government was expected to reduce public support, at a time when Rover needed resources to develop a new product range. Without new product development Rover was likely to experience further decline in sales. Product quality was also a problem.

For its part Honda was looking for a partner to help it gain experience of the European market, the one 'Triad' market in which it was poorly represented. At the same time both protectionist policies and overcapacity in Europe made market development more difficult. Rover was attractive as it had an established dealer network in the UK and Europe, and significant spare capacity in its plants.

The first limited agreement between the two companies was signed at the end of 1979, and enabled Rover to make the Triumph Acclaim model in the UK from kits supplied by Honda.

The subsequent development of the alliance has seen the use of Honda platforms by Rover in renewing its model range, followed by the joint development of new product platforms by both companies, co-production and cross-sourcing of components. Honda also acquired a 20 per cent equity stake in Rover. The alliance has thus undergone significant development since 1979, although both companies continue to retain their distinctive identities.

Its alliance with Honda has been a major reason for Rover moving back into profit, having started to re-establish its reputation for making quality cars. The improvement in the company's quality strongly reflects its relationship with Honda and the organisational learning which has taken place from the Japanese company.

The sale of Rover by British Aerospace, its parent company with an 80 per cent interest, to the German car producer BMW in early 1994 has put the future continuation of the existing alliance between Honda and Rover at risk. Honda has publicly stated that it will honour existing agreements, but when these are concluded there will be no further development. Honda strongly feels that the sale of Rover to BMW has broken the mutual trust both Honda and Rover had worked so hard to develop since 1978, and that they do not wish to see the alliance continue.

Source: The authors, based on Faulkner (1995)

- joint ventures;
- non-joint ventures (collaboration); and
- consortium.

Joint ventures   A joint venture is a separate legal entity, with the partners to the alliance normally being equity shareholders. To form the joint ventures the partners will usually provide the resources to allow it to become established, and may subsequently provide additional resources. The intention of establishing a joint venture is generally to enable the company to become a free-standing organisation in its own right.

Joint ventures can be highly successful, but can cause difficulties if the corporate ambition of one or more the partners diverges and it, for example, wishes to acquire full control of the geographical area and/or product range developed by the joint venture. Where this happens, finding a way to break up or leave the joint venture can cause difficulties depending on the situation and attitude of the other partners.

Non-joint venture (collaboration)

Non-joint ventures are forms of collaboration where a separate legal entity has not been created, although there may be cross-company shareholdings. Such forms of collaboration may be very limited in their scope and scale, or alternatively be much more significant. One of the advantages of such agreements is that, given their flexibility, they are capable of being extended and developed over time if the initial relationship between the partners to the agreement proves successful. Correspondingly, collaborative agreements of this nature tend to be much more flexible to all partners than joint ventures, which by their very nature tend to have much clearer boundaries.

Consortium

In respect of an international strategic alliance, a consortium describes a situation where a number of partners come together to undertake what is often a large-scale activity. Perhaps a good example of a consortium arrangement is the development of the European Airbus, whereby a number of national aerospace manufacturers have joined together in an attempt to compete with their larger North American rivals. In this case the rationale is that each company is individually unable to fund new product development or to achieve the necessary volumes to recoup the level of investment made. Collectively the companies believe that by pooling their resources they can compete. Industries characterised by large and expensive technological projects often see the emergence of consortium arrangements.

Together with considering the rationale for and the form which co-operation between organisations takes, research has been carried out in an effort to determine what factors may contribute to the success or failure of an international strategic alliance (see, for example Faulkner, 1995; Lewis, 1993). Some of the common factors identified include:

- *Strategic need.* There should not only be a mutual need for the alliance at the time at which it is established, but if the degree of collaboration is to be maintained or developed each partner's ongoing interests must be met. In other words, each partner must have a continuing need for the other.
- *Shared objectives.* Below the overall strategic need, the partners to the alliance must have shared objectives. Otherwise there is likely to be conflict as to the future direction of the alliance and ultimately, in all probability, its demise.

- *Shared risk and commitment.* Each of the partners to the organisation must accept a degree of risk in making the alliance work and be committed to ensuring its success. Unless both risk and commitment are necessary, it is unlikely that the will to invest at both a personal and corporate level in the alliance in order to make it work will be present.

- *Agreed procedures for resolving disputes.* Inevitably disputes between the partners to an alliance can be expected to arise. The test, as in any relationship, is whether the partners to the alliance can find ways of resolving any difficulties in ways which strengthen rather than undermine the relationship. In an attempt to do this successfully, procedures for resolving disputes have to be clarified and operated in a way which is agreed by all parties. Together with the use of formal procedures, there is a high probability that informal systems and networks for resolving problems will need to be evolved in order to ensure problem resolution takes place at the appropriate level. This emphasises the importance of personal relationships and trust.

- *Trust.* This is perhaps the most critical element if an international strategic alliance is to endure. By its very nature an alliance is dependent on all partners working together so that in total the outcomes are greater than any one party is able to achieve on its own. If one partner loses its belief that it is able to trust its partners, the whole basis of the relationship is likely to be threatened. In practice, trust is likely to build up slowly over time, but is always vulnerable to being eroded quickly by the action of one party to the alliance.

In addition to the factors listed above, it is also probably advisable for all partners to have a clear understanding of the circumstances in which they might terminate the alliance, in the event of, for example, shared need and commitment no longer being present for all partners.

As the globalisation process continues for many technologically driven industries in particular, the expectation is that international strategic alliances both to complete a company's global network and to develop new products will increase. As one Japanese company has recently stated publicly:

> Strategic alliances are attractive for a number of reasons. For example, the digital revolution and the development of multimedia can only reach fruition through the cross-fertilisation of technologies, bringing together partners from the media, communications and computing. We are contributing here through our links with Time Warner and other companies. Another consideration is cost. New technologies require enormous investments in research, plant and equipment. Alliances like ours with IBM and Siemens for development of 256-megabit DRAMs allow partners to maximise the use of their resources, realise cost of advantages and speed up development. Moreover, the diffusion of the developed technology also encourages competition at the production stage. Finally, the dynamic pace and vast extent of modern technology is just too much for any single company. Today, no company can avoid incorporating technologies from other companies in its products. The best way to do that is by building up trust and working together in design-in and similar projects. (F Sato, President and Chief Executive Officer, Toshiba Corporation, 1994)

As Mr Sato emphasises, international strategic alliances are likely to become a more important feature of the future, and not just for relatively weak companies. Even the largest and best resourced organisations are likely to seek to develop some form of international strategic alliance in some aspects of their business.

Organisational forms for worldwide competitors

Research carried out into how worldwide competitors organise themselves emphasises the divergence of organisational structures and cultures. Drawing on the work of Bartlett and Ghoshal (1989), it is possible to discern a number of separate organisational forms used by different worldwide competitors. To the three principal organisational forms identified by Bartlett and Ghoshal a fourth – the co-ordinated international regional – has been added. Each of these organisational forms, their associated structures, cultures and systems have both strengths and weaknesses, which a fifth organisational form, the *transnational,* seeks to overcome. The transnational will be discussed after each of the following organisational forms has been examined separately in detail:

- global company
- multi-local
- international
- co-ordinated international region

It is important to understand that, while each of the four organisational forms can clearly be differentiated in theory, in practice there is inevitably a degree of overlap between them. This point not only recognises the uniqueness of each organisation, its structure, culture and systems, but also that the organisations are constantly adapting and modifying their organisational forms. Figure 8.5 illustrates the overlap between the different organisational forms.

Figure 8.5 The overlap between different organisational forms employed by worldwide competitors

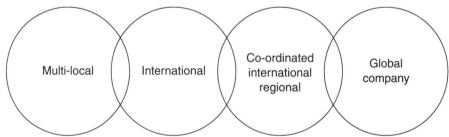

To establish the continuum of organisational forms, culture and systems, the two extremes of the spectrum – global company and multi-local – will be examined. Using four key discriminators – *product/service offer; resources, responsibilities and control; dominant power groups and culture;* and *research and development and innovation* – these two organisational forms can be distinguished as set out in Figure 8.6.

Figure 8.6 Distinguishing between the global company and multi-local organisation

1. Product

Multi-local   Global

Localised for a national market   Standardised for the global market

2. Resources, responsibilities and control

Multi-local   Global

Decentralised to a national organisation   Centralised on a global basis

3. Dominant power group and culture

Multi-local   Global

Country-based managers;   Centralised functions;
independent culture   dependent culture

4. Research and development and innovation

Multi-local   Global

National facilities;   Centralised R&D and new
'local' new product development   product development

Global

In many respects the global company is the organisational form which springs most readily to mind when managers and consultants refer to worldwide competitors. As Figure 8.6 shows, the global company offers its customers an essentially standardised product or service. Any product or service custom-isation for a national market is essentially cosmetic. Hence the global company relies upon customer preferences being broadly uniform across the globe.

In respect to production facilities, if the global company is a manufacturer, the extreme case will be that it is wholly reliant on its home-country base. Where this is the case, the organisation is essentially a *global exporter*. This makes the company highly vulnerable if factor costs (e.g. labour, raw materi-als, utilities, etc.) and/or the exchange rates move in such a way as to undermine the viability of producing in its 'home' country. Many Japanese companies have experienced this difficulty in the 1980s and 1990s, and as a result have attempted to disperse their production base across the globe.

Where the global company is producing outside its home country, the role of such plants is essentially to assemble products developed by the parent company situated in the 'home' country. In other words, cross-border subsidiaries depend on the corporate centre for resources and direction. The dominant power group in the organisation tends to be the centralised product divisions, which in turn are based in the 'home' country. Correspondingly the culture is one where cross-border subsidiaries are highly dependent on the parent company and the national culture of its home location.

In the global company research and development facilities are normally largely or wholly centralised in the home location, so that national subsidiaries do not have the facilities to develop new products independently. If national subsidiaries sense opportunities in their market, and believe the company should develop new products to exploit such a gap in the market, then the subsidiary must first convince the corporate centre that its idea should be adopted for the whole organisation. Diagramatically, the global company can be illustrated as in Figure 8.7.

In the global company the national subsidiaries are concerned largely with implementing the plans and policies developed by the corporate centre. The primary strength of the global company is its ability to gain economies of scale by operating on a global scale. Using such an organisational form many Japanese companies, usually with a relatively narrow product focus, were highly successful in the 1970s and 1980s. These companies used their low cost home manufacturing base and centralised product development to bring new products quickly to the market and undercut the prices set by rivals. Consequently, Japanese companies were able to increase their market share in many international product-markets.

One of the weaknesses of the global company is the tendency, reflecting the nature of its development, to rely upon managers from its 'home' country. This reliance means that organisations are denying themselves the benefit of interpreting and learning from other national cultures by offering 'non-home' country nationals appropriate positions of responsibility. Illustration 8.4 describes how one Japanese company is trying to overcome this problem.

Despite the global company's intrinsic weaknesses, where global scale and new product development are primarily requirements of the globalisation process this organisational form can be highly effective in securing global competitive advantage. For example, in civil aircraft production the US company Boeing concentrates production in its 'home' country, having sales offices strategically located across the world in order to gain these advantages. As the case of Boeing demonstrates, typically the global company has a stronger product rather than geographical focus.

Multi-local

The multi-local organisational form is at the other end of the spectrum to the global company. One of its virtues is that each national subsidiary is focused strongly on the local market and its needs. Products/services offered by national subsidiaries are developed for local markets, although where appropriate these may be adopted by the overall organisation and subsequently 'customised' for other national contexts. Multi-local organisations may use

Figure 8.7 The organisation of the global company

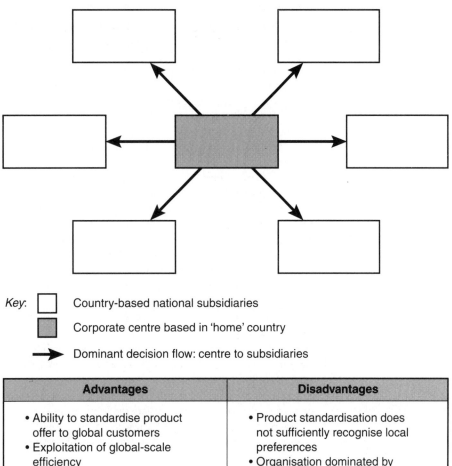

Key: ☐ Country-based national subsidiaries

  ▨ Corporate centre based in 'home' country

  ➜ Dominant decision flow: centre to subsidiaries

Advantages	Disadvantages
• Ability to standardise product offer to global customers • Exploitation of global-scale efficiency • Centralised functions enable resources to be concentrated and new products quickly developed and diffused	• Product standardisation does not sufficiently recognise local preferences • Organisation dominated by single nation culture • Centralised functions and power may prevent organisation reacting to external stimuli first identified in cross-border markets

'local' rather than global brands, and be managed so as to accommodate significant national cultural differences.

To enable the organisation to respond to local needs resources are largely decentralised, with each national organisation being highly autonomous. The role of the corporate centre tends to be much more one of keeping a watching brief and monitoring financial outcomes. The dominant power group in the multi-local is normally the country-based national managers, who operate as general managers and control the resources decentralised to them. This is reflected in the corporate culture, which places strong emphasis on the independence of the national organisations. Country-based general managers

Illustration 8.4

Mitsubishi – international human resource development

The use of senior foreign management by many Japanese companies is still comparatively rare. Traditionally in Japanese companies there has been a very tightly knit corporate culture in which seniority tended to be an important element in the choice of managers for senior positions.

One of the problems for foreigners seeking senior positions is that they tend to enter companies via a joint venture or subsidiary, often in mid-career. Mitsubishi is one company which has recognised this problem and is trying to do something about it. In particular the company, which operates some 600 cross-border joint ventures and subsidiaries, realises that the managers of such operations do not have to be Japanese. With the supply of Japanese managers beginning to fall because of the age structure of Japan's population, Mitsubishi is attempting to retain and make better use of its foreign executives.

Without a clearly defined process of rotating managers through the organisation, one of the difficulties in the past has been that an increasing number of foreign staff have become frustrated and left the company after a single posting. To begin to overcome these difficulties Mitsubishi has set up a new head office group, the International Human Resources Development Unit, to influence how the company can make better use of its non-Japanese employees worldwide. One of the first tasks of this unit will be to establish a clearly understood system for transferring foreign executives between divisions. The new unit is also considering how foreign executives can be given exposure to the corporate centre. Knowledge of head office and how it works is vital if a manager is to be effective, given the centralisation of authority in the company.

Despite these intended changes, the composition of the company's main board of directors remains for the present wholly Japanese.

Source: Based on Dawkins (1994)

have profit and loss responsibility for the full range of the company's sales to their national market.

In essence, the multi-local is a decentralised federation of loosely integrated national subsidiaries. Further, the multi-local form emphasises a geographical rather than product focus. Diagramatically, the loose control exercised by the corporate centre over national subsidiaries can be illustrated by Figure 8.8.

A major strength of the multi-local is its ability to sense local market opportunities and to develop new products to meet these newly emerging needs. This is made possible by each national subsidiary having its own R&D facilities. Consequently, the organisation is highly responsive to local needs, and the decentralisation of assets and responsibilities encourages national subsidiaries to be proactive in seeking to develop new market opportunities. Even where national subsidiaries are managed by expatriate managers, these tend to spend a relatively long period with the country subsidiary and develop a strong commitment to the national organisation. The nature of the multi-local, however, encourages and provides the opportunity for the advancement of foreign nationals. Further, new market opportunities and new products developed for

Figure 8.8 The multi-local organisation

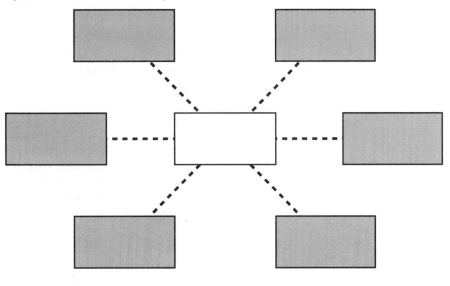

Key:

▨ Country-based national subsidiaries

☐ Corporate centre based in 'home' country

▬ ▬ ▬ Dominant decision flow: loose control of subsidiaries by corporate centre

Advantages	Disadvantages
• Product strongly focused to meet local market needs • Local companies are encouraged and have the resources to engage in the product development • Local managers strongly committed to the local organisation	• Inability to exploit competitive interdependencies and gain global-scale efficiencies • Duplication of costly facilities • New product diffusion across the organisation can be difficult as subsidiaries exert independence

one market may prove to have wider application, emphasising the benefits of having an organisation which is sensitive to newly emerging trends in different areas of the world, given that these may subsequently become global trends.

The multi-local organisation has been a feature of a number of European companies who initially internationalised in the inter-war period when trade barriers were much more prevalent and transportation more costly. The Dutch company Philips, the subject of the case study at the end of Chapter 4, traditionally operated with a multi-local organisational form. Illustration 8.5 on Nestlé provides a current example of a company using largely a multi-local organisational form.

329

Illustration 8.5

Nestlé

Nestlé operates as a holding company with in excess of 200 operating companies. The company, which was established in the nineteenth century, operates a policy of decentralisation and dispersion of activities.

While the original business was based on milk and dietetic foods for children, numerous other food and drink products have been added over the years. In addition the company produces pharmaceutical products and has interests in cosmetics. The company operates 482 factories and sells its products in more than 100 countries. Less than 2 per cent of the company's total 1993 sales of SFr57.5 occurred in Switzerland, its country of origin.

Nestlé's corporate management is responsible for giving strategic direction to the organisation. The corporate centre decides in which geographical areas to allocate resources and manages all acquisitions. R&D is also strongly centralised. Despite these centralised roles, the company's organisational structure, systems and culture continue to emphasise the importance of local interpretation, and in many matters local managers have considerable discretion. Within this structure personal relationships between the heads of the operating companies and the holding company's executives are central in binding the company together.

The table below gives some indication of how the supply of two of the company's products – milk powder and dietetics, and chocolate and confectionery – to a number of national markets is organised.

Manufacture and sale of products: position in 1993 in markets manufacturing and selling products under Nestlé processes and trademarks

Country	Number of factories	Milk powder and dietetics	Chocolate and confectionery
Europe			
Germany	35	•	•
Portugal	6	•	¶
Switzerland	12	Δ	Δ
Middle/Far East			
Saudi Arabia	1	Δ	¶
Thailand	5	Δ	Δ
North America			
Canada	12	•	Δ
South America			
Ecuador	3	Δ	Δ
Africa			
South Africa	12	Δ	•
South Pacific			
Pacific Islands	5	Δ	Δ

Key: • Local production; Δ local production and imports; ¶ imports.

Source: Nestlé Annual Report 1993, p 39

> Nestlé's organisational structure and culture have strongly fitted the company's external context. For most of the company's products the key features of demand have been the diversity of consumer tastes and national regulations. These have been complemented by the absence of sufficient economies of scale to warrant centralised production on a global scale. Equally, while R&D is important constantly to improve and update products, many of Nestlé's brands were introduced many years ago. Nescafé, although a very different product today, for example, was introduced in 1938.
>
> With the increasing convergence of tastes, and national regulations in at least some areas of the world being standardised, the company recognises the need to co-ordinate some aspects of its operations across different markets.
>
> > At market level, co-ordination has been established between our principal company in a given region and the company or companies in one or more neighbouring markets, which that principal company supervises by delegation from the central management – for example, Spain and Portugal. This leads to a better integration of the markets with all the advantages of decentralisation. (Nestlé Annual Report 1992, p 7).
> >
> > The company has also taken steps to strengthen its regional management, and strategic business units have been created for various product groups with the emphasis on integrating marketing, research and production at the country level for related products. Nevertheless, despite these changes the company continues to emphasise the advantages of decentralisation in prompting and maintaining local responsiveness.
>
> *Source:* The authors

As the example of Nestlé demonstrates, where local responsiveness remains important and global-scale efficiency less important, multi-local structures continue to offer advantages over other organisational forms.

Between the extremes of the continuum as represented by the global company and multi-local are two organisational forms – international and co-ordinated international regional – which attempt to blend both geographical and product perspectives through the worldwide competitive strategies they facilitate.

International   The international company as an organisational form characterised many US international companies for much of the post-war period. It relies upon centrally developed products, which could then, if required, be customised for local market conditions. In the case of US companies, the size of their home market meant that this tended to be the dominant factor in developing new products. As a result of this, national subsidiaries placed far greater reliance on the corporate parent than the multi-local, although there was more autonomy than in the case of the global company. In the international company, domestic sales tended to be organised into product divisions, while national subsidiaries were structured under an international division. Within the international division, national subsidiaries tended to be relatively independent, with a limited attempt to co-ordinate sales between subsidiaries in close geographical proximity.

The parent company normally influenced and controlled the national subsidiaries through the use of specialist corporate staff located in the home country. Often sophisticated management information systems, going beyond the communication of financial data, have been used by international companies for the purposes of planning and control. Since the parent company's core competences are centralised, ways have had to be found to convey these to the national subsidiaries. In particular, the parent company seeks to transfer knowledge, understanding and skills to its cross-border subsidiaries in the form of, for example:

- technology
- marketing
- managerial capabilities

Reflecting the emphasis on the transfer of knowledge, understanding and skills to the national subsidiaries, the functional managers, especially technical and marketing, tended to be the dominant power group in the organisation. Further, the parent company's management often adopted a superior and parochial attitude to the company's international operations, which almost inevitably, taking one country at a time, are smaller than domestic sales.

> Historically, North American companies have suffered a major handicap as they expanded internationally – they were located in the world's largest, richest and most sophisticated market. This benign curse led managers in a large number of US based multi-national corporations to regard their international operations somewhere along the spectrum between attractive side-bet and distractive nuisance. At best they were thought of as organisational appendages that generated incremental revenue, but whose role was tangential to the mainstream corporate strategy. (Bartlett and Ghoshal, 1991, p 5)

Regarding cross-border operations as an appendage in the 1950s and 1960s, when the US was by far the most dominant market in the world, did not present major difficulties. In the 1990s, however, the US economy is no longer as dominant, and other 'Triad' markets – EU, Japan/Asia-Pacific – are much more significant. Continuing to regard these markets as 'appendages' is no longer appropriate in many industrial contexts.

The strength of the parent company is emphasised by the centralisation of R&D facilities in the home country, and normally the lack of separate facilities to support national subsidiaries. As a result, products developed centrally are 'given' to the national subsidiaries to sell or customise for their markets.

The culture of dependence on the corporate parent may be emphasised further by the use of expatriate managers who typically spend only a relatively short period in a particular national subsidiary before returning 'home'. Where this happens, the danger is that managers do not identify with the national organisation, seeing it only as a temporary assignment and adopting a 'custodial approach' to managing the national subsidiary. Diagrammatically, the international organisation is illustrated in Figure 8.9.

Figure 8.9 The organisation of the international company

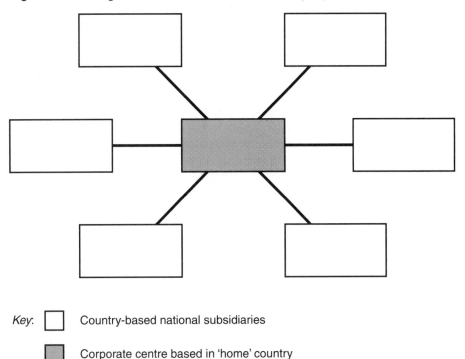

Key: ☐   Country-based national subsidiaries

▓   Corporate centre based in 'home' country

━━   Dominant decision flow: largely from corporate centre to subsidiary, but with some independence on key aspects of local strategy

Advantages	Disadvantages
• Able to transfer and leverage core competences, knowledge, understanding and skills • Centralisation of R&D avoids resource duplication • Able to diffuse new products speedily to geographically diverse markets	• Product/services focus many overly focused on 'home' country needs • 'Home' country managers tend to operate cross-border subsidiaries by adopting a custodial approach • Dependent on 'home' country hegemony in key business areas

The strength of the international company is its ability to leverage its core competences and transfer knowledge, understanding and skills to its international subsidiaries. Against this, however, there may be an over-dependence on meeting the needs of the 'home' country, and not recognising the need to accommodate actual and emerging needs which develop elsewhere in the world.

Co-ordinated international regional strategy

Some companies, including Ford, the US automotive vehicle producer, have employed a co-ordinated international regional strategy for many years. In the case of Ford, its European operations have been integrated on a co-ordinated basis since 1967 (see Illustration 1.1, p. 10). For other companies a co-ordinated international regional strategy is an emerging structure, evolving out of one of three other organisational forms. Unilever, for example, has more recently moved to a co-ordinated international regional strategy, having recognised some to the weaknesses inherent in its previous organisational structures. For Unilever, a compelling trigger to moving from its previous multi-local form was the difficulties this presented in competing with its main rival, Procter and Gamble, who had already established a co-ordinated international regional strategy. Illustration 8.6 discusses how Procter and Gamble has been evolving its worldwide strategy using a series of co-ordinated international regional strategies.

Illustration 8.6 indicates how using a co-ordinated international regional strategy to manage both geographical and product perspectives may result in a complex matrix structure, whereby both regional (geographical) and product reporting lines are established. There are inherent contradictions in such structures which can prove difficult to manage, as the Philips case demonstrated.

Companies operating with a co-ordinated international regional strategy essentially standardise their product or service offer for an international region, allowing minor modifications for national markets where necessary. To enable this to happen key resource areas are centralised and configured to meet the needs of the region, rather than any one national market. The centralisation of key functions reduces the range of business functions undertaken and controlled by country-based subsidiaries. Consequently, the dominant power group tends increasingly to be the regional product managers, who are responsible for managing pan-regional operations.

Worldwide competitors operating with co-ordinated international regional strategies will have a series of business strategies covering different regional needs, but only loosely, if at all, linked. Hence a company operating in the three 'Triad' markets will have separate strategies covering the EU, NAFTA and Japan/East Asia. As a consequence, while a series of co-ordinated international regional-strategies enable regional scale efficiencies to be achieved, they do not allow global-scale efficiencies to be gained.

Table 8.4 Co-ordinated international regional strategy

Advantages	Disadvantages
• product/service offer focuses on regional preferences	• potential loss of contact with national markets
• avoid costly duplication of facilities by configuring functions on a regional basis	• inability to gain global-scale efficiencies
• achieve regional-scale efficiencies	• organisational structures may become highly complex and potentially contradictory

Illustration 8.6

Procter and Gamble

Procter and Gamble (P&G), the US detergents company, continues to rely upon the use of an international division to manage its international operations. This division is responsible for managing the company's range of packaged goods outside its domestic market.

Within the division there are four continental groups, two in Europe covering different product groups, and one each in Asia and Latin America/Canada. The continental groups are an important element of the company's co-ordination on a continental basis, attempting to blend product and geographical perspectives. Each of these groups has a dual reporting responsibility. They are charged with reviewing the product needs of the region in which they are located, while contributing to the development of the company's worldwide business. In Europe, the European Technical Centre is responsible for laundry detergents, household cleaners and fabric softeners. Within this structure three vice-presidents/general managers are responsible for the North Europe, South Europe and Central Europe regional offices. Additionally, each has a pan-European responsibility for one of the three product categories covered by the European Technical Centre. For the present, however, country-wide managers remain responsible for 'bottom-line' performance. This matrix of responsibilities can be illustrated as below.

Product focus: regional vice-presidents

Geographical focus: country based managers	Laundry detergents	Household cleaner	Fabric softeners
France			
Germany			
United Kingdom			

Since the early 1980s the company has standardised its European products, and rationalised production and marketing on a European-wide basis. Equally, P&G no longer depends upon Americans to fill its top positions and host-country nationals head most of its national organisations. While recognising the emergence of world brands, the company continues to manage its business both regionally and locally.

Source: The authors, based on Humes (1993)

Recognising some of the limitations of operating a series of co-ordinated international regional strategies as a worldwide competitor, Illustration 8.7 describes how Ford is now attempting to merge its North American and European operations in order to achieve global-scale efficiencies.

As the case of Ford illustrates, the co-ordinated international regional company may offer insufficient attractions when the industry of which it is part requires companies to operate with global scale. In such circumstances,

Illustration 8.7

The Ford Motor Company

The Ford Motor Company is the world's second largest motor vehicle producer. In 1994 it announced its intention to move away from its existing international regional structures and processes in an attempt to become a global car company. When compared to its Japanese rivals Ford faces formidable challenges. Its administrative heritage includes its European operation, Ford of Europe, which has developed as a fully integrated and independent vehicle maker. As a result, new products have been largely designed and produced to meet the needs of a regional market, and in particular for the company's main European and North American markets.

What Ford is now trying to achieve is to bring together its worldwide operations in a way which will enable the company to achieve global rather than regional-scale efficiency. In the place of its largely independent regional organisations, the company intends to organise itself to achieve global efficiencies through the designation of five vehicle programme centres (VPCs): four in North America and one in Europe.

The European VPC will be divided between Germany and the United Kingdom and will be responsible for small and medium front wheel drive cars. The other VPCs will be located with the company's US R&D facilities in Dearborn, near Detroit. These centres will cover large front wheel drive cars, rear wheel drive cars, personal-use trucks, and commercial vehicles. Following the changes each VPC will have worldwide responsibility for the design, development and engineering of vehicles in its defined area.

In making these changes the company is attempting to integrate currently separate processes and avoid duplication of effort and resources. Ford anticipates being able to reduce the number of basic chassis platforms – from which all car products are derived – from the current number of sixteen to four by the end of the century. This is expected to realise savings of between $2–3 billion over the same time scale, helping the company to manage the ever increasing cost of developing new models. It will also achieve the additional economies of scale associated with larger volumes. Ford's strategy recognises that the competitive pressures in the industry are driving the industry to become truly global.

Ford's announced strategy is a development of changes which have already seen the development of the Mondeo model, sold in both Europe and North America. The Mondeo/Ford Contour/Mercury Mystique is assembled in Belgium, the USA and Mexico. The project represents a major move towards integrating the company's worldwide operations. The company is planning to sell around 250,000 units a year in North America, and another 420,000 cars in Europe. The Mondeo project challenges the traditional idea that the world's leading car manufacturers need to make a vehicle for each key market, namely the USA, Japan and Europe. Around 90 per cent of the hidden parts of the Mondeo – underbody, suspension and powertrain – are common to both European and US versions of the car. The company's next challenge will be to develop a single replacement vehicle for its two Escort models, one sold in the American market and the other in Europe.

Beyond the company integrating its North American and European operations, Ford is expected to consider how its 25 per cent owned affiliate in Japan, Mazda, might be brought into its new organisational form, together with its joint venture operation with Volkswagen in Latin America. Interestingly, both Ford and VW announced that they would move towards separating their joint operations in Brazil and Argentina. It was expected that this would take the whole of 1995 to complete.

Like many US vehicle producers, Ford has tended to neglect the Asian market allowing its Japanese rivals to gain a strong competitive position in the region. The recognition that this region now offers some of the best growth prospects for the future is focusing the minds of many Western vehicle producers, including Ford. The company intends to increase substantially its manufacturing presence in Asia, with a particular emphasis on Taiwan, China and India. Announcing the company's third joint venture in the production of automotive components in China during 1994, Frank Macher, Ford's Vice-President and general manager of the automotive components division publicly stated, 'we are eager to establish vehicle assembly projects in China at the earliest opportunity.'

Source: The authors, based on press reports

regional scale does not allow the organisation to compete with companies which are organising as global companies.

To summarise the characteristics of the alternative organisational forms adopted by worldwide competitors, Table 8.5 applies the four key discriminator – product/service offer; resources, responsibilities and control; dominant power groups and culture; and research and development and innovation – to position each organisational type relative to each other. The details of Table 8.5 emphasise the continuum between organisational forms, with the multi-local organisation at one end of the spectrum and the global company at the other.

Reconciling the irreconcilable: the search for the transnational company

Each of the organisational forms described above for the worldwide competitor offers both advantages and disadvantages. The strength of the global company is that it is able to achieve global scale while its centralised product divisions allow rapid new product development. By contrast, the multi-local company is highly responsive to national market conditions, and is able both to sense market opportunities and develop new products which may have broader geographical applicability. The international company's strength is its ability both to transfer and leverage its core competences, by sharing with its national subsidiaries the range of knowledge, understanding and skills it has developed. Finally, the co-ordinated international regional company is able to achieve regional scale, but retains the ability to shape its products for the preferences of customers in different regions of the world.

The relative strength of each organisational form is matched by weaknesses which emphasise that none of the organisational forms is equally effective in all dimensions of competition. Rather, as Bartlett and Ghoshal (1988) suggest, each form tends to be uni-dimensional in its strengths, when

Table 8.5 Distinguishing between alternative worldwide business strategies

| | Worldwide competitor | | | |
Dimension	Multi-local	International	Co-ordinated international regional	Global company
Product/service offer	Developed for local markets.	Centrally developed products, customised for local needs.	Product, standardised for the region, with minor modifications for national markets where necessary.	Standardised product sold world-wide, with possible cosmetic changes for local markets.
Resources, responsibilities and control	Resources largely decentralised to local organisation. Local organisations highly autonomous, with little intervention from the corporate centre.	Greater dependence on corporate centre than for multi-local, but more autonomy than global. Core competences centralised. Sophisticated management systems and specialist corporate staff to control subsidiaries.	Key resource areas centralised on an international regional basis, with some relatively minor functions left with country-based operations.	Centralisation of assets, resources and responsibilities. Overseas subsidiaries depend on corporate centre for resources and direction.
Dominant power group and culture	Country-based national managers. Independent culture based on national organisations.	Functional managers, especially technical and marketing. Parent company management often superior and parochial in attitude to international operations.	Regional product managers. Emerging culture of international regional interdependence.	Centralised product divisions. Highly dependent culture based on parent company's home location.
Research and development and innovation	National R&D facilities to support local product development.	R&D facilities centralised and many likely to be located in the country of the corporate parent. Products developed centrally 'given' to national subsidiaries to customise.	At least some R&D facilities regionally based.	R&D facilities wholly centralised in 'home' location. National subsidiaries unable independently to develop new products. New ideas need to be adopted by corporate centre.
Overall	Each national subsidiary managed as an independent entity. Highly responsive national organisation. Independence of subsidiaries encourages innovation and development of new products to meet local needs.	Foreign subsidiaries often seen as appendages. Parent company seeks to leverage transfer of knowledge, understanding and skills to national subsidiaries.	Strong co-ordination and integration of functions on a regional basis. Able to achieve regional scale. Little or no co-ordination between international regions.	Role of local units is to assemble and/or sell products developed centrally. National subsidiaries largely concerned with implementing plans and policies developed by corporate centre. Strength is ability to achieve global scale.

what is required for the future worldwide competitor are organisational forms to yield multi-dimensional advantages. For a company to do this it needs to have highly complex structures, systems and cultures to achieve this aim, and be able to manage these elements dynamically. Such a company is able to use its people and processes to manage both product and geographical needs, and to reconcile the tensions inherent in doing this. The name which Bartlett and Ghoshal (1989) give such an organisational form is the *transnational*. Figure 8.10 suggests how the transnational organisation can be related to the other organisational forms.

Figure 8.10 indicates how the transnational is related to the other structures, systems and cultures adopted by worldwide competitors, and suggests that it may emerge out of any of the other organisational forms – multi-local, international, co-ordinated international regional, and global. There may also be occasions when organisations adapt to different external contexts across the world by organising differently for the purposes of individual countries. For example, subsidiaries in highly regulated countries may be managed much more as a multi-local, while the organisation adopts another form for the majority of its operations.

Figure 8.10 The relationship between the transnational and other organisational forms

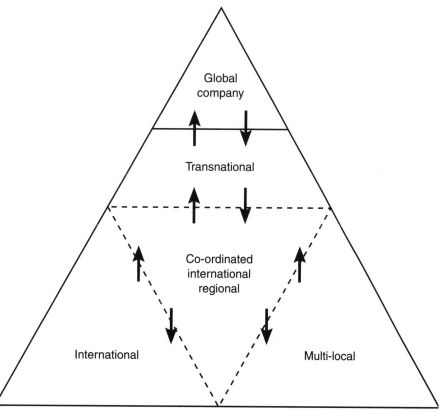

The characteristics of the transnational are that is able to achieve:

- global-scale efficiencies;
- local responsiveness;
- a leveraging of the parent company's knowledge and competences.

In other words, the transnational seeks to gain all the relative advantages of each of the organisational forms previously discussed. The central task for an organisation seeking to develop as a transnational is the need to build organisational capability. The transnational needs to build and manage its decision-making process in a way which is not just about whether functions are centralised or decentralised. In short, the transnational is:

> less a structural classification than a broad organisational concept or philosophy, manifested in organisational capability and management mentality. (Bartlett and Ghoshal, 1989, p 209)

The decision to attempt to move towards the transnational as an organisational form will again be informed by both external and internal triggers to change. Once more, while the external context may indeed require, for example, both global scale and local responsiveness, the ability of the organisation to move to a new organisational form and change fundamentally its way of operating will very much depend upon its internal context, and in particular its administrative heritage. In the context of worldwide competitors, is worth recognising that an organisation's administrative heritage is likely to have elements of national culture, as well as those relating to other aspects of the organisation's history.

Transforming a company so that it becomes a transnational is likely to require almost all organisations who have not been through a lengthy conditioning process to consider very carefully how such a fundamental change, which represents a significant discontinuity to how the organisation has operated in the past, can be managed. In considering the processes required to achieve an effective organisational transformation, the framework for managing organisational change presented in Chapter 4 is helpful. In the context of a transnational this framework helps to focus on the need to:

- build a new shared mindset;
- develop additional competences/capabilities; and
- change the corporate culture.

Clearly, each of these tasks is inter-related and significant in its own right. At the heart of the changes which need to be achieved is the requirement to change corporate culture, which holds in place the existing paradigm or mindset. To do this successfully, both individually and collectively, the elements of the cultural web need to be acted upon. The individual elements of the cultural web can be clustered into three groups, namely:

- formal structure;
- systems and information;
- culture and values.

Transforming an organisation into a transnational requires action in respect of each of the three elements identified. The need is to change each in ways which develop, and collectively reinforce, the new organisational form and philosophy. This emphasises the interlinkage between the three clusters, and how collectively they may enable a transformation to be effective. Figure 8.11 illustrates the relationship between the three clusters of factors.

Figure 8.11 *The developing transnational*

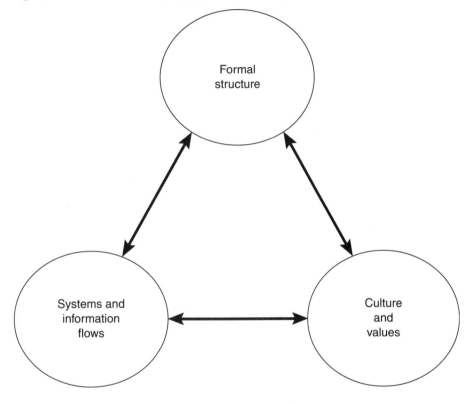

Formal systems   This element of the organisation defines the formal decision-making channels, responsibility and authority. The process embedded in the formal structure tends to be defined in static terms, and there is often a need to use taskforces, committees and project teams to solve particular problems.

Systems and information flows   The information systems must support the transnational's need to be able to deal with the transfer of complex data, often between geographically spread locations. This recognises the requirement to gather, exchange and process large volumes of information in order to ensure the effective operation of the organisation. Additionally, a vital role is played by informal information channels and relationships. Indeed globally, improved communications have greatly facilitated personal contacts, which can be an important aspect of this process.

Culture and values

The importance of shared values, which are either implicit or explicit, cannot be underestimated. In the development of the transnational arguably three areas of management action are particularly important in influencing corporate culture, namely:

- a shared understanding of the company's mission and objectives;
- the demonstrative behaviour of senior managers, emphasising what they value highly; and
- the human resource policies adopted by the organisation, including the extent to which recruitment takes place outside the 'home' country; management development programmes; posting managers to develop knowledge and experience and a personal network of contacts.

As has been stressed throughout the text, the modification of corporate culture, encompassing as it does core values and beliefs, is inevitably a slow process. Figure 8.11 suggests why modifying only one component of the internal context is unlikely to be successful in trying to transform an organisation to become a transnational. For example, attempts to change only the formal structure are likely to prove of limited value, to the extent that the informal relationships and networks are vital to the effective functioning of the organisation. Indeed, it is often helpful to ask the simple question as to which is more important in the completion of normal everyday activities: the formal or informal structures and relationships.

For many the informal aspects of the organisation are as, if not more, important to the functioning of the organisation. Consequently, failure to change these informal aspects is likely at best to render changes to the formal structure limited in their effectiveness, and at worst undermine the functioning of the organisation. Even more serious is that the informal aspects of the organisation may completely neutralise the intended changes arising out of the formal structure, leaving the organisation no closer to achieving its goal. An understanding of this potential difficulty emphasises that informal changes have to accompany formal ones, and often precede them.

In thinking about how to change an existing organisational form to create a transnational organisation, a number of key elements are likely to be central. First, there is a need within the complex configuration of organisational assets and capabilities to create an organisation which is integrated through a set of strong interdependencies. Mutual dependency helps to create an interdependent culture, and this may well require both the distribution of capabilities throughout the organisation and the specialisation of roles. Hence in some aspects of the organisation's capability one subsidiary may act as the *lead country*, while in another aspect a subsidiary located elsewhere in the world may be more important. Consequently, the transnational may be considered to be an integrated network of interdependent elements, as shown in Figure 8.12, with dependency between subsidiaries being reciprocal. The reciprocal nature of the interdependencies allows co-operation to be self-sustaining as each element of the organisation depends on the other.

Figure 8.12 The transnational organisation

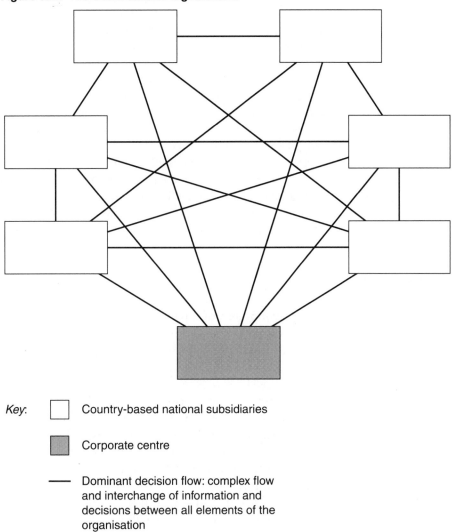

Key: ☐ Country-based national subsidiaries

▨ Corporate centre

—— Dominant decision flow: complex flow and interchange of information and decisions between all elements of the organisation

The transnational is therefore based upon dispersing assets and capabilities in a way which emphasises their interdependence, but recognises the varied contributions that different elements of the organisation can offer by assigning different tasks to individual subsidiaries and locations. For this integrated network to function effectively and efficiently, there is the need to integrate three key flows, namely:

- components and raw materials;
- the flow of funds and skills; and
- intelligence, ideas and knowledge.

Within the transnational organisation centrally designed products and processes are likely still to be important, but innovations are also likely to be created outside the 'home' country by subsidiaries in dispersed locations. The organisation's customers may well demand differentiated products, but at the same time the level of quality that low cost global companies are able to deliver. In managing these needs the transnational may well seek to develop products with a modular structure which are capable of being styled for individual markets, while at the same time ensuring that the basic elements of the product and design are standardised. Further, the use of flexible manufacturing systems can be a key component in managing the scale–flexibility tension.

The development of a transnational organisation poses formidable challenges for an organisation. The specific nature of the challenge will vary according to the organisation's context and current stage of development. In all cases the extent of the challenges to developing a transnational should not be underestimated. In particular, there is the need to ensure its managers and staff can offer an individual commitment which goes beyond national or self-interest and allows the organisation to achieve much wider objectives.

Summary

The development of a worldwide competitor represents the final phase of international business development. The need to achieve worldwide scope and scale is driven by the globalisation process. Examining how organisations are able to manage the demands of globalisation requires an examination of three dimensions: product, geography, and people and processes.

The globalisation process is being driven both by external factors and by development of worldwide competitors who have the necessary vision and organisational dynamics to move beyond earlier stages of international business development. The extent to which the globalisation process is advanced can be examined by considering the three key dimensions – product, geography, people and processes – as they relate to a specific industrial context and companies operating in the industry. Undertaking a full strategic assessment will enable the strength and weakness of individual competitors to be assessed.

Global competitors are likely to enjoy significant advantages over national and international regional players, suggesting that the former need to consider their competitive position. Where the situation dictates and companies are unable to achieve world scale, forms of co-operation/collaboration may be considered. International strategic alliances offer many advantages for companies faced with such a situation.

For the worldwide competitor there are a number of organisational forms, each of which offers some advantages and disadvantages. The search for a new organisational form with appropriate structure, systems and culture simultaneously to achieve global-scale efficiencies, local responsiveness and leverage core competences is the search for the transnational. This arguably, for many contexts, suggests that this is the organisational form for the future worldwide competitor.

Checklist

- Worldwide competitors have reached the final phase of international business development.
- Companies operating on a worldwide scale need to consider how they will configure their business in respect of product, geography, and people and processes.
- To capture global competitive advantage organisations must develop a global vision and have supporting organisational dynamics.
- Global competitive assessment will enable competitive trends and the strategic position of companies in the industry to be assessed.
- The global competitor has distinct advantages if compared to national or international regional players when configuring its competitive moves.
- International strategic alliances offer an alternative option to competing with rivals.
- The forms of international strategic alliances include joint venture, collaboration and consortium.
- Alternative organisational forms can be differentiated on the basis of product/service offer; resources, responsibilities and control; dominant power groups and culture; and research and development and innovation.
- A global company is able to achieve global-scale efficiencies through product standardisation.
- The multi-local company is highly responsive, but unable to achieve global-scale efficiencies.
- An international company is able to leverage core competences.
- A co-ordinated international regional strategy enables international regional rather than global-scale advantages to be achieved.
- The transnational organisation seeks to develop global-scale efficiencies, local responsiveness and the ability to leverage core competences.
- Transforming an organisation into a transnational represents a fundamental discontinuity, requiring change to structures, systems and culture.
- A transnational is based upon mutual dependency between units, resulting in the development of an integrated network of subsidiaries.
- Changing informal systems and relationships is often as important as the altering the formal structure.

SKF AB

Introduction

SKF is the world's leading company in the roller bearing industry. The company's share of the world market is around 20 per cent, which is attributable to an unparalleled global sales, distribution and manufacturing presence. With a long-standing philosophy of 'the right bearing in the right place', SKF is a full line bearing producer aspiring to leadership across virtually all applications and markets for bearings.

In deciding how to manage its products and processes worldwide, SKF has undergone a number of fundamental organisational changes. Without ever changing the basic strategy, periodic changes in organisational structure have focused on the inherent tensions of global efficiency, local responsiveness and transfer of knowledge. Long-standing Chairman Mauritz Sahlin has crafted such organisational realignments in the belief that 'if SKF is to successfully adapt to the new market conditions of the future, it must be highly flexible.'

Background

SKF owes its existence to Sven Wingquist's invention of the double-row self-aligning ball bearing. Some 2200 of this newly invented type of bearing, which were subsequently to dominate world markets, were produced in Sweden in 1907. With limited low sales potential in Sweden, SKF's future development depended on establishing a strong export market. In the first year alone Wingquist visited 100 potential customers throughout Europe. By 1910 sales offices had been set up in France, Germany and the United Kingdom, with agents appointed in locations as diverse as Helsinki, Finland and Melbourne, Australia.

In order to establish first mover advantage in world markets, manufacturing facilities were established outside Sweden. By 1918 SKF had established plants in the United Kingdom (1911), France (1911 and 1917), Germany (1916), the United States (1916 and 1917) and Russia (1918). It was also operating sales and service subsidiaries in more than 100 countries. With some 12,000 staff, SKF's annual bearing production from its 12 plants exceeded 5 million units. After this initial expansion the company recognised that it needed time to consolidate, and no further plant extensions were undertaken for the next decade.

SKF's continuing history of innovation in bearing design was the driving force behind product range expansion in the inter-war years. In this period SKF developed a complete assortment of roller bearings to suit all applications. By 1939 the combined bearing output of the twelve SKF manufacturing facilities had increased to 25 million a year. More than 27,000 people were employed throughout the world, of which only 7300 worked in Sweden. The company was unquestionably the market leader in the roller bearing industry, a position it has maintained to the present day.

Like other bearing manufacturers, since 1990 SKF has suffered heavily as falling industrial production has manifested itself in reduced demand for its products in virtually all the sectors it supplies. This has prompted the company to

Case Study 8

undertake a far-reaching restructuring programme, aided by the adoption of 'lean' manufacturing techniques, to achieve a radically lower break-even point. The last couple of years have also seen significant changes to its organisational structure, so the company feels that it is now well placed to benefit from any recovery in world industrial production.

Geographical coverage

SKF is an archetypal worldwide business. Not only is its sales organisation practically universal geographically, but also market penetration is high across most product lines in almost all areas of the world. Moreover, there are substantial manufacturing facilities in all major industrial world regions. Table C8.1 shows that geographical sales exposure is concentrated in Europe and North America. Swedish sales account for only 5 per cent of the group total, but exports from Sweden amount to some SEK3 billion. This represents some 10 per cent of total group sales, with North America being the principal export market.

Table C8.1 Geographical breakdown of sales, 1989–93 (%)

Country/region	1989	1990	1991	1992	1993
Sweden	4	4	4	4	4
Other Europe	56	60	55	56	49
North America	21	17	21	23	27
Rest of the World	19	19	20	16	19
Total	100	100	100	100	100

Source: SKF Annual Reports, 1991 and 1993, Note 27

SKF has a broad production base. Table C8.2 shows that 85 per cent of the company's identifiable asset base is located outside Sweden. Even so, some 60 per cent of the asset base is located in Europe. The asset base in North America has doubled in the last five years, as a result of a strategic decision to boost US sourcing from about 80 per cent of sales to around 90 to 95 per cent. Driving the decision was a combination of dollar weakness, growing protectionist measures and a need to move nearer the customer in an era of just-in-time manufacturing.

Table C8.2 Geographical breakdown of total assets, 1989–93 (%)

Country/region	1989	1990	1991	1992	1993
Sweden	11	10	15	13	15
Other Europe	63	62	55	51	46
North America	12	16	17	21	23
Rest of the World	14	12	13	15	16
Total	100	100	100	100	100

Source: SKF Annual Reports, 1991 and 1993, Note 27

SKF has a well-established distribution network and sizeable manufacturing operations in Argentina, Brazil, Mexico, South Africa, India and Malaysia. Capacity has been considerably expanded in recent years in Brazil, India and on a new greenfield site in Malaysia. SKF's most recent bearing facility was opened in Malaysia in 1992, and there is the expectation that more capacity will be added in Asia through a joint venture in China. The rationale for these sizeable investments has been to gain exposure to rapidly growing markets which cannot be supplied from outside due to outright prohibitions, unduly long supply lines and/or high local tariffs.

In short, SKF's senior management sees the world in three zones: Europe, North America and Asia. This vision has prompted the concept of currency zone production. The German deutschmark, US dollar and Japanese yen have been identified as the three key currencies. Mauritz Sahlin, SKF's Chairman, would like to be in a position of matching what is sold with production in each zone. Future capital expenditure can be expected to be directed to ensuring that within each currency zone production and consumption are closely aligned.

Customer groups and trading prospects

The company divides its bearing market into two segments which are approximately equal in sales terms. The automotive and general machinery sectors depicted in Table C8.3 belong to the so-called *original equipment manufacturing (OEM)* category. These customers purchase bearings in large volumes as components to be incorporated in the products they are producing. The high volumes purchased mean that customers are highly price sensitive and margins are brought down by competition. The *after-market* (replacement demand) category conducted through industrial distributors is much less price sensitive. SKF holds a world-leading position in this higher value-added market segment.

Table C8.3 Breakdown of SKF's sales by customer base, 1993.

	% of total sales
Automotive	33
General machinery	24
After-market	32
Others	11
Total	100

Source: SKF Annual Report, 1993

SKF's most important OEM is Europe, given that the majority of the company's automotive customers are based in this international region. Analysts estimate that SKF has a hefty 50 per cent market share, with strong positions in all major car and truck producers other than Renault, which has its own in-house source of bearings. The current state of the automotive industry, however, and the bleak

Case Study 8

outlook for significant volume expansion imply that profitability improvements for SKF must be gained predominantely on the cost side. Table C8.4 shows both the current and forecast levels of European and North American automotive output.

Table C8.4 Automotive manufactures, production volumes: millions of units: 1992 and 1993 actuals; all other years estimates

Region	1992	1993	1994	1995
Europe	15,135	12,565	12,950	13,650
North America	11,757	12,930	13,780	13,800
Total	26,892	25,495	26,730	27,450

Source: Industry sources

SKF's current weak trading environment in Europe is derived primarily from Germany and France (20 per cent and 10 per cent of sales respectively). These two markets jointly accounted for a pre-tax loss of SEK660 million in 1993. Although 1994 is expected to be better, volumes in Germany are likely to continue to decline. This is not encouraging, as Germany is SKF's largest single market. Furthermore, the company has 25 per cent of its production capacity based in Germany. SKF will therefore be adversely affected by being a hard currency producer. This will lead to further price pressure and erode margins on bearings exported from Germany.

North America has been a major success story for SKF over the past few years. Since 1990 SKF's sales volume growth has been consistently outpacing the market, so that market share has been increasing. This advance has been based to a considerable extent on new automotive business. The recent 20 per cent surge in US truck production has greatly benefited the company, since it is a leading producer of taper bearings used by the industry. The company has also gained significant new business from General Motors and Ford, including in the case of the latter the Mondeo hub bearing component contract.

SKF's position as the exclusive worldwide supplier of all Mondeo wheel-hub bearing units is particularly significant for the company. The size of the contract is reflected in the expected sales of the Mondeo: up to 420,000 cars per annum in Europe and 250,000 in North America. It also illustrates the company's highly regarded capabilities as a global component supplier. In this context global manufacturing capacity is becoming increasingly important for component suppliers, given the rapid geographic expansion of the automotive majors and their growing tendency to unify product development geographically.

Market leadership

Overall, SKF has around 20 per cent of the world bearing market, making it by far the largest player in the industry. There are almost 150 firms worldwide operating in the bearings industry, of which only ten (three in North America, three in Japan and four in Europe), each with a world market share greater than 2 per cent, account for more than 80 per cent of the world output of bearings. Table C8.5 shows that three of these, SKF (Sweden), NSK (Japan) and NTN (Japan), account for almost 50 per cent of world production. The two Japanese majors are particularly strong in their domestic market, while SKF has built up a strong position in both Europe and North America.

Table C8.5 Market shares of leading manufacturers of roller bearings, 1993

		Market share (%)		
Manufacturer	Domestic base	Western Europe	North America	Western Europe and North America
SKF	Sweden	35	16	21
NSK/RHP	Japan	7	–	13
NTN	Japan	–	–	12
FAG	Germany	22	7	10
Koyo (Toyota)	Japan	–	–	8
Timken	USA	5	21	6
Torrington	USA	2	15	5
INA	Germany	7	3	3
NDH (GM)	USA	0	6	2
SNR (Renault)	France	7	0	2
Other		15	33	18
Total		100	100	100

Source: Trade estimates

In Europe, SKF has a commanding 35 per cent market share and is strong or very strong across virtually all applications and in all markets. It is almost twice the size of the next largest competitor, FAG Kugelfischer. It is widely felt in 1994 that there is overcapacity in the market, with a 35 per cent volume decline from the peak in 1989 representing the deepest downturn in the post-war history of the European bearings industry. The market shares of non-indigenous (largely Japanese) competitors has risen from 5 per cent in the 1970s to around 15 per cent in 1994.

SKF's share in North America is lower than in Europe, but still substantial at about 16 per cent, having recently displaced Torrington from the number two position. As Table C8.5 shows, Timken is easily the most important player in North America. Timken has also significant market share in Europe, and is the world leader in taper bearings. While volume upturn occurred in 1993, prices are soft on the basis of considerable excess capacity. Japanese competition (primarily NSK and NTN) exacerbates the position of indigenous producers in the North American market. The market share held by Japanese producers has risen from under 10 per cent in the 1970s to over 25 per cent by the end of 1994.

Elsewhere in the world, SKF is number one or two in several major developing markets including Argentina, Brazil, India and Mexico. In these countries SKF's market share varies between 30 and 50 per cent. The main gap in the company's global network, in common with other American and European bearing producers, is Japan and the rapidly industrialising countries of the Asian Rim. At present, the Japanese and Far Eastern bearing markets are very much the preserve of the three local majors: NSK, NTN and Koyo. Although these companies have continued to make money throughout the downturn, profits have largely come from non-bearing activities.

With overcapacity in the market and the influx of Japanese competition into both Europe and North America, it has become increasingly difficult for SKF to maintain market share. Its market share of these markets has fallen from around 26 per cent in 1975, to 24 per cent in 1985 and 21 per cent in 1994. Historical figures suggest that scale does confer significant cost advantages and assist profitability. During the 1980s SKF's average operating margin was close to 7 per cent; FAG, its nearest European competitor, struggled to better 6 per cent; and Japanese producers were close to 5 per cent (in the case of NSK, well below this figure), while Koyo and Timken found 4 per cent difficult to achieve.

Finally, worldwide there has been much pressure from customers, themselves under increasing pressure, to reduce prices. In order to address this, over the last couple of years manufacturers have been forced to reduce prices, in the case of SKF perhaps even more than others, in the pursuit of market share. Even so, SKF has been able to use its size and influence to attract customers into working more closely with it; to enter into longer-term contracts; and undertake more value-added product applications (such as supplying whole wheel units for cars and trucks), which offer the opportunity to offset the overall price reduction felt. Table C8.6 explains why changes in the level of economic activity have such a profound influence on product prices and the reasons that SKF's strategy of trying to win longer-term supply contracts is so vital to the company.

Financial performance

SKF's track record shows dramatic growth throughout the late 1980s. In the five years to 1989, Table C8.7 reveals that sales increased by well over 40 per cent, operating profit grew almost 2.4 times and margins increased by more than 50 per cent to a peak of 10.4 per cent in 1989. The peak in profits was short lived. The years between 1989 and 1992 saw average volumes fall by 25 per cent, and from the best to worst month they actually fell by as much as 40 per cent. Operating profit turned the wrong way to the tune of SEK3.8 billion, with the severity and swiftness of the collapse prompting further rationalisation of manufacturing capacity. In 1993 these continuing efforts to address internal problems resulted in the scale of losses diminishing. In 1994 increased volumes from a surge in European automotive output should enable SKF to translate cost cuttings into earnings recovery.

Table C8.6 *Relationship between bearing production and profitability and the level of economic activity*

Since the early 1970s there have been three peaks and troughs in bearing markets in Europe and North America. The peaks occurred in 1973, 1979/80 and 1989/90. The troughs can be charted in 1975/76, 1983 and 1993/94. These all coincide with the high and low points for industrial activity. Upswings and downswings have been considerably more pronounced than for the economy as a whole. This reflects the

Bearing producers: comparison of profitability

	1986	1987	1988	1989	1990	1991	1992	1993
SKF (SEK billion)								
Operating profit	1.32	1.31	1.56	2.60	1.92	(0.06)	(1.19)	0.10
Margin (%)	7.3	6.7	7.3	10.4	6.9	(0.2)	(0.4)	0.3
Timken (US$ million)								
Operating profit	(36.7)	46.7	94.1	102.4	102.3	33.9	N/A	N/A
Margin (%)	(4.9)	5.6	9.4	9.8	8.7	3.0	N/A	N/A
FAG (DM million)								
Operating profit	228.6	189.3	197.7	259.0	218.1	135.3	N/A	N/A
Margin (%)	7.3	6.1	8.6	6.6	5.4	3.5	N/A	N/A

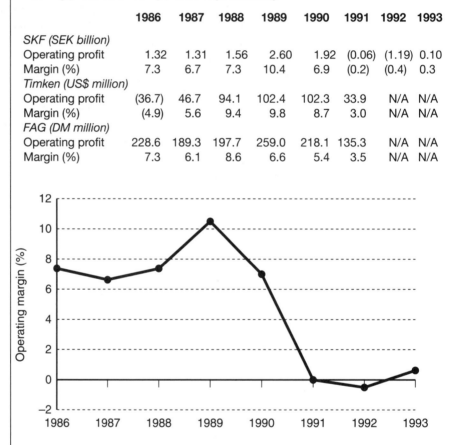

powerful influence of inventory changes in bearing markets and the intrinsically volatile nature of the demand for durable consumer goods and capital equipment.

SKF's operating margin from all operations closely correlates with the level of activity in the bearings market, which in turn reflects the overall health of economic activity.

SKF's operating profit trend in recent years, showing a strong build-up from the 1980s, a peak in 1989, followed by a sharp dip, has been broadly replicated by its key competitors, including Timken and FAG. In FAG's case the 1989 peak was less marked than for SKF and Timken. The subsequent downturn has been sharply felt by all three companies.

The long and severe downturn in European bearings demand should bottom out in 1994, primarily reflecting the cessation of a sharp inventory rundown. The mid-1990s may therefore prove to be a more profitable period for all three companies.

Case Study 8

Writing in the company's 1992 Annual Report Mauritz Sahlin, SKF's Chairman, stated:

the message from a number of loss-making companies in the bearings industry is unequivocal – a number will be forced to leave the industry, either completely or in part. . . It is this climate that we are continuing to develop SKF, in order to create a structure and cost levels that are compatible with customer demands. During the past two years, both our focus and our operating methods have undergone radical changes. We are continuing to implement action programmes, which will also affect the Group during 1993. The tangible results of these programmes will be reduced costs and shorter decision-making channels.

Table C8.7 Eight-year financial review of SKF, 1986–93 (SEK millions unless otherwise stated)

	1986	1987	1988	1989	1990	1991	1992	1993
Income statements								
Net sales	18,180	19,604	21,248	25,066	27,766	26,302	26,649	29,200
Other income	261	212	177	305	164	238	148	273
Other operating expenses	(17,120)	(18,504)	(19,865)	(22,772)	(26,015)	(26,596)	(27,982)	(29,376)
Operating income	1,321	1,312	1,560	2,599	1,915	(56)	(1,185)	97
Income after financial income and expenses	1,247	1,154	1,519	2,470	1,750	(221)	(1,777)	(669)
Net income	599	739	979	1,513	1,014	(1,177)	(1,704)	(381)
Product areas								
(i) Net sales								
Bearings	17,176	18,515	20,115	23,754	26,476	24,347	22,690	27,199
Others	1,004	1,089	1,133	1,312	1,290	1,955	3,959	2,001
Total	18,180	19,604	21,248	25,066	27,766	26,302	26,649	29,200
(ii) Income after financial income and expenses								
Bearings	1,129	1,073	1,399	2,399	1,709	(135)	(1,264)	(329)
Others	118	81	120	71	41	(86)	(513)	(340)
Total	1,247	1,154	1,519	2,470	1,750	(221)	(1,777)	(669)
Average number of employees								
Bearings	38,933	40,134	40,115	43,138	45,889	40,841	39,337	36,881
Others	3,059	3,559	3,216	3,529	3,416	4,444	7,335	2,558
Total	41,997	43,693	43,331	46,667	49,305	45,285	46,672	39,439
Total salaries, wages and social charges	7,398	8,106	8,468	9,658	11,142	11,279	11,845	12,277

Source: SKF Annual Reports; previously published values from 1986 through to 1991 have been restated to conform with the current group structure

Cost cutting

Strategically, SKF is focused firmly on cost cutting and the disposal of non-core activities. The chief disposal in 1992 was the sale of CTT Tools to another Swedish company Sandvik, AB. This action shed a business which in 1992 employed some 4000 workers, achieved sales of approximately SEK2 billion, but had incurred a loss in each of the previous two years of around SEK100 million. Prospectively, the core bearings business will account for about 95 per cent of the group sales, with Ovako Steel (which reported as an associate company between 1987 and 1991) representing the bulk of the remainder.

An indication of the far-reaching impact of the cost-cutting programme on the bearings division can be discerned from Table C8.7. From the announcement of the first cost-cutting programme in late 1990 until 1992, the headcount in bearings fell by around 6500. In 1993 a further 2500 jobs were shed, with another 1000 planned to go in 1994. This will take the cumulative headcount decline in bearings between 1990 and 1994 to about 10,000, a figure approaching 25 per cent of the labour force.

Table C8.8 shows that headcount reductions across all group activities have been broadly based. Although the figures include more than just bearings, the relative composition of the geographical spread of the labour force was unchanged between 1990 and 1993. By reducing the headcount by around 10,000 employees worldwide, the company has saved well over 10 per cent of operating expenses through cost reductions since 1990. Senior management believe that even with continuing downward pressure on prices, SKF should aim in better times to achieve a 10 per cent operating margin.

Table C8.8 Average number of employees of SKF worldwide

Region	1987 Number	%	1990 Number	%	1993 Number	%
Europe	29,593	68	29,223	59	23,443	59
North America	5,888	14	8,125	17	7,200	18
Rest of the World	8,212	18	11,957	24	8,796	23
Total	43,693	100	49,305	100	39,439	100

Source: SKF Annual reports 1987, 1990 and 1993, Note 28

In order to break even at current volume levels, it was deemed necessary to close a major bearings facility in Germany in 1993. The high wage costs in Germany have increasingly made production uneconomic, which is confirmed by a brief comparison of FAG's and SKF's costs, as set out in Table C8.9.

The figures in Table C8.9 concurred with SKF's management's view that it is around 30 per cent more expensive to operate in Germany. Given that SKF has 25 per cent of its total production in Germany, it is not at all surprising that one of the three bearing facilities in Schweinfurt, Germany was closed in 1993. This reduced the German headcount from a peak of 10,237 in 1990 to 6842 in 1993, a fall of 3395 in three years.

Table C8.9 Comparative wage costs, SKF and FAG, 1992 (1992 US$ equivalent)

Sales/personnel costs per employee	SKF	FAG	Difference (%)
Sales per employee	74,200	66,500	+11.5
Personnel cost per employee	32,800	40,300	−19.0

Source: Annual Reports

Lean production

It is intended that the bulk of the headcount reduction will be permanent. This is partly attributable to continued investment in well-developed manufacturing technology, coupled with a new approach for establishing the optimal flow of production from raw materials to the customer. SKF's *channel concept*, highlighted in Figure C8.1, has allowed the company to become faster and more efficient, with teamwork and initiative being encouraged on the 430 production channels in its manufacturing plants. The group's leading market position is based on strong quality awareness, with the new way of working assisting in achieving productivity and quality goals.

Figure C8.1 The channel concept

The objective of the channel concept is to achieve shorter lead times, increased flexibility and reduced inventory, together with attaining higher and more consistent quality. 'Really, it is more a matter of mental channels and a total change in our perception of production,' says Chairman Mauritz Sahlin.

Old system	**Channel production**
• *pressure from organisation*	▯ stimuli from customers' orders
• *others monitor quality*	▯ team measures own improvement
• *cost point based accounting*	▯ accounting by channel
• *functional organisation*	▯ flow organisation
• *achieve best results*	▯ eliminate faults
• *major improvement campaigns*	▯ many small regular improvements

In addition to promoting new thinking at workshop level – where responsibility, teamwork and initiative are encouraged – the channel concept has also reduced unplanned downtime by close to 50 per cent. Increased motivation of employees has resulted in less absenteeism.

Case Study 8

One of the goals when implementing the channel concept in SKF's plants worldwide was to reduce lead times in production by 50 per cent, from 18 weeks in 1989 to 9 weeks in 1993. This goal has been achieved. The company is continuing to devote intensive efforts to further reducing lead times. At the start of the 1994 fiscal year, the lead time in production was 8.5 weeks. Some channels have now established new targets, involving an additional 50 per cent reduction in lead times.

As a percentage of annual sales, SKF's inventories are high compared to industry standards. SKF aims to reduce its inventories further in relation to sales, which are depicted in Table C8.10. In relation to the channel concept a new target for inventories has been set to represent 25 per cent of sales (or SEK1.9 million below present levels). This is expected to be reached in 1996.

A new European distribution centre in Tongeren, Belgium was completed at the beginning of 1994. With the further rationalisation of warehouses planned by 1997, the number of European inventory points will have been reduced from the current level of 24 to just 5, consisting of Tongeren and four other international warehouses. The number of deliveries dispatched directly to customers from SKF plants will increase substantially, with the logistics contracted out to Frans Maas.

Table C8.10 Inventory levels, selected years, 1981–93

	1981	1984	1987	1990	1993
Inventories	6,448	6,346	7,550	9,954	9,220
Sales	13,570	15,682	19,604	27,766	29,200
Inventories to sales (%)	48	40	39	36	32

Source: SKF Annual Reports

Organisational form

It is not enough to create a cost structure that is compatible with customer demands, it is also necessary to create an appropriate organisational structure, systems and values. In the first 25 years of its history, when SKF laid the foundation for its presence in the international market – which is one of the company's major current strengths – the world was divided into a large number of national markets. Most important markets demanded a presence in the form of manufacturing operations. Until low priced Japanese bearings began to erode SKF's customer base in the early 1970s, the company's operating philosophy had always included a strong measure of local autonomy. Company records for the early 1960s show that, with the exception of Sweden (which exported 70 per cent of its output), 'on average, the Group was selling 80 per cent of its products

Case Study 8

locally.' Moreover, until 1972 each plant worldwide had its own research unit geared mainly to deal with local projects.

Faced with the rapid internationalisation of Japanese bearing manufacturers, SKF began to recognise the need to centralise planning and co-ordinate manufacturing and sales. In 1967 a group headquarters was established in Sweden, 'the first of several progressive moves to streamline administration, to increase international co-operation and overall awareness of group policies, and to eliminate production duplication and bottlenecks.' At the beginning of the 1970s, companies with the same or similar product ranges were divisionalised. This structure was later modified, and in 1974 the European Bearing Division announced an SEK250 billion plan to rationalise production. Between 1974 and 1979 6 out of 22 plants were closed, and manufacturing focused on 5 large plants located in Germany, Italy, France, Sweden and the United Kingdom.

These five large manufacturing plants specialised in different bearing applications in order to avoid duplicate production. As a result, each manufacturing unit obtained the necessary production volumes required to strengthen its competitive position. Simultaneously, this production organisation entails an extensive internal trade between the various SKF companies. At the same time SKF installed a global forecasting and supply system (GFSS) with the aim of co-ordinating global production. Administrative changes were also made to deal with growing inter-group trade, with SKF International AB formed to act as a clearing house for financial matters. This reduced exchange and other costs and enabled group companies to transact business in their own currencies.

As national markets became organised into trading areas, a production configuration of one plant per product worldwide began to be questioned. SKF transferred entire production lines from Europe to the United States in 1988. This strategic response was linked to organisational restructuring. Although it was felt that the full impact of the new market-oriented organisation would not be experienced until 1990, the need to have a strong customer orientation was seen as critical to meet the demand of various target groups. Each unit within SKF's bearing operation was required to establish its own objectives and priorities.

Throughout the 1990s the group has continued to develop its organisational form. Each annual report records further adjustments to evolving structures and systems, resulting in the decentralisation of operational activities and centralisation of service functions. By establishing business divisions which correspond to its key customer groups, SKF has sought to develop a coherent approach to customers around the world. Each business division has total responsibility for product development, production and planning in Europe and for co-ordinating the corresponding manufacturing unit in the rest of the world. Marketing and sales are organised into two divisions, one focusing on automotive and the other on industrial customers.

Conclusion

In the 1982 Annual Report it was stated that 'in order to defend this leading position we must offer customers the fullest range of bearing products, we must develop this range in line with new requirements, we must be cost effective and quality conscious with reliable delivery and good service.' The challenge for SKF remains unchanged today; its response is in a continual state of organisational flux as the company seeks to adapt itself to optimise service to customers worldwide.

Questions

(1) *What are the reasons for the roller bearings industry becoming increasingly global?*

(2) *To what extent have the major companies in the industry managed to achieve worldwide market coverage? Where do you expect the different companies to invest over the next decade?*

(3) *Why is the industry so vulnerable to changes in the level of economic activity? What can companies do to manage fluctuations in the level of demand?*

(4) *Explain what you understand by the 'channel concept'. How does it differ from the previous methods of production and what advantages does it bring?*

(5) *Which of the organisational forms discussed in the chapter best describes SKF? Why do you think the company has developed the form that it currently has?*

BIBLIOGRAPHY

Albaum, G S *et al.* (1992), *International Marketing and Export Management*, Addison-Wesley.

Baden-Fuller, C and Stopford, J M (1992), *Rejuvenating the Mature Business*, Routledge.

Bartlett, C A and Ghoshal, S (1988), 'Organising for worldwide effectiveness: the transnational solution', *California Managment Review*, Fall, pp 54–74.

Bartlett, C A and Ghoshal, S (1989), *Managing Across Borders*, Harvard Business School Press.

Bartlett, C A and Ghoshal, S (1991), 'Global strategic management: impact on the new frontiers of strategy research', *Strategic Management Journal*, Vol 12, pp 5–16.

Blackwell, N *et al.* (1991), 'Shaping a pan-European organisation', *McKinsey Quarterly*, Vol 2, pp 94–111.

Blake, J and Amat, O (1993), *European Accounting*, Pitman Publishing.

Boland, V, (1994), 'Mappin & Webb opens new store', *Financial Times*, 10 September, p 2.

Bovet, D (1993), 'Logistics strategies for Europe in the nineties', in Halliburton, C and Hunerberg, R (eds), *European Marketing: Reading and Cases*, Addison-Wesley, pp 246–54.

Brookes, M (1994), *Measuring World GDP*, Goldman Sachs.

Calori, R and Lawrence, P (1992), *The Business of Europe*, Sage.

Carr, C (1993), 'Global, national and resource-based strategies: an examination of strategic choice and performance in the motor components industry', *Strategic Management Journal*, Vol 14, pp 551–68.

Collis, D (1991), 'A resource-based analysis of global competition: the case of the bearings industry', *Strategic Management Journal*, Vol 12, pp 49–68.

Cronshaw, M *et al.* (1990), 'On being stuck in the middle or good food costs less at Sainsbury's', London Business School Working Paper Series, Number 83, August.

Daniels, D, and Radebaugh , D (1994), *International Business*, 6th Edition, Addison-Wesley.

Daniels, J L and Daniels, N C (1993), *Global Vision*, McGraw-Hill.

Davies, G (1994), 'The new world order in economics as G7 is brought down a size or two', *The Independent*, 31 January.

Dawkins, W (1994), 'Career moves in Tokyo', *Financial Times*, 12 September, p 22.

De Jonquieres, G (1991), 'Unilever adopts a clean sheet approach', *Financial Times*, 21 October, p. 13.

Delbridge, R *et al.* (1994), *Worldwide manufacturing competitiveness study – the second lean enterprise report*, Andersen Consulting.

Dent, J (1990), 'Strategy, organisation and control: some possibilities for accounting research', *Accounting Organisation and Society*, Vol 15, pp 3–25.

Dicken, P (1986), *Global Shift: industrial change in a turbulent world*, Harper & Row.

Done, K (1994), 'Monster challenge for cut-price Kia', *Financial Times*, 20 January.

Drucker, P (1994), 'The theory of business', *Harvard Business Review*, Sept–Oct, pp 95–104.

Eilon, S (1988), 'Editorial: three prominent performance ratios', *International Journal of Management Science*, Vol 16, No 6 pp 503–8.

Ellis, J and Williams, D (1993), *Corporate Strategy and Financial Analysis*, Pitman Publishing.

Ernst and Young (1995), *Integrated European Logistics: the barriers to overcome*, Ernst & Young European Consulting Group.

Faulkner, D (1995), *International Strategic Alliances*, McGraw-Hill.

Garratt, B (1987), *The Learning Organisation*, Fontana.

GATT (1993), Background paper prepared by the GATT Secretariat, November.

Ghoshal, S (1987), 'Global strategy: an organising framework', *Strategic Management Journal*, Vol 8, pp 425–40.

Gray, B and Clark, B (1994), 'The best lines of defence', *Financial Times*, May 17, p. 19.

Goold, M and Campbell, A (1987), *Strategies and Styles*, Blackwell.

Goold, M and Campbell, A (1989), 'Good "corporate parents" can see off "unbundlers"', *Financial Times* letter, 6 November.

Grant, R M (1991), *Contemporary Strategy Analysis*, Blackwell.

Grinyer, P and Spender, J (1979), 'Recipes, crises and adaptation in mature businesses', *International Studies of Management and Organisation*, Vol 9, pp 113–23.

Halliburton, C and Hunerberg, R (1993), 'Pan-European marketing – myth or reality?', in Halliburton, C and Hunerberg, R (eds) *European Marketing: Reading and Cases*, Addison-Wesley, pp 26–44.

Hamel, G (1994), 'The concept of core competence', in Hamel, G and Heene, A *Competence Based Competition*, Wiley.

Hamel, G and Prahalad, C K (1985), 'Do you really have a global strategy?' *Harvard Business Review*, July–August, pp 139–48.

Hamel, G and Prahalad, C (1994), *Competing for the Future*, Harvard Business School Press.

Hampden-Turner C (1990), *Corporate Culture for Competitive Edge*, Economist Publications.

Herman, H (1988), *The Creative Brain*, Brain Books.

Holmes, G and Sugden, A (1991), *Interpreting Company Reports and Accounts*, Woodhead Faulkner.

Humes, S (1993), *Managing the Multinational*, Prentice-Hall.

Johnson, G (1987), *Strategic Change and the Management Process*, Blackwell.

Johnson, G (1992), 'Managing strategic change – strategy, culture and action', *Long Range Planning*, Vol 25, No 1, pp 28–36.

Kaplan, R S and Norton, D P (1992), 'The balanced scorecard – measures that drive performance', *Harvard Business Review*, January–February, pp 71–9.

Kay, J (1993), *Foundations of Corporate Success*, Oxford University Press.

Kehoe, L, (1994a), 'Change while you are ahead', *Financial Times*, 19 March.

Kehoe, L (1994b), 'IBM drags itself out of the mire', *Financial Times*, 28 March, pp. 15–16.

Ketelhohn, W (1993), *International Business Strategy*, Butterworth Heinemann.

Kotter, J P and Schlesinger, H P R (1979), 'Choosing strategies for change', *Harvard Business Review*, March–April.

Lapper, R (1994), 'Hard work to be free and single', *Financial Times*, 1 July, p 19.

Levitt T, (1983), 'The globalisation of markets', *Harvard Business Review*, May–June, pp 92–102.

Lewin, K (1951), *Field Theory in Social Science*, Harper and Row.

Lewis, J (1993), *Partnerships for Profit*, Free Press/Macmillan.

Lorenz, C (1993), 'Here, there and everywhere', *Financial Times*, 21 October, p 13.

Lorenz, C (1994), 'A mesh of formal and the flexible', *Financial Times*, 4 November, p 11.

Madura, J (1992), *International Financial Management*, 3rd Edition, West Publishing Company.

Mintzberg, H (1994), *The Rise and Fall of Strategic Planning*, Prentice-Hall.

Mintzberg, H and Waters, J (1985), 'Of strategies, deliberate and emergent', *Strategic Management Journal*, Vol 6, pp 257–72.

Monnich, H (1991), *The BMW Story*, BMW AG.

Nakamoto, M (1994), 'The rising yen means pain for a supplier', *Financial Times*, 1 January.

Nobes, C (1993), *International Guide to Interpreting Company Accounts*, FT Management Report.

Ohmae, K (1990), *Borderless World*, Collins.

Pascale, R T (1984), 'The Honda effect', *California Management Review*, Vol XXVI, No 3, pp 47–72.

Pascale, R T (1990), *Managing on the Edge*, Penguin.

Pera International (1993), *Opportunity or Threat: the single market reality for SMEs*, Pera International.

Pettigrew A, (1985), *The Awakening Giant*, Blackwell.

Philips (1992), Some basic issues relating to Europes futures in electronics, (International Briefing Document).

Porter, M (1980), *Competitive Strategy*, Free Press.

Porter, M (1985), *Competitive Advantage*, Free Press.

Quinn, J B, Mintzberg, H and James, R M (1995), *The Strategy Process*, Prentice-Hall International.

Root, F R (1987), *Entry Strategies for International Markets*, Lexington Books.

Rumelt, R P (1979), 'Evaluation of strategy: theory and models', in Schendel, D E and Hofer, C W (eds), *Strategic Management*, Little, Brown.

Shenkman, M H (1992), *Value and Strategy*, Quorum Books.

Skapinker, M and Ridding, J (1993), 'Unlucky or unwise?', *Financial Times*, 13 November, p 4.

Slatter, S (1984), *Corporate Recovery*, Penguin.

Snyder, A and Ebeling, H (1992), 'Targeting a company's real core competences', *Journal of Business Strategy*, Nov–Dec, pp 26–32.

Stacey, R (1993), *Strategic Management and Organisational Dynamics*, Pitman Publishing.

Stalk, G and Hout, T (1990), *Competing Against Time: how time based competition is reshaping global markets*, Free Press.

Theuerkauf, I (1991), 'Reshaping the global organisation', *McKinsey Quarterly*, Vol 3, pp 103–19.

Tichy, N (1983), *Managing Strategic Change*, Wiley.

Tomkins, R (1994), 'A long walk to the shops', *Financial Times*, 11 April, p 15.

Troer, T (1994), 'Creditanstalt rediscovers its former eastern markets', *The European*, May.

Trompenaars, F (1993), *Riding the Waves of Culture*, Economist Books.

Watson, G W (1993), *Strategic Benchmarking: How to rate your company's performance against the world's best*, Wiley.

Wegstyl, S (1994), 'Spares lead the way in India car parts exports', *Financial Times*, 28 January.

Yip, G S (1989), 'Global Strategy . . . in a world of nations', *Sloan Management Review*, Fall, pp 29–41.

Yip, G S (1993), *Total Global Strategy: managing for worldwide competitive advantage*, Prentice-Hall.

Yip, G S and Coundouriotis, G A (1991), 'Diagnosing global strategy potential: the world chocolate confectionery industry', *Planning Review*, January/February.

INDEX OF COMPANIES

INDEX